GLOBAL MARKETING

GLOBAL MARKETING

Practical Insights & International Analysis

Carlyle Farrell

Los Angeles | London | New Delhi
Singapore | Washington DC

Los Angeles | London | New Delhi
Singapore | Washington DC

SAGE Publications Ltd
1 Oliver's Yard
55 City Road
London EC1Y 1SP

SAGE Publications Inc.
2455 Teller Road
Thousand Oaks, California 91320

SAGE Publications India Pvt Ltd
B 1/I 1 Mohan Cooperative Industrial Area
Mathura Road
New Delhi 110 044

SAGE Publications Asia-Pacific Pte Ltd
3 Church Street
#10-04 Samsung Hub
Singapore 049483

Editor: Matthew Waters
Assistant editor: Nina Smith/Molly Farrell
Production editor: Sarah Cooke
Copyeditor: Sharon Cawood
Proofreader: Audrey Scriven
Indexer: Silvia Benvenuto
Marketing manager: Alison Borg
Cover designer: Francis Kenney
Typeset by: C&M Digitals (P) Ltd, Chennai, India
Printed and bound in Great Britain by Ashford
Colour Press Ltd

Library of Congress Control Number: 2014946244

British Library Cataloguing in Publication data

A catalogue record for this book is available from the British Library

ISBN 978-1-44625-263-5
ISBN 978-1-44625-264-2 (pbk)

At SAGE we take sustainability seriously. Most of our products are printed in the UK using FSC papers and boards. When we print overseas we ensure sustainable papers are used as measured by the Egmont grading system. We undertake an annual audit to monitor our sustainability.

To the memory of my brother Trevor Farrell

GET ONLINE FOR MORE

LECTURER RESOURCES

- PowerPoint slides per chapter
- Multiple choice questions and short Q&As per chapter

STUDENT RESOURCES

- Multiple choice questions per chapter
- SAGE Pinterest marketing pins

 companion website

study.sagepub.com/farrell

CONTENTS

ABOUT THE AUTHOR

Carlyle Farrell is an Associate Professor in the Global Management Studies Department at the Ted Rogers School of Management, Ryerson University. He teaches international marketing at both undergraduate and MBA levels and is a frequent media commentator on international business issues. Carlyle holds a BSc degree from the University of the West Indies, an MSc degree from the University of Guelph and a PhD from the University of Manitoba. Dr Farrell has over 15 years of private sector experience as an international management consultant and senior executive. As an international management consultant, he has worked for private and public sector clients in over 20 countries across Europe, Africa, South America and the Caribbean. His clients have included Rabobank International, the African Development Bank, the Inter-American Development Bank and the United Nations, as well as numerous small and medium-sized companies. Carlyle has also served as president of the Canadian subsidiary of a US-based e-commerce company where he had full responsibility for marketing and brand development in the Canadian market. Working with Nelson Education, Dr Farrell co-authored the textbook *Global Marketing: Foreign Entry, Market Development and Strategy Implementation* which was targeted at the Canadian market. His current research interests center on the marketing and corporate strategies of emerging market multinationals. He has published in a number of journals including the *Journal of Business Research*, *Journal of Global Marketing*, *Marketing Education Review*, *Atlantic Economic Journal*, *Journal of Teaching in International Business*, *International Journal of China Marketing* and the *Journal of African Business*. Carlyle is a serious collector of Caribbean art and spends much of his spare time visiting museums and studying art history.

GLOBAL MARKETING EXPLAINED

1

LEARNING OBJECTIVES

After reading this chapter you should be able to:

- Define the term 'global marketing' and explain how it differs from other terms such as 'international marketing', 'multi-domestic marketing' and 'glocal marketing'

- Explain the EPRG framework

- Define the term 'globalization'

- Discuss the major forms of globalization

- Discuss the main drivers of globalization

- Explain the perspective of the anti-globalization movement.

INTRODUCTION

In today's business environment, firms may face competition from companies located in their own home market as well as from those based halfway around the world. Also, customer trends which take root in one country may quickly spread to other parts of the world, creating either new marketing opportunities or potential threats to a firm's established products and business models. In addition, political and economic crises in one region may have important implications for consumer and business confidence around the world. One need look no further than the sovereign debt crisis in Europe that began to unfold in 2009 or the sub-prime mortgage crisis in the USA that first came to light some two years earlier, to appreciate the impact of such events on economic growth, consumer spending and prosperity. Economic and political events taking place around the world may have a profound effect on a company's prospects for survival and growth. It should be noted that whether or not a firm elects to operate internationally, it is still vulnerable to changes taking place in the global marketplace. A focus only on its domestic market does not make a firm immune to global competitive pressures or exogenous shocks that stem from political and economic events originating outside the borders of its home country.

   This text will introduce you to the field of global marketing. As you read through the following chapters, you will learn how to identify opportunities in foreign markets and develop effective strategies to capitalize on those opportunities. You will begin to appreciate the cultural differences between consumers in your home market and those in markets around the world, and you will learn how those differences impact a company's ability to succeed abroad.

You will also learn how to formulate and execute effective marketing strategies in foreign countries while mitigating the political and economic risks involved in doing business abroad.

The study of global marketing is as exciting as it is important. For many firms based in developed countries, penetrating fast-growing emerging markets such as India and China is a matter of survival. The mature markets of Western Europe and North America offer little prospect for rapid growth with their aging populations and low population growth rates. Firms operating in these established markets also face intense competitive pressures which effectively limit expansion possibilities. These competitive pressures, it should be noted, come not only from established western firms but also from emerging market multinationals headquartered in countries such as Brazil, China and India.

Box 1.1

Foreign direct investment (FDI) and strategic alliances are both institutional arrangements used by firms to penetrate foreign markets. When a firm engages in FDI, it is making a long-term capital investment in a new or existing foreign business. For example, in June 2012 the Belgian company Anheuser-Busch InBev SA agreed to purchase the 50 percent of Mexican brewer Grupo Modelo it did not already own for $20 billion. The deal gave Anheuser-Busch InBev a stronger presence in the fast-growing Mexican beer market. Strategic alliances, on the other hand, involve two or more companies collaborating over the short to medium term in order to achieve some mutually beneficial corporate objective. In February 2011, for example, US-based Microsoft and the Finnish handset maker, Nokia, announced a broad strategic alliance between their firms. As part of the deal, Microsoft developed applications to run on Nokia's handsets and Nokia adopted Windows Phone as its smartphone strategy. Of course, a strategic alliance may be the first step towards FDI. For example, in August 2013 Microsoft opted to deepen its commitment to the handset market by purchasing Nokia's entire hardware business for over $7 billion.

In some cases, firms may be forced to adopt a global marketing perspective simply based on the nature of their products. High research and development (R&D) costs involved in bringing some pharmaceutical drugs to market, for example, necessitate that they be marketed globally if those costs are to be recouped. There is considerable debate around the cost of developing new pharmaceutical drugs. Indeed, one recent study estimated the cost at over $1 billion.[1] To be financially feasible, clearly such products must be marketed globally. Also, some high technology products, such as Apple's iPhone 6, are themselves inherently global and demand that the firm adopt a global marketing perspective. With robust demand from consumers around the world, it would make little sense for Apple to market its products only in its home market of the USA.

GLOBAL MARKETING DEFINED

One may define **global marketing** as the systematic planning, coordination and implementation of the firm's marketing activities across national borders. From this definition, we note that global marketing involves the implementation of marketing activities across national borders, i.e. outside the firm's home country. What this means is that the firm is no longer dealing with the familiar environment of its home country but is now confronted with environments with significant differences in terms of culture and level of economic development, and perhaps major differences in political structures and approaches to government regulation. In attempting to

---

[1] Adams, C.P. and Brantner, V.V. (2010) 'Spending on new drug development', *Health Econ.*, 19: 130–41.

implement marketing activities in these new host countries, the firm may also face unfamiliar competitors and marketing channels as well as consumers with decidedly different needs and purchasing behaviors. Business practices may also be found to differ significantly from what obtains in the firm's home country. Understanding regulations governing foreign direct investment and dealing with strategic alliances with foreign partners are likely to prove taxing for the firm new to global marketing. These inter-country differences clearly make global marketing considerably more challenging for firms that have historically focussed on their domestic markets.

Global marketers are generally concerned with several issues that are of little relevance to the purely domestic firm. For example, the global marketing firm has to consider issues such as:

- the selection of foreign countries that offer the best prospects for the products marketed by the firm
- the choice of strategies and approaches, e.g. foreign direct investment, exporting or a more loosely structured strategic alliance, which the firm may employ to penetrate international markets
- the need for changes to the firm's products so that they fit more closely with the needs of consumers in the foreign countries selected
- the need for the firm's advertising strategies to be adjusted to better communicate with consumers who are culturally dissimilar to those in its home market
- the need to contract and work with foreign intermediaries in order to get the firm's products into the hands of customers in the various host countries
- the need to adjust the firm's pricing strategies in response to differences in the structure of marketing channels in the foreign countries and differences in the purchasing behavior of consumers in those markets
- the need to identify countries in which to locate the firm's value-added activities, e.g. research and development
- the need to evaluate and mitigate the political risks inherent in doing business in foreign countries
- the need to consider opportunities for the firm to coordinate its marketing activities across the various countries in which it plans to conduct business.

Domestic marketing is not concerned with the issues identified above. In essence, the 'liability of foreignness'[2] a firm faces when operating outside its home market adds an additional layer of complexity and risk to its marketing decisions (Zaheer, 1995).

⭐ **Box 1.2**

The term **'liability of foreignness'** generally refers to the inherent disadvantages that multinational firms face when operating in a new host country. As a foreign entity, the multinational firm will face additional costs which are not borne by other firms which are indigenous to the host country. Local firms have a good understanding of the political, cultural and regulatory environments in which they operate and also have the knowledge necessary to navigate their environment. Foreign firms, on the other hand, do not possess such in-depth knowledge and are put at a competitive disadvantage. Further, some multinational firms may face resistance from consumers who may favor the products of local firms. Host governments too may favor local firms in the tendering of contracts. Foreign multinationals may again be placed at a competitive disadvantage. Building on the work of scholars such as Hymer (1960) and Kindleberger (1969), the term liability of foreignness was coined by Zaheer in 1995. It encapsulates all of the additional costs multinationals must bear in order to compete with local firms in a new host country.

---

[2] See Box 1.2, as well as the following publications:

Zaheer, S. (1995) 'Overcoming the liability of foreignness', *Academy of Management Journal*, 38, 2: 341–63.

Hymer, S. (1960) *The International Operations of National Firms: A Study of Foreign Direct Investment*. Cambridge, MA: MIT Press.

Kindleberger, C. (1969) *Industry Consolidation and Global Competition: Multiple Market Competition in the Tire Industry*. New Haven, CT: Yale University Press.

The definition of global marketing presented above implies that the firm is conducting marketing activities in a number of countries outside of its home market. The definition is, however, deliberately silent on the precise number of countries a firm must operate in to be considered a global marketer. One should note that a company does not need to market its products in every country in the world to be considered a global marketing company. Given that there are roughly 200 countries around the world, even major multinationals such as McDonald's, Nike and Coca-Cola would not meet such a strict criterion. Research published in the *Journal of International Business Studies* has shown that the vast majority of large firms generate most of their sales in their home region of the Triad (the USA, Japan and Western Europe), i.e. they do not have the breadth of foreign market coverage to be considered truly 'global' (Rugman and Verbeke, 2004).[3] Of course, despite the above finding, firms do need to market their products in a number of foreign countries simultaneously in order to satisfy the definition of global marketing. It is also necessary for the firm to engage in systematic planning and coordination of its activities in these foreign markets. This systematic planning and coordination may be manifested in, for example, the sale of a standardized product in all international markets, the use of a consistent brand name and advertising message across all foreign markets, or a coherent pricing strategy that must be followed by all of the firm's subsidiary managers, regardless of geographic location. Systematic planning and coordination may also be demonstrated by the firm adopting an integrated approach to foreign market entry and the utilization of resources, such as manufacturing facilities and sales personnel, in ways which maximize efficiency and overall corporate profitability.

The need for systematic planning and coordination of marketing activities across country markets is central to the concept of global marketing but is not at all relevant to purely domestic marketing. There are, however, similarities between domestic and global marketing. Both share a focus on the satisfaction of consumer needs and the exchange of something of value. These basic principles which are, of course, central to the discipline of marketing apply equally whether marketing activities take place in a domestic or global context. In the case of global marketing, transactions take place between entities in different countries, making it significantly more difficult to apply these basic marketing principles. The cross-border nature of global marketing transactions adds an additional layer of complexity to the process of exchange and the satisfaction of customer needs.

⭐ **Box 1.3**

The term **economies of scale** refers to the reduction in per unit cost of production as the firm expands its level of output. Longer production runs and increased output translate into a lower cost per unit. The firm which is able to exploit these scale economies may be more price-competitive in global markets as it faces a lower per unit cost structure than competing firms. The concept differs from **economies of scope** which refers to a reduced cost per unit as the firm spreads its total costs (production, marketing and R&D) over a larger number of brands, product lines or target markets.

EVOLUTION OF THE CONCEPT

The concept of 'global marketing' owes much to the work of Harvard Business School professor and consultant Theodore Levitt.[4] In a 1983 article published in the *Harvard Business*

---

[3] Rugman, A.M. and Verbeke, A. (2004) 'A perspective on regional and global strategies of multinational enterprises', *Journal of International Business Studies*, 35, 1: 3–18.

[4] This section draws heavily from Czinkota, M., Ronkainen, I., Farrell, C. and McTavish, R. (2009) *Global Marketing: Foreign Entry, Market Development and Strategy Implementation*. Toronto: Nelson Education.

Review[5] titled 'The globalization of markets', Levitt argued in favor of a convergence of cultural and national preferences in consumer markets around the world. The implication of this convergence is that companies need not customize their product offerings but should instead service markets around the world with standardized products and a uniform marketing strategy. There is no need to adapt to unique national differences. Global markets, according to Levitt, could be serviced with standardized products, allowing the firm to exploit the economies of scale that would result from longer production runs. Indeed, doing so would have a positive impact on the firm's price competitiveness in international markets as cost per unit declined in response to increased output. This notion of convergence of national preferences and the new era of 'homogenized demand' would force business executives to re-think their foreign market strategies.

Prior to Levitt popularizing the nation of global marketing, companies would attempt to pursue foreign market opportunities by essentially extending their domestic marketing strategies to international markets. The nuances of individual foreign markets and the preferences of consumers in those markets were largely ignored. Firms expended little intellectual or financial capital to cater to the unique preferences of customers in the various foreign markets in which they did business and viewed international sales as secondary to their core domestic operations. These strategies were largely unsuccessful.

▣ Expand Your Knowledge

Levitt, T. (1983) 'The globalization of markets', *Harvard Business Review* (May–June): 92–102.

This classic article argues that technology is driving the world towards commonality. As consumer tastes and preferences around the world converge, the strategy of tailoring products to the needs of multiple markets may actually put multinational firms at a disadvantage. Levitt suggests that firms should focus on providing standardized products at the right price to consumers around the globe.

Companies pursuing foreign market opportunities would eventually recognize the importance of national differences and would opt to pursue a **multi-domestic** or country-by-country marketing strategy. With this approach, each of the firm's foreign subsidiaries or divisions was viewed as a profit center and individual marketing strategies were developed for each country in which the company operated. Significant differences were observed in the brands marketed in each country, as well as in the approaches used to pricing and advertising. While this strategy was effective in recognizing and catering to the unique characteristics of consumers in each country market, there was little or no coordination of marketing activities across countries – even across those that were closely related. As a result, the potential synergies and cost savings that would derive from more coordinated and integrated approaches to the firm's marketing efforts were foregone.

The inefficiencies inherent in developing and implementing separate marketing strategies in each foreign market would eventually become more apparent and would drive firms to examine ways to exploit the similarities in the various foreign markets they served. Executives began to question whether advertising messages could not be crafted that could be utilized in multiple countries and whether products could not be designed with features that appealed to consumers in all of the countries in which they wished to do business. Questions also began to surface with respect to the duplication of manufacturing facilities across various country markets and the possibilities of leveraging resources

---

[5] Levitt, T. (1983) 'The globalization of markets', *Harvard Business Review* (May–June): 92–102.

across markets in a more coordinated and integrated manner. Firms also began to recognize that they were facing the same competitors in all of the major markets in which they had operations and that an increasing number of their customers were operating globally. The above insights would lead firms to embrace the notion of global marketing with its focus on the development and implementation of a coordinated and integrated approach to foreign markets.

It should be recognized that capitalizing on the notion of global marketing with its emphasis on standardization implied that there was little need to adapt the marketing mix to the unique characteristics of customers in the various country markets. Consumers were essentially homogeneous, all wanting the same product features and brands. This, however, ran counter to the **marketing concept** which espoused the need to identify and satisfy unique customer needs. The marketing concept was, of course, well entrenched in the marketing literature at the time and was at the heart of the strategic approach used by practitioners.

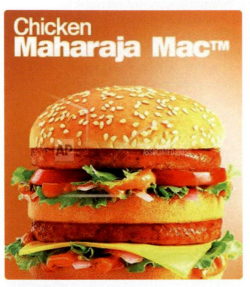

PHOTO 1.1

PHOTO 1.2

By the late 1980s, marketers began to recognize that differences between consumers in the various countries they served could not easily be ignored. These differences were real and demanded that they be considered, if global marketers were to be successful outside their domestic markets. The marketing concept was still relevant and marketers would, therefore, ignore consumer differences at their peril. 'Think global, act local' became the new mantra of global marketers. Companies were now encouraged to 'act local' by, for example, reformulating their products to suit the tastes and preferences of local consumers or acquiring and re-launching well-established local brands. This recognition of the salience of culture and local market differences gave rise to the concept of '**glocal marketing**' which reflects the need for balance between global marketing with its emphasis on standardization and local marketing with its focus on catering to individual country differences (see Figure 1.1). Companies such as McDonald's and Coca-Cola are well known for their efforts to localize their global product offerings. In India, for example, McDonald's serves the Maharaja Mac made with mutton or chicken instead of beef, while in some tropical countries guava juice has been added to the menu. In Latin America, banana pies have found their way onto this US company's menu, while in Germany customers are offered beer with their meals. The latter is, of course, a major departure for a business globally positioned as a family-oriented restaurant. McDonald's recognized, however, that attitudes towards alcohol are very different in Germany, and across Europe, compared to the USA.

Coca-Cola has also recognized that the ability to adapt to local country differences is a source of competitive advantage. New products have been introduced for specific local markets. The firm's Japanese unit, for example, markets Qoo, a noncarbonated beverage which is manufactured in a range of flavors such as grape and orange. Other companies such as Disney have also had to find ways to localize their product in an effort to resonate with local customers (see Case Study 1.1).

FIGURE 1.1   The Evolution of Global Marketing

Extension of domestic strategy to international markets

Separate and uncoordinated multidomestic strategy for each country market

Coordinated and intergrated global strategy

Global strategy with adjustments for local country difference

case study 1.1: Disney Hong Kong theme park

Disney's Hong Kong theme park has finally turned a profit, reporting net earnings of some $14 million during the fiscal year ending September 2012. Jointly owned by Walt Disney (48 percent) and the Hong Kong government (52 percent), the theme park has consistently lost money since it opened in 2005. These latest financial results may be giving the Walt Disney Company and its government partner some hope that measures taken to localize the theme park experience have begun to produce the desired effect. Hong Kong Disney is the smallest of the Disney theme parks and featured just three 'lands' when it first opened – Fantasyland, Tomorrowland and Adventureland. The park is, however, being expanded to keep visitors coming back. A new 'land' based on the Toy Story movies opened to the public in 2011 and a Wild West-themed 'land' dubbed Grizzly Gulch opened in 2012.

In addition to the physical expansion, Hong Kong Disney has had to make other changes to localize its content and customer experience. The company is now incorporating Feng Shui, an ancient Chinese discipline that governs spatial arrangement and the flow of energy, into the design of its parks. This necessitated, for example, that the main entrance to the park be moved so that it faced the 'right' direction. The company also added a curve from the train station to the new entrance in order to trap chi (or energy) and prevent it flowing into the South China Sea. Feng Shui experts were also brought in to lay out the design of the rides. While Disney kept its globally recognized characters such as Mickey and Minnie Mouse, they were given a make-over to appeal to the local audience. Mickey was outfitted in a red Mao

PHOTO 1.3

suit and Minnie in a cherry blossom red dress to appeal to a Chinese audience. Cast members speak both English and the local Hong Kong and Chinese dialects (Cantonese and Putonghua) and maps and brochures are printed in simplified and traditional Chinese characters, in Japanese and English. In addition, various shows incorporate local scenes such as Victoria Harbor and Honk Kong skyscrapers to foster a connection with an Asian audience. Park restaurants serve primarily Chinese foods such as sushi and roast suckling pig. Also, when Disney executives recognized that Chinese patrons take 10 minutes more to eat their meals, compared to American visitors, they decided to add 700 more seats to the park dining areas.

Sources

Business Week (2013) Disney's Hong Kong Theme Park Finally Turns a Profit. Available at: www.businessweek. com/articles/2013-02-19/disneys-hong-kong-theme-park-finally-turns-a-profit, accessed May 24, 2013.

(Continued)

(Continued)

Matusitz, J. (2011) 'Disney's successful adaptation in Hong Kong: A glocalization perspective', *Asia Pacific Journal of Management*, 28: 667–81.

Discussion Questions

1. Given that there are a number of competing theme parks in mainland China, do you believe that Disney's glocalization strategy will provide the company with a competitive advantage in this market?
2. From your own research on Disney's Hong Kong theme park, are there elements of the firm's global strategy, other than those discussed above, that should be localized?

MANAGEMENT ORIENTATION

A firm's approach to global markets is heavily dependent on its management orientation. The EPRG framework illustrates various management orientations and how these translate into strategic approaches for the management of foreign affiliates (Perlmutter, 1969;[6] Chakravarthy and Perlmutter, 1985[7]). Some firms take the position that headquarters should exercise a significant degree of control over international operations. Important decisions are localized at head office and the firm is largely driven by the needs of consumers in its home market. Foreign subsidiaries utilize technologies and business processes transferred from headquarters in serving their local customers. Described as an **ethnocentric** management orientation, this approach differs markedly from that used by firms that provide their foreign affiliates with substantial latitude to make decisions in their local markets. Firms which have adopted a **polycentric** management orientation essentially provide their foreign subsidiary managers with considerable flexibility to make decisions with respect to marketing, production and technology choices in serving their local customers. Head office views each foreign market as unique and distinct and exercises little centralized authority over its operation.

Firms subscribing to a polycentric (or multi-domestic) management orientation make little attempt to coordinate the activities of their foreign affiliates. In some cases, however, firms may take a **regiocentric** approach to the management of their foreign operations. Such firms view the world as a set of distinct regional markets, such as Europe, Latin America, North America and Asia. Regiocentric firms attempt to coordinate their activities and business strategies within these defined regions but not across them. A UK-based subsidiary manager, for example, would have little opportunity to coordinate her activities with those of counterparts in Asia but would be expected to execute on the firm's pan-European business strategy. In contrast, some companies may view the world as a global market but recognize the importance of catering to local cultural differences. **Geocentric** firms, therefore, attempt to offer standardized global products with adaptations to the various country markets they serve.

GLOBALIZATION DEFINED

The term **globalization** refers to the increasing integration and inter-dependence of economies, national institutions, firms and individuals around the world. The trend became obvious during the

---

[6] Perlmutter, H.V. (1969) 'The tortuous evolution of the multinational corporation', *Columbia Journal of World Business*, 4, 1: 9–18.

[7] Chakravarthy, B.S. and Perlmutter, H.V. (1985) 'Strategic planning for a global business', *Columbia Journal of World Business*, XX, 2: 3–10.

oil price shocks in the 1970s during which the Arab members of the Organization of Petroleum Exporting Countries (OPEC) imposed an embargo on western nations to protest their support of Israel in the Yom Kippur war against Egypt. The trend towards integration has continued to intensify ever since. The Asian financial crisis of 1997 and the Argentine crisis of 2002 are also important reminders of our growing interconnectedness. More recent manifestations of the phenomenon that may be cited include the US sub-prime financial crisis which began in 2007 and which sent shock waves around the world, adversely affecting countries as far away from the epicenter of the crisis as Iceland. One may also cite the European sovereign debt crisis which began in 2009 and initially only impacted the peripheral EU countries of Greece and Ireland but which quickly spread to other countries of the eurozone including Spain and France.

The trend towards increased globalization is unlikely to abate any time soon. Despite the economic dislocations associated with the trend, globalization has also presented firms with unparalleled opportunities to expand and tap into foreign markets. These opportunities are available to both small and large firms and companies headquartered in any country around the world. Indeed, national governments in both the developed and developing worlds are actively positioning their local firms to take advantage of these opportunities. Consumers also benefit from this trend by having access to a wider selection of products at competitive prices, as well as greater access to employment opportunities around the globe.

FORMS OF GLOBALIZATION

One may make a distinction between two basic forms of globalization: the **globalization of markets** and the **globalization of production** (see Figure 1.2). The convergence of consumer tastes and preferences recognized by Levitt in the early 1980s describes what we now refer to as the globalization of markets. Essentially, consumers around the world seem to have similar tastes and demand the same global brands. Major brands such as Nike and Apple are able to capitalize on this phenomenon with standardized products and marketing campaigns that appeal to consumers in countries around the world. Products such as the Apple iPhone and iPad are as popular in Asia and the Middle East as they are in North America.

Globalization of production, on the other hand, refers to the ability of companies to shift the location of their manufacturing operations to any country around the world in response to

FIGURE 1.2   Forms of Globalization

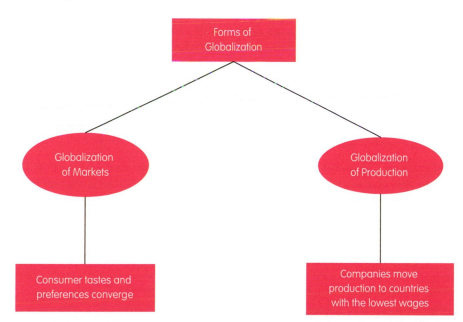

wage rates and government incentives. Nike, for example, has for many years used China as the manufacturing base for its trainers in order to take advantage of that country's low wage rates. In recent years, however, wages in China have begun to increase by as much as 20 percent per year and Nike has seen many of its competitors shift their production to countries with even lower wage rates such as Vietnam, Cambodia, Indonesia and Bangladesh. Nike has followed suit and in 2010 Vietnam became the company's largest production base worldwide.[8] Firms may shift production to any part of the world to take advantage of cost savings in various countries.

THE DRIVERS OF GLOBALIZATION

One may identify five key drivers of the process of globalization: market, cost, environmental, competitive and technological factors[9] (see Figure 1.3).

Market factors

The existence of consumers around the world with similar tastes and preferences is a powerful driver of globalization. These consumers, many with high levels of disposable income, engage in international travel and are exposed to brands not found in their home markets. This puts significant pressure on global marketers to expand their product offerings to those markets. Further, as already noted, some products are inherently global which necessitates a global marketing approach. High technology firms such as Apple continue to see strong global demand for their products, as witnessed by the successful September 2014 launch of the iPhone 6 and iPhone 6 Plus which sold some 10 million new units in the first three days after the models were launched in the USA, Australia, Canada, France, Germany, Hong Kong, Japan, Puerto Rico, Singapore and the UK.

Cost factors

The need to contain cost is a major driver of globalization. Firms are encouraged to expand beyond their home jurisdictions in order to capitalize on low wage rates in other countries. A significant number of North American and European companies, many of them well-known manufacturers of branded consumer products, have elected to move their manufacturing operations to China in order to take advantage of that country's low wage structure. Clothing and shoe manufacturing firms such as Nike have been producing in China for many years but so also have companies in other sectors such as consumer electronics, food and industrial products. While China's wage rates are considerably lower than those in western industrialized economies, they have been rising significantly in recent years. As noted above, this has prompted some companies such as Nike to seek out even lower wage jurisdictions for its manufacturing operations, and interestingly has also encouraged American firms such as Chesapeake Bay Candle and Peerless AV to move production back to the USA.

Environmental factors

As will be shown in Chapter 5, government barriers to trade and investment have fallen dramatically in the last several years and this has further facilitated the globalization of markets. Significant progress made in the reduction of tariff and non-tariff barriers to trade has served to spur the trend towards globalization, as have government efforts to reduce barriers to direct foreign investment.

---

8   *The Economist* (2012) 'The boomerang effect as Chinese wages rise, some production is moving back to the rich world'. Available at: www.economist.com/node/21552898, accessed September 25, 2012.

9   This section draws heavily from Czinkota, M., Ronkainen, I., Farrell, C. and McTavish, R. (2009) *Global Marketing: Foreign Entry, Market Development and Strategy Implementation*. Toronto: Nelson Education.

FIGURE 1.3   The Drivers of Globalization

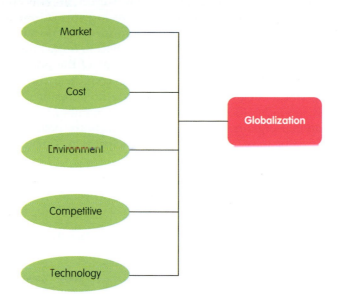

Competitive factors

Companies may have little choice but to pursue global opportunities. With ever-shortening product life cycles, firms must continuously innovate and seek new markets if they are to defend themselves from foreign competition. Firms without an efficient global distribution network will find it increasingly difficult to maintain market share and profitability as rivals execute their aggressive global expansion strategies. Companies headquartered in the mature markets of North America and Western Europe now face more intense competitive pressures from emerging market multinationals, which are rapidly expanding outside their traditional regional bases of operation.

Technological factors

Technological factors are a powerful driver of globalization. Technical innovation makes it possible for firms to operate in multiple countries and connect with consumers in various parts of the world. The Internet, for example, allows firms to create an awareness of their brands among consumers in foreign markets and gain insights into their needs and product preferences. Social media websites such as Facebook and Twitter allow consumers in various countries to not just search for product information but also share ideas and perspectives with others with similar interests. Social media websites are providing global marketing managers with a significant advertising opportunity. The use of social media in a global communication strategy is discussed in Chapter 12.

THE MEASUREMENT OF GLOBALIZATION

The extent of globalization can be measured. One research study authored by Axel Dreher measures overall globalization on three dimensions: economic integration, social integration and political integration.[10] Dreher's KOF[11] globalization index and its three sub-indexes range from 1 to 100, with increasing values denoting greater globalization. The economic integration dimension examines factors such as the trade and investment flows between countries and the

---

[10]   Dreher, A. (2006) 'Does globalization affect growth? Evidence from a new Index of Globalization', *Applied Economics*, 38, 10: 1091–110.

[11]   This index is named after the KOF Swiss Economic Institute, an economics think-tank based in Zurich, Switzerland. KOF is an acronym for the German word *Konjunkturforschungsstelle*, which means 'business cycle research institute'.

extent to which the country uses policy measures to restrict these flows. This sub-index is constructed from data on variables such as foreign direct investment, imports and exports, portfolio investment, average tariff rates and income payments to foreign nationals. Social integration reflects the flow and movement of ideas, people and information. This sub-index captures data on variables such as tourism flows between countries, telecom traffic, the numbers of international letters sent, the number of Internet users, percentage of the population with television sets and the number of McDonald's restaurants in various countries. The final dimension of the globalization index is political integration which captures the diffusion of government policies around the world. This sub-index incorporates data on the number of embassies in a country, the number of international organizations to which the country belongs and the number of United Nations peace-keeping missions the country participates in. Table 1.1 presents a ranking of countries on the KOF scale.

TABLE 1.1   Country Ranking on the KOF Globalization Scale, 2012

Overall globalization:

Rank	Country	Globalization score
1	Belgium	92.76
2	Ireland	91.95
3	Netherlands	90.94
4	Austria	90.55
5	Singapore	89.18
6	Sweden	88.23
7	Denmark	88.11
8	Hungary	87.38
9	Portugal	86.73
10	Switzerland	86.64
14	United Kingdom	85.54
15	Canada	85.53
21	Australia	81.60
27	New Zealand	78.31
35	United States	74.88
73	China	59.37

Economic globalization:

Rank	Country	Globalization score
1	Singapore	97.39
2	Luxembourg	94.63
3	Ireland	93.27
4	Malta	92.23
5	Belgium	92.15
6	Netherlands	91.91
7	Hungary	90.50
8	Sweden	88.98
9	Bahrain	88.96
10	United Arab Emirates	88.74
22	New Zealand	80.79
32	Australia	76.26
35	Canada	76.05
44	Germany	72.52
45	France	72.41
79	United States	60.83
107	China	51.25

Social globalization:

Rank	Country	Globalization score
1	Cyprus	91.76
2	Ireland	91.43
3	Singapore	91.04
4	Austria	90.28
5	Belgium	89.75
6	Switzerland	89.43
7	Canada	88.72
8	Netherlands	87.87
9	Denmark	86.19
10	France	85.65
16	Germany	82.16
24	Australia	79.65
29	United States	76.24
35	New Zealand	72.77
51	Japan	64.57
93	China	48.09

Political globalization:

Rank	Country	Globalization score	Rank	Country	Globalization score
1	Italy	98.43	9	Portugal	94.36
2	France	98.21	10	Canada	94.16
3	Belgium	97.91	17	Germany	93.15
4	Austria	97.31	22	United States	92.47
5	Spain	96.68	25	Australia	91.77
6	United Kingdom	96.43	33	Japan	88.91
7	Sweden	95.86	41	China	86.70
8	Poland	95.17	56	New Zealand	82.73

Source: KOF Index of Globalization (2012) Available at: http://globalization.kof.ethz.ch/static/pdf/rankings_2012.pdf, accessed October 5, 2012.

THE ANTI-GLOBALIZATION MOVEMENT

Globalization has been heavily criticized. This criticism has been centered on the impact of the trend on the poor, the environment, women and the ability of sovereign states to make independent decisions. Anti-globalists have used opportunities presented by international meetings of policy makers to express their concerns and vent their anger. The December 1999 World Trade Organization (WTO) meeting in Seattle, USA, for example, attracted some 50,000 protestors. While their initial objective was to express their displeasure at global trade liberalization and the free movement of capital, their protest quickly turned violent, spilling out into the streets of Seattle in a spate of rioting and looting. A similar protest was organized in Davos, Switzerland, in February 2000 at the World Economic Forum. This protest would also turn violent with angry mobs attacking a McDonald's restaurant – which, to many, is a symbol of globalization and a persistent reminder of the low wages paid to workers by some multinational companies. The protest in Davos was quickly followed by others at the joint IMF–World Bank meeting in Prague, Czech Republic, and the G8 meeting in Genoa, Italy. The latter is usually marked as a low point for the anti-globalization movement. At that meeting, a protestor was shot and killed by police.

More recently, and in the wake of the sub-prime mortgage crisis in the USA, a new global protest movement was formed. The Occupy Movement began on September 17, 2011, when a small group of protestors set up camp in Zuccotti Park in New York's financial district.[12] Inspired by the Arab Spring protests in countries such as Tunisia and Egypt and the Spanish *Indignants*, the protestors vowed to take a stand against corporate greed, social inequality and the influence of big banks and other large corporations on the democratic process. Canada-based Adbusters Media Foundation is reported to have been the catalyst for the movement when it used social media tools such as Twitter and Facebook to urge Americans to occupy Wall Street to protest against economic inequality.[13]

United under the banner of 'We are the 99%', the protests quickly grew, sweeping across the USA, Canada, Europe and Asia. The 99 percent referred to the vast majority of people who were struggling to make ends meet financially, while the 1 percent referred to the investment banks on Wall Street and the corporate elite. Thousands protested in cities around the world including Rome, Frankfurt, Toronto and Sydney. In fact, protests surfaced in some 900 cities around the world and on almost every continent.[14] Visible symbols of capitalism such as the European Central Bank were the scene of large-scale protests. Protestors' attempts to occupy the London Stock Exchange were, however, frustrated by police. The Occupy Movement was clearly a grassroots uprising with no identifiable agenda, mandate or leadership structure. Despite this, the Movement's strong commitment to non-violence and participatory democracy was seen as a core strength and resulted in substantial media attention and public support.

PHOTO 1.4

Anti-globalization protests continue to attract attention by the media. The violence and looting that have become associated with the movement typically make headlines in newspapers around the world and garner much discussion in social media. Many anti-globalists argue, however, that violence at international meetings is not what their movement is about and that those who engage in such activities do not speak for them. It is true that the protestors at anti-globalization events are not monolithic. Various groups are represented, each with its own agenda and approach. Some groups, for example, are concerned with

[12] *New York Times* (2012) Occupy Movement (Occupy Wall Street). Available at: http://topics.nytimes.com/top/reference/timestopics/organizations/o/occupy_wall_street/index.html, accessed October 3, 2012.

[13] *The Guardian* (2011) Occupy America: Protests against Wall Street and Inequality Hit 70 Cities. Available at: www.guardian.co.uk/world/2011/oct/08/occupy-america-protests-financial-crisis, accessed October 4, 2012.

[14] *Washington Post* (2011) Occupy Wall Street Protests Continue Worldwide. Available at: www.washingtonpost.com/world/europe/occupy-wall-street-protests-continue-world-wide/2011/10/16/gIQAcJ1roL_story.html, accessed October 4, 2012.

the impact of globalization on women and children, some are concerned about the impact on the environment, while others are concerned about the poor in developing countries and their working conditions. Some anti-globalization groups advocate for the preeminence of the state, while others are viscerally opposed to any form of state authority and argue in favor of anarchy. While some anti-globalization groups raise valid and serious concerns, the tactics adopted by others are less than constructive and do not contribute to rational debate.

SUMMARY

This chapter has provided an introduction to the field of global marketing. The term global marketing has been defined and the evolution of the concept has been discussed. The chapter has also explored the concept of globalization and has identified its major forms and drivers. The anti-globalization movement has also been discussed in this chapter.

The study of global marketing is important. With increasing globalization, marketing managers can no longer afford to focus solely on their home-country markets. Competition is now global and consumers around the world are more aware of world-class brands and are certainly more demanding. Also, the repercussions of economic and political events taking place in one part of the world can quickly spread to countries around the globe, creating opportunities for, or threats to, a company's established business models. This puts tremendous pressure on today's marketing manager to adopt a global perspective.

This text will provide you with the tools needed to make effective global marketing decisions. Given the practical decision-making orientation of the text, the chapters that follow are written from the perspective of the global marketing manager, i.e. the individual charged with the responsibility for planning and implementing the firm's global marketing strategy. The text also seeks to bridge the gap between theory and practice. This is done throughout the text by highlighting a number of research studies that have attempted to shed light on topics of interest to practicing global marketing managers.

? discussion questions

1. What is global marketing and how does it differ from other concepts such as international marketing and multi-domestic marketing?

2. What is the EPRG management orientation framework? From your own research, how would you describe the management orientation of a company such as Apple?

3. What are the key factors driving globalization? Do you think that the globalization trend will eventually fizzle out?

4. Overall, do you see globalization as good or bad for society in the long run?

5. Do you think that the Occupy Movement will have a meaningful impact on global income inequality?

6. In making foreign market entry decisions, how would you use the KOF globalization index?

7. How should firms balance the benefits of standardization with the importance of satisfying the needs of consumers in various country markets?

8. With countries as different as Saudi Arabia and the USA, can marketers really find homogeneous consumer segments in various countries around the world?

FURTHER READING

Freidman, T.L. (2007) *The World is Flat: A Brief History of the Twenty-First Century*. Vancouver, BC: Douglas & McIntyre. (First published by Farrar, Straus and Giroux, 2005.)

Ohmae, K. (1991) *The Borderless World: Power and Strategy*. New York: Harper Perennial.

2

THE CULTURAL ENVIRONMENT

LEARNING OBJECTIVES

After reading this chapter you should be able to:

- Define the term 'culture' and discuss the various elements of the construct

- Explain why culture is central to the study of global marketing

- Discuss approaches used to classify and analyze a society's culture

- Discuss various techniques that firms may use to improve cross-cultural management within their organizations

- Discuss the relationship between culture and ethical decision making.

INTRODUCTION

Global marketing involves transactions between parties in different countries and this necessitates interacting with people from different cultural backgrounds. To be successful in global marketing, one must have an in-depth understanding and appreciation of these cultural differences. For example, culture has a profound impact on consumer behavior. What consumers buy and their approach to the purchase decision are heavily influenced by their culture. An individual's approach to business and negotiation is also influenced by her cultural framework. Further, in today's global business environment, managers are likely to have employees from different cultural backgrounds as well as competitors and partners from different countries. This presents a challenge to the global marketer because the resultant differences in cultural contexts impact approaches to conducting business. To be effective, therefore, global marketers must strive for **cultural literacy**, i.e. a detailed knowledge of the culture of the host country that allows the global manager to live and work effectively in the new environment. While this should be the goal, some managers choose to adopt an **ethnocentric** orientation, i.e. a perspective that their culture is in some way superior to others. Approaching global marketing with an ethnocentric orientation is not likely to lead to success in the market. As will be discussed later in this chapter, an ethnocentric perspective will likely blind the marketer to opportunities in foreign countries and cause her to overlook or minimize differences in consumer preferences and buyer behavior.

The literature contains numerous examples of blunders which could have been avoided had managers paid closer attention to cultural differences (see Ricks, 2006).[1] These range from advertising messages and brand names which do not translate well in foreign languages to the use of inappropriate colors and designs in the packaging of products destined for sale in foreign markets. The popular '*Got Milk?*' advertising campaign developed for the California Milk Processor Board by the agency Goodby Silverstein & Partners is a case in point. The advertisements featured celebrities and others sporting a milk mustache and was designed to promote the nutritional benefits of the beverage. When the campaign was launched in Mexico, however, the tagline translated to 'Are you lactating?' which was obviously not the intended message. Such blunders are amusing but multimillion-dollar cross-border investments have failed because managers did not consider the cultural differences between their home and the target country. This chapter will provide several examples. Understanding the pace at which business transactions can be completed in some countries also requires cultural literacy. In some societies, Mexico for example, business transactions tend to proceed slowly in order to allow sufficient time for the parties to get to know each other on a more personal level. In North America, such personal relationships are not nearly as important and transactions tend to proceed at a much faster pace.

For the above reasons, it is critically important for global marketers to have a deep appreciation of the cultural environment within which they must operate. Cultural differences must be incorporated into the firm's global marketing strategy and this requires that managers approach foreign markets with an open mind and a willingness to adapt. It should also be noted that the global marketer has no control over the culture of the target market. Culture is an uncontrollable variable for the global marketing manager but one which has significant implications for the success of the firm's marketing strategies.

This chapter will introduce you to the concept of culture and its various elements. Several approaches to the classification and analysis of culture are also presented in this chapter. These are useful in assisting global marketers in understanding the cultural environment within which they operate. Also discussed below are techniques that firms may adopt to improve cross-cultural management practices within their organizations. The relationship between culture and ethical decision making is also an important issue and is touched on at the end of this chapter.

CULTURE DEFINED

So what is 'culture'? We know that culture is complex and influences virtually everything we do, how we see the world, how we respond to challenges and interact with others. The types of rewards, i.e. monetary or otherwise, that motivate us are also influenced by culture, as is our tolerance for risk and our sense of equity and justice. As Kroeber and Kluckhohn (1952) have noted, there are literally hundreds of definitions of the term 'culture'.[2] Geert Hofstede, a recognized scholar in this area, defines culture as: 'the collective programming of the mind that distinguishes the members of one human group from another'.[3] According to Hofstede (1980), the term culture is reserved for societies or nations. For specific groups within a society,

---

[1]   Ricks, D. (2006) *Blunders in International Business*, 4th edn. Chichester: Wiley-Blackwell.

[2]   Kroeber, A. and Kluckhohn, C. (1952) 'Culture: A Critical Review of Conceptions and Definitions.' Peabody Museum Papers 47, Harvard University, Cambridge, MA.

[3]   Hofstede, G. (1980) *Culture's Consequences: International Differences in Work-Related Values*. Newbury Park, CA: SAGE, p. 21.

FIGURE 2.1   The Forces of Enculturation

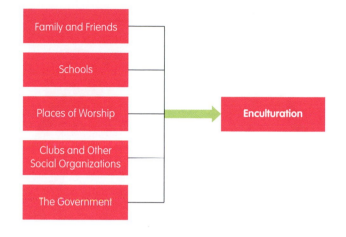

e.g. based on religion or language, it is more appropriate to use the term sub-culture. Culture determines the identity of human groups in much the same way as an individual's personality forms the basis of his identity. For our purposes, culture may be defined as an 'integrated system of learned behavior patterns that are distinguishing characteristics of members of a given society'.[4] Several aspects of the latter definition need to be examined. First, culture is learned. Every person is **encultured** into their particular culture, i.e. each of us is subject to numerous influences that teach us the 'right' way to behave from a cultural perspective. From birth, several individuals, groups and institutions work in concert to teach an individual his culture. These include family and friends, churches and other places of worship, schools, the government and social groups (see Figure 2.1). Culture is, therefore, shared among members of the same society and is passed down from one generation to another. Culture tends to resist change and remains fairly stable over time.

Enculturation is a fairly natural process and is complete at a very early age. Problems do arise, however, when an individual who has been encultured into one culture has to adjust to another. Managers working for large multinational corporations, for example, are often assigned to foreign subsidiaries for periods as long as several years. To be effective in their new, albeit temporary, work environment requires adaptation. This process of adaption, known as **acculturation**, may be extremely difficult for some but is essential if one is to be successful as a global marketer. Indeed, the inability to adapt may be very costly not only for the individual and his family but also for the firm. These costs are discussed in more detail when we examine global organizational structures and staffing in Chapter 13.

While cultural differences are extremely important, it is also interesting to note that there are common traits which cut across all cultures. These so-called **cultural universals** include mourning, body adornment, decorative art, music, religious rituals and courtship. Research shows that these are common across cultures but how they are practiced varies from culture to culture (Murdoch, 1945).[5]

---

[4]   Czinkota, M., Ronkainen, I., Farrell, C. and McTavish, R. (2009) *Global Marketing: Foreign Entry, Market Development and Strategy Implementation*. Toronto: Nelson Education, p. 65.

[5]   Murdoch, G.P. (1945) 'The common denominator of cultures', in R. Linton (ed.) *The Science of Man in the World*. New York: Columbia University Press, pp. 123–42.

FIGURE 2.2 The Elements of Culture

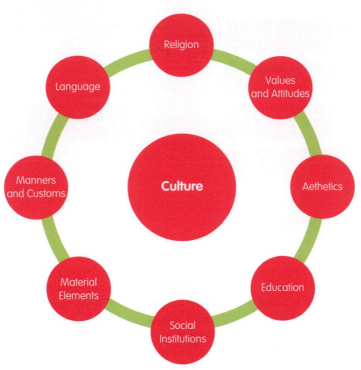

THE ELEMENTS OF CULTURE

Culture is a multidimensional construct. As shown in Figure 2.2, culture is generally regarded as being composed of eight elements[6] – language, religion, values and attitudes, manners and customs, aesthetics, education, social institutions and the material.

Language

Language consists of the words used to convey a message as well as the way in which the words are communicated, i.e. tone of voice. It is difficult for someone to be properly acculturated into a new culture without mastery of the language. As Levine and Munsch (2010) note, at 1 year of age babies typically know only a few words. By age 2, that number increases to 200–500 words and by age 3, most children are putting together multi-word sentences.[7] Mastery of one's native language takes place fairly quickly. Becoming an expert in a foreign language is, however, more difficult. Mastery of a foreign language involves going beyond mere word recognition and must include a deeper understanding and appreciation of the nuances with which words are used. Despite the fact that it is more difficult, proficiency in the language gives one a unique insight into the foreign culture, which is

---

6   Czinkota et al. (2009) op cit.

7   Levine, L.E. and Munsch, J. (2010) *Child Development: An Active Learning Approach*. London: SAGE.

not possible otherwise. Mastery of the host-country language gives the global marketing manager the ability to independently assess the economic and political environment in which the firm is operating without reliance on local counterparts. It also allows the global manager to engage directly with customers and channel members which leads to a better understanding of their needs. Given that people are generally more comfortable communicating in their native language, foreign language capability gives the global marketing manager a major advantage in gathering information about the host country's business environment. Mastery of the host-country language also gives the global manager the tools needed to engage in local communities and become embedded in the society. Of course, if the company's executives are perceived as a part of the local community, this may well represent a major reputational advantage for the firm.

Mastery of the host-country language also allows the firm to communicate more effectively in its promotional literature and avoid the types of translation errors that have plagued the advertising campaigns of so many multinational firms. Ford, for example, was surprised by the cool reception to its Pinto automobile in Brazil until it was pointed out that Brazilians do not wish to be seen driving a vehicle with a name that literally translates to 'tiny male genitals'. Similarly, Dell experienced communication difficulties in its foray into China when it tried to promote its direct sales business model. The phrase 'direct sales' translated to *zhi xiao* which is often used to mean an illegal pyramid scheme. To address the problem, Dell adopted a new phrase, *zhi xian ding gou*, which means direct orders. Traficante, an Italian brand of mineral water, received an interesting reception when launched in Spain as the name translates to '(drug) dealer' and Kellogg's had to rename its Bran Buds cereal in Sweden where the name translates to 'burnt farmer'. The technique of **translation-back-translation** is an effective approach in reducing the possibility of such errors (see Box 2.1).

Box 2.1

Translation-back-translation is a technique used to ensure an accurate translation of the firm's message. The message is first translated from the original language to the foreign language by one person. A different person then translates the foreign language version of the message back into the original language. The two versions in the original language are then compared to assess the quality of the translation exercise. The technique is effective in alerting the firm to omissions and potential blunders which may impact its reputation in the host country. In this regard, it is important to note that translation must effectively communicate emotion and that this may often lead to the use of very different words.

While English is generally regarded as the language of business, mastery of the host-country language will pay significant dividends for the global marketing manager. Table 2.1 provides a ranking of the most important business languages, other than English, based on multiple factors: the number of countries in which the language is official; the number of individuals who speak the language; the population of the countries in which the language is official; GDP; international trade; number of schools; life expectancy; literacy rates; number of Internet users/Internet penetration among native speakers; geographic continuity; and tourism receipts. Languages are awarded points from 0 to 100 based on their position relative to each other and these points are summed to arrive at the overall score. Mandarin is ranked first despite the fact that it is the official language of only one country. French, which is the official language of 27 nations, is ranked second, followed by Arabic.

It is important to recognize that language is not only verbal. Non-verbal forms of communication, such as hand gestures and body language, are often equally important in getting one's message across. For example, a North American manager engaged in negotiation may use the finger-and-thumb OK sign to indicate that everything is acceptable and that the deal can be completed. Depending on the country, however, this sign may have a very different interpretation. To a Japanese manager, the sign means that a bribe is being requested, while to a manager from the South of France it indicates that the North American executive believes that the deal is worthless. A Brazilian executive would find the sign to be rude and deeply offensive. Facial expressions also carry different meanings in different parts of the world. In Latin America, winking has romantic or sexual overtones, while the Chinese consider it to be rude and some Nigerians wink when they want their children to leave the room.

Edward Hall, a pioneer in the study of non-verbal communication, recognized five aspects of non-verbal, or silent, communication: time, space, material possessions, friendship patterns and business agreements. Managers should become familiar with the use of these forms of non-verbal communication if they are to be successful in foreign markets. In many parts of the world, such as Latin America, the Caribbean and the Middle East, time is viewed as flexible. People routinely arrive late for meetings or may not show up at all and they would be quite taken aback if an expatriate manager reacted negatively to their tardiness or absence. In other parts of the world, such as Germany, one is expected to be on time and tardiness is severely sanctioned. Space is also regarded as an important form of non-verbal communication. In some societies, people prefer to maintain a safe distance when interacting with others and react negatively when their personal space is invaded. In other countries, such as those in Latin America and the Middle East, people generally

TABLE 2.1   Ranking of Business Languages Other than English, 2011

Language	Score	Number of countries in which the language is official
Mandarin	57	1
French	51.7	27
Arabic	50.1	23
Spanish	49.2	20
Russian	44.6	4
Portuguese	37.7	8
Japanese	34.1	1
German	24.0	6
Italian	19.6	4
Korean	16.0	1
Turkish	13.7	1

Source: Bloomberg (n.d.) Mandarin Chinese Most Useful Business Language After English. Available at: http://media.bloomberg.com/bb/avfile/roQlgEa4jm3w

come quite close to each other when speaking. If a foreign executive, who may not be comfortable with such proximity, backs away from an Arab or a Latin American, this might incorrectly be taken as a negative reaction.

In some cultures, touching is quite acceptable, even between two people who have just met. A light touch on the arm or a kiss would not alarm most Latin Americans or Eastern Europeans but would not be taken kindly by Asians. Gender is also important. For example, Indian women would shake hands with a foreign woman but not with a foreign man and western women should not initiate a handshake with an Indian man. The global marketing manager also needs to be sensitive to the issue of non-verbal communication in advertising, as we see in the case of Drakkar Noir (Case Study 2.1).

case study 2.1: Drakkar Noir ad

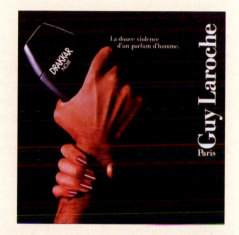

PHOTO 2.1   Drakkar Noir Ad – Saudi Arabia   **PHOTO 2.2**   Drakkar Noir Ad – Europe

Global marketers must often adjust their advertising approaches and their use of non-verbal cues depending on the country. Guy Laroche, manufacturer of the men's cologne, Drakkar Noir, is a case in point. The firm's European ads show a woman firmly grasping a man's bare forearm. In Saudi Arabia, the firm modified the ad so that the man's forearm is clothed in the sleeve of a dark suit and white shirt and the woman's fingers are barely touching.

Source

Jandt, F. (2013) *An Introduction to Intercultural Communication Identities in a Global Community*, 7th edn. London: SAGE.

Discussion Questions

1. In modifying the Drakkar Noir ad for Saudi Arabia, what problem is the company attempting to solve?
2. Do you believe that the company was able to achieve its objective with the modified advertisement? Why/why not?

Societies also differ in terms of the level of importance attached to material possessions. In some societies, the type of car one drives, the business suit one wears and the mobile phone one uses are regarded as important tools of non-verbal communication. In other societies, however, such symbols have much less relevance and may even send the 'wrong' message. The importance of friendship patterns also varies depending on the societal context. In some countries, individuals must first be friends before business transactions are undertaken and your network of personal relationships becomes a powerful means of communication with prospective business partners. Similarly, in some countries business agreements tend to be informal. Western managers would be extremely uncomfortable closing a deal with just a handshake and would certainly prefer a more formal written contract. Asian managers, in contrast, are likely to be far more comfortable with an informal agreement.

Religion

Most individuals have a belief in the existence of a higher power and subscribe to some form of organized religion. Religion provides people with a sense of purpose and a set of ideals to which they should aspire. There are several major religions which are shared by people around the world, including Christianity, Islam, Hinduism, Confucianism and Buddhism. Other religions such as Judaism have few followers but have had a significant impact on world history. For example, while there are only 13 million Jews worldwide, the religion has a history dating back some 3,000 years and has had a profound impact on Middle Eastern politics and international relations. Some countries, such as China and Cuba, officially hold to a tradition of secularism but religious beliefs still exert a powerful influence. Global marketers need to understand the differences between the various religions as well as divisions that may exist within particular religions.

Christianity is the largest organized religion and is comprised of two major groups – Catholics and Protestants. Most Christians are to be found in the Americas and Europe as well as Africa. The religion is founded on the life and teachings of Jesus of Nazareth. There are roughly 2 billion Christians in the world, roughly one-third of the population of the planet. Roman Catholics make up roughly 50 percent of the total number of Christians, or one billion people. Catholics and Protestants are united in their belief in Jesus Christ as the messiah prophesized in the Bible and in the doctrine of the Holy Trinity, i.e. God as Father, Son and Holy Spirit. The two groups differ significantly, however, in their attitudes to money. Catholics have generally downplayed, if not discouraged, the individual pursuit of money, while Protestants have emphasized the importance of hard work and the accumulation of wealth. Protestants argue in favor of living a frugal lifestyle, saving and investing.

Islam is the second largest organized religion (with roughly 1.6 billion adherents) and is comprised of two major sects – Sunni and Shia. Followers of Islam, known as Muslims, believe that Muhammad was the last of God's prophets and that the Qur'an is the last and final articulation of God's teachings. Muslims believe that Jesus, Moses and Abraham were prophets and do not subscribe to the Christian belief in the divisibility of God as reflected in the Holy Trinity. Islam has five pillars – prayer performed five times a day; fasting during the holy month of Ramadan; pilgrimage to the city of Mecca; alms giving; and testimony. Islam is supportive of business but frowns on any business practices that may be viewed as exploitative. Islamic banking, for example, is not based on charging interest to borrowers as is traditional western banking. Interest (or riba) is viewed as being socially unjust. *Sharia* (the law of Islam) governs trade, economics and business, as well as many other aspects of Muslim life. Women, for example, may face constraints in terms of participating in business activities, participating in market research surveys or even interacting with male salespeople. The types of products sold, or whether they can be sold at all, will also be determined by *Sharia*. The sale of alcohol, for example, is prohibited and meat and poultry exported to Muslim countries must be *halal*, i.e. the animal must be slaughtered in the name of God (Allah) and certified as such. There is significant sensitivity among followers of Islam surrounding the portrayal of their religion in western media, and in some cases these sensitivities have impacted firms' business operations in Muslim countries (see Case Study 2.2).

case study 2.2: Danish cartoon row

Over the last few years, protests have erupted around the world in response to what have been described as slights against the Muslim faith and the Prophet Muhammad. In September 2006, the Danish newspaper *Jyllands-Posten* published a series of cartoons which Muslims found to be deeply offensive. Islamic tradition forbids depictions of the Prophet Muhammad. Despite this, several newspapers across Europe reprinted the cartoons to support their belief in freedom of the press in a secular society. As a result of the uproar, the Danish–Swedish dairy processor, Arla Foods, reported that its sales to the Middle East had plummeted to zero as consumers boycotted its products. Arla Foods exports mostly cheese, milk and butter to the Middle East and is one of the most visible Danish companies in the region. The firm immediately became the poster child for the crisis, despite the company's efforts to distance itself from the controversy. The firm, for example, ran full-page advertisements in a number of Arab newspapers condemning the cartoons and criticized the Danish media for publishing them. While the firm's efforts did cause some Arabs to adopt a softer stance, many others remained unconvinced.

PHOTO 2.3

In 2012, an amateur trailer for a video titled the Innocence of Muslims was posted on YouTube and also sparked outrage in the Muslim world. The YouTube video which again ridiculed the Prophet Muhammad also sparked a wave of protests across the Middle East. These and other incidents dating back to the 1980s demonstrate individuals' sensitivity to attacks against their religious beliefs and the need for sensitivity on the part of the global marketer and the general public.

Source

BBC (2012) Muhammad Cartoon Row Intensifies. Available at: http://news.bbc.co.uk/2/hi/europe/4670370.stm, accessed October 16, 2012.

Discussion Questions

1. Should western media demonstrate greater cultural sensitivity towards adherents of the Muslim faith? Why/why not?
2. How should a company such as Arla Foods respond to the loss of sales from the controversy over the Danish cartoons?

Hinduism is the third largest organized religion with roughly 1 billion followers. It is the dominant religion in India, as well as in countries such as Nepal and Mauritius. Hindus do believe in the notion of a God or Supreme Being but followers also subscribe to the existence of lower-level deities. Hinduism is not only a religion but is also a way of life predicated on the caste system, a rigid form of social stratification which severely restricts upward mobility and economic advancement. While still in existence, the caste system is, however, much less relevant today as a determining factor in one's success.

Buddhism is the world's fourth largest religion with an estimated 350 million followers. Buddhism emphasizes spiritual enlightenment over material possessions and teaches that life is a series of rebirths into one of several planes of existence. Unlike Christianity and Hinduism, Buddhists do not subscribe to the notion of a soul. Buddhism derived from Hinduism but, unlike the latter, does not argue in favor of a caste system.

Confucianism has over 150 million followers, mainly in China, Japan and Korea. Developed by the Chinese philosopher Confucius, the religion stresses loyalty and community relationships. Confucianism does not involve a belief in the supernatural, in deities or gods, and from this perspective may be viewed more as a code of ethical conduct than as a traditional religion.

Values and attitudes

Values are beliefs or norms that have been internalized and are shared among a group of individuals. Attitudes, on the other hand, represent the evaluation of alternatives based on these values.[8] Our values and attitudes determine what we see as being right or desirable. For example, traditional animosity between China and Japan has spilled over into consumer purchase decisions, with some Chinese refusing to purchase Japanese products and vice versa. The concept of ethnocentricity was introduced earlier in this chapter. In some countries, however, the global marketer may encounter **consumer ethnocentricity** (Shimp and Sharma, 1987),[9] i.e. consumers who believe that it is unpatriotic or even immoral to purchase foreign products (see Box 2.2). In such countries, there is strong resistance against those who produce and market foreign products.

Box 2.2

The term consumer ethnocentricity was coined by Terence Shimp and Subhash Sharma in 1987 as an extension of the concept of ethnocentricity. Since that time, it has become well entrenched in the global marketing and international business literature. The CETSCALE is the instrument developed by Shimp and Sharma to measure the tendency towards being consumer ethnocentric. It was originally developed to understand American views on purchasing foreign products and consisted of 17 items which consumers ranked on a scale of 1 (= strongly agree) to 7 (= strongly disagree). Below are some of the items in the scale:

'We should purchase products manufactured in America instead of letting other countries get rich off us'

'It is not right to purchase foreign products, because it puts Americans out of jobs'

'A real American should always buy American-made products'

'Only those products that are unavailable in the USA should be imported'.

The CETSCALE is useful in understanding negative consumer reactions to foreign products – a problem that a global marketer may well have to confront. It is not uncommon for animosities between countries to lead to increased patriotism and for these sentiments to spill over into commercial transactions. This may result in resistance on the part of some consumers to purchase foreign products. In 2012, for example, Japanese auto manufacturers reported a marked slowdown in sales to China, which some analysts have linked to a territorial dispute over two islands in the East China Sea. In this case the negative consumer reaction of Chinese consumers to Japanese products had little to do with their value proposition and everything to do with their country of origin.

Strongly held values and attitudes tend to be rooted in core beliefs such as religious teachings. These change only very slowly over time and the global marketer needs to understand and appreciate this. The global marketer may, however, find that attitudes towards change tend to be more positive in developed countries such as the USA, Canada, Japan and those in Western Europe.

---

8   Czinkota et al. (2009) op cit., p.75.

9   Shimp, T.A. and Sharma, S. (1987) 'Consumer ethnocentrism: Construction and validation of the CETSCALE', *Journal of Marketing Research*, XXIV, August: 280–9.

case study 2.3: Dara and Sara dolls in Iran

To counter the perceived influence of Mattel's Barbie and Ken dolls on Iranian values, a government agency (the Institute for the Intellectual Development of Children and Young Adults) affiliated with Iran's Ministry of Education is marketing its own line of dolls, dubbed Dara and Sara. The new toys, a brother and sister, are modeled on well-known Iranian school-book characters. Sara typically wears a white headscarf and is dressed in a full-length chador – a traditional garment worn by devout Muslim women. One toy seller, Masoumeh Rahim, argued that playing with Mattel's skimpily dressed Barbie may lead girls to grow up into women who reject traditional Iranian values. The toy seller goes on to state: 'I think every Barbie doll is more harmful than an American missile.' Initially, store owners were instructed to hide the leggy, buxom American dolls behind their Iranian competitors but in the wake of US sanctions the Iranian government has completely banned sales of Barbie.

Dara and Sara were introduced in 2002 and the government agency responsible initially manufactured 100,000 dolls. The dolls retail for about $15 – less than half the price of Mattel's Barbie. Reports suggest, however, that Iranian girls are not impressed with the new toys. One Iranian mother is quoted as saying, 'my daughter prefers Barbies. She says Sara and Dara are ugly and fat'. While pointing to dolls covered in long black veils in the store window, one retailer said, 'we still sell Barbies but secretly and put these in the window to make the police think we are just selling these kinds of dolls'.

PHOTO 2.4

Barbie also faces competition from Fulla in the Middle East. Named after a type of jasmine that grows in the Levant, Fulla is also supposed to reflect Muslim values. NewBoy Design Studio, a Syrian firm, is the creator of Fulla. The doll came to market a year after Dara and Sara were introduced and retails for around $16. Fulla has dark eyes and is marketed wearing an abaya with matching headscarf and a pink prayer mat. In advertisements, Fulla is portrayed as loving, caring and respectful of her mother and father. In commercials, the doll is often shown praying as the sun rises, baking a cake to surprise her friend or reading a book at bedtime. Unlike Barbie, Fulla does not have a boyfriend.

Mattel markets collectors' dolls, including a Moroccan Barbie and a doll called Leila, intended to represent a Muslim slave girl in an Ottoman court. A spokesperson for NewBoy notes, however: 'This isn't just about putting the hijab on a Barbie doll … You have to create a character that parents and children will want to relate to. Our advertising is full of positive messages about Fulla's character'. As a result of the firm's marketing efforts, Fulla's popularity has been growing across the Middle East.

Sources

BBC News (2002) Muslim Dolls Tackle 'Wanton' Barbie. Available at: http://news.bbc.co.uk/2/hi/middle_east/1856558.stm, accessed July 28, 2006.

Israeli National News (2012) Iran Bans Barbie: Meet Dara and Sara. Available at: www.israelnationalnews.com/News/News.aspx/151804#.UaPqzdl3uSo, accessed May 27, 2013.

New York Times (2005) Bestseller in Mideast: Barbie with a Prayer Mat. Available at: www.nytimes.com/2005/09/22/international/middleeast/22doll.html?_r=0, accessed May 31, 2013.

Reuters (2012) Iran Cracks Down on Moral Peril of Barbie Peddlers. Available at: www.reuters.com/article/2012/01/16/us-iran-barbie-ban-idUSTRE80F0SI20120116, accessed May 27, 2013.

Discussion Questions

1. How likely is it that the Iranian government's efforts to police the sale of Barbie dolls will be successful?
2. What (if anything) should Mattel do to compete with new market entrants such as Fulla and Sara?

Manners and customs

Understanding the manners and customs of the host country is extremely important for the global marketing manager. For example, manners and customs have a major impact on the process of business negotiations. Japanese executives are noted for remaining silent for long periods during negotiations, which is likely to unnerve less seasoned western negotiators, prompting them to lower their prices or offer other inducements to get the deal done. Similarly, in the Middle East, negotiations may drag on for extended periods because Arab executives may want to spend some time getting to know their western counterparts.

Manners and customs also play a part in the area of gift giving. The type of gift given and how it should be presented will vary based on the host country. In China, for example, a

PHOTO 2.5

gift is presented by extending it to the recipient with both hands. The color of the wrapping also has to be carefully considered as certain colors are not well received in some countries (see below). Cultural superstitions also play a role in gift giving and purchase decisions. The number of units in a package may have implications for what gifts are bought and how those gifts are perceived in countries with strong cultural superstitions. In China, for example, the number 8 is regarded as lucky while the number 4 is not. In western societies, the number 7 is associated with good luck and the number 13 with bad luck. In fact, research suggests that cultural superstitions may in fact override economic rationality (Block and Kramer, 2009).[10] It has been shown, for example, that for the same price consumers in some countries may prefer to purchase a product with fewer but a lucky number of units in the package, as opposed to one with a greater number of units.

Q Spotlight on Research 2.1   Consumer Ethnocentrism

Consumer ethnocentrism may present global marketers with significant obstacles to the penetration of what would otherwise be lucrative international markets. Because of its practical importance, researchers have expended considerable effort in better understanding this phenomenon. An article by Josiassen, Assaf and Karpen (2011), published in the *International Marketing Review*, is an example of the work undertaken in this area. These researchers focus on the influence of consumer demographic variables, i.e. age, gender and income, noting that the influence of these variables on consumer ethnocentrism is unclear in the extant literature. They also note that consumers of different income, gender and age profiles may well vary in their propensity to allow consumer-ethnocentric tendencies to influence their willingness to buy domestically produced products and that this too represents a research gap in the literature. The literature does suggest that consumer-ethnocentric consumers will have more favorable evaluations of domestic products than non-ethnocentric consumers. The moderating effect of demographic variables on this relationship is not, however, well understood.

Hypotheses

The authors test the following **hypotheses**:

---

[10] Block, L. and Kramer, T. (2009) 'The effect of superstitious beliefs on performance expectations', *Journal of the Academy of Marketing Science*, 37: 161–9.

H1. Older consumers are more consumer ethnocentric than younger consumers.

H2. Women are more consumer ethnocentric than men.

H3A. Lower-income consumers tend to be more consumer ethnocentric than higher-income consumers.

H3B. Higher-income consumers tend to be more consumer ethnocentric than lower-income consumers.

H4. The impact of consumer ethnocentrism on willingness to buy decreases with the consumer's age.

H5. The impact of consumer ethnocentrism on willingness to buy is moderated by gender so that the relationship is stronger for women than for men.

H6A. The impact of consumer ethnocentrism on willingness to buy increases with the consumer's income.

H6B. The impact of consumer ethnocentrism on willingness to buy decreases with the consumer's income.

The authors' conceptual model is illustrated in Figure 2.3.

FIGURE 2.3   Conceptual Model – Impact of Consumer Demographics on Consumer Ethnocentrism and Willingness to Buy

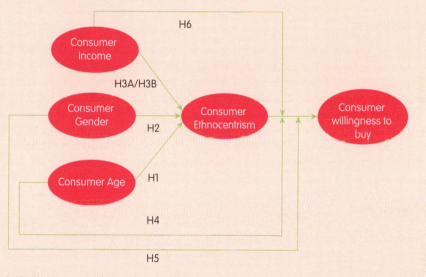

Source: Usunier, J. C. (2000) *International Marketing.* London: Pearson Education

Method

Data for the study were generated from a mall intercept survey of consumers. The authors used a convenience sample of 361 consumers who were shopping in a major capital city in Australia. Systematic sampling was used in which every tenth individual was stopped and asked to complete a questionnaire. To qualify for inclusion in the study, individuals had to be between 17 and 70 years of age and been living in Australia for more than one year. The sample was found to adequately represent the Australian population. Reflective scales with a seven-point response format were developed. The authors followed Shrimp and Sharma (1987) in their construction of their consumer ethnocentrism scale and Klein et al. (1998) for their willingness to buy scale. The consumer ethnocentrism scale included items such as: 'purchasing foreign-made products is un-Australian' and 'it is not right to purchase foreign products because it puts Australians out of jobs'. The willingness to buy scale included items such as: 'whenever possible I avoid buying Australian products' and 'whenever available I would prefer to buy products made in Australia'. Both scales showed high levels of reliability – $\alpha = 0.861$ and $\alpha = 0.949$ respectively. Confirmatory factor analysis was used to ascertain unidimensionality. Overall model fit was found to be satisfactory (Chi-squared = 1.329, RMSEA = 0.04, IFI = 0.99, CFI = 0.99).

(Continued)

(Continued)

Results

The authors utilize linear regression with interactions to test their hypotheses. The authors find that age had a significant and positive impact on consumer-ethnocentric tendencies ($\beta = 0.11$, $\rho < 0.05$). H1 was, therefore, supported. The results of the regression also showed support for H2, i.e. the authors find that female consumers are more ethnocentric than male consumers ($\beta = 0.11$, $\rho < 0.05$). The study did not, however, find evidence for a relationship between income and ethnocentric tendencies. Note that the income relationship was stated as two opposing hypotheses (H3A and H3B). As may be expected, consumer ethnocentrism was found to have a significant impact on consumer willingness to buy domestically produced products ($\beta = 0.74$, $\rho < 0.001$). Age was found to be a significant moderating factor in that relationship ($\beta = 0.51$, $\rho < 0.001$). Slope analysis showed that the relationship between consumer ethnocentrism and willingness to buy is stronger for younger consumers than for older consumers. The study finds support for H4. On the other hand, the results of the regression analysis do not support H5 or H6, i.e. gender and income do not have a significant impact on the focal relationship between consumer ethnocentrism and willingness to buy.

Implications

Given that consumer-ethnocentric tendencies were stronger for older consumers (than for younger consumers), the authors argue that older consumers represent an important segment for domestic firms. It should, however, be noted that older consumers are less willing to let their ethnocentric perspective influence their willingness to buy. The authors explain this by appealing to the crystallized abilities theory which suggests that older workers are more likely to focus on their past experience in evaluating key product features as opposed to product origin. As a result, the authors argue that firms need to be cautious in allocating resources to consumer-ethnocentric segments of the market without first understanding whether these efforts are likely to result in the desired change in consumer behavior. Consumer demographics do matter.

References

Josiassen, A., Assaf, A.G. and Karpen, I.O. (2011) 'Consumer ethnocentrism and willingness to buy: Analyzing the role of three demographic consumer characteristics', *International Marketing Review*, 28, 6: 627–46.

Klein, J.G., Ettenson, R. and Morris, M.D. (1998) 'The animosity model of foreign product purchase: An empirical test in the People's Republic of China', *Journal of Marketing*, 62, 1: 89–100.

Shimp, T.A. and Sharma, S. (1987) 'Consumer ethnocentrism: Construction and validation of the CETSCALE', *Journal of Marketing Research*, XXIV, August: 280–9.

Discussion Questions

Read Josiassen et al. (2011) and answer the following questions:

1. One of the key limitations of this study is that it does not take into account the impact of culture on the relationship between demographic variables and consumer ethnocentrism. Do you believe the results of this study will hold true in a non-western society such as China? Why/why not?
2. How would you re-design this research project to empirically investigate the role of culture on the relationship between consumer ethnocentrism and consumer willingness to buy?
3. Why do you believe gender and income did not have a significant moderating impact on the relationship between consumer ethnocentrism and willingness to buy domestically produced products?

TABLE 2.2   Color Associations in Global Marketing

Color	Anglo-Saxon	Germanic	Latin	Nordic	Chinese	Japanese
White	Purity and happiness				Death and mourning	Death and mourning
Blue	High quality Corporate	Warm Feminine		Cold Masculine	High quality Trustworthy	High quality Trustworthy
Green	Envy Good taste		Envy		Purity Reliability	Love Happiness
Yellow	Happiness Jealousy	Envy Jealousy	Envy Infidelity		Purity Good taste Royalty Authority	Envy Good taste
Red	Masculinity Fear Love Lust Anger	Fear Anger Jealousy	Masculine	Positive	Love Happiness Luck	Love Anger Jealousy
Purple	Authority Power				Expensive Love	Expensive Sin Fear
Black	Expensive Fear Grief	Fear Anger Grief	Fear Anger Grief		Expensive Powerful	Expensive Powerful

Source: Adapted from Aslam, M. (2006) `Are you selling the right colour? A cross-cultural review of colour as a marketing cue', *Journal of Marketing Communications*, 12, 1: 15–30.

Aesthetics

Every society has its own view of what is considered beautiful or in good taste. The global marketing manager needs to understand what is considered aesthetically appealing to consumers in the host country. The use of sex in advertising is a case in point. Images and messages featuring sexual content may play well in Western Europe but are not likely to be well received in China. As noted above, the use of various color associations in packaging and promotional material needs to be considered. Color influences consumer perceptions as it induces specific moods and emotions as well as perceptions of price and quality. As noted by Aslam (2006), the choice of the 'wrong' color may lead to customer rejection and business failure.[11] Black is the traditional color of mourning in countries such as the USA and Canada, whereas white carries that symbolic meaning in Japan and some other Asian countries. Red is associated with love, happiness and luck in China but fear, anger and jealousy in Germanic societies (see Table 2.2). In African countries such as Nigeria and Chad, red is associated with bad luck.

Education

Education is an important vehicle for cultural change and the transmission of cultural values. Educational institutions such as universities and colleges have an important role to play in the

---

[11] Aslam, M. (2006) 'Are you selling the right colour? A cross-cultural review of colour as a marketing cue', *Journal of Marketing Communications*, 12, 1: 15–30.

transmission of cultural values but at the same time are instrumental in exposing students to new ideas and ways of thinking. Students who study in foreign countries will bring back to their home countries many of these new ideas and approaches which, over time, may lead to cultural change.

The global marketer should become familiar with educational levels in the host country by analysis of objective data on literacy rates, percentage of the population with a university education, etc. The type of education and training emphasized by the society also needs to be considered. Countries such as Japan tend to place relatively more emphasis on math and the sciences compared to western countries, and this may have implications for the production and use of technological innovations.

Social institutions

Social institutions are extremely important determinants of culture. In some societies, the family has a major impact on consumption patterns, both in terms of the speed with which purchase decisions are made and the products purchased. In western societies, the family unit is usually comprised of parents and children but in other parts of the world grandparents and other relatives are included. In some cultures, it is not uncommon for all members of the extended family to be consulted on major purchase decisions. In the workplace, familial relationships are also important. In Latin American countries, family members are routinely hired because the assumption is that they can be trusted. The same holds true in India where the hiring of one's family members is very much a cultural norm. To western managers, the practice is viewed as nepotism, which can lead to misunderstandings when doing business in countries in Latin America or in India.

An important aspect of the process of socialization is the role of **reference groups**, i.e. groups of individuals who play an important role in imparting values and attitudes and who thereby shape behavior in their societies. One may distinguish between **primary reference** groups which include family and coworkers, and **secondary reference** groups such as professional associations. In the case of primary reference groups, there are continuous and ongoing interactions and opportunities to influence, while in the case of secondary reference groups interaction is more sporadic. Both, however, provide the social interaction that is important in shaping an individual's value system and attitudes. These values and attitudes in turn have an impact on the types of products which are purchased and the source of these products.

In western business, there is a heavy reliance on formal structures and power relationships. Lines of authority, rules and contracts serve to provide order and integrity to business relationships. In China, the emphasis is more on the acquisition and use of political capital in order to get things done. While formal contracts are important in the measurement of progress, the Chinese tend to emphasize *guanxi* in their relationships.[12]

★ Box 2.3

The concept of guanxi is generally regarded as a Chinese term for interpersonal relationship. Guanxi is rooted in Confucian philosophy and is essentially a concept with six principal attributes:

- Guanxi binds two individuals through an exchange of favors rather than through sentiment and emotion.

- Guanxi stresses reciprocity in the exchange of favors between parties to the guanxi relationship, although the favors exchanged are not necessarily of equal value.

---

12   See Box 2.3; Tsui, A. (2001) 'Book review: Guanxi and Business', *Asia Pacific Journal of Management*, 18: 407–13; and Luo, Y. (2000) *Guanxi and Business*. Singapore: World Scientific.

- It is also possible, through personal introductions and recommendations, for an individual to be connected to the guanxi network of her friends or colleagues.

- Guanxi is regarded as a personal concept which operates at the level of the individual and is heavily influenced by other constructs such as trust, respect, commitment, face and social status.

- Guanxi is associated with the concept of relational capital and may be best viewed as a long-term intangible asset that can be augmented over time by successive personal interactions and drawn down in times of difficulty.

- Participants in a guanxi relationship operate on the basis of an unwritten code of conduct where the only sanction for violation is the loss of one's respectability and standing in Chinese society.

The material

The extent to which a society places an emphasis on the material can have a significant impact on global marketing strategy. Generally, societies in which material possessions matter will present better marketing opportunities for the global firm. Of course, the nature of the economic system chosen by a particular country has a bearing on its ability to provide for the material well-being of its citizens. The material is often related to technological progress. Access to the Internet and mobile devices has a profound impact on an individual's desire for material goods, as the ability to observe how others around the world live, work and play can be a powerful driver of materialism.

Expand Your Knowledge

Wong, Y.H. and Leung, T. (2001) *Guanxi: Relationship Marketing in a Chinese Context*. New York: International Business Press, an imprint of Haworth Press Inc.

This book provides a more detailed treatment of the guanxi construct and how it differs from western views.

CULTURAL ANALYTICS

Global marketing managers need to understand and explain differences in the cultures of the societies in which they do business. Several scholars have sought to develop frameworks and typologies to allow managers to more easily understand the culture within which they are working.

HIGH VS. LOW CONTEXT

One relatively simple approach to classifying cultures is based on the writings of Edward Hall.[13] Hall (1976) divides cultures into **high context** and **low context** based on their approach to communication. In high-context cultures, the context surrounding the message is just as important as the actual message itself. The setting in which the communication is delivered and the status and importance of the person delivering the message are all part

---

[13] Hall, E.T. (1976) *Beyond Culture*. Garden City, NY: Anchor Press.

FIGURE 2.4   The Context Continuum

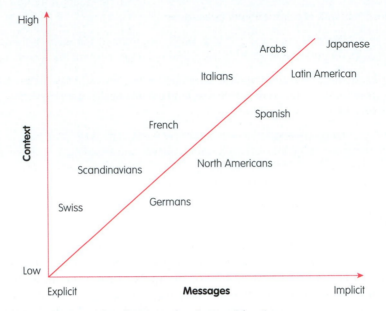

Source: Usunier, J. C. (2000) *International Marketing.* London: Pearson Education

of the communication. Effective communication, therefore, depends on the receiver's ability to decode these contextual cues without an overreliance on the words used. In low-context societies, on the other hand, communication is much more explicit, i.e. the words used are meant to accurately and precisely convey meaning. Most of the relevant information is embodied in the words used and context provides much less insight. As Hall has pointed out, no society exists on one end of the scale or the other. Americans, however, engage in low-context communication, while Japanese and Arabs tend to engage in high-context communication (see Figure 2.4).

Where a country falls on the continuum between low and high context has important implications for the global marketer. Western managers conducting market research to launch a new product in a high-context country such as Japan need to be aware of the fact that respondents may not be blunt in expressing their true feelings about the product. Respondents may be reluctant to express negative opinions out of a desire not to offend the interviewer. Similarly, a Middle Eastern expatriate manager working in the USA may well be put off by direct criticism from a supervisor during a performance appraisal. An understanding of where countries fall on the continuum is, therefore, extremely useful to the global manager.

HOFSTEDE'S FRAMEWORK

A second approach to the analysis of culture is Hofstede's framework (Hofstede, 1981).[14] Hofstede argues that four dimensions account for observed differences in national culture. This finding came out of a major study of IBM employees which Hofstede undertook to shed light on what motivated individuals from various societies. Hofstede's pioneering study involved conducting some 100,000 interviews with IBM employees based in over 70 countries. The study was conducted from 1967–1973. Hofstede's dimensions are described below.

14   Hofstede, G. (1981) *Culture's Consequences.* London: SAGE.

Individualism

The individualism dimension of Hofstede's framework reflects the extent to which people in a given society are focused on individual achievements and accomplishments as opposed to the overall success of the group to which they belong. In an individualistic society, personal success is highly valued and people are rewarded for their initiative and ability to act for themselves. In contrast, individuals from more collectivist societies are oriented towards teamwork and the success of the group. In such societies, one's ability to work as a member of a team and contribute to its success is highly valued and individual accomplishments are generally downplayed.

Power distance

The power distance dimension is reflective of the extent to which individuals are willing to accept inequality in their society. In societies which score high on the power distance dimension, individuals are more willing to accept significant differences in wealth and influence. Individuals are more comfortable with the notion that a few in society are privileged and materially very successful while others may be living in abject poverty. However, in those societies which score relatively lower on the power distance dimension, inequality is not accepted so easily. Individuals in such societies may be expected to argue strongly for a more equitable distribution of their society's wealth, for greater decision-making authority within organizations and for an equitable distribution of corporate profits among managers, workers and other stakeholders.

Uncertainty avoidance

Hofstede proposed the uncertainty avoidance dimension to reflect the extent to which individuals in a society expect to be guided by formal rules and regulations. Societies which score relatively higher on this dimension expect structure and organization and have little appetite for risk and ambiguity. Individuals from such societies will tend to seek out plans and policies to guide their actions and are unlikely to exhibit high-risk entrepreneurial behavior. In contrast, individuals from societies which score relatively lower on this dimension are far more likely to exhibit initiative and risk-taking behavior and will be less tolerant of bureaucratic policies and procedures. They are likely to embrace situations in which the payoff and consequences are not known in advance.

Masculinity

This dimension of Hofstede's framework reflects the extent to which a society tends to emphasize and reward 'masculine' values such as competition, success and performance as opposed to 'feminine' values such as nurturing and caring for others. It should be emphasized that this dimension has little to do with the gender of the individual and only reflects the values of the society to which the individual belongs.

Time

In subsequent writing, Hofstede added a fifth dimension, 'time', to reflect a society's long-term versus short-term orientation. Countries which score relatively high on this dimension are typically Asian (e.g. China, Hong Kong, Taiwan, Japan and South Korea). Most western countries (such as the USA and the UK) score relatively low on the time dimension. This dimension of Hofstede's framework may well reflect the orientation of Japanese and Chinese firms which tend to adopt a long-term time horizon in their investment decisions. While western firms are driven by the pressure to meet quarterly profit expectations, Japanese and Chinese firms are more focused on building market share and shareholder value over the long term.

Figures 2.5 and 2.6 present summaries of where various countries fall on the power distance and individualism, and the uncertainty avoidance and masculinity scales respectively.[15]

---

[15]   For countries not included in Figures 2.4 and 2.5, readers may access their scores at: http://geert-hofstede.com/countries.html

FIGURE 2.5

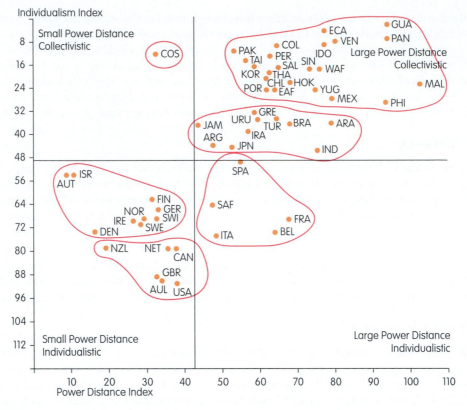

FIGURE 2.6

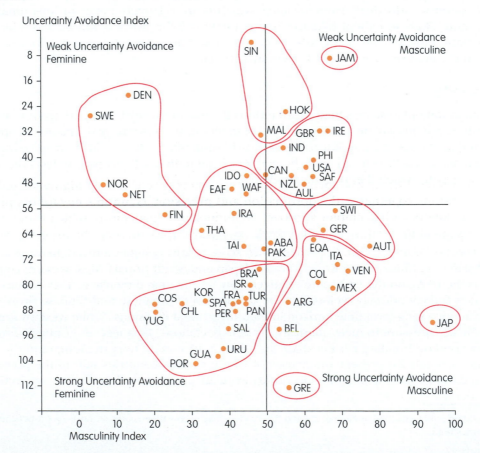

> ## ★ Box 2.4
>
> **C**ultural distance may be defined as the degree to which cultural values in one country differ from cultural values in another country (Sousa and Bradley, 2008). A country's cultural values are usually measured using Hofstede's dimensions. For example, to measure the cultural distance between the home country (A) and the host country (B), one could calculate a composite measure using the method developed by Kogut and Singh (1988).
>
> $$\text{Cultural Distance} = \sum_{j=1}^{4} \frac{(H_{Aj} - H_{Bj})}{4 \times V_j}$$
>
> where $H_{A,j}$ is the home-country score for Hofstede's cultural dimension j, $H_{B,j}$ is the score for the corresponding cultural dimension j in the host country, and V_j is the variance of the index score of cultural dimension j.
>
> A related concept is that of **psychic distance**. This may be thought of as the distance between two countries in the mind of the individual. Individuals will likely differ in their perceptions of the distance between two countries based on their own life experiences and world view.

GANNON'S METAPHORS

Hofstede's framework is the most widely used tool for the analysis of cultural differences and is often used in the academic literature to measure the **cultural distance** between countries (Kogut and Singh, 1988; Sousa and Bradley, 2008).[16] A simpler approach was, however, proposed by Gannon (2001).[17] Gannon argued that it is possible to describe a society's culture with a single descriptive metaphor. These metaphors are designed to capture in a simple but holistic manner the true essence of the culture of any given society. When heard, these metaphors should conjure up a mental image that accurately encapsulates the culture of the society under consideration. Gannon argued, for example, that American football is an appropriate metaphor for US culture. The sport is hard driving and competitive and features strong leaders calling the plays and directing the team's strategy on the field. The sport is also characterized by select individuals, who, based on their skill and abilities, are able to achieve glory and substantial monetary rewards. In contrast, the classical symphony is typically the metaphor used to describe German culture. The mental image conjured up in this case is that of highly skilled individuals working together with coordination and precision. Gannon's metaphors provide global marketers with a simpler approach to understanding a culture which is unfamiliar. While not a substitute for more thorough analysis, metaphors may be an effective way of providing managers with a quick mental image of the culture of a host country that may be of interest.

---

[16] Sousa, C.M.P. and Bradley, F. (2008) 'Cultural distance and psychic distance: Refinements in conceptualisation and measurement', *Journal of Marketing Management*, 24, 5–6: 467–88; and Kogut, B. and Singh, H. (1988) 'The effect of national culture on the choice of entry mode', *Journal of International Business Studies*, 19, 3: 411–32; see also Box 2.4.

[17] Gannon, M. (2001) *Understanding Global Cultures: Metaphorical Journeys Through 23 Nations*, 2nd edn. Thousand Oaks, CA: SAGE.

KLUCKHOHN-STRODTBECK (KS) FRAMEWORK

The KS framework examines cultural differences based on six dimensions.[18] According to Kluckhohn-Strodtbeck, cultural differences may be assessed from the standpoint of whether people believe that they are in control of their environment; whether individuals in society are future oriented or fixated on the past; whether they can be relied upon to act freely and responsibly; whether individuals in the society are more interested in material as opposed to spiritual goals; whether people in the society believe that they are collectively responsible for each other's welfare; and whether people prefer to conduct their affairs in private or in public (Kluckhohn and Strodtbeck, 1961). Some of the dimensions in the KS framework do have parallels in Hofstede's dimensions of masculinity and power distance but some, such as whether people prefer to conduct their affairs in private or public, have no counterpart in Hofstede's model.

THE GLOBE PROJECT

The Global Leadership and Organizational Behavior Effectiveness (GLOBE) project was a ten-year research exercise conducted by a team of scholars to study the relationship between culture and leadership effectiveness (House et al., 2004).[19] Seventeen thousand middle managers in the banking, food processing and telecommunications industries in 64 countries were interviewed as part of the project. The GLOBE researchers identified nine dimensions of culture.

Performance orientation

This dimension relates to the extent to which society places a high value on innovation and performance. Societies with high ratings on this dimension tend to be competitive and materialistic and engage in direct communication. Such societies tend to value training and development as a means of improving business performance.

Uncertainty avoidance

Societies with high levels of uncertainty avoidance emphasize rules, norms and formal procedures to reduce unpredictability. Such societies thrive on predictability and not on ambiguity and rely on rules to minimize uncertainty. Members of these societies take only well-calculated risks, tend to engage in formal communication, rely on rules and maintain meticulous records. Note that uncertainty avoidance is also one of the dimensions of Hofstede's framework.

In-group collectivism

The GLOBE researchers defined this dimension as 'the degree to which individuals express pride, loyalty, and cohesiveness in their organizations or families'.[20] Societies which score high on this dimension make a clear distinction between individuals who are members of the in-group and those who are members of the out-group. There is a strong commitment and a sense of loyalty to members of the in-group which does not exist for out-group members. Societies which score low on in-group collectivism make little distinction between

---

[18]   Kluckhohn, F. and Strodtbeck, F. (1961) *Variations in Value Orientations*. Evanston, IL: Row, Peterson & Co.

[19]   House, R.J., Hanges, P.J., Javidan, M., et al. (eds) (2004) *Culture, Leadership, and Organizations: The GLOBE Study of 62 Societies*. London: SAGE.

[20]   House et al. (2004) op cit., p. 12.

in-groups and out-groups and focus more on personal needs as opposed to obligations to a particular group.

Power distance

This dimension also has a parallel in Hofstede's framework. The GLOBE researchers define this dimension in terms of the extent to which society accepts authority, power differences and status privileges. In societies with high power distance, there is marked social stratification and upward mobility tends to be limited. Power is associated with social class and only a few have access to relevant information and society's limited resources. In contrast, societies which are low on this dimension tend to have a large middle class, upward mobility is common and a wider base of people have access to information and resources.

Gender egalitarianism

This dimension relates to the extent to which the society stresses gender equality. Societies which scored high on this dimension in the GLOBE study had a higher proportion of women in positions of power, fewer gender-segregated occupations and a similar level of educational achievement among males and females.

Humane orientation

The GLOBE researchers defined this dimension in terms of 'the degree to which individuals in organization or societies encourage and reward individuals for being fair, altruistic, friendly, generous, caring, and kind to others'.[21] Societies which score high on humane orientation sanction all forms of discrimination and members put the interests of others above their own. Societies with low scores on this dimension are far more materialistic and driven by power and self-interest.

Institutional collectivism

This dimension of the GLOBE framework is designed to capture the extent to which institutional and organizational procedures are focused on achieving an equitable distribution of society's resources. In these societies, according to the researchers, the economic system is geared to maximizing the interests of groups rather than individuals. Individuals see themselves as highly interdependent with the organization and the reward system emphasizes seniority and within-group equity.

Future orientation

This dimension of the GLOBE project has its parallels with the time dimension of Hofstede's framework. The GLOBE dimension captures the extent to which society rewards future-oriented behavior such as planning, saving and working towards long-term success. Societies which score high on this dimension exhibit a propensity to save and are flexible and adaptable in reaching their long-term goals. Societies which score low on this dimension, in contrast, exhibit low savings rates, a focus on instant gratification and inflexibility.

Assertiveness

The final dimension in the GLOBE study is assertiveness. Individuals from societies high on the assertiveness scale are confrontational and aggressive in their dealings with others. Such

---

[21]　House et al. (2004) op cit., p. 13.

FIGURE 2.7   Stages in the Development of Cultural Knowledge and Skill

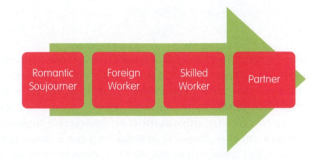

societies value competition and success, communicate directly and expect subordinates to take the initiative. Societies which are low on the assertiveness dimension communicate indirectly and allow others to 'save face'. Cooperation is favored over competition and subordinates are expected to be loyal.

CROSS-CULTURAL MANAGEMENT

As previously noted, global marketing managers must strive for cultural literacy. An ethnocentric approach to conducting business in foreign markets is unlikely to pay dividends for the multinational firm. Managers who are culturally literate are more likely to negotiate effectively with foreign counterparts, as they will have a command of the language and sensitivity to non-verbal communication. Culturally literate managers are also more likely to recognize unique differences in preferences of foreign consumers and appreciate subtle differences in buyer behavior. Further, managers who are acculturated will be able to better assess political and economic risk in the host country and more easily recognize important marketing opportunities.

   Research suggests that the development of cultural knowledge and skills proceeds in a series of stages. For example, in an empirical study of buyers in the fashion industry, western mangers were seen to develop cultural sensitivity in Asia according to a sequence of well-defined steps (Shapiro et al., 2008).[22] These are illustrated in Figure 2.7. The first was the **romantic sojourner**. In this stage, the manager is driven by a passion for travel and a desire to learn more about various cultures. Individuals at this stage have a fascination with different cultures but totally unrealistic expectations with respect to these new cultures. Carnivals, parades, exotic foods and beaches captivate the imagination of the romantic sojourner, and while they are engaged in business they lack the skills needed to truly understand the new culture at a deep level. At this stage, the business manager relies on two types of knowledge – **declarative** and **procedural**. Use of declarative knowledge involves an appeal to simple facts about the culture, while procedural knowledge consists of rules of thumb on what should be done in particular situations.

   The next stage in the process is that of the **foreign worker**. Unlike the romantic sojourner, the foreign worker has a much more realistic view of the foreign culture and a deeper understanding. The foreign worker begins to participate in the rituals and ceremonies of the new culture and has developed an in-depth understanding of the local business environment. At this stage, the manager has learned to control her western manners, postures, verbal and

---

22   Shapiro, J.M., Ozanne, J.L. and Saatcioglu, B. (2008) 'An interpretive examination of the development of cultural sensitivity in international business', *Journal of International Business Studies*, 39: 71–87.

non-verbal communication skills and has developed a comfortable relationship with the new culture. The love affair is, however, essentially over at this stage. Foreign workers who persevere deepen their understanding of the culture and become **skilled workers**. Skilled workers have developed the requisite diplomatic skills needed to react effectively in building relationships with host-country partners. They truly understand the host-country environment and can pick up on changes which may have an adverse impact on their business. Skilled workers have a more participatory style and are more tolerant of misunderstandings and mistakes. Despite the progress made in understanding the host-country culture, skilled workers eventually recognize that they will always be outsiders. A few skilled workers, however, do progress to the final stage of **partner**, characterized by the highest level of cultural sensitivity. The partner has developed an appreciation of the various nuances of the host culture and has also developed an intimate understanding of the differences between various sub-cultures.

TRAINING

The development of cultural literacy may be enhanced by various types of training. Foreign language training is certainly extremely useful in developing a manager's cultural literacy, as are country briefings and field visits. Broadly, there are two types of knowledge that managers may acquire about foreign cultures. Managers may acquire objective or **factual knowledge** of a foreign culture by, for example, learning about the meaning associated with different cultures' non-verbal symbols. Individual research and participation in cross-cultural training exercises are important in developing a manager's factual knowledge of a foreign culture. **Experiential knowledge** is the second type of knowledge that may be acquired by the global manager. The acquisition of this type of cultural knowledge, however, requires that the manager live in the foreign country and become immersed in its culture. Living in a country for an extended period of time, interacting with locals in the community, attending business meetings, etc. will lead to the development of experiential knowledge. Over time, experiential knowledge becomes **interpretive knowledge** as the manager learns to appreciate the nuances of the new culture, such as how time and space are interpreted and attitudes to foreigners.

CULTURE AND ETHICS

There is a strong correlation between culture and one's approach to ethical decision making. A society's core cultural values provide the basis for the assessment of alternatives and for decisions on whether some action is right or wrong (Beekun et al., 2010).[23] Research has shown that societies have different views on which issues fall in the moral domain requiring an ethical decision, and which do not (Haidt et al., 1993).[24] Further, the approach used by individuals to resolve ethical dilemmas also depends on culture. Whether a society is individualistic or collectivistic, for example, will have an impact on the process of ethical decision making.

It is imperative that the global marketing manager understand the relationship between ethics and culture in all countries in which business is conducted. As firms expand internationally, global managers will be confronted with situations in which ethical decisions must be

---

[23]   Beekun, R., Stedham, Y., Westerman, J. and Yamamura, J. (2010) 'Effects of justice and utilitarianism on ethical decision making: A crosscultural examination of gender similarities and differences', *Business Ethics: A European Review*, 19, 4: 309–25.

[24]   Haidt, J., Koller, S.H. and Dias, M.G. (1993) 'Affect, culture, and morality, or is it wrong to eat your dog?', *Journal of Personality and Social Psychology*, 65, 4: 613–28.

made. These may range from acceptance of the use of child or prison labor in some cultures to local expectations that bribes will be offered. How these ethical problems are perceived depends heavily on one's cultural perspective. Should the global marketing manager go along with practices that are viewed as unethical in the home country because they are tolerated or accepted in the host country?

SUMMARY

Culture is one of the most important aspects of the uncontrollable environment. This integrated system of learned behavior patterns has a profound impact on every aspect of an individual's life. The type of products purchased, the purchase decision process and one's approach to business negotiations are all influenced by culture. The point was made that culture is in fact a multidimensional construct and includes elements such as language, values and attitudes, religion, and manners and customs. It was also argued that culture remains fairly stable over time and that the goal of the global marketing manager is to develop an acceptance and comfort level that allows him to function effectively in the new environment, i.e. to develop cultural literacy.

Various models and frameworks are available to assist the global marketing manager in better understanding the culture of the host country. These range from fairly comprehensive approaches, such as that proposed by Hofstede and researchers associated with the GLOBE project, to the much simpler Gannon metaphors. Culture is complex and the process of acculturation, while necessary, is time-consuming and difficult. Cross-cultural training is useful in assisting the global manager to adapt to the various cultures in which the firm operates.

 Real World Challenges

Tecmo Koei Exports Japanese Culture to Canada

Sam Richardson was not quite sure what he should do. He knew it would have happened sooner or later but as he stared at the email from head office the decision was still a bit of a shock. Sam had been appointed General Manager of Koei Canada about eight months ago and since that time it was clear that the company was not performing according to expectations. Maybe he should have raised his concerns with the executives at head office sooner before the decision was made to close the Toronto office.

Koei Canada is a wholly-owned subsidiary of Japan-based Tecmo Koei Co. Ltd. The company, a videogame developer, operates from an office in downtown Toronto, Canada, and employs roughly 50 people. Koei Canada develops games for personal computers, as well as home and hand-held game consoles. The company's software development team has completed development of *Fatal Inertia*, a futuristic aerial combat racing game which has been released for Xbox 360™ consoles. The company has also worked on aspects of two other games – the *Dynasty Warriors* series and *Crimson Sea*.

The email from head office alluded to the fact that Koei Canada's recent games were not selling well and that the company had to make tough financial decisions. As Sam met with his team to discuss the situation, it was clear that no one agreed with the assessment of the Japanese executives. It was 'culture', shouted

Susan from across the room on learning about the studio's closing. 'How are we expected to be productive when morale in this office is so low?', chimed in Jeff. Despite the protests, however, it was clear that Koei Canada had gone from working on major projects such as *Fatal Inertia* to producing low-end titles for mobile devices.

To Susan's point, when Koei Co. Ltd established its production studio in Canada, it attempted to infuse Japanese culture into its new subsidiary's operations. Several times each week, company employees would begin their day by greeting their boss with a collective 'Good morning' while standing at their desks. With the morning greeting out of the way, the company's general manager would then provide employees with a briefing on the company's plans and major initiatives. This ritual is quite common in Japanese corporate settings and is termed *chorei*. The practice is designed to encourage open dialogue within the organization and motivate employees to give their best to the company. *Chorei* is, however, quite alien to western culture and not practiced by Canadian firms. In order to ensure punctuality, Tecmo Koei also required its software programmers in the Toronto office to log into a digital clock. While 'punching' a clock is common among blue collar workers in a factory setting, it is generally not required of IT professionals. Tecmo Koei's decision to have these knowledge workers sit together in a large open room without cubicles also raised concerns among company employees. Further, the company's practice of having female employees serve tea to guests of the company's senior executive struck many in the Toronto office as sexist and antiquated. At the end of every year, both senior and junior employees of Koei Canada were expected to participate in *o soji* – a cleanup of the office. This too was a practice common in Japan but which had no parallel in a western corporate environment. Koei Canada had a free rein in terms of creative content. Despite this freedom, however, attempts to impose Japanese culture on westerners made it difficult to maintain staff morale and also made it difficult for Koei Canada to retain valuable and highly skilled employees. Members of the game developer community were aware of the morale problems at Koei Canada and, as a result, the company also experienced significant challenges in recruiting top new talent. Sam and his team were convinced that there were extenuating circumstances that led to the subsidiary's poor performance.

Sam knew that he would have to call the president of the company to explain his position but was unsure about what his approach should be. He knew that the Japanese engaged in high-context communication and were ethnocentric. How could he get his point across without offending his Japanese boss?

Sources

Czinkota, M., Ronkainen, I., Farrell, C. and McTavish, R. (2009) *Global Marketing: Foreign Entry, Market Development and Strategy Implementation*. Toronto: Nelson Education.

Financial Post (2013) Tecmo Koei Canada Closing its Toronto Studio. Available at: http://business.financialpost.com/2013/03/01/tecmo-koei-canada-closing-its-toronto-studio/, accessed June 4, 2013.

Gaming Blend (2013) Tecmo Koei's Canadian Studio Shutting Down Because Mobile Games Didn't Sell. Available at: www.cinemablend.com/games/Tecmo-Koei-Canadian-Studio-Shutting-Down-Because-Mobile-Games-Didn-t-Sell-53266.html, accessed June 4, 2013.

The Wall Street Journal (2007) A Firm's Culture Can Get Lost in Translation When It's Exported. Available at: www.goinglobal.com/hot_topics/general_dvorak_culture.asp, accessed February 23, 2007.

Questions

1. State the problem that Sam Richardson faces.
2. Identify the options available to Sam. Be sure to identify more than one.
3. Based on the options identified above, recommend a course of action. Be sure to provide a rationale and make a decision.

? discussion questions

1. As a global marketer, how would you deal with strong tendencies towards consumer ethnocentricity in a foreign country in which you wished to do business?

2. How important is it for the global marketing manger to speak more than one language?

3. In conducting business abroad, should global marketing managers be guided more by rules of moral conduct in their home country or by those in the host country?

4. Is it the job of the global marketer to change a country's cultural values and attitudes?

5. A western manager working in Iran gave the 'thumbs up' to his Iranian counterpart not knowing that it is considered a vulgar gesture there. How could this slight have been avoided?

FURTHER READING

Hall, E.T. (1981) *The Silent Language*. New York: Anchor Books.

Hofstede, G. (1980) *Culture's Consequences: International Differences in Work-Related Values*. Newbury Park, CA: SAGE.

ECONOMIC AND FINANCIAL ENVIRONMENTS

INTRODUCTION

The economic and financial environments are central to the design and implementation of global marketing strategy. The level of interest rates in the home and host countries has an impact on the firm's investment decisions, exchange rates have implications for the competitiveness of a country's exporting firms and income levels in the host country have a bearing on consumers' ability to purchase foreign products. Other macroeconomic variables such as inflation and unemployment rates also have a bearing on consumer demand for foreign goods and services. Economic variables such as interest rates, exchange rates, inflation, income and unemployment levels are important determinants of global marketing success but are clearly beyond the control of the global marketing manager. These uncontrollable variables need to be carefully monitored by the firm and factored into key strategic decisions.

A firm's decisions on the allocation of resources to foreign markets, and when to enter and exit those markets, are heavily influenced by economic factors. All economies go through periods of prosperity and recession. In some cases, downturns may extend for protracted periods of time and be quite severe. In such situations, some global marketing firms may choose to cut back on their foreign expansion plans or even exit non-core markets altogether. For other global firms, major economic and financial dislocations present unprecedented opportunities to acquire foreign assets at discounted prices and secure positions in important foreign markets.

With unprecedented economic and financial problems in Europe, a number of foreign multinationals have moved to acquire struggling European firms. For example, in 2012 Sany Heavy Industry, China's largest construction equipment group, acquired the German firm Putzmeister for €360 million excluding debt. Putzmeister is a Mittelstand company that manufactures high-tech concrete pumps and employs roughly 3,000 people. Although Putzmeister is the world's largest concrete pump manufacturer by sales, the company has seen its revenues decline by 50 percent since the global recession began in 2007. Also in 2012, Walgreens, the US pharmacy chain, announced plans to acquire an almost 50 percent stake in European pharmacy giant Alliance Boots GmbH for $6.7 billion. Alliance Boots is based in Switzerland and operates more than 3,300 stores, most of which are in the UK.

ECONOMIC FACTORS IN ASSESSING FOREIGN MARKETS

In making decisions with respect to which foreign markets to enter, and the level of resources to allocate to each, the global marketing firm must consider a number of economic variables. Population and market size, income and income distribution, as well as exchange rates and debt levels, are key factors to be considered. These are discussed in turn below.

MARKET SIZE AND POPULATION

The overall size of the market, as measured by its population, clearly has a bearing on market attractiveness. More populous countries such as China and India may point to stronger and more stable demand for foreign products and, therefore, present a more attractive opportunity for the global marketer. World Bank data suggest that the world's population approximated 7 billion in 2011, with China and India being the most populous countries (see Table 3.1). These two countries combined represent almost 40 percent of the world's population and 70 percent of the population of Asia. The USA, with a population count just in excess of 300 million, is ten times more populous than its neighbor to the north and provides Canadian exporters with a large and attractive target market.

The global marketer should recognize that the bulk of the world's population actually live in low- and middle-income countries. Such countries account for roughly 5.8 billion people, most of whom reside in Asia and Sub-Saharan Africa. High-income countries account for only 16 percent of the global population. The unique challenges faced, and opportunities presented, in marketing to low-income consumers are explored later in this chapter.

TABLE 3.1   Top 25 Most Populous Countries in the World, 2011

Country	Population ('000s)
China	1,344
India	1, 241
United States	311,592
Indonesia	242,326
Brazil	196, 655
Pakistan	176, 745
Nigeria	162, 471
Bangladesh	150, 494

Country	Population ('000s)
Russian Federation	141, 930
Japan	127, 817
Mexico	114, 793
Philippines	94, 852
Vietnam	87, 840
Ethiopia	84, 734
Egypt, Arab Rep.	82,537
Germany	81,726
Iran	74,799
Turkey	73,640
Thailand	69,519
Congo	67,758
France	65, 437
United Kingdom	62, 641
Italy	60, 770
South Africa	50, 587

Source: Data.worldbank.org (2013) World Development Indicators | Data. Available at: http://data.worldbank.org/data-catalog/world-development-indicators, accessed June 6, 2013.

The global manager is not, however, only interested in total population size in making decisions on resource allocations to foreign markets. Population growth rates are also critically important. The United Nations projects that the global population will reach 9 billion by the year 2050 with most of the increase concentrated in the developing world.[1] The population of developed countries is expected to increase only marginally by 2050. Interestingly, in both developed and developing countries, the UN projects that the population segment over age 60 will be the fastest growing over the next four decades. In developed countries, this segment of the population is expected to grow by 2 percent annually, while in the developing world the segment of the population over age 60 is expected to increase by 3 percent annually. China is an extreme case – with its one child policy the country is expected to stop growing entirely by 2032. The older segment of the population will become increasingly significant over the next several decades. The global marketing manager is well advised to take note of this trend, as it has implications for the types of products which will be in demand over the next few decades and how these products should be advertised and promoted. In China, for example, one may expect to observe a shrinking in the size of households over time as children become adults and leave home, or as one parent dies. Products that rely on use by multiple family members for volume may not fare well in that environment and marketers will be forced to focus not only on the retention of existing customers but also on the acquisition of new users. Opportunities to simply grow volume among existing households may prove to be quite limited.[2]

---

[1] United Nations Department of Economic and Social Affairs Population Division (2009) *World Population Prospects: The 2008 Revision.* Population newsletter no. 87, June.

[2] Nielsen.com (2013) *The Aging Chinese Marketplace: Lessons for Marketers.* Available at: www.nielsen.com/us/en/newswire/2010/the-aging-chinese-marketplace-lessons-for-marketers.html, accessed June 6, 2013.

The UN notes that currently the number of children and young adults (15–24 years) is a significant proportion of the populations of developing countries, which puts considerable pressure on these governments to provide educational resources and a climate that favors job creation and growth. In the more developed countries, the number of children is expected to remain relatively constant in the coming decades while the number of young adults is actually expected to decrease. Again, this trend has implications for global marketing firms targeting consumers in this age group.

INCOME AND INCOME DISTRIBUTION

In assessing foreign markets, the global marketer must consider not only population but also income and the distribution of that income. Income levels along with price levels, savings and access to credit determine consumer purchasing power. Global marketers should evaluate a country's level of income in making their judgments on consumers' ability to purchase their products. Income may be measured in a number of ways. The broadest measure is the country's **gross national product** (GNP), which is the total value of goods and services produced by the country over the course of a one-year period. This figure includes the value of the country's goods and services which are produced abroad. **Gross domestic product** (GDP) is a slightly more narrow measure and refers to the total value of goods and services produced domestically over a one-year period, i.e. it excludes the value of the country's international activities. In assessing a country's income level, GNP and GDP may be calculated on a per capita basis by dividing by the country's population.

Countries are usually classified by income. The World Bank, for example, classifies countries according to GNP (also referred to as Gross National Income or GNI) as low income ($1,025 or less); lower-middle income ($1,026 to $4,035); upper-middle income ($4,036 to $12,475); and high income ($12,476 or more). Low-income countries include many in Sub-Saharan Africa such as Uganda, Tanzania and Zimbabwe, while high-income countries include many in Europe such as Norway, Germany, France, Sweden and Luxemburg (see the income distribution in Figure 3.1). For example, Norway's GNI per capita was roughly US$89,000 in 2011, while that for the Democratic Republic of the Congo was just US$190 in that year. Interestingly, the two most populous countries in the world have relatively low per capita incomes compared to the USA, Canada, Germany and other industrialized countries. In 2011, China's GNI per capita stood at US$4,930 and India's at only US$1,420.

While the World Bank's country classification is based solely on income levels, various other organizations use alternative schemes to classify countries in their economic policy analyses. Countries such as Haiti, Afghanistan and Bangladesh are classified as **Least Developed**

FIGURE 3.1   World Bank Income Grouping of Countries

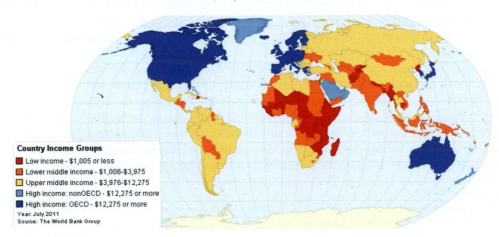

Source: ChartsBin, (2011) *Country Income Groups (World Bank Classification* [online]. Available at: http://chartsbin.com/view/2438, accessed: June 6, 2013.

Countries (LDC) by the United Nations. Such countries are characterized not only by low per capita incomes but also by weak infrastructural development, poor access to healthcare and education, and weak transportation and communication linkages. The term **Transition Countries** refers to countries which are in the process of moving away from central planning to more market-oriented economies. This group of countries includes Azerbaijan, Ukraine and Croatia. Countries such as the USA, Canada, Germany, France, Italy, Japan and the UK are referred to as **Developed Countries**. This group is also referred to as the **Group of Seven** (G7) and is characterized by high standards of living, well-developed physical infrastructure and advanced technology. Developed countries not only have well-developed service sectors but also a broad industrial base and high GDP per capita. The term **Newly Industrialized Countries** (NICs) refers to those which have not yet reached advanced status but have clearly outpaced their developing country counterparts. Included in this group are Brazil, China, India, Malaysia, Mexico, Thailand, the Philippines and South Africa. Brazil, Russia, India and China are now commonly referred to as the **BRIC Countries**. This group of four countries has rapidly developing economies and is gaining economic and political power on the world stage.

Box 3.1

The GINI coefficient is commonly used to measure income inequality. A GINI coefficient of 0 represents total equality while a value of 1 indicates total inequality.

The GINI coefficient is calculated from the Lorenz curve which plots cumulative family income (i.e. the studied variable) against the cumulative percentage of the population from poorest to richest. The index is the ratio of the area between a country's Lorenz curve and the 45-degree line (A) and the entire triangular area under the 45-degree line (A+B).

FIGURE 3.2   Lorenz Curve

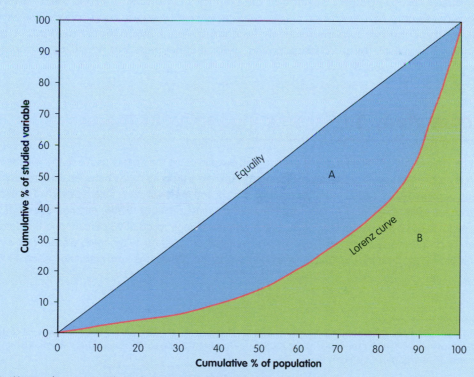

Source: http://www.rrh.org.au/articles/subvieweuro.asp?articleid=457

Depending on the nature of the firm's products and the characteristics of the market, some global marketers may opt to focus their marketing efforts exclusively on developed countries. Some executives may argue that these markets offer a deep pool of potential customers with the requisite purchasing power that allows their companies to operate profitably. Global marketers at other firms may choose to pursue customers in developing country markets, pointing to the significant populations in those countries, rapid growth rates and the possibility of modifying the firm's products to make them more affordable to low-income segments of the market.

Global marketers are not only interested in the level of income in a potential target market. An understanding of the distribution of that income is also important if the firm's marketing strategies are to be effective. In a 2011 study, the Organization for Economic Cooperation and Development (OECD) found that average incomes of the richest 10 percent of the population in its member countries were roughly nine times that of the poorest 10 percent.[3] The OECD also noted that this average 9:1 ratio was higher in some countries such as Italy, Japan and the UK (10:1), as well as Israel and the USA (14:1), and significantly higher in Mexico and Chile (27:1). A cursory examination of aggregate national income does not, therefore, provide the global marketer with complete information. An understanding of income distribution is clearly important to the firm as it formulates its product, pricing and advertising approaches for the foreign market.

EXCHANGE RATES

An exchange rate is the price of one country's currency expressed in terms of another. Exchange rates have a profound impact on the demand for imported goods and services and, therefore, have implications for global marketing strategy. When a country's currency is weak relative to, say, the US dollar, consumers in that country are required to relinquish more of their local currency to finance imports denominated in US dollars. The price of imported goods increases with a weak currency and this has the effect of dampening demand. By the same token, exporters do benefit from a weak currency as their exports are now relatively cheaper and more price-competitive in international markets. Indeed, governments may deliberately devalue their currency in order to improve the competitive position of the country's exporters. A strong local currency has the opposite effect to that described above, making imported goods and services less expensive but making the country's exports relatively less attractive on international markets. A revaluation, therefore, increases the purchasing power of local consumers but penalizes exporters.

case study 3.1: Income inequality in Japan

Japan has been mired in recession for over a decade, and despite being the third largest economy in the world now faces serious problems of poverty and income inequality. There is a growing divide between Japanese citizens able to afford luxury condominiums priced at almost a million dollars and others living in abject poverty. For example, the number of Japanese millionaires has increased more than 10 percent from 2001 to 2011 and now stands at 1.6 million. On the other hand, in 2011, the percentage of Japanese with no savings stood at 23 percent and the percentage of the population living in poverty stood at 16 percent. The number of households receiving welfare has increased to 2 million – a record for the country – and there have been a reported 700 deaths from starvation since 2000.

---

[3] Organization for Economic Cooperation and Development (OECD) (2011) *An Overview of Growing Income Inequalities in OECD Countries: Main Findings. Divided We Stand: Why Inequality Keeps Rising.* Available at: www.oecd.org/els/soc/49499779.pdf

Several factors contribute to the growing income inequality in Japan. One may point to the country's aging population and the movement away from lifetime employment that many Japanese enjoyed prior to the onset of the recession. As companies struggled to survive, traditional loyalties to workers were abandoned, leading to layoffs and marked reductions in household incomes. At the same time, pressure on government finances led to the scaling back or elimination of public works programs that have traditionally provided employment for unskilled workers. With Japanese companies essentially breaking their social contract with employees and the government unable to compensate, workers, particularly younger workers, have had to resort to part-time or temporary employment. These new employment arrangements have been cost-effective for Japanese companies but have put significant strains on household finances.

Sources

Adapted from: Watanabe, C. (2006) Emergence of Rich and Poor Rattles Japan, April 5. Available at: http://mdn.mainichimsn.co.jp/features/archive/news/2006/04/20060418p2g00m0fe006000c.html, accessed July 29, 2006.

Boston Consulting Group (2012) *Global Wealth 2012: The Battle to Regain Strength*. Boston, MA: Boston Consulting Group.

Japan Times (2012) Attitudes Hardening toward the Welfare State. Available at: www.japantimes.co.jp/text/fd20120708bj.html, accessed November 18, 2012.

PHOTO 3.1

The Global Intelligence (2012) Poverty in Japan: A Starvation Case Highlights the Problem. Available at: http://theglobalintelligence.com/2012/04/03/poverty-in-japan/, accessed November 18, 2012.

Discussion Question

1. What are the implications of Japan's income distribution for foreign firms interested in entering this market?

From the standpoint of the global manager, exchange rate stability is more important for strategic planning than the absolute value of the exchange rate. Fluctuating exchange rates distort standard of living and purchasing power statistics, making it difficult to make sound strategic marketing decisions. Comparing standards of living and purchasing power across countries using nominal exchange rates will lead to poor decisions. **Purchasing power parity** (PPP) exchange rates provide a more robust basis for making inter-country comparisons. PPP is defined as the number of units of a foreign country's currency required to purchase an identical basket of goods and services in the local country. The concept is based on the **Law of One Price**, which argues that products should have the same price in all countries when that price is expressed in a common currency. This assumes, of course, that the product is tradable, transportation costs are negligible and product quality is the same in all countries. In order to ensure comparability across countries, it is, therefore, important to adjust national income figures by the PPP exchange rate. Such data are readily available from secondary sources such as the OECD for all countries in which the global marketing manager would have an interest (see Table 3.2).

TABLE 3.2   GDP (PPP), selected countries

Country	Gross domestic product, constant prices, PPP (S million)				
	2007	**2008**	**2009**	**2010**	**2011**
Australia	771,686	782,228	800,452	816,962	835,364
Canada	1,189,564	1,197,757	1,164,582	1,202,022	1,230,938
France	1,950,171	1,948,598	1,887,274	1,918,660	1,951,233
Germany	2,747,927	2,777,692	2,635,279	2,744,847	2,827,986
Italy	1,722,353	1,702,439	1,608,899	1,638,043	1,645,183
Japan	4,042,140	4,000,035	3,778,954	3,946,555	3,916,763
Mexico	1,404,955	1,422,065	1,332,706	1,406,829	1,461,844
United Kingdom	2,110,446	2,090,019	2,006,953	2,043,064	2,058,558
United States	13,144,400	13,097,200	12,690,000	12,992,000	13,225,900
China	6,899,442	7,564,180	8,261,159	9,124,201	n.a
Russian Federation	1,991,696	2,096,219	1,932,276	2,016,135	2,103,541

Source: Oecd.org (2009) Statistics: Organization for Economic Co-operation and Development. Available at: www.oecd.org/statistics/, accessed June 6, 2013.

DEBT LEVELS

In assessing foreign markets, it is also essential to consider debt levels. Excessive debt constrains the ability of consumers, industrial buyers and government departments to purchase foreign products. High government debt loads dampen public-sector demand for goods and services, both domestically produced and imported, and may lead to the imposition of stringent austerity measures to achieve fiscal balance. High household debt also has a negative impact on the demand for foreign goods and services. Faced with heavy debt service obligations, consumers will likely be forced to cut back significantly on purchases of both domestic and foreign products. Global marketing firms may well see declines in their overall volume of sales in such markets.

FIGURE 3.3   Government Debt as a Percentage of GDP in Selected Countries

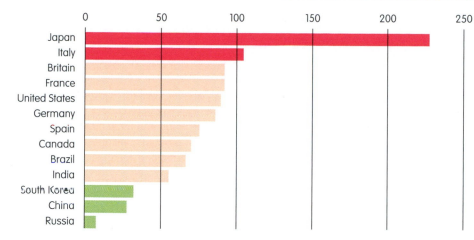

Source: The Economist. n.d. The Debtors' Merry-go-round (online). Available at: http://www.economist.com/blogs/graphicdetail/2012/09/daily-chart-10, accessed June 6, 2013.

FIGURE 3.4   Household Debt as a Percentage of GDP in Selected Countries

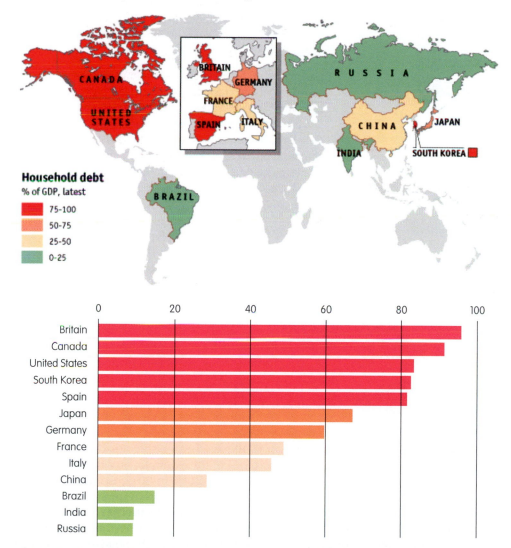

Source: The Economist. n.d. The Debtors' Merry-go-round (online). Available at: http://www.economist.com/blogs/graphic detail/2012/09/daily-chart-10, accessed June 6, 2013.

case study 3.2: Cate and Levi puppets in Canada

Levi & Crate is a small specialty toy manufacturer based in Toronto, Canada. The firm manufactures a line of puppets, 'pillow pals', backpacks, beach towels, 'animal hats' and accessories targeted at the high-end segment of the toy market. The company's products are handmade and use reclaimed wood and other materials. The color and texture of the reclaimed wood are individually selected to ensure that each product is unique. Further, all materials are sourced close to the firm's manufacturing facility which reduces fuel consumption and the firm's carbon footprint.

PHOTO 3.2

Since inception, the company has relied almost exclusively on the US and Canadian markets. In fact, owners of the company estimate that 70% of their business comes from the USA, 20% from Canada and the remaining 10% from other foreign countries. The heavy reliance on the US market has, however, proven to be a challenge for the firm. The downturn in the economy sparked by the sub-prime financial crisis has resulted in a sharp contraction in demand from American consumers. The high end of the toy market has been particularly hard hit as US consumers struggle with a weak job market and declining disposable incomes. At the time the company's exports to the USA also suffered as a result of a strong Canadian dollar, which translated into higher import prices for the firm's American consumers.

Executives of the company believe that they have little choice but to target new markets outside of North America. In fact, the company has signed agreements with distributors in the UK, New Zealand and Australia and is also targeting the Mexican market. Over time, the company also plans to have its puppets in homes across Europe. A spokesperson for the company notes that 'high-end markets in Europe especially value made-in-Canada, green products'. The firm plans to market its 'animal hats' in colder countries and its beach blankets in warmer climates. The spokesperson goes on to add: 'I don't think it's unreasonable to think that overseas could represent 40% to 50% of our sales.'

Sources

Cateandlevi.com (2013) About Us: Cate and Levi. Available at: www.cateandlevi.com/about-us_198cms.htm, accessed June 7, 2013.

Money.canoe.ca. (n.d.) Untitled. Available at: http://money.canoe.ca/money/business/canada/archi ves/2011/07/20110708-123008.html, accessed June 7, 2013.

Discussion Question

1. Is diversification into markets such as the UK, Australia, New Zealand and Mexico the correct strategic response to the economic downturn in the US market? Why/why not?

Government debt levels as a percentage of GDP have been rising steadily over the last few years. OECD data indicate that debt levels in Greece, for example, stood at 170% of GDP in 2012, up from 117% in 2006, while in Japan it stood at 214% in 2012, up from 167% in 2006. The debt level in the USA was 109% of GDP in 2012, which is up dramatically from the 2006 figure of 66% of GDP. Figure 3.3 illustrates the government debt situation for a select group of countries, while Figure 3.4 shows household debt levels for a number of countries. The UK, Canada and the USA stand out for their high levels of household debt relative to GDP. The BRIC countries, on the other hand, are seen to have relatively low levels of household debt to GDP.

The high levels of consumer and government debt in the developed world are not sustainable and do not augur well for the long-term growth in demand for goods and services. The global marketer is well advised to factor this into her company's strategic marketing plans. This may be accomplished by, for example, exploring potential new markets in developing countries or the deployment of new technologies with the potential to reduce manufacturing costs and which will allow the firm to respond to the needs of an increasingly cash-strapped consumer.

ECONOMIC SYSTEMS

In doing business around the world, the global marketer will encounter a variety of economic systems. Societies have devised a number of systems of organization to address the central economic problem of scarcity. These economic systems define the role of government in regulation of the economy, the role and motivation of the private sector in producing goods and services, as well as issues related to property rights, the distribution of profits and fundamental constructs such as equity and freedom for its citizens. Most countries around the world embrace a **free enterprise** or **capitalist** economic system in which private firms seek to maximize profits and factors of production, such as where land and capital are privately owned. Governments, however, are expected to play a key role in the regulation of private business activities and the protection of disadvantaged members of society. Free enterprise systems differ in the extent of government involvement. Some, such as the USA and Germany, adopt a more laissez-faire approach, while others, such as Canada and Norway, have much more of a focus on promoting income equality and social programs that benefit all their citizens.

Socialist or **planned** economies differ from free enterprise economies in that the means of production are primarily under the control of the state. Production and distribution decisions are made centrally and are driven, not by the pursuit of individual profit, but by the state's much broader economic and political agendas. Governments play a central role in the operation of such economies and private initiative is neither valued nor encouraged. Countries of the former Soviet Union have been transitioning to more market-based outcomes for several decades, while China now pursues its own brand of **market socialism** in which we see private firms making production and investment decisions but within a broad framework of state ownership.

Capitalism and socialism may be viewed as opposite ends of the spectrum of economic systems. Most countries operate somewhere in the middle and are referred to as **mixed economies**. In such economies, both private enterprise and the state are involved in making production and investment decisions and the 'animal spirits' of private firms are tempered by strong government regulation. The central government, for example, holds the reins of fiscal and monetary policy and uses these tools to moderate business cycles, control inflation and maintain employment levels.

BUSINESS CYCLES

All economies go through business cycles of growth and contraction. It is usual to measure these fluctuations in economic activity using changes in GDP over time. Free enterprise economies generally progress through five stages. The growth or expansion phase features rising GDP and economic prosperity, as well as declining rates of unemployment. Economic activity eventually peaks and GDP growth rates moderate, as do employment gains. A recession invariably follows as the next stage and we witness a contraction in GDP and a rise in unemployment. Consumers' confidence begins to wane and they cut back their spending on non-essential goods and services and increase savings. Businesses faced with a drop in consumer demand now cut back on production and reduce their demand for raw materials, intermediate inputs and, of course, labor. With even more workers losing their jobs, the demand for goods and services continues to drop. At some point, the economy hits rock bottom and the rate of job losses begins to subside. Firms begin to rebuild their inventories of finished products. With fewer people losing their jobs, consumer confidence slowly begins to return and demand picks up. The economy is now in its recovery phase with positive rates of GDP growth and declining unemployment rates.

The business cycle, as described above, is regarded as a normal feature of capitalist economies and may last from three to five years as economic activity goes from peak to trough and back to peak. Japan is, however, a notable exception as that country has been mired in recession since the collapse of its real estate and stock markets two decades ago. Greece is also proving to be an exception as in 2012 that country was still experiencing significant negative GDP growth more than five years into the start of its recession. The situation in the USA is also worrisome as that country has exhibited only weak positive growth several years following the end of the recession precipitated by the sub-prime financial crisis.

Box 3.2

Income per capita is certainly an important measure of a country's level of economic development. However, in assessing countries in which to conduct business, the global marketing manager may wish to consider broader measures of economic welfare. One such measure is the Human Development Index (HDI) which was developed in 1990. The HDI measures welfare on three dimensions: literacy rates, life expectancy and Gross Domestic Product (GDP) at PPP. HDI scores range from 0 to 1. A score of less than 0.5 indicates that the country is at a low level of development, while a score greater than 0.8 is indicative of higher development. Canada, the USA, Australia, Japan, France, the UK, Hong Kong and Germany all score 0.8 or above on the HDI scale, while low-ranked countries include most in Africa as well as Haiti and Yemen.

An alternative to the HDI as a measure of economic development is the Physical Quality of Life Index (PQLI). The PQLI is also a composite measure of welfare and has three components: life expectancy, infant mortality and adult literacy rates. The global marketing manager may find both the HDI and the PQLI to be useful in tracking the development progress of target countries over time.

MARKETING TO LOW-INCOME COUNTRIES

There are over 4 billion poor people in countries around the world living on a per capita income of $2 per day. There has been considerable debate as to whether these income-constrained consumers can be profitably targeted or are best ignored as a marketing opportunity. C.K. Prahalad was a major proponent of the idea that multinational corporations can successfully market to low-income consumers, alleviating poverty while also contributing to the firm's bottom line. According to Prahalad and Hammond (2002), consumers at the **base of the economic pyramid** (BoP) represent a vast untapped market which has historically been ignored by multinational firms.[4] The reasons for this are not difficult to understand. The poor have little money to spend and what they do spend is directed at satisfying basic needs. There are also problems of illiteracy, poor marketing infrastructure, corruption, currency fluctuations and bureaucracy that tend to plague developing countries. Prahalad and Hammond (2002) argue, however, that these assumptions made by multinational firms are not correct. They note, for example, that while individual consumers in the developing world may be poor, the combined income of the community is significant. The poor in Rio de Janeiro, for example, have a combined purchasing power of $1.2 billion or $600 per person and purchasing power is similarly high for shanty towns in Mumbai and Johannesburg.

The issue of the poor's money only being spent on basic needs also needs to be reexamined, according to these scholars. They point to Dharavi, a shanty town in Mumbai, where 85% of the residents own a television set, 75% own a pressure cooker and a mixer and 56% own a gas stove. Prahalad and Hammond (2002) also argue against the notion that the products sold to the poor are cheap, making it difficult for firms to be profitable, and that these consumers are difficult to reach at a reasonable cost. The poor in fact pay more for a range of products

---

4   Prahalad, C.K. and Hammond, A. (2002) 'Serving the world's poor profitably', *Harvard Business Review*, September.

including food and drinking water when compared to upper- and middle-income consumers. Also, given the fact that the poor tend to live in densely populated cities, it makes it easier to market and deliver products to them than is conventionally thought. The rapid adoption of mobile communication technologies among the poor also facilitates this process.

Some multinational companies have been convinced by the arguments made by BoP protagonists. Whirlpool, for example, has marketed a line of inexpensive but stylish washing machines in India, China and Brazil which cost half the price of those retailed in North America.[5] Hindustan Lever, the Indian subsidiary of Unilever, has also experienced success in marketing candy, detergent and salt to the poor in India. The company's confectionary product, which is made with real fruit and sugar and retails for a penny per serving, soon became the fastest selling product in its portfolio. The company estimates that the product has the potential to generate revenues of $200 million per year in India and similar markets.

Several analysts have taken issue with the arguments and evidence presented by supporters of the BoP thesis. Karani (2007) questions the overall size of the BoP market, suggesting that estimates used by Prahalad and Hammond (2002) of 4 billion consumers are exaggerated.[6] Karani (2007) suggests that the BoP market may be as small as $1.2 trillion at PPP and not the $13 trillion claimed by Prahalad and his supporters. At market exchange rates (not PPP rates) in 2002, this translated into a target market of only $0.3 trillion, a much less attractive opportunity for multinational firms. Karani (2007) also questions the ease of marketing to the poor, stating that apart from the urban poor concentrated in slums the poor are generally geographically dispersed and culturally heterogeneous, which drives up the cost of delivering goods and services to them. The notion that they are consumers of luxury goods is also a problematic assumption, given that the poor tend to spend as much as 80 percent of their income on basic needs such as food. This is consistent with **Engel's law** which suggests that as a family's income increases, the percentage spent on food will decrease, the percentage spent on housing and household operations will be roughly constant, and the amount saved or spent on other purchases will increase. With 80 percent of the poor's income devoted to food and other basics, there will be little left over to purchase non-essentials.

Simanis (2012) has also alluded to problems with the BoP concept, arguing that if the firm's strategy is one of low price–low margin–high volume, then penetration rates need to be exceptionally high.[7] Procter & Gamble (P&G), for example, achieved market penetration rates of between 5 and 10 percent in a number of low-income test markets for its Pur water-purification powder but was unable to earn competitive returns. Dupont's subsidiary Solae, a manufacturer of soy protein, is reported to have had similar problems in marketing its products in India. In the case of the company's soy fortified snacks, margins were so low that to make a profit the firm would have had to sell quantities that significantly exceeded the amounts that could be consumed by communities within reach of the business.

Simanis (2012) argues that a low price–low margin–high volume strategy is able to work but only if the firm is able to lever an existing marketing infrastructure that is already supporting high-income consumers, and its low-income consumers already know how to use the product. Unilever, for example, experienced success with its Wheel detergent in India because the company was able to use its existing distribution and retail infrastructure to reach both middle- and low-income consumers. Wheel was sold alongside the firm's other products in the small grocery stores frequented by both low- and middle-income consumers. Revenues from poor customers were, therefore, only required to cover the incremental cost of having Wheel on the store shelves. In addition, poor consumers already knew how to use detergent

[5] Sachet Marketing. Available at: www.trendwatching.com/trends/SACHET_MARKETING.htm, accessed February 26, 2007.

[6] Karani, A. (2007) 'The mirage of marketing to the bottom of the pyramid: How the private sector can help alleviate poverty', *California Management Review*, 49, 4.

[7] Simanis, E. (2012) 'Reality check at the bottom of the pyramid', *Harvard Business Review*, June.

so Unilever did not have to invest any money in creating a demand for Wheel or educating consumers on its use. If a firm has to invest in new marketing infrastructure or create a demand for the product among the poor, the prospects for commercial success may be limited.

Expand Your Knowledge

Prahalad, C.K. and Hammond, A. (2002) 'Serving the world's poor profitably', *Harvard Business Review*, September.

This is a classic article that lays out the case for marketing to consumers at the base of the pyramid.

case study 3.3: Unilever in Europe

PHOTO 3.3

Unilever is the third largest packaged goods company in the world, marketing a portfolio of well-known brands such as Dove, Hellmann's, Surf, Ben & Jerry's, Wishbone, Knorr, Lifebuoy, Sunlight and Pond's and Lipton. The company markets 400 brands, 14 of which generate sales in excess of €1 billion a year. The company's products are sold in over 190 countries around the world and in 2012 generated sales of €51 billion. Developing countries account for some 55 percent of the company's business.

Despite the company's size and global brands, the economic crisis in Europe has caused the firm to radically change its marketing strategy. In response to the rise in unemployment, crushing consumer debt, falling incomes and declining consumer confidence, Unilever has had to adopt marketing strategies in Europe usually used in developing countries. The company has begun to sell its products in smaller sizes and has introduced a number of low-priced brands. As the head of Unilever's European business pointed out, 'If a consumer (*sic*) in Spain only spends €17 when they go shopping', he notes, 'then I'm not going to be able to sell them washing powder for half their budget'. The company spokesperson goes on to add: 'Poverty is returning to Europe.' In Spain, Unilever markets its Surf laundry detergent in five-wash packages and in Greece mayonnaise is sold in small packs. Low-cost brands of tea, olive oil and other products have also been introduced. Unilever has mastered the strategy of marketing to low-income consumers. In Indonesia, for example, the firm markets sachets of shampoo for 2–3 cents and the company is still able to generate a profit. Prior to the economic crisis, however, there was no need to consider such strategies in Europe.

Sources

Goldman, B. (2012) *Economic Crisis brings Third World Marketing Strategies to First World*. Available at: www.examiner.com/article/economic-problems-bring-third-world-marketing-strategies-to-first-world, accessed June 7, 2013.

Unilever.com (2012) *Unilever Facts* | About Us | Unilever Global. Available at: www.unilever.com/aboutus/introductiontounilever/unileverataglance/, accessed June 7, 2013.

Discussion Question

1. Do you believe that Unilever's BoP marketing strategy will be successful in the developed countries of Western Europe? Why/why not?

FIGURE 3.5   Forms of Economic Integration

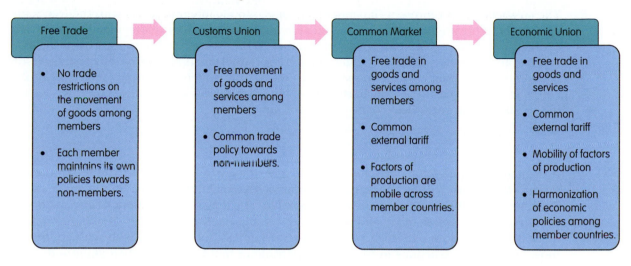

MODELS OF REGIONAL ECONOMIC INTEGRATION

Since World War II, countries around the world have attempted to engage in regional economic integration in order to increase efficiency and provide more attractive marketing opportunities for members. Economic integration may be conceptualized as a continuum from very loose arrangements involving only the elimination of trade restrictions to more complex and ambitious alliances which seek to harmonize economic policies and even achieve political union. As shown in Figure 3.5, economic integration may be viewed as a sequence of four stages from free trade areas to customs unions, common markets and finally economic unions.[8]

FREE TRADE AREA

The least restrictive form of economic integration among countries is the free trade area. Countries comprising a free trade area agree to eliminate all restrictions on the movement of goods and services between member countries. There are no barriers to trade among member countries. Tariffs, which are taxes on traded goods, and quotas which are quantitative restrictions on traded goods are not permitted between member countries of a free trade area. It should be noted, however, that member countries are free to set their own policies with respect to trade with non-member countries, i.e. discriminatory taxes and quotas may be imposed. Further, membership in a free trade area does not preclude a country from establishing preferential trading relationships with other countries or groups of countries. Mexico, for example, is a member of the North American Free Trade Agreement (NAFTA) but has established bilateral trading relationships with another bloc (the European Union), as well as with individual countries such as Chile. Canada, while a member of NAFTA, has also established trading relationships with other countries including Chile. It should further be recognized that free trade areas may be established only for select products or services. Canada and the USA, for example, had already established a free trade area in automobiles and auto parts prior to the execution of the more comprehensive North American Free Trade Agreement. Additional detail on the so-called Auto Pact is provided in a later section.

---

[8] This section draws heavily from Czinkota, M., Ronkainen, I., Farrell, C. and McTavish, R. (2009) *Global Marketing: Foreign Entry, Market Development and Strategy Implementation*. Toronto: Nelson Education.

CUSTOMS UNION

The customs union represents a deeper form of economic integration. As with the free trade agreement, there are no restrictions on trade in goods and services among member countries. Unlike a free trade agreement, however, member countries are not free to establish their own restrictions on trade with non-member countries. Rather, member countries must agree on a common trade policy with non-member countries. Agreement is typically in the form of a common external tariff (CET) against non-members with imports from third countries subject to the same tariff, regardless of the country of importation.

COMMON MARKET

A common market contains all the characteristics of a customs union, i.e. the removal of all discriminatory restrictions on trade and a common external tariff against non-member states. However, in addition a common market provides for the free movement of the factors of production, i.e. capital, labor and technology among member countries. Member countries are required to adopt extremely accommodative immigration policies, with workers free to move between jurisdictions in search of opportunities that best match their skills and experience. Similarly, member countries are required to adopt a liberal approach to cross-border investment with minimal restrictions on the movement of capital across jurisdictions.

ECONOMIC UNION

Further along the spectrum of integration is the economic union. Economic unions embody all of the characteristics of a common market but members are also mandated to harmonize their monetary, tax and fiscal policies. Member countries may also be required to adopt a common currency. In essence, economic unions represent a deep form of integration with the elimination of barriers to trade in goods and services, a common external tariff, free movement of the factors of production and the harmonization of macroeconomic policies. From the above, it is clear that the implementation of an economic union will require member countries to give up a great deal of their individual sovereignty to the overarching policy and regulatory framework that governs the group as a whole.

THE NEXT PHASE OF INTEGRATION

Some argue that in fact the final step in the process of economic integration would be a political union. Such a union would require the complete harmonization of political policies and government institutions. This would indeed be an ambitious undertaking and there are no known examples in the real world.

PROS AND CONS OF ECONOMIC INTEGRATION

Engaging in economic integration carries certain benefits and costs. These advantages and disadvantages may, however, only become evident over the long term and may not impact each member country equally. Also, within countries various sectors may be impacted differently as integration policies come into effect.

Advantages

Trade creation: Economic integration leads to an overall expansion in trade between member countries. Because of the elimination of trade restrictions, countries substitute imports from beneficiary countries within the bloc for their own domestic production. Such trade creation effects benefit consumers in member countries who now have access to goods at more competitive prices.

Political power: Members of an economic bloc share common interests. Acting as a group, member states have a greater opportunity to influence the course of negotiations in multilateral forums such as the World Trade Organization (WTO), an umbrella organization consisting of 149 countries with a mandate to improve trade and investment flows around the world. As individual member states, smaller countries are able to wield far less political clout on the world stage but as a group their influence is increased.

Enhanced cooperation and consensus: Economic blocs may consist of 2–3 member countries or upwards of 50. Given their relatively small size, it is far easier to achieve consensus on shared goals as opposed to in larger multilateral groupings such as the WTO.

Disadvantages

Trade diversion: While integration increases trade among member countries, this is clearly not the case for non-members. There is a trade diversion effect as countries divert imports from more efficient non-beneficiaries outside the bloc to less efficient preferred countries within the bloc. Imports from non-member countries are now more expensive as they do not enjoy preferential treatment which leads to a loss of market share to those countries which are part of the bloc.

Shifts to low-wage countries: The formation of an economic bloc may result in a shift of production to low-wage countries that are part of the economic grouping. With the removal of restrictions on the movement of labor, capital and technology, firms are free to relocate production to countries with the lowest wage rates. While an advantage for those industries employing low-skilled workers, such shifts in the locus of production may well result in increased unemployment in high-wage countries. This is often a politically sensitive issue in the negotiation of economic integration agreements, as was seen during the NAFTA negotiations.

Loss of sovereignty: Economic integration requires that member countries give up some measure of independence if the interests of the group are to be maintained. Agreements on the use of a common currency may, for example, prove quite difficult for some countries, and surrendering aspects of a nation's monetary policy may prove to be equally challenging for some states.

MAJOR ECONOMIC BLOCS

Table 3.3 summarizes key features of the major economic blocs. It should, of course, be noted that these may change over time as groupings add new members, evolve in terms of their mission or cease to exist altogether and are replaced by entirely new blocs. The trade blocs listed in Table 3.3 are certainly not an exhaustive list of the agreements between trading partners. The World Trade Organization reports that, as of January 2012, it had received over 500 notifications of regional trade agreements and of these more than 300 were already in effect. These may be between two or more individual countries or between individual countries and previously established trading blocs and include agreements covering both goods and services.[9]

Integration in Europe

Economic integration in Europe began in the 1950s with the European Coal and Steel Community playing an active role in uniting European countries in the aftermath of World War II.[10] The founding members of the integration movement were Belgium, Germany, France, Italy, Luxembourg and the Netherlands, and in 1953 they formed the European Economic Community (EEC). The EEC would eventually be renamed the European Union and see its membership expand. Denmark, Ireland and the UK joined the European Union in 1973. Greece

---

[9]   See www.wto.org/english/tratop_e/region_e/region_e.htm

[10]   Europa.eu. (n.d.) EUROPA: the official European Union website. Available at: http://europa.eu/index_en.htm, accessed June 7, 2013.

TABLE 3.3   Major Regional Economic Blocs

Economic grouping	Population	GDP (at PPP) $US m	Number of member states
Europe			
European Union (EU)	496,198,605	12,025,415	27
North America			
North American Free Trade Agreement (NAFTA)	450,495,039	15,279,000	3
Latin America & the Caribbean			
MERCOSUR	275,499,000	3,324,501	5
Caribbean Community (CARICOM)	14,565,083	64,219	16
Africa			
Economic Community of West African States (ECOWAS)	251,646,263	342,519	15
East African Community (EAC)	97,865,428	104,239	3
Southern African Customs Union (SACU)	51,055,878	541,433	5
Middle East			
Gulf Cooperation Council (GCC)	35,869,438	536,223	6
Asia			
Association of Southeast Asian Nations (ASEAN)	553,900,000	2,172,000	10
South Asian Association for Regional Cooperation (SAARC)	1,467,255,669	4,074,031	8

Source: Alon, I. and Jaffe, E. (2013) *Global Marketing: Contemporary Theory, Practice and Cases*. New York: McGraw-Hill/Irwin.

Data for MERCUSOR retrieved from: Imf.org (2012) *Report for Selected Countries and Subjects*. Available at: www.imf.org/external/pubs/ft/weo/2012/01/weodata/weorept.aspx?sy=2011&ey=2011&scsm=1&ssd=1&sort=subject&ds=.&br=1&prl.x=64&prl.y=12&c=213%2C223%2C288%2C298%2C299&s=NGDPD%2CNGDPDPC%2CPPPGDP%2 CPPPPC%2CLP%2CBCA&grp=0&a=, accessed June 8, 2013.

joined the Union in 1981, with Spain and Portugal becoming members five years later. The enlargement of the EU has been a heavily debated issue, with policy makers expressing their concerns about the cost of integration and the implications of the free movement of labor among member countries. In 2004, ten countries simultaneously joined the EU and by 2007 that number had ballooned to 27 – Austria, Belgium, Bulgaria, Cyprus, the Czech Republic, Denmark, Estonia, Finland, France, Germany, Greece, Hungary, Ireland, Italy, Latvia, Lithuania, Luxembourg, Malta, the Netherlands, Poland, Portugal, Romania, Slovakia, Slovenia, Spain, Sweden and the UK. Other countries, such as Croatia, Macedonia, Turkey, Albania, Bosnia and Herzegovina, Serbia and Montenegro, are candidates for membership. Iceland has also expressed an interest in joining the bloc.

Passage of the Single European Act of 1986 put in train the process for the removal of trade and investment barriers in Europe and the creation of a single market. This process was completed in 1993. The Maastricht Treaty on European Union was also executed in that year, leading to the launch of a single currency – the euro (€). Creation of the single market and economy was expected to lead to significant benefits for consumers and businesses on the continent. Transaction costs were to decline with the elimination of trade and investment restrictions. Manufacturing firms, faced with a larger 'domestic' market, would be able to reap economies of scale as they expanded output. Competition within Europe would lead to an increased focus on efficiency and consumers would benefit from access to a wider range of goods and services. With a single currency, firms and consumers within the eurozone would benefit from greater pricing transparency and reduced foreign exchange risks. Foreign firms from non-EU countries were expected to be put at a severe disadvantage in trying to tap into this market of almost 500 million people. The term **Fortress Europe** was coined to articulate the fears that many had that the EU would raise trade restrictions against non-members and present foreign firms with an almost unassailable target.

The EU began to face a number of financial challenges beginning in 2010 which have raised concerns about the stability of the bloc and the fate of the single currency. With the collapse of real estate markets on the continent, commercial banks with significant exposure to this sector had to be rescued by government bailouts. This in turn gave rise to the so-called sovereign debt crisis as governments attempted to shore up a weakened financial sector and counteract a marked slow-down in economic activity. In countries such as Greece, public-sector wages and pension commitments exacerbated the financial crisis which would eventually spread from the peripheral EU countries to larger economies such as those of Spain and France. The sovereign debt crisis has roiled the continent. The International Monetary Fund (IMF), the European Central Bank (ECB) and the European Commission, the so-called troika, have tried to contain the evolving situation with successive bailouts of national governments and the imposition of severe austerity measures. As a result of these measures, the world has witnessed mass protests and demonstrations as unions and their workers, pensioners and the general public have reacted in outrage to the economic situation.

Private firms have also had to make adjustments in the wake of the financial crisis. Azkoyen, a small Spanish manufacturer of vending machines and security systems, has been struggling with declining sales in Spain, Portugal and Italy and its Italian unit has been forced to focus on markets outside of Europe.[11] Large multinational companies have also had to react to the changed economic environment in Europe and have closed plants and reduced production. Ford, for example, has decided to end vehicle manufacturing in the UK on the heels of announcements that it has also closed its car manufacturing plant in Belgium.[12] The company has reduced production in Europe by 18 percent. On the other hand, Dienes Group, a German industrial-knife manufacturer, is cautious about the situation in the EU but has no plans to retrench workers and cut back on production. Instead, the firm plans to increase its marketing efforts in a bid to attract more customers.[13]

INTEGRATION IN NORTH AMERICA

Integration in North America began with the Auto Pact – a trade agreement in automobiles between Canada and the USA. The Canada–United States Automotive Products Agreement or Auto Pact was executed in 1965 and removed tariff barriers on cars, trucks and automotive parts traded between the two nations. The Auto Pact gave Canadian consumers access to a wider range of vehicles, while simultaneously providing US car manufacturers with access to a larger market free of tariffs. The Auto Pact was a very limited agreement as it was confined to one sector and contained safeguards for Canada – for example, each car manufactured in Canada had to have at least 60 percent Canadian content. Despite its limited scope, however, the Auto Pact proved to be the forerunner for the Canada–US Free Trade Agreement (FTA) which was signed in 1987. The FTA was much broader in scope as it eliminated tariff

[11] Horobin (n.d.) *Euro-Zone Economy Contracts in Third Quarter*. Available at: http://online.wsj.com/article/SB10 00142412788732455630457812020100944359B.html, accessed June 7, 2013.

[12] Ottawacitizen.com (n.d.) Untitled. Available at: www.ottawacitizen.com/business/Ford+closing+plants+cutting+jobs/7452693/story.html, accessed June 7, 2013.

[13] Horobin (n.d.) op cit.

and many non-tariff barriers on a range of products including textiles, wine and agricultural products. The FTA was eventually replaced by NAFTA in 1994.

The ratification of NAFTA created a free market with some 450 million consumers. The accord not only created a substantial free trade area but also represented a bold experiment as it brought together industrialized countries (Canada and the USA) and a developing country (Mexico) in a single economic bloc. Prior attempts at economic integration were always between countries at roughly the same level of development. NAFTA liberalized trade flows between the three member countries and contributed to economic growth in the USA and Canada as well as in Mexico. Mexico, in particular, has experienced rising incomes and a reduction in poverty as a result of the accord as firms in that country gained access to a large pool of high-income consumers in the USA and Canada.

In general, the corporate view of NAFTA has been positive. It should, however, be noted that when first proposed there was considerable opposition to the accord. Objections tended to center around two issues – the potential for the USA and Canada to lose jobs to Mexico because of the latter country's lower wages and work standards, and the potential for damage to the environment. Despite opposition, the agreement would be signed by the Bush Administration using that president's fast-track authority. However, in order to allay fears and win broader support for the agreement, two side agreements were subsequently incorporated into the accord. Prior to a vote in the US Senate, the Clinton Administration added the North American Agreement for Environmental Cooperation (NAAEC) and the North American Agreement on Labor Cooperation (NAALC) to the legislation. These side agreements were crafted in order to address concerns about labor and the environment and make the accord more palatable to skeptical US and Canadian voters.

The North American Agreement on Labor Cooperation (NAALC) provided a mechanism to air complaints about worker abuse and a means of promoting consultation and dialogue among labor, business and government groups in all three countries. One of the principal objectives of the NAALC is to improve working conditions and living standards in each of the signatory countries. The North American Agreement for Environmental Cooperation (NAAEC) was similarly established to address concerns about the environmental impact of the agreement. The focus here was on ensuring consistency in environmental regulations across all three member countries, thereby precluding firms from relocating their operations to jurisdictions with less stringent environmental regulations. It should be recognized that the NAALC and the NAAEC have little by way of real enforcement authority. The Secretariats responsible for the implementation of both agreements engage in fact finding and provide a forum for the discussion of complaints. These discussions are non-adversarial and do not constitute a dispute-resolution mechanism, i.e. the parties are not legally bound to carry out any remedial action.

It is clear that NAFTA has provided firms in both Mexico and Canada with greater access to the expansive US market. While some analysts question its success, others have argued that the accord did what it was designed to do, i.e. promote economic growth by fostering competition in domestic markets and stimulating domestic and foreign investment. As a result of the agreement, North American firms have restructured and streamlined their operations and are now more productive and efficient.[14] While it is difficult to ascribe precise performance metrics to the agreement, the Council on Foreign Relations, a non-partisan think tank, reports that the value of intra-North American trade has more than tripled since NAFTA came into effect. Business investment in the USA has increased by 117 percent between 1993 and 2007, compared to only a 45 percent increase in the 14 years prior to the execution of the agreement. Trade between NAFTA members now represents 80 percent of overall Mexican and Canadian trade and 33 percent of US trade.[15]

---

[14]   Hufbauer, G.C. and Schott, J.J. (2005) *NAFTA Revisited: Achievements and Challenges*. Washington, DC: Institute for International Economics.

[15]   See www.cfr.org/economics/naftas-economic-impact/p15790

INTEGRATION IN LATIN AMERICA AND THE CARIBBEAN

Efforts at economic integration in Latin America date back to the formation of the Latin American Free Trade Association (LAFTA) in 1960. The goal of LAFTA was to create a common market with the eventual elimination of tariffs on trade between its members. The initial signatories to the agreement were Argentina, Brazil, Chile, Mexico, Peru, Paraguay and Uruguay. Ecuador, Venezuela, Bolivia and Columbia would subsequently join the bloc. In 1980, LAFTA was transformed into the Latin American Integration Association (ALADI). These early attempts at integration were not particularly successful as political upheaval in the region disrupted efforts at economic cooperation.[16]

In the early 1990s, Argentina, Brazil, Paraguay and Uruguay formed the Common Market of the South (Mercosur) in yet another attempt at integration. Venezuela became a full member in 2012, while Bolivia, Chile, Colombia, Ecuador and Peru currently hold associate member status in the group. Mercosur presents a market of some 276 million consumers and a per capita GDP of US$12,600. Despite their own economic challenges and disagreements over trade policy, the Mercosur members and the five associate members have agreed to economic-convergence targets similar to those the EU set as a precursor to the euro. These are in the areas of inflation, public debt and fiscal deficit.

Many Latin nations are realizing that if they do not unite, they will become increasingly marginalized in the global market. Integration has, however, not been smooth. Bolivia, Chile, Colombia, Ecuador and Peru formed the Andean Community of Nations (originally the Andean Pact) in 1969. Chile eventually withdrew in 1979. Venezuela joined in 1973 and withdrew in 2006, claiming that the trade agreements signed between Columbia, Peru and the USA were not tolerable. Several other regional groupings have been formed in Latin America, including the G3 Free Trade Agreement between Mexico, Columbia and Venezuela. Countries in the Caribbean have also been included in discussions on the establishment of the Free Trade Area of the Americas (FTAA) which will stretch from Point Barrow, Alaska, to Patagonia. Fifteen Caribbean countries are currently members of the Caribbean Community (CARICOM) which came into effect with the execution of the Treaty of Chaguaramas in August 1973. The current members of this group are: Antigua and Barbuda, Bahamas, Barbados, Belize, Dominica, Grenada, Guyana, Haiti, Jamaica, Montserrat, Saint Kitts and Nevis, Saint Lucia, Saint Vincent and the Grenadines, Suriname and Trinidad and Tobago.

INTEGRATION IN ASIA

With Europe mired in recession and the USA experiencing a protracted period of slow growth, the Asia-Pacific region has put renewed emphasis on economic integration.[17] The Association of South East Asian Nations (ASEAN) is the most established of the regional economic groupings in Asia. Formed in the late 1960s, ASEAN was a fairly loose association of Asian countries which attempted to promote economic growth, peace and stability in the region. In 1992, however, the ASEAN Free Trade Area (AFTA) was formed. AFTA seeks to eliminate tariff and non-tariff barriers among its ten member countries: Brunei, Indonesia, Malaysia, Philippines, Singapore, Thailand, Myanmar, Cambodia, Laos and Vietnam.

In 1989, with Australia acting as a catalyst, the Asia Pacific Economic Cooperation (APEC) was formed to facilitate trade negotiations in the region. APEC consists of 21 countries on both sides of the Pacific. The forum is credited with reducing tariffs between member countries

---

[16] Basnet, H.C. and Sharma, S.C. (2010) Economic integration in Latin America. Working Paper, Department of Economics, South Illinois University.

[17] Asian Development Bank (2012) *Asian Economic Integration Monitor*. Mandaluyong City, Philippines.

from 17 percent in 1989 to 5.8 percent in 2010.[18] The organization has also worked to reduce non-tariff barriers between its member countries.

The South Asian Association for Regional Cooperation (SAARC) is a grouping of south-Asian countries formed by Bangladesh, Bhutan, India, the Maldives, Nepal, Pakistan and Sri Lanka to promote economic and social cooperation among its members. Formed in 1985, the seven founding members were joined by Bangladesh and Afghanistan in 2007. In 2004, the founding members agreed to the formation of the South Asian Free Trade Area (SAFTA) which sought to eliminate trade barriers and promote the free flow of goods between the member states.

INTEGRATION IN AFRICA

Economic integration in Sub-Saharan Africa has faced a number of political and economic challenges over the years. Because of historical colonial ties, African nations have tended to trade more with the countries of the developed world and intra-regional trade flows have remained weak. Attempts at integration on the African continent include the formation of the Economic Community of West African States (ECOWAS) in 1975. The stated goal of this 15-member group is to promote economic integration in a broad range of fields such as energy, telecommunications, transportation, agriculture, culture, industry and monetary and financial matters. The member states are: Benin, Burkina Faso, Cape Verde, Cote D'Ivoire, Gambia, Ghana, Guinea, Guinea Bissau, Liberia, Mali, Niger, Nigeria, Senegal, Sierra Leone and Togo.[19] The group has a combined population of 250 million and GDP at PPP of over $340 billion. In 1980, ECOWAS members agreed to the establishment of a free trade area in unprocessed agricultural products and handicraft, and by 1990 tariffs on a range of products had been eliminated. In 1994, several ECOWAS member countries entered into an agreement to form the West African Economic and Monetary Union (UEMOA). The member states of this grouping are: Benin, Burkina Faso, Côte d'Ivoire, Mali, Niger, Senegal, Togo (all founding members) and Guinea Bissau which joined in 1997. All UEMOA member countries share a common currency – the West African CFA franc. UEMOA is both a customs union and a currency union and the group has implemented a common external tariff against non-member countries.

In 1999, Burundi, Kenya, Rwanda, Tanzania and Uganda established the East African Community (EAC) to promote economic and social integration among its members. To this end, the EAC established a customs union in 2005 and plans to eventually form an economic and political union of east African states. The EAC has a combined population of 98 million and GDP at PPP of $104 billion. It should be noted that attempts at east African integration had been made in the late 1970s but collapsed due to jockeying for political power within the group and differences in economic systems among the members.[20]

The Southern African Development Community (SADC) was formed in 1992 to promote economic and social integration among its member countries. The member states of SADC are: Angola, Botswana, the Democratic Republic of the Congo, Lesotho, Madagascar, Malawi, Mauritius, Mozambique, Namibia, the Seychelles, South Africa, Swaziland, Tanzania, Zambia and Zimbabwe. In 2000, SADC created a free trade area which eventually included all of its member countries with the exception of the Democratic Republic of the Congo and the Seychelles.

---

[18]   Apec.org (n.d.) *Achievements and Benefits: Asia-Pacific Economic Cooperation.* Available at: www.apec.org/About-Us/About-APEC/Achievements-and-Benefits.aspx, accessed June 7, 2013.

[19]   Comm.ecowas.int (2013) Untitled. Available at: www.comm.ecowas.int/sec/index.php?id=about_a&lang=en, accessed June 7, 2013.

[20]   McLaughlin, A. (2006) 'East African trade zone off to creaky start', *The Christian Science Monitor*, March 9.

INTEGRATION IN THE MIDDLE EAST

Countries in the Middle East have made some efforts at economic integration. The Gulf Cooperation Council (GCC) is the major regional grouping and was formed in 1981 by founding members Bahrain, Kuwait, Oman, Qatar, Saudi Arabia and the United Arab Emirates. Members of the GCC share a common language, culture and history and, with the exception of Bahrain, are all major oil producers. The GCC has as its objective facilitating cooperation between member states in areas such as finance, economics, trade, tourism and culture. In the wake of the Iran–Iraq war, military cooperation is also a priority for the group. The GCC established a common external tariff in 2003 and formed a common market in 2008 to facilitate the flow of goods, services and investment between the countries of the bloc. An overriding objective of the GCC has been monetary union and the creation of a single currency.[21]

Two other regional groupings exist in the Middle East. The Arab Maghreb Union (AMU) is comprised of Algeria, Libya, Mauritania, Morocco and Tunisia in northern Africa. Although established in 1989, the bloc has been beset by economic and political problems and remains largely inactive. The Arab Cooperation Council (ACC) was also founded in 1989 and its members are North Yemen, Iraq, Jordan and Egypt. This organization too, however, is largely inactive.

SUMMARY

This chapter has examined the economic and financial environment within which the global marketer must operate. The multinational firm has little control over the economic environment of either the home or the host countries but is profoundly impacted by them. Key aspects of the economic environment which have an impact on the global marketing firm include population and population growth rates, income and income distribution as well as exchange rates and debt. Each of these variables will have a bearing on the decisions the firm makes with respect to which markets to enter and the level of resources that should be devoted to each.

As the firm assesses various markets for entry, it will encounter a range of economic systems in effect in various countries. It is important for the global marketer to have a basic understanding of these, as they will determine in part how host governments react to foreign investment and imported goods and services. In this chapter, we examined a range of economic systems from free enterprise to centrally planned. The point was made that these are polar opposites and most countries will operate somewhere in the middle, i.e. they are mixed economies that feature a blend of private-sector decision making and government regulation and oversight. A feature of all free enterprise or capitalist economies is the business cycle. Market economies follow cycles of boom and bust which may be moderated by government policies but not avoided altogether. An understanding of where the host country is in the business cycle is important to market planning and the timing of foreign market entry decisions.

This chapter has also introduced the notion of marketing to the bottom of the economic pyramid. The targeting of consumers in low-income countries has its proponents who believe that firms can not only make a profit but also contribute to poverty alleviation in those countries. Other analysts, however, question the premise and suggest that the base of the marketing pyramid is only profitable under highly restrictive conditions.

Finally, the chapter examined economic integration movements around the world. The advantages and disadvantages of integration were examined and specific examples of the more important groupings were discussed.

---

[21] Peterson Institute for International Economics (2009) *The GCC Monetary Union: Choice of Exchange Rate Regime.* Washington, DC.

Real World Challenges

Michelin Faces Plant Closure Decisions in Europe

Pierre Lagarde knew that he would have to come up with a workable solution before the start of the emergency executive meeting set to begin in just under two hours. As Senior Vice President, Global Marketing for Michelin, he was going to have a major role to play in any decisions on the company's operations in Europe. It was clear that some of the company's senior executives were in favor of outright plant closures in France but Pierre was reluctant to add to the pain his countrymen were already experiencing. These workers did not cause the financial crisis sweeping across Europe, Pierre thought to himself, as he looked over a Deutsche Bank analyst report suggesting that the company would have to close two plants and lay off 2,500 people. There must be a better solution, Pierre surmised, as he looked out of the window of his 10th floor office at the company's headquarters in Clermont-Ferrand, France.

Michelin is among the largest tire manufacturers in the world. The company produces 166 million tires annually at some 69 production facilities in 18 countries around the world. The firm employs in excess of 113,000 people and has a roughly 15 percent share of the global tire market. Passenger car and light truck tires account for 52 percent of the company's consolidated sales, while the truck tires market accounts for 31 percent and the company's specialty businesses make up the remaining 17 percent of global sales.

With the onset of the financial crisis, Michelin has seen demand stall and market share come under pressure across Europe. The situation is seen to be more acute in the truck segment of the market. Deutsche Bank reports that since the start of the financial crisis in 2007, the European truck tire market has declined by 8 percent (from 22 million in 2007 to 20 million units in 2012) and Michelin has seen its share of this market drop precipitously from 36 percent to 29 percent. As a result of this slippage, the report notes that seven plants across Western Europe are running at 60 percent of their capacity. Plants are producing 5.5 million units as opposed to their capacity of 9.9 million units. The Deutsche Bank analyst report also notes, however, that the passenger car tire segment of the market is generally more profitable for tire manufacturers. Truck tire sales volumes are lower than passenger car tire volumes and their raw material (especially natural rubber) content is higher. Michelin's selling price for its truck tires is higher than those of its European peers but, as the Deutsche Bank analysts point out, its margins are lower than those of the competition.

Pierre knew that a definitive decision would have to be based on a detailed financial analysis of the firm's European operations. As a French company, Michelin had always been reluctant to cut jobs at home but the firm was now under considerable pressure. Pierre was convinced there would be a backlash as was seen when Goodyear made the decision to close its Amiens-Nord plant. In response to the American firm's decision to close plants in France, there was a series of legal challenges from the CGT (General Confederation of Labor) union and violent clashes between workers and the police. Pierre wanted Michelin to avoid that scenario but what other options could he suggest?

Sources

Lerougetel, A. (2013) Police Clash with Workers Fighting Closure of Goodyear Amiens-Nord Plant. Available at: www.wsws.org/en/articles/2013/03/09/good-m09.html, accessed June 8, 2013.

Michelin.com (n.d.) Michelin Corporate | Tires, Motorsport, Finance, Careers, Travel & News. Available at: www.michelin.com/corporate/EN, accessed June 8, 2013.

Tyrepress.com (2013) Is Michelin Considering European Plant Closures? Available at: www.tyrepress.com/News/business_area/25/27586.html, accessed June 8, 2013.

Questions

1. State the problem that Pierre Lagarde faces.
2. Identify the options available to Pierre. Be sure to identify more than one.
3. Based on the options identified above, recommend a course of action. Be sure to provide a rationale and make a decision.

? discussion questions

1. How does a rapidly growing population over age 60 impact the global marketing of goods and services in developed and developing countries?

2. Does the fact that India and China, the two most populous countries in the world, have relatively low incomes per capita make them less attractive to the global marketer? Why/why not?

3. Do firms need to change their marketing strategy when operating in countries such as Mexico and Chile with significant income inequality? Why/why not?

4. Are Europeans right to take to the streets to protest austerity measures, even when their governments have little choice but to impose them?

5. Who bears more responsibility for the alleviation of poverty: multinational firms targeting consumers at the bottom of the pyramid, national governments or the poor themselves?

FURTHER READING

Prahalad, C.K. (2005) *The Fortune at the Bottom of the Pyramid: Eradicating Poverty through Profits.* Upper Saddle River, NJ: Prentice Hall.

POLITICAL AND LEGAL ENVIRONMENTS

LEARNING OBJECTIVES

After reading this chapter you should be able to:

- Discuss the major forms of government organization

- Discuss the importance of the home-country political and legislative environments on the development and execution of global marketing strategy

- Discuss the importance of the host-country political and legal environments on the development and execution of global marketing strategy

- Define the term 'political risk', identify its various forms and describe how the concept may be quantified

- Discuss strategies for mitigating the impact of political risk.

INTRODUCTION

Global marketing strategy is not immune to changes taking place in the political and legal environments. In fact, these can have a major impact on global marketing success. As is the case with the economic environment and the culture of the host country, the political environment is outside the control of the global marketing manager. The global marketer, therefore, needs to monitor political developments in the host environment very carefully when making market-entry decisions and must stay alert to changes that could impact the firm's ongoing operations. For example, host-country governments may institute policies to seize control of the assets of foreign firms, block the repatriation of their profits or attempt to influence their ongoing operations. These policy changes may be instituted quickly, with little warning, and have potentially devastating consequences for the foreign firm. US-based Cargill, a global agribusiness firm, experienced this problem first hand when the government of Venezuela seized control of some of the firm's assets in response to alleged violations of the country's price-control rules.[1] Similarly, the Spanish petroleum company Repsol has seen the government of Argentina seize a controlling interest in its YPF subsidiary, despite protests from the European Commission and other international organizations.[2] While the Argentine

1   The Associated Press (2009) *President Hugo Chavez Orders Expropriation of Cargill Rice Plant.* Available at: http://finance.sympatico.msn.ca/investing/news/businessnews/article.aspx?cp-documentid=18316829 , accessed March 4, 2009.

2   Seekingalpha.com (2012) What Does Argentina's Impending Expropriation of YPF Tell Us? Available at: http://seekingalpha.com/article/502111-what-does-argentina-s-impending-expropriation-of-ypf-tell-us, accessed June 8, 2013.

government would eventually agree to pay Repsol $5 billion in compensation,[3] the seizure sent shock waves through the international investment community. In many cases, these types of actions are driven by strong nationalistic sentiments and the need for governments to appease their political constituents at home. Regardless of the government's motivation, however, the impact on the firm will undoubtedly be negative.

It should be noted that it is not only the political environment of the host country that should concern the global marketing firm. Home-country political decisions may also have a bearing on the operations of the multinational firm. A company's home government may, for example, impose **sanctions** on a foreign country in retaliation for its military aggression or perceived terrorist threats. In such situations, the multinational firm will be prohibited from doing business with that foreign country. The US government has, for example, imposed sanctions on the Caribbean island of Cuba since 1960 following the seizure of US assets by the Castro government. Under the 1996 Helms-Burton Act, American firms and individuals are prohibited from conducting business in Cuba.[4] It is only recently that the relationship between these two countries has begun to thaw with an agreement reached to reopen embassies in each other's capitals.[5] Countries around the world have also united in enforcing sanctions on Iran in order to deter that country's nuclear ambitions.

The global marketing manager also needs to consider the general global environment and the state of international relations between the home country, the host country and the rest of the world[6] (see Figure 4.1). The general global environment and political events taking place in third countries will also have an impact on the success of firm strategy in foreign markets. Geo-political uncertainty can undermine business and consumer confidence and create a much more challenging environment for the global marketing manager. Outright military conflict may, of course, be expected to dampen trade flows between the combatants and perhaps globally as well (Gowa, 1994).[7] Interstate military conflicts may also be expected

FIGURE 4.1   Home Country-Host Country Influence on Global Marketing Strategy

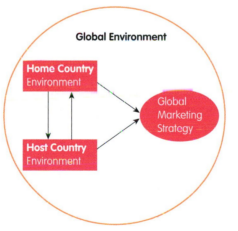

3   *New York Times* (2014) Repsol in $5 Billion Settlement with Argentina. Available at: www.nytimes.com/2014/02/26/business/international/repsol-said-to-reach-settlement-with-argentina.html?_r=0, accessed June 24, 2013.

4   Historyofcuba.com (1959) Economic Embargo against Cuba. Available at: www.historyofcuba.com/history/funfacts/embargo.htm, accessed June 11, 2013.

5   *Wall Street Journal* (2015) U.S., Cuba Reach Agreement to Establish Full Diplomatic Relations. Available at: www.wsj.com/articles/u-s-cuba-reach-agreement-to-establish-formal-diplomatic-relations-1435702347, accessed July 1, 2015.

6   Czinkota, M., Ronkainen, I., Farrell, C. and McTavish, R. (2009) *Global Marketing: Foreign Entry, Market Development and Strategy Implementation*. Toronto: Nelson Education

7   Gowa, J. (1994) *Allies, Adversaries and International Trade*. Princeton, NJ: Princeton University Press; see also Gowa, J. and Mansfield, E.D. (1993) 'Power, politics and international trade', *American Political Science Review*, 87, 2: 408–20.

to have a deleterious impact on foreign direct investment (Biglaiser and DeRouen, 2007).[8] This chapter will examine these and other issues but we begin with a brief discussion of the various forms of government organization.

GOVERNMENT ORGANIZATION AND POLITICAL STABILITY

Multinational firms can usually adjust to any political environment as long as there is some stability and clarity around the rules of engagement. Different societies have different forms of government organization. In a few cases, countries are run by a monarchy or **dictatorship** with political (and military) power concentrated in the hands of a single individual. Decisions are made autocratically and those governed have little say in how they are governed. In other societies, power is concentrated in the hands of a few and decisions are made by members of an **oligarchy**, also with little or no input from those being ruled. What is more common, however, is a democratic form of government organization in which all eligible members of the society have an equal say in how they are governed. In a **democracy**, citizens have the right to vote and the right to serve as elected government representatives. Most countries around the world now embrace a democratic form of government organization in which political and economic freedoms are emphasized. While there are a few notable hold-outs, such as North Korea, the world seems to have embraced democracy as the superior form of government. In fact, the dissolution of the Union of Soviet Socialist Republics (USSR) in 1989 and the creation of the Commonwealth of Independent States (CIS) resulted in several countries in Eastern Europe beginning the long journey towards democratic government. China, however, has been much slower to commit to democratic reforms, with little choice for its citizens but to accept the ruling People's Communist Party and a closed system of selecting political leaders.

In democratic societies, citizens will have the option of voting for one of perhaps several political parties. These political parties represent groupings of voters who support the party's political platform or agenda. In countries such as the USA, there are only two major political parties while countries such as India have a multi-party system. In some cases, the agendas of the various parties are significantly different while in other cases differences may be more subtle. In the USA, the Republican Party is generally viewed as more business friendly, with policies that focus on reducing corporate taxes and government regulations. The Democratic Party is considered to favor an agenda that emphasizes stronger social programs and support for the disadvantaged in society. In the UK, the Conservatives tend to be supportive of trade liberalization, while the Labour Party is much more likely to impose restrictions on free trade. It is important for the global marketing manager to appreciate these differences between political parties and consider how changes in the governing party will impact firm operations at home and abroad.

THE HOME-COUNTRY ENVIRONMENT

As previously noted, the home-country environment can have a significant impact on the operations of the multinational firm. Political positions and legislative measures adopted by the firm's home country are generally not designed to inhibit global market activity but may have just that effect. Governments are for the most part supportive of the global activities of their multinational companies and do what is required to promote their ambitions. The activities of these firms do create jobs at home and generate foreign exchange

---

[8]   Biglaiser, G. and DeRouen, K. (2007) 'Following the flag: Troop deployment and US foreign direct investment', *International Studies Quarterly*, 51, 4: 835–54; see also Blanton, S.L. (2000) 'Promoting human rights and democracy in the developing world: US rhetoric versus US arms exports', *American Journal of Political Science*, 44, 1: 123–31.

and tax revenues that may be used to fund social programs. The successful foreign market expansion of multinational firms also generates national pride in their home countries, and governments are, therefore, supportive of their efforts.

National governments do, however, have objectives other than the economic and commercial success of their multinationals. Ensuring national security for its citizens and supporting its multilateral obligations to organizations such as the United Nations also need to be factored into the equation. In some situations, these objectives may supersede the commercial interests of the individual company. Government-sponsored measures, such as sanctions, boycotts, export restrictions and measures to prohibit unethical behavior abroad, may have an impact on firm operations in foreign countries.

EMBARGOES AND SANCTIONS

The terms sanction and embargo refer to actions taken by national governments which disrupt the free flow of goods, services and money in order to force a target country to coexist peacefully with its neighbours and the rest of the world. These measures are instituted by governments for political, not economic, reasons and work most effectively when applied multilaterally. Sanctions and embargoes do not involve the use of military force but may be the last step before armed conflict becomes a reality. The basic premise is that by causing deprivation the international community will be able to force the target country to change its behaviour. Sanctions are usually considered, however, only after all efforts at diplomatic negotiation have broken down.

Sanctions have been used throughout history. The Hanseatic League or Hansa, a North European trading confederation originating in the 13th century, illustrates the early use of this tool. The Hansa became a dominant force in the trading of grain and established a trading post in the Norwegian port of Bergen. This trading post would eventually become a German settlement. The Hansa demanded that Norway extend trading privileges to them, to the exclusion of other nations, notably the Dutch and the English. The Norwegians refused. In 1368, the Hansa's navy simply blockaded Norwegian ports, preventing the importation of grain. Norway, dependent on imported grain to feed its population, would eventually be forced to give in to the Hansa's demands.[9]

The United Nations Security Council applies mandatory sanctions under Chapter VII of its Charter. These sanctions may be comprehensive, prohibiting all trade and investment with the target country, or more targeted involving only an arms embargo, ban on travel to the country or financial or diplomatic restrictions.[10] With Security Council authorization, the Charter also allows sanctions to be imposed by regional bodies such as the Organization of American States and the Organization of African Unity. The most high profile and successful sanctions by the United Nations were those applied against Iraq prior to and following the first Gulf war in 1991. In that case, the majority of Iraq's trading partners, including many Arab nations, supported the United Nations trade embargo and ceased trade with the target in an attempt to force Iraq to withdraw its troops from Kuwait. The Council has also applied more targeted sanctions banning the importation of conflict diamonds from Angola and Sierra Leone. These so-called 'blood diamonds' are used by rebel forces to finance arms purchases. Travel bans have also been implemented against the leaders of rebel groups such as the National Union for the Total Independence of Angola (UNITA) and their families after failure to comply with UN demands to disarm.

Once the Council adopts a resolution to apply sanctions, the decision is binding on all member countries. Each permanent member of the Security Council, however, has the right to veto efforts to impose sanctions. As noted above, in order to work sanctions need to be

---

[9]   History Today (2013) The First Common Market? The Hanseatic League. Available at: www.historytoday.com/stephen-halliday/first-common-market-hanseatic-league, accessed June 11, 2013.

[10]   United Nations, Section U. (1907) United Nations Security Council Sanctions Committees. Available at: www.un.org/sc/committees/index.shtml, accessed June 11, 2013.

imposed multilaterally. Only when virtually all nations in which a product is produced agree to deny it to a target can there be a true deprivation effect. Without such denial, sanctions do not have much impact. Yet to get all producing nations to agree can be quite difficult. Typically, individual countries have different relationships with the country subject to the sanctions due to economic, geographic or historic ties. As a result of these ongoing relationships, there may be a reluctance to terminate trade with the target. China's reluctance to support the imposition of UN Security Council economic sanctions on oil-rich Sudan, despite that country's record of human rights abuses, is a case in point. China is a major investor in Sudan's oil industry and a significant consumer of its petroleum exports. According to Tull (2006), China is also an active investor in other African countries such as Nigeria and Angola with significant oil deposits and as a result is not motivated to jeopardize its economic relationships in the region.[11]

Humanitarian groups and various governments have been vocal in their opposition to sanctions, indicating that they have a disproportionate impact on the poor and vulnerable in the societies in which they are applied. They also allude to the negative impact sanctions may have on the economies of third countries. In response to these concerns, the UN Security Council has adopted a more refined approach to the implementation of sanctions which includes humanitarian exceptions and more targeted approaches, such as the freezing of assets of those responsible for the conflict.

EXPORT CONTROLS

Several national governments impose export controls in order to restrict access by adversarial countries to strategically sensitive products such as uranium. These export controls in effect become instruments of foreign policy designed to keep dual-use materials out of the hands of rogue states or terrorist groups. Materials such as enriched uranium may be used in nuclear reactors both to generate electricity for peaceful purposes and to manufacture weapons of mass destruction. The European Union, the USA and Canada, for example, have implemented export controls against Iran for its failure to cooperate with the International Atomic Energy Agency and suspend its uranium-enrichment activities. Under these restrictions, it is an offense to export to Iran any products, services, equipment or technologies that could assist that country in the enrichment of uranium or the development of a nuclear weapons delivery system.

IMPORT CONTROLS

The global marketer may also have to contend with import controls imposed by its home government. Such regulations limit the quantity of a product that can be imported into the multinational firm's home market and are implemented to protect a domestic industry or to correct trade imbalances. The firm's home-country government may impose these restrictions on a specific foreign country, as was seen in the case of Chinese textiles coming into the EU, or on a group of countries. Import controls imposed by the home-country government become problematic for the multinational firm when they impact the firm's ability to source inputs. If the import controls are directed at countries which are key input suppliers, the multinational firm may be forced to seek alternative supplies which may be more expensive

---

[11] Tull, D.M. (2006) 'China's engagement in Africa: Scope, significance and consequences', *Journal for Modern African Studies*, 44, 3: 459–79.

or of lower quality. Either situation will have a deleterious impact on the international competitiveness of the firm's products.

BOYCOTTS

Countries may also institute **boycotts** of the goods and services produced by another country as a form of political protest. Firms may refuse to do business with companies from countries subject to a boycott and consumers may refuse to purchase products from those countries. Tensions between Israel and the Arab world, for example, have resulted in Arab countries developing a list of firms which conduct business with Israel. Arab companies will generally not conduct business with any firm on that list. The boycott was organized by the Arab League following the 1948 Arab–Israeli war and sought to ban the importation of any product or service originating in Israel. Arab companies are also discouraged from conducting business with non-Arab businesses with commercial ties to Israel. These positions are not driven by economic considerations but are purely political and designed to punish and isolate Israel.

Because of its close ties to Israel, the US government has adopted anti-boycott legislation designed to prevent its companies and private citizens from complying with the Arab boycott. The Bureau of Industry and Security is the government organization charged with the implementation of the anti-boycott laws which came into effect in the mid-1970s. Under these laws, it is an offense for US firms or individuals to refuse to do business with Israel or any company on the Arab League's prohibited list. If convicted, fines may be imposed and companies could lose their foreign income tax benefits. US firms and individuals are also required under law to report any requests made to comply with the boycott. It should be noted that Israel has passed its own anti-boycott legislation which allows any person or organization calling for a boycott of Israel, or the settlements, to be sued by the boycott's target without having to prove that it sustained any material damage. The Israeli law also states that any person or organization calling for a boycott of Israel will be ineligible to bid on any contracts with the Israeli government.[12] The European Union has voiced its opposition to the legislation on the grounds that it may impinge on the freedom of Israeli citizens and organizations to express their political views. At the same time, positions in Europe appear to be hardening with several calls for the boycott of products originating in the settlements.[13]

Historical tensions between Japan and China have similarly led to boycotts of Japanese products sold in mainland China. Japan's occupation of parts of China in the 1930s has fuelled anti-Japanese sentiments, and a more recent territorial dispute over two islands in the East China Sea has led to public outrage and boycotts of Japanese products. Japanese companies such as Panasonic and Toyota have also been the target of violent protests. While calling for calm and an end to attacks on Japanese businesses operating in China, the Chinese government has generally supported the boycott of Japanese products. Interestingly, many of the Japanese-branded products being boycotted are actually made in China so the action may well have more of a negative material impact on the Chinese economy.[14]

---

[12] Lis, J. (2013) Netanyahu: Boycott Law Reflects Democracy in Israel. Available at: www.haaretz.com/news/diplomacy-defense/netanyahu-boycott-law-reflects-democracy-in-israel-1.373058, accessed June 11, 2013.

[13] Harman, D. (2013) European Union Expresses Concern over Israel's Boycott Law. Available at: www.haaretz.com/news/diplomacy-defense/european-union-expresses-concern-over-israel-s-boycott-law-1.373076, accessed June 11, 2013.

[14] CBC.ca. (2012) Angry Chinese Protesters Ransack Japanese Businesses. World – CBC News. Available at: www.cbc.ca/news/world/story/2012/09/16/china-japan-protests.html, accessed June 11, 2013.

case study 4.1: Wal-Mart's Mexican Unit

Wal-Mart has become embroiled in a major controversy involving allegations of corruption and bribery in its Mexican unit. Wal-Mart is one of the world's largest retailers with over 10,000 stores under 69 banners in 29 countries. The company reported sales of $466 billion in the financial year 2013 and employs some 2.2 million associates around the world. The company's Mexican unit, Wal-Mart de Mexico SAB, is that country's largest private employer with well over 200,000 employees across 2,000 retail outlets.

It is alleged that lawyers retained by Wal-Mart handed out $156,000 in cash to Mexican government officials to speed up the approval of environmental permits to build new stores. The bribes were paid over a two-year period. The firm is also alleged to have paid $117,000 in bribes to managers of Luz y Fuerza del Centro – a now defunct energy company – to allow Wal-Mart to receive electricity for a new distribution center ahead of other customers. The *New York Times* has also reported that the company paid a total of $341,000 in bribes to build a Sam's Club warehouse store in a densely populated neighborhood near the Basílica de Guadalupe, without a construction license, an environmental permit, an urban impact assessment or a traffic permit. The company is also alleged to have paid some $765,000 in bribes to build a refrigerated distribution center in an environmentally sensitive flood basin north of Mexico City and an additional $200,000 in bribes to build a supermarket near to the pyramids of Teotihuacán, one of Mexico's cultural landmarks. The latter payment included a bribe of $52,000 to alter Teotihuacán's zoning map to allow for commercial development of the area.

PHOTO 4.1

As a result of the allegations, the US Justice Department and the Securities and Exchange Commission have launched investigations of possible violations of the Foreign Corrupt Practices Act, the federal law that makes it a crime for US corporations or their subsidiaries to bribe foreign officials. Wal-Mart has also launched its own internal investigations, not only in Mexico but also in all the foreign countries in which it does business. The company reports that it has found evidence of wrongdoing not only in Mexico but also in India, China and Brazil. Senior executives in Mexico and India have been suspended or forced to resign as a result of the investigations. The firm also reports that it is spending millions on anti-corruption training and background checks on lawyers and lobbyists hired to represent the company in negotiations with foreign government officials.

Sources

Bloomberg (2013) Wal-Mart Accused of Using Mexican Governor to Push Bribes. Available at: www.bloomberg.com/news/2013-01-29/wal-mart-accused-of-using-mexican-governor-to-push-bribes.html, accessed 10 June 10, 2013.

Nytimes.com (2013) The Bribery Aisle: How Wal-Mart Got Its Way in Mexico. Available at: www.nytimes.com/2012/12/18/business/walmart-bribes-teotihuacan.html?pagewanted=all&_r=0, accessed 10 June 10, 2013.

Walmart Corporate (1996) Walmart Corporate: Our Story. Available at: http://corporate.walmart.com/our-story/, accessed June 10, 2013.

Discussion Question

1.   Given Wal-Mart's size and scale of operation, is there any way for the company to ensure that its employees don't engage in bribery and other corrupt business practices?

BRIBERY AND CORRUPTION

Home-country governments exert considerable influence over the international behavior of their firms in foreign markets. This is clearly seen in government attempts to regulate bribery and other corrupt business practices. **Corruption** is generally viewed as the abuse of public office for private gain. In some countries, the payment of government officials for their services is expected and considered just another cost of doing business. In many other countries, however, the practice is frowned upon and may lead to serious problems for the firm and its executives.

Corruption, if rampant, may have a negative impact on foreign direct investment (Cuervo-Cazurra, 2006).[15] Multinational firms generally prefer to invest in countries where corruption is not likely to be a major problem. Firms may also have to alter their foreign market entry strategies and other business practices when considering countries with high levels of corruption (Uhlenbruck et al., 2006).[16] The firm may have to partner with a local firm in order to more effectively navigate the host-country environment. In some cases, however, the firm may believe that it has little choice but to give in to corrupt practices in order to survive and compete in the foreign market.

★ Box 4.1

One should note that there is a distinction between bribery and extortion. While both represent corrupt practices, the latter carries with it an implicit threat of harm and may not necessarily involve a government official. For example, Chiquita Brands International, a US banana company, was fined $25 million by the US Justice Department for the payment of protection money to terrorist groups in Columbia. The company admitted to providing extortion payments to the United Self-Defense Forces of Colombia (AUC) in return for the protection of its workers in Columbia. The AUC is a right-wing militia which is responsible for a significant proportion of Columbia's cocaine exports and is implicated in some of the worst massacres in the country's history. In 2001, the US government branded the AUC a terrorist organization. Chiquita also admitted to paying for protection from the National Liberation Army and the leftist Revolutionary Armed Forces of Colombia which control some of the banana-growing areas in the country.[17]

Many governments are signatories to international agreements that attempt to fight bribery and corruption in international business. For example, the Organization for Economic Cooperation and Development (OECD) convention on Combating Bribery of Foreign Public Officials in International Business Transactions seeks to eliminate the flow of bribes to corrupt foreign government officials and remove corruption and bribery as **non-tariff barriers** to international trade. Non-tariff barriers restrict trade flows and are discussed in the following chapter. Under the OECD Convention, which became effective on December 17, 1997, it is an offense for a company to bribe a public official to get or retain business or other improper advantage, whether or not the company was the best qualified for the job. 'Other improper advantage' may, for example, refer to the granting of building permits for the construction of new facilities without the required government approvals and oversight. It is important to note that under the Convention it is an offense, whether the advantage is given to the person offering the bribe or is received on behalf of some other person or company (see Case Study 4.2).

---

[15] Cuervo-Cazurra, A. (2006) 'Who cares about corruption?', *Journal of International Business Studies*, 37: 807–22.

[16] Uhlenbruck, K., Rodriguez, P., Doh, J. and Eden, L. (2006) 'The impact of corruption on entry strategy: Evidence from telecommunication projects in emerging economies', *Organization Science*, 17, 3: 402–14.

[17] Chiquita Agrees US$25m Fine to Settle Case: Alleging Extortion Payment to Terrorists. Available at: www.jamaica-gleaner.com/gleaner/20070317/business/business3.html, accessed March 17, 2007.

Interestingly, the OECD Convention notes that the value of the advantage received or whether officials in the host country are tolerant of such payments is immaterial to the determination of whether or not an offense has been committed. The Convention does argue, however, that small 'facilitation' payments do not fall within the definition of bribery and are accepted in some countries even though they may be used to induce services from government officials. Signatory governments to this Convention, of course, have jurisdiction to prosecute their nationals for offenses committed abroad.

The OECD offers a number of tips to multinational companies for strengthening their internal controls, ethics and compliance programs to deal with issues of corruption in foreign countries:

- The company must develop a clear corporate policy against foreign corruption.
- Senior management must communicate a strong and visible commitment to the company's programs and policies dealing with foreign corruption.
- It must be communicated that all individuals in the company, regardless of level, have a duty to comply with the company's prohibition against corruption and the related policies.
- The company's compliance program must be applicable to all directors, officers and employees of the company, as well as all entities over which the company has control, e.g. foreign subsidiaries, and should cover the areas of: gifts; hospitality, entertainment and expenses; customer travel; political contributions; charitable donations and sponsorships; facilitation payments; and solicitation and extortion.
- Subject to contractual arrangements, the company's compliance program should also be applicable to third-party contractors, agents, consultants, joint venture partners and distributors.
- The company should maintain financial and accounting systems, with appropriate controls, to ensure that they cannot be used for bribery and corruption or concealing such activities.
- The company should institute appropriate disciplinary procedures to address violations of the company's program.
- The company should provide guidance to employees, officers and directors on complying with the company's policy and urgent advice when they are confronted with specific difficult situations.
- The company should provide protection for those who report violations.[18]

Other international agreements targeting bribery and corruption include the Organization of American States' convention against corruption, the United Nations Convention against Transnational Organized Crime and the United Nations Convention against Corruption. The WTO has also been active in trying to stamp out the practice. The work done by Transparency International (TI) also needs to be noted. This non-profit organization regularly publishes information about the perception of corruption in countries around the globe. Table 4.1 shows the country rankings for 2011. The TI Corruption Perception Index (CPI) is based on 16 surveys from 10 independent institutions which collect information from businesspeople and country analysts. Scores range from 0 for countries which are perceived as being highly corrupt to 10 for those viewed as being not at all corrupt. New Zealand, Denmark, Finland and Sweden are among the top countries perceived as 'clean', while corruption is perceived as rampant in countries such as North Korea and Somalia.

It should be recognized that the TI scores presented in Table 4.1 represent the perceptions of those interviewed for the survey and these may be at variance with the actual experience of corruption on the ground in the countries. Corruption is a sensitive topic and individuals involved are generally reluctant to admit to the practice. This makes the reality of corruption somewhat difficult to measure objectively. Critics of the CPI also note that the scores are widely reported in the media every year, which may have an impact on the perceptions of the very businesspeople and analysts who are asked to complete the surveys. A country's low CPI score in one year reinforces the negative view of survey participants, leading to a

---

[18]   OECD (2011) *Convention on Combating Bribery of Foreign Public Officials in International Business Transactions and Related Documents*. Paris: OECD.

low score the following year. A vicious cycle is, therefore, created. It should also be recognized that the methodology used to compute the CPI may change and, therefore, year-to-year comparisons may not be appropriate. Same-year comparisons between countries are also problematic given that the sources of information used for the index will be different for each country. In addition, the CPI is based on aggregate measures and, therefore, does not provide information on the level or type of corruption that is believed to exist in a country.[19]

TABLE 4.1   Transparency International Corruption Perception Index, selected countries, 2011

Rank	Country	CPI score
1	New Zealand	9.5
2	Denmark	9.4
2	Finland	9.4
4	Sweden	9.3
5	Singapore	9.2
6	Norway	9.0
7	Netherlands	8.9
8	Australia	8.8
8	Switzerland	8.8
10	Canada	8.7
11	Luxembourg	8.5
12	Hong Kong	8.4
13	Iceland	8.3
14	Germany	8.0
14	Japan	8.0
16	Austria	7.8
16	Barbados	7.8
16	United Kingdom	7.8
19	Belgium	7.5
19	Ireland	7.5
21	Bahamas	7.3
22	Chile	7.2
22	Qatar	7.2
24	United States	7.1
25	France	7.0
25	Saint Lucia	7.0
25	Uruguay	7.0
28	United Arab Emirates	6.8
29	Estonia	6.4
30	Cyprus	6.3
175	Iraq	1.8
177	Sudan	1.6

(Continued)

[19] Byrne, E., Arnold, A-K. and Nagano, F. (2010) *Building Support for Anti-Corruption Efforts: Why Anti-Corruption Agencies Need to Communicate and How.* Washington, DC: World Bank.

TABLE 4.1   (Continued)

Rank	Country	CPI score
177	Turkmenistan	1.6
177	Uzbekistan	1.6
180	Afghanistan	1.5
180	Myanmar	1.5
182	Korea (North)	1.0
182	Somalia	1.0

Source: Transparency International (2011) Bribe Payers Index. Available at: http://bpi.transparency.org/bpi2011/in_detail/, accessed June 9, 2013.

Transparency International also publishes the Bribe Payers Index (BPI). The BPI provides a measure of the likelihood that firms headquartered in various countries will bribe when operating in a foreign country. In essence, the BPI measures the supply side of corruption. The index ranges from 0 to 10. The higher the score, the less likely it is that firms from that country will engage in bribery when doing business abroad. Transparency International computes the BPI annually for the largest economies in the world. As with the CPI, the BPI is also based on the perceptions of business executives responding to questions about the likelihood that companies from various countries will engage in bribery when doing business in their country. Results for 2011 are shown in Table 4.2. Companies from Russia, China and Mexico are perceived to be the most likely to engage in bribery when operating outside their home country, while firms from the Netherlands, Belgium and Switzerland are perceived to be the least likely to engage in such corrupt practices.

TABLE 4.2   Transparency International Bribe Payers Index, 2011

Rank	Country	BPI score
1	Netherlands	8.8
1	Switzerland	8.8
3	Belgium	8.7
4	Germany	8.6
4	Japan	8.6
6	Australia	8.5
6	Canada	8.5
8	Singapore	8.3
8	UK	8.3
10	USA	8.1
11	France	8.0
11	Spain	8.0
13	South Korea	7.9
14	Brazil	7.7
15	Hong Kong	7.6
15	Italy	7.6
15	Malaysia	7.6
15	South Africa	7.6
19	Taiwan	7.5
19	India	7.5
19	Turkey	7.5

Rank	Country	BPI score
22	Saudi Arabia	7.4
23	Argentina	7.3
23	UAE	7.3
25	Indonesia	7.1
26	Mexico	7.0
27	China	6.5
28	Russia	6.1

Source: Transparency International (2011) What is the Corruption Perceptions Index? The Report. Available at: http://cpi.transparency.org/cpi2011/in_detail/, accessed June 9, 2013.

case study 4.2: IKEA in Russia

IKEA, the Swedish furniture retailer, ran into trouble in Russia in 2010. Two of the company's executives were fired after they paid a bribe, through a local contractor, to get electrical permits. IKEA was expanding in Russia and wanted to ensure that construction in St Petersburg would not be stalled because it did not have the necessary permits. IKEA has a zero-tolerance policy regarding corruption and its IWAY standard of business ethics was in place at the time. This policy states in part:

The values of trust, integrity and honesty are at the foundation of IWAY and are keys to its sustainable implementation. It is on this basis that we begin the relationships and through continued respect of these values that it will grow. It is important that all IKEA co-workers and external business partners understand the IKEA position on corruption and its prevention. This has been established in the IKEA Corruption Prevention Policy and The IKEA Rules on Prevention of Corruption and communicated in the IKEA Way of Doing Business and the vendor letter which shall be signed by all business partners.

PHOTO 4.2

Even though in this case corruption was 'outsourced' to a local contractor, IKEA's integrity was called into question and the company had to move quickly to terminate the employment of the executives involved.

Sources

IKEA Supply AG (2008) IWAY Standard: Minimum Requirements for Environment and Social and Working Conditions when Purchasing Products, Materials and Services. Available at: www.ikea.com/ms/en_CA/about_ikea/pdf/SCGlobal_IWAYSTDVers4.pdf, accessed November 21, 2014.

New York Times (2010) Ikea Fires 2 Officials in Russia Bribe Case. Available at: www.nytimes.com/2010/02/16/business/global/16ikea.html, accessed February 17, 2010.

Discussion Questions

1. Should IKEA have fired the two executives involved in this scandal? Why/why not?
2. Are corporate anti-corruption policies really effective in preventing problems of corruption, given that IKEA did have such a policy in place at the time?
3. What can IKEA do now to prevent a reoccurrence of this problem?
4. Based on the BPI scores, should IKEA have anticipated this problem and done more to prevent it?

🔍 Spotlight on Research 4.1   Laws Against Bribery Abroad

Cuervo-Cazurra (2008) argues that in theory laws against bribery are supposed to induce foreign investors to reduce their investments in corrupt countries. These laws are expected to raise the cost of bribery, thereby making the practice less attractive and reducing the supply. The increase in costs is expected to make foreign investors more sensitive to the consequences of bribing abroad and lead to a decrease in investment in more corrupt countries. One would expect these laws to be effective given that most multinational companies are domiciled in countries with low levels of corruption and a judicial system that actually works. The author points out that while most countries have laws banning corruption at home, very few have laws banning corruption abroad. To be effective, however, implementation of laws banning corruption abroad must be coordinated among countries. If not, corrupt government officials will simply demand bribes from investors from countries with lax (or no) bribery legislation. Investors from countries with laws against bribery will face a prisoner's dilemma and will be encouraged to find ways around the legislation in order to remain competitive in the foreign market. The (2008) article by Cuervo-Cazurra attempts to settle the debate on the effectiveness of laws against bribery abroad in stemming the flow of investment to corrupt countries. The Organization for Economic Cooperation and Development (OECD) Convention on Combating Bribery of Foreign Public Officials in International Business Transactions and the US Foreign Corrupt Practices Act are considered in the analysis.

Hypotheses

Cuervo-Cazurra (2008) tests the following hypotheses:

Hypothesis 1a: US investors will invest less in corrupt countries than investors from other countries.

Hypothesis 1b: US investors will not invest less in corrupt countries than investors from other countries.

Hypothesis 2a: Investors from countries who are signatories to the OECD Anti-Bribery Convention will invest less in corrupt countries than investors from other countries.

Hypothesis 2b: Investors from countries who are signatories to the OECD Anti-Bribery Convention will not invest less in corrupt countries than investors from other countries.

Method

The above hypotheses are tested using FDI data from 103 host countries. Cross-sectional panel data covering a seven-year period (1996–2002) are used. Most of the FDI data comes from the United Nations Conference on Trade and Development (UNCTAD) country profiles but OECD data are also used. The author's empirical models are specified as follows:

$$FDI_{ijt} = \gamma_1 \text{ Home country has laws against bribery abroad (US FCPA or OECD Anti-Bribery Convention)}_{it-1} \times \text{Host corruption}_{jt-1} + X_{ijt-1}\beta + \varepsilon_{ijt}$$

The dependent variable in this research is the natural logarithm of bilateral FDI inflows from a home country to a host country, measured in US$ using the average foreign exchange rate for the year. The author utilizes two measures of corruption – Transparency International's corruption perception index and the World Bank's control of corruption measure: γ_1 is the coefficient of interest, X_{ijt-1} is a vector of the control variables, β is a vector of the coefficients of the control variables, and ε_{ijt} is the error term. In the above specification, the author controls for the size of the country using indicators of gross domestic product and population. The geographic distance between the countries is controlled for using an indicator of the great circle distance, which measures distance on the surface of the earth using longitude and latitude coordinates. The distance measure is complemented by indicators that the country is landlocked or an island, or has a common border with the host country. Cultural similarities are captured with an indicator of the existence of a common language between home and host country, while commonalities in administration are measured with indicators of the existence of a colonial relationship and of a common colonizer. The author uses a double-log model with quasi-fixed effects and one-year lag to analyze the data.

Results

The author finds support for hypothesis 2a but not for 2b, i.e. investors from countries which are signatories to the OECD Anti-Bribery Convention have reduced their investment in corrupt countries. The coefficient of the interaction between the independent variable 'the home country implemented the Convention into its national laws' and the variable measuring host-country corruption is negative and statistically significant ($\beta = -0.142$, $\rho < 0.001$). This hypothesis is supported whether the World Bank or Transparency International measure of corruption is used. Similarly, the author also finds support for hypothesis 1a but not for 1b. The coefficient of the interaction between the variable 'the host country is the USA' and the variable 'host-country corruption' is negative and statistically significant ($\beta = -0.698$, $\rho < 0.01$). Again, this hypothesis is supported whether the World Bank or Transparency International measure of corruption is used. The analysis suggests that the US Foreign Corrupt Practices Act has been effective in reducing US investment in corrupt countries, a result which is contrary to earlier studies, such as Wei (2000) and Smarzynska and Wei (2000). The author notes that one explanation for the difference in result from previous studies may be the period of analysis. Earlier studies utilized data prior to the execution of the OECD Convention when US investors would have had an incentive to bypass the US legislation in order to remain competitive. To determine whether time period really was the driver for the difference in results, the author ran additional regressions for the period before and after 1998 – the year when the US legislation was modified to incorporate the requirements of the OECD Convention. The results confirmed that US investors became more sensitive to the issue of corruption after 1998 and reduced their investment in corrupt countries. The coefficient of the interaction between the variable 'the host country is the USA (after 1998)' and the variable 'host-country corruption' is negative and statistically significant ($\beta = -0.336$, $\rho < 0.01$). Prior to 1998, the results are similar to earlier studies with US investors, demonstrating no greater sensitivity to corruption than with investors from other jurisdictions. The coefficient of the interaction between the variable 'the host country is the USA (before 1998)' and the variable 'host-country corruption' is negative but not statistically significant ($\beta = -0.027$, $\rho > 0.05$).

Implication

The study by Cuervo-Cazurra (2008) suggests that laws against bribery are effective but only when implemented within a coordinated, multilateral framework. The efforts of individual governments are unlikely to reduce the supply of bribes flowing into corrupt countries.

Read the complete article by Cuervo-Cazurra and answer the following questions.

Sources

Cuervo-Cazurra, A. (2008) 'The effectiveness of laws against bribery abroad', *Journal of International Business Studies*, 39: 634–51.

Smarzynska, B.K. and Wei, S.J. (2000) Corruption and composition of foreign direct investment: Firm-level evidence. NBER Working Paper No. 7969. Cambridge, MA: National Bureau of Economic Research.

Wei, S.J. (2000) 'How taxing is corruption on international investors?', *The Review of Economics and Statistics*, 82, 1: 1–11.

Discussion Questions

1. Cuervo-Cazurra (2008) assesses the effectiveness of laws against bribery abroad by examining whether investors reduced their presence in corrupt countries as opposed to the number of identifications or prosecutions. How would you overcome this limitation of the study in future research?
2. The article by Cuervo-Cazurra (2008) does not address the issue of regulatory stringency. Do you believe that greater stringency in the US Foreign Corrupt Practices Act (as opposed to incorporating the requirements of the OECD Convention) would be more effective in reducing investment in corrupt countries? Why/why not? How would you test this hypothesis empirically?

THE HOST-COUNTRY ENVIRONMENT

While the firm needs to be aware of and monitor political developments at home, it is in the host country that most problems may arise. Conducting business in a foreign country carries with it a certain level of **political risk**. This political risk may be defined as the risk of loss when investing in a foreign country due to changes in that country's political structure, policies, regulations or laws.[20] These changes have an adverse impact on the firm and its operations and may range from confiscation of assets by the state to restrictions on the transfer of profits out of the country. It should be noted that there is political risk associated with doing business in all countries but that the level of risk will vary significantly between countries. Countries such as the USA, Canada, Switzerland, Norway and Japan with stable democracies and respect for the rule of law are considered low risk. Other countries, however, such as Venezuela, Iran and Russia, are considered high risk.

As illustrated in Figure 4.2, political risk may be broken down into three types: ownership risk, transfer risk and operating risk. **Ownership risk** refers to the risk associated with the government seizing control of the firm's assets in the host country and jeopardizing property, as well as the lives and well-being of its employees. **Transfer risk** refers to government actions which make it difficult or impossible for the firm to transfer financial capital into or out of the host country. **Operating risk** involves government interference with the day-to-day business decisions made by the firm.

Firms may face political risk because of the actions of the host-country government but also because of actions that are outside the state's control. In terms of deliberate government actions, the global marketer must consider the possibility of expropriation of its assets by the state. **Expropriation** involves the seizure of the company's assets with the payment of compensation. In such situations, it is unlikely that the compensation offered by the government will be close to the market value of the assets and may well be below their book value. Payment may also be offered in a non-convertible local currency or in virtually worthless government bonds. Companies faced with this situation often accept the payment offered by the government rather than engage in a protracted legal battle. In some cases, however, the firm is not offered any form of compensation. **Confiscation** refers to the seizure of the firm's assets without the payment of compensation. Both confiscation and expropriation have extremely damaging effects on the multinational firm. Fortunately, the frequency of such actions has diminished over time as they are severely frowned upon by the international community.

Rather than engage in extreme forms of interference such as confiscation, some governments have resorted to more subtle forms of control such as domestication. With **domestication** (or nationalization), partial ownership of the foreign firm is transferred to the government along with day-to-day management responsibilities. The company is allowed to continue operating

FIGURE 4.2   Types of Political Risk

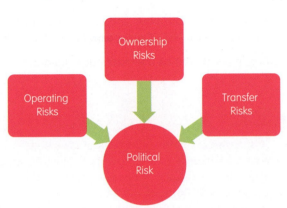

---

20   Czinkota, M., Ronkainen, I., Farrell, C. and McTavish, R. (2009) *Global Marketing: Foreign Entry, Market Development and Strategy Implementation*. Toronto: Nelson Education.

in the country but the government may place a number of its own nationals on the board of directors, changing the balance of power and giving the state de facto decision-making authority. Along with changes in the composition of the board may also be new directives from the government on the hiring of nationals in key management positions and the purchase of local raw materials and supplies to ensure that a larger share of the profits of the firm is retained within the country. While domestication may bring much needed revenue and employment to the host country, it may have a deleterious impact on the multinational firm and its operations. Placing inexperienced nationals in key executive positions may lead to poor decision making which may jeopardize the firm's long-term competitiveness and profitability. Also, imposing restrictions on the use of local raw materials may drive up the firm's cost of production and/or jeopardize the quality of the final product (see Case Study 4.3).

case study 4.3: Crystallex mining in Venezuela

Located in southeastern Venezuela is one of the world's largest gold deposits. Las Cristinas is the site of these gold deposits, estimated at some 18 million ounces. Crystallex International Corporation, a Canadian mining company, has, since 2002, been embroiled in a series of legal and political battles with the government of Venezuela over the ownership of the Las Cristinas mine. In that year, Crystallex signed a mining operation agreement with Corporacion Venezolana de Guayana (CVG) which supposedly gave Crystallex the exclusive right to exploit the mineral resources at Las Cristinas. Despite having completed all the regulatory requirements in terms of feasibility studies and environmental impact assessments, the Venezuelan government has steadfastly refused to issue the permits necessary for production to begin.

The legal ownership of Las Cristinas has been in dispute as far back as 1982 when Mrs Culver-Lemon, the original holder of a 25-year concession, sued her business partner for alleged violations of the terms of their contract. Following a series of legal battles, the property would eventually be expropriated by the Venezuelan government with the National Guard seizing the mine in 1999. CVG, a state-owned Venezuelan conglomerate, was tasked with deciding the fate of the mine and would eventually grant Crystallex the concession.

Despite having control over the mine, Crystallex has been denied the opportunity to work it. As the company waited for government approval, concerns were raised about the possibility that the mine may in fact be nationalized. Indeed, the late Hugo Chavez is quoted as saying: 'They [Crystallex] go around the world saying they have this much in gold reserves, but they are never going to exploit it.' The company's contract to operate the mine was unilaterally terminated by CVG in 2007. Crystallex filed for bankruptcy in 2011 and the Venezuelan government has since announced plans to develop the mine jointly with a Chinese company.

Sources

Vcrisis.com (2006) Venezuela: Crystallex Out. Available at: www.vcrisis.com/index.php?content=letters/200509261713, accessed June 9, 2013.

Worldpress.org (2013) Venezuela: The Saga That Is Las Cristinas. Available at: www.worldpress.org/Americas/2268.cfm#down, accessed June 9, 2013.

Discussion Questions

1. Should Crystallex have attempted to conduct business in Venezuela with such a high level of political risk?
2. Would development of the Las Cristinas mine in Venezuela be any easier for a Chinese company? Why/why not?
3. Do you think that partnering with the Venezuelan government would have been a better strategy for Crystallex in its attempts to develop the Las Cristinas mine? Why/why not?

Apart from confiscation, expropriation and domestication, governments may take other actions against foreign firms which may result in material losses. In the case of certain sensitive products, such as staple foods or medicine, the government may impose price controls which will have an impact on foreign companies operating in those sectors. **Price controls**, in essence, put a ceiling on what the foreign company can charge for its products on the local market, which has implications for overall profitability. If the firm is unable to reduce its cost of production, it will have to decide whether it can continue to operate in the host country. Companies such as Coke and PepsiCo, for example, have had to make such decisions with respect to their operations in Mexico.

Host-country governments may also impose **import restrictions** on foreign firms operating in their jurisdictions. In these situations, the foreign firm is not able to freely import raw materials, equipment, parts and other inputs and is forced to rely on local suppliers. This government action can provide local industry with a significant boost but have a negative impact on the efficiency and cost competitiveness of the firm's operations. The problem may become even more acute if local input suppliers are unable to keep up with the demands of foreign firms. Closely associated with import restrictions may be government demands that products sold in the country embody a certain percentage of local content. **Local content requirements** necessitate that the foreign company utilize local parts and labor in its assembly operations and not rely 100 percent on foreign inputs. This is seen, for example, in the case of Chinese investment projects in Africa. Projects in Africa sponsored by Chinese state-owned firms have typically used imported labor from China, despite the abundance of skilled and unskilled labor available on the African continent. The African Union has now called for a reversal of this policy and has demanded that 70 percent of all of Africa's raw materials be processed on African soil and that Sino-African joint ventures use 80 percent African labor. While China is unlikely to accept these targets, they do represent a starting point for negotiation between the two sides (Amosu, 2007).[21]

In addition to actions such as price controls, local content requirements, confiscation and domestication, there may be other elements in the host-country environment, such as terrorist acts, that create uncertainty for the foreign multinational but are beyond the control of the government. **Terrorism** has been defined as 'the premeditated, systematic threat or use of violence by sub-national groups to attain a political, religious or ideological objective through intimidation of a large audience' (Czinkota et al., 2010).[22] It should be recognized that terrorism is not normally carried out as part of a government's official policy agenda, whereas measures such as expropriation and confiscation are. Terrorist acts may lead to the loss of lives and property. In addition, such acts may also result in a number of indirect effects such as:

- dampened consumer demand as a result of fear and panic following such events
- increased transaction costs for the multinational firm as it attempts to comply with various government regulations put in place to increase the security of commercial activities
- interruptions in the proper functioning of the firm's global supply chain which may lead to shortages and customer dissatisfaction
- reduced foreign direct investment in the affected country.[23]

Terrorist attacks tend to be concentrated in a few countries such as Iraq, Pakistan and Afghanistan but are fairly widespread (see Figure 4.3). Indeed, of the 158 countries studied by the Institute for Economics and Peace (IEP), only 31 have had no terrorist attacks in the ten years ending in 2011.

---

[21]   Amosu, A. (2007) Foreign Policy in Focus. China in Africa: It's (Still) the Governance, Stupid. Available at: www.fpif.org/fpiftxt/4068, accessed March 1, 2013.

[22]   Czinkota, M., Knight, G., Liesch, P.W. and Steen, J. (2010) 'Terrorism and international business: A research agenda', *Journal of International Business Studies*, 41, 50: 828 .

[23]   Czinkota et al. (2010) op cit., p. 831.

FIGURE 4.3

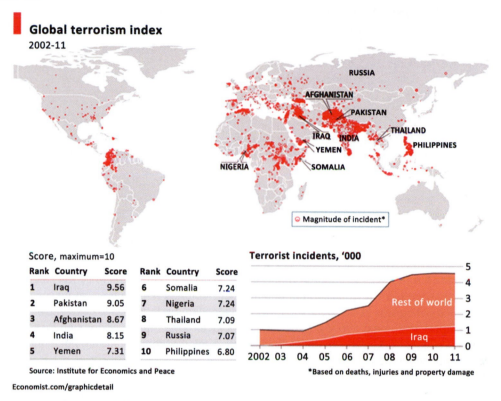

Global terrorism index
2002-11

RUSSIA
AFGHANISTAN
PAKISTAN
THAILAND
PHILIPPINES
IRAQ INDIA
YEMEN
NIGERIA SOMALIA

◎ Magnitude of incident*

Score, maximum=10

Rank	Country	Score	Rank	Country	Score
1	Iraq	9.56	6	Somalia	7.24
2	Pakistan	9.05	7	Nigeria	7.24
3	Afghanistan	8.67	8	Thailand	7.09
4	India	8.15	9	Russia	7.07
5	Yemen	7.31	10	Philippines	6.80

Terrorist incidents, '000

Rest of world

Iraq

2002 03 04 05 06 07 08 09 10 11

Source: Institute for Economics and Peace   *Based on deaths, injuries and property damage

Economist.com/graphicdetail

The Economist. n.d. Fear and loathing (online) Available at: http://www.economist.com/blogs/graphicdetail/2012/12/daily-chart-0, accessed June 9, 2013.

The analysis of political risk is extremely important. A government in power when a country is being evaluated for investment may be overthrown in a coup d'état after the investment has been made. With a change in government, considerable uncertainty is introduced for the foreign firm with respect to economic policies and the new government's attitude towards foreign investment and foreigners.

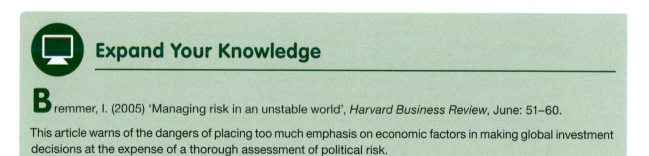

Expand Your Knowledge

Bremmer, I. (2005) 'Managing risk in an unstable world', *Harvard Business Review*, June: 51–60.

This article warns of the dangers of placing too much emphasis on economic factors in making global investment decisions at the expense of a thorough assessment of political risk.

THE MEASUREMENT OF POLITICAL RISK

In order to properly assess the political risks they face in specific countries, global marketers need access to current factual information. Several organizations, such as the Economic intelligence Unit and Export Development Canada, develop and disseminate quantitative data on the level of political risk that firms face in various countries around the world. The Profit Opportunity Recommendation Index (POR) developed by Business Environment Risk Intelligence SA (BERI) is one of the more widely used measures of political risk. The POR is comprised of three sub-indices that attempt to capture different facets of a country's political risk profile. These sub-indices follow:

(a) The Political Risk Index (PRI) is focused on political risk that stems from sociopolitical conditions in the country under analysis. The PRI considers six internal causes of political risk:

- fractionalization of the political spectrum and the power of these fractions
- fractionalization along language, ethnic or religious lines and the strength of these fractions
- restrictive measures used to retain power in the society
- the mentality of the people (tendencies toward xenophobia, nepotism, corruption, etc.)
- social conditions, e.g. wealth distribution
- strength of forces for a radical government.

In addition, the PRI also considers two external causes of political risk: dependence on a major hostile power and negative influences that stem from regional politics.

(b) The Operations Risk Index (ORI) assesses the operations climate for foreign businesses. A total of 15 variables are considered which attempt to capture the degree to which nationals are given preferential treatment over foreigners and the overall quality of the business climate. Specific variables used in this sub-index include: policy continuity; attitude towards foreign investors and profits; degree of privatization; bureaucratic delays; and the enforceability of contracts.

(c) The R Factor is concerned with remittances and repatriation. Several criteria are used in this measure to assess the country's willingness and capacity to allow foreign firms to convert their profits in the local currency into foreign exchange and transfer the funds back to their home country. It also assesses the willingness of the country to provide foreign firms with access to convertible currency in order to import equipment and raw materials. The R factor takes into consideration factors such as the country's legal framework, its ability to generate foreign exchange, accumulated international reserves and foreign debt.

TABLE 4.3   POR Scores, selected countries, 2012

Country	POR score
Low risk (POR: 70–100): *'Political changes will not lead to conditions seriously adverse to business. No major sociopolitical disturbances are expected.'*	
Switzerland	76
Singapore	78
Norway	73
Moderate risk (POR: 55–69): *'Political changes seriously adverse to business have occurred in the past, but governments in power during the forecast period have a low probability of introducing such changes. Some demonstrations and strikes have a high probability of occurring.'*	
Canada	63
USA	58
UK	62
France	55
China	57
Australia	55
Germany	68
Japan	56

Country	POR score
High risk (POR: 40–54): *'Political developments seriously adverse to business exist or could occur during the forecast period. Major sociopolitical disturbances, including sustained rioting, have a high probability of occurring periodically.'*	
Chile	54
India	42
Russia	48
Brazil	41
Columbia	41
Indonesia	43
Italy	42
Prohibitive risks (POR: 0–39): *'Political conditions severely restrict business operations. Loss of assets from rioting and insurgencies is possible. Disturbances are part of daily life.'*	
Iran	36
Mexico	35
Venezuela	38
Greece	27
Argentina	39

Source: Business Environment Risk Intelligence

The POR is an average of the three sub-measures discussed above. The scale ranges from 0 to 100 and is computed for 50 countries. Sample scores are provided in Table 4.3. BERI relies on the judgment of experts drawn from organizations such as private-sector firms, including financial institutions, government departments and international institutions.

STRATEGIES FOR MITIGATING POLITICAL RISK

Apart from closely monitoring political developments in the host country, the global marketer also has the option of purchasing political risk insurance. Industrialized countries such as the USA, the UK, Germany and Canada offer insurance coverage to their domestic firms when operating abroad. For example, in the USA, OPIC, a development finance company, provides insurance coverage for businesses operating in foreign markets. Coverage may be purchased for risks associated with currency inconvertibility, expropriation, political violence and changes in the regulatory environment such as tax policies and operating licenses. Lloyd's of London provides similar coverage for UK-based companies operating around the world, while Export Development Canada offers coverage for Canadian exporters.

While insurance is useful in covering the risks associated with operating in foreign countries, the multinational firm should also strive to build good working relationships with the host-country government. It is often useful for the multinational company to have a well-selected local partner with a superior understanding of the political environment in the host country and well-developed contacts in government. Canada's Bema Gold, for example, has operated successfully in high-risk countries by paying attention to its selection of strategic partners. Bema operates successfully in Russia because it has partnered with a regional Russian government which holds 25 percent of the equity in the venture.[24] Building support within the local community in which the multinational firm operates is also a useful strategy. Firms which contribute to their communities and are successful at building relationships will be perceived differently by host-country governments. Companies may also have the option of lobbying the host-country government for regulatory or policy changes that have a positive impact on their operations. The multinational firm may hire professional lobbyists whose mandate would include meeting with local politicians and government officials in order to influence their opinions on policy and regulatory matters that impact the firm. Companies with a solid track record of community engagement and which can point to concrete benefits to the local economy are more likely to be successful in their lobbying efforts. The multinational firm may also have the option of licensing its technology to a local firm, thereby obviating the need to operate in the foreign country. The multinational will receive a royalty payment for its technology, so is able to build market share in the foreign country without direct exposure to the political risks involved. Licensing is discussed more fully in Chapter 8.

GENERAL GLOBAL ENVIRONMENT

The global marketing manager must consider not only the political and legal environment in the home and host countries but also the general global environment. Global political tensions can undermine business and consumer confidence and make international sales more challenging for the multinational firm. On the other hand, a thawing of political animosity, as experienced at the end of the Cold War, can lead to entirely new market opportunities for globally oriented firms.

Legal disputes between nations may also occur from time to time and are usually related to international trade or territorial boundaries and resources. These may also be damaging to international business because of the uncertainty they create. While there is no global legislative framework to which all countries subscribe, there are a number of international agreements to which many countries are signatories. The World Trade Organization (WTO), discussed in the following chapter, for example, is instrumental in dealing with global disputes involving trade in products and services. Discussions and negotiations at the level of the WTO take place among sovereign states and individual companies do not participate directly. The individual firm may, however, raise its concerns with its home-country government.

Intellectual property protection is another area that is extremely important to the global marketing firm. The Paris Convention for the Protection of Industrial Property was the first major treaty for the protection of intellectual property and came into force in 1884 with just 14 members. In 1886, the Berne Convention for the Protection of Literary and Artistic Works came into effect for the protection of copyrighted materials such as architectural drawings. The offices which administer the Paris and Berne Conventions were eventually merged to form the United International Bureaux for the Protection of Intellectual Property. This latter organization would eventually become the World Intellectual Property Organization (WIPO). WIPO, a United Nations agency, now administers some 25 treaties and has over 180 member countries.

Generally, firms need to obtain protection for their trademarks, designs and other intellectual property in every country in which they operate. Registering a patent in the UK, for example, does not offer the firm protection in the USA, Mexico or Canada. WIPO can, however, assist firms in protecting their intellectual property in a large number of jurisdictions. The Patent Cooperation Treaty (PCT) makes it possible for a

---

24 Canada.com (2011) Bema Gold Victim of its own Success. Available at: www.canada.com/nationalpost/financialpost/story.html?id=5b7e1850-c047-48a5-8b78-41a6a0b7114b, accessed June 11, 2013.

firm to seek patent protection in over 145 contracting states simultaneously. Nationals or residents of a contracting state may file an application either at their local patent office or through WIPO's International Bureau. WIPO also administers the Madrid System for the International Registration of Marks which offers protection to trademark holders in over 80 countries. It should be noted that the WTO is also active in the protection of intellectual property. The Agreement on Trade-Related Aspects of Intellectual Property Rights (TRIPS) was negotiated in 1986–94 and marked the first time that intellectual property rules were introduced into a multilateral trading system.

THE LEGAL ENVIRONMENT

The political and legal environments are closely intertwined. Laws and regulations which impact international business are usually the result of political decisions. It is imperative that the global marketer understands the laws and regulations that govern how business is to be conducted in each foreign country in which it operates. There is no uniform law that governs how business is to be conducted in all countries. Major differences in the legislative environment do exist and will have significantly different impacts on the firm's operations. Countries differ, for example, in the emphasis they place on resolving disputes through the legal system. In countries such as China and Japan, the role of the courts and lawyers is minimized, while in the USA the opposite is true. The USA is generally regarded as being extremely litigious and has the highest number of lawyers per capita.

While the multinational firm is better served by retaining competent legal counsel, the global marketing manager should at least be aware of some of the major differences in legal systems around the world. For example, business in Muslim countries is conducted under *Sharia* law which is opposed to the payment of interest, referred to as riba in the Quran. Interest is considered to be usurious and socially unjust. This restriction has severe implications for western banking practices that revolve around interest charged on loans to debtors. Islamic finance is based on notions of shared risk and the ownership of assets. A bank lending money to a business becomes an equity partner in that business and is entitled to share in the profits (or losses) of that business. Payments made to the bank are not interest and, therefore, do not contravene *Sharia* law. Traditional mortgages, as used in western societies, are not workable in Muslim societies because they also rely on interest payments. A prospective home owner will need to work with a financier who is able to purchase the property. The financier would then re-sell the property at a higher price which includes an amount that would have been considered interest in a traditional western mortgage transaction.

Sharia law also forbids investment in certain industries such as alcoholic beverages, pork, tobacco and gambling which are considered *haraam* or impermissible. In western societies, investment in industries such as gambling and alcoholic beverages may be considered by some to be immoral but it is certainly not illegal. Of course, investments in other industries such as prostitution and pornography are also off limits in Muslim societies. Conventional western banks and investment companies that utilize riba in their business models are also problematic as are businesses such as insurance companies that transfer risk from one party to another. Under *Sharia* law, risk must be shared.

While it is important to understand the basics of *Sharia* law if the firm operates in a Muslim country, most international business transactions are conducted under either common law or code law. Common law and code law are the two major legal systems found around the world. Common law (also termed English law) originated in England at the time of the Norman Conquest and is now practiced in the UK, as well as in a number of countries with colonial ties such as India, the USA, Canada, Pakistan, Australia and Hong Kong. Common law is based on precedents, so previous court rulings become the legal basis for resolving future disputes. Courts are required to review how similar cases were decided in the past and apply the same logic to cases being adjudicated. The goal is to have consistency in the decisions made by the courts when confronted with similar legal problems. If there are no similar cases, then the judge hearing the case is empowered to make a decision which then sets a precedent for future cases. Code law, on the other hand, relies on a comprehensive set of written statutes against which cases are evaluated. When confronted with a legal problem, judges are mandated to consult the existing statutes for guidance in making a decision. If the existing statutes are silent on the specifics of the case, then the judge may reason by analogy to arrive at a decision. Code law is derived from Roman law and is practiced in countries such as France, Germany and Japan.

The global marketer will be confronted with a number of laws which must be understood and adhered to when doing business in foreign markets. **Antidumping legislation**, for example, may prohibit the sale of products at prices below their cost of production, and health and safety legislation may place restrictions on the labelling of products that are allowed into the foreign market. The multinational firm will also be confronted with legislation that places restrictions on the advertising and promotion of products in the foreign country, as well as laws on the treatment of workers and the payment of taxes. **Antitrust** legislation also exists in all developed countries and in many developing countries and is designed to prevent anti-competitive behavior. Mergers and acquisitions (M&A), for example, which may give a firm an unfair advantage in a particular market or industry, are generally subject to approval by local authorities. Transactions may be approved but subject to conditions such as a requirement that the combined firm divest some of its assets. For example, in the $41 billion merger of Merck and Schering-Plough, two US pharmaceutical firms, the European Commission mandated that Merck divest its stake in Merial to Sanofi-Aventis. Merial, which is a player in the animal health industry, was a 50/50 joint venture between Merck and Sanofi-Aventis. While the Commission did not have concerns about competition in the human health sector, it was concerned about the overlap in animal health products between Merck and Schering-Plough. Divestment of Merial became a requirement for approval of the merger in Europe.[25] The deal was also approved by the US Federal Trade Commission. With antitrust legislation, the underlying principle is that firms should not have such a dominant market position that they are able to dictate prices and exploit consumers. Competition must exist in order to protect the consumer as well as rival firms.

The global marketing manager needs to note that it is not only M&A transactions which are scrutinized by regulators. Other business practices such as predatory pricing, product tying and the gouging of consumers are also policed by authorities. For example, the European Commission fined Intel, the US chip manufacturer, a record 1.06 billion euros for anti-competitive behavior which denied consumers choice. Intel was found to have offered rebates to computer companies such as Acer, Dell, Hewlett-Packard, Lenovo and NEC on the condition that these firms purchase all or almost all of their chips from Intel. Intel was also found to have made payments to Media Saturn Holding, owner of a chain of superstores, in order to entice the retailer to only sell Intel-based computers in its stores in Germany, Belgium and other countries. Computer manufacturers were also paid by Intel to cancel or postpone the distribution of computers with rival AMD chips.[26] Microsoft has similarly run foul of EU antitrust rules for its bundling of Windows Media Player with its popular Windows software. Microsoft was fined $613 million.

---

[25]   Reuters (2009) Merck Takeover of Schering-Plough Wins EU Approval. Available at: www.reuters.com/article/2009/10/23/us-schering-merck-eu-idUSTRE59M1DP20091023, accessed June 11, 2013.

[26]   NYtimes.com (2013) Europe Fines Intel $1.45 Billion in Antitrust Case. Available at: www.nytimes.com/2009/05/14/business/global/14compete.html?pagewanted=all&_r=0, accessed June 9, 2013.

DEALING WITH CROSS-BORDER LEGAL DISPUTES

In cross-border transactions, conflict will invariably arise. Parties from different cultures will see the world differently, will have differing ethical standards and will have to deal with rules and regulations in a country which are not always clear to outsiders. When conflicts arise, business partners must find a way to resolve them and move on. As previously noted, the USA has the most lawyers in the world and is generally regarded as an extremely litigious country. **Litigation** is certainly one way for firms to resolve cross-border disputes but may not be the best approach as it is expensive and time-consuming. Firms will need to retain legal counsel and, given a backlog of cases, it may be months or even years before a matter is finally resolved in court. Also, given that the firm may be dealing with a foreign legal system, the outcome of the process will be far from certain. Further, even if the outcome of legal proceedings in a foreign country is positive, there will be issues of enforceability of the judgment in the home country. For these reasons, firms tend to avoid litigation as a means of settling cross-border disputes, if at all possible.

Firms involved in cross-border disputes may utilize **alternative dispute resolution** (ADR) to solve the problem. **Mediation** (or conciliation) is one such approach. Mediation is a voluntary, non-binding process in which the disputants retain the services of a neutral third party to help them work through their differences and arrive at an acceptable compromise. The mediator or conciliator is expected to meet with each of the parties involved and listen to their proposals for resolving the dispute. Each proposal is then shared with the opposing side in an attempt to find common ground. The conciliation process is confidential and any information shared is generally inadmissible in any subsequent dispute-resolution process such as litigation.

Arbitration is another alternative to litigation in the settlement of international disputes between firms. The process involves the selection of a neutral but informed third party who will review the merits of the case presented by both sides and render a judgment which is binding on the parties. Prospects for successful arbitration are increased if the business partners have included the provision for arbitration in their original agreement and have, therefore, committed to be bound by the arbitrator's decision. In other words, it is important that both parties commit to the process of arbitration before disagreements emerge. However, even when an arbitration clause is not included, it is still possible to refer a dispute to arbitration, with the agreement of both parties. Arbitration is viewed favorably by firms because it is far less expensive than litigation, and it is faster and much less adversarial than settling the dispute in the courts. In addition, arbitral awards are more easily enforced in foreign countries compared to court judgments.[27] The United Nations Conference on International Trade Law (UNCITRAL) is active in the area of international arbitration and has developed guidelines that are used by countries around the world.

SUMMARY

This chapter has examined the political and legal environment in which global marketing transactions are conducted. The global marketing manager must be aware of how political and legal factors both at home and abroad may affect the design and implementation of the firm's strategies. Positions taken by the firm's home-country government may have a negative impact on its marketing success, as is the case where sanctions are imposed or there is a government-supported boycott of a target country. In some situations, the firm's

---

[27] Nicholson, M.J. (2007) *Legal Aspects of International Business: A Canadian Perspective*. Toronto: Emory Montgomery Publications.

home-country government may impose export controls which restrict the products that can be sold to a target country. The multinational firm's government may also have in place legislation designed to regulate firm behavior in foreign countries and this would need to be respected. Many governments, for example, are signatory to international agreements on the bribery and corruption which will impact a firm's operations abroad.

This chapter has also examined the impact of host-country government actions on firm operations. The multinational firm will be exposed to political risk when operating in foreign markets. The major types of political risk were examined above and the impact of actions such as confiscation, expropriation and domestication were explored. The point was also made that political risk can be measured and readers were introduced to two measures – the corruption perception index and the bribe payers index – which may be used to better assess prospective foreign markets. Strategies for minimizing political risk were also considered.

The legal system was discussed next and the major legal systems found around the world were briefly described. The point was made that the global marketing firm will need to be acutely aware of national legislation with respect to issues such as anti-competitive behaviour and antidumping and the potential implications for its business. As careful as the company may be, there is still the potential for disagreements between business partners. It is, therefore, important for the global marketing manager to be aware of the various approaches available for resolving cross-border disputes. A discussion of mediation, arbitration and litigation closed the chapter and the point was made that the latter approach is best avoided, if at all possible.

Real World Challenges

The Nationalization of Servicios de Aeropuertos Bolivianos S.A. (Sabsa)

Mary Rodriguez was startled by the commotion outside. As she looked up from her laptop, she was surprised to see heavily armed Bolivian soldiers entering her office. A quick glance out the window revealed that the entire building was surrounded by Bolivian troops. As Mary and her staff were being escorted out of the building, she knew she had to get to a phone immediately to inform head office about these latest developments. It was unlikely, however, that any of the executives back at the Abertis headquarters in Barcelona, Spain would be surprised by her story. Sabsa was being nationalized and her company and the Spanish government would need to decide what, if anything, should be done about it.

Sabsa is a joint venture between the Spanish conglomerate Abertis Infrastructuras SA and Spain's airport authority, AENA. Sabsa operates airports in three of Bolivia's major cities – La Paz, Santa Cruz and Cochabamba. Abertis owned 90% of the equity in Sabsa and, therefore, had the most to lose as a result of the nationalization. Sabsa had been awarded a 25-year contract to operate Bolivia's three major airports in 1997. Since the award, the company had changed hands twice – from US-based Airport Group International to the UK's TBI in 1999 and then to the Abertis-AENA joint venture some five years later.

As she made her way back to her apartment, Mary wondered why she was even rattled by the day's events. As General Manager and head of Bolivian operations, she had certainly heard the rumors about an impending nationalization and listened to the fiery rhetoric from the leftist president, Evo Morales. Mary, of course, had no doubt that the Bolivian government would carry through on its plans to nationalize the airports. Since coming to power, the Morales government had seized control of four business units belonging to Spain's largest utility company, Iberdrola SA. Transportadora de Electricidad, owned by the Spanish company Red Electrica, had also been nationalized. That company controlled 74 percent of energy transmission in Bolivia. The Bolivian operations of Spain's Repsol and France's Total had already been taken over by the Morales administration. The country's largest telephone operator controlled by Italy's ETI has also been transferred to the state.

Back at her apartment, Mary turned on the television just in time to see President Morales announce, 'I want to let the people of Bolivia know about the nationalization of Sabsa'. He went on to tell his television audience that Sabsa had made 'an exorbitant profit with a derisory capital input'. He noted that Abertis-AENA had committed to invest $26 million in the airports over the period 2006–2011 but had only invested $5.6 million. In a press release later that day, Abertis shot back that the company 'denies accusations about inadequate investment in Bolivia, where more than $12 million has been invested in the last few years'. The company went on to add that the Bolivian government was the source of the problem as it had raised the salaries of airport staff by 140% since 2005 and had frozen airport tariffs in 2001, causing the firm to sustain losses. As the war of words heated up, Spain's Foreign Minister chimed in that the country would mobilize its resources and that of the European Union against Bolivia's act of 'aggression' and that Madrid would have to 'rethink bilateral relations as a whole'. As far as the Morales administration was concerned, however, the state would proceed with the nationalization and appointed the Ministry of Public Works, Services and Housing to take over the operations of the company. An independent audit would also be commissioned to decide on the level of compensation Abertis-AENA should receive for Sabsa. This latter statement suggested that the Bolivian administration's intention was in fact expropriation and not nationalization.

As the most senior Abertis executive on the ground in Bolivia, Mary had been asked to come up with a strategy for dealing with the problem. Her mind was racing as she settled in for the night. What should she recommend? Should her company fight or quietly comply with the government order? What would be the implications of either course of action? Was there a third option?

Sources

Before It's News | Alternative News | UFO | Beyond Science | True News| Prophecy News | People Powered News (2013) Bad for Business: Bolivia Nationalizes Spanish Firm Running Its Airports | Alternative. Available at: http://beforeitsnews.com/alternative/2013/02/bad-for-business-bolivia-nationalizes-spanish-firm-running-its-airports-2569608.html, accessed 10 June 10, 2013.

NDTV.com (2012) Bolivia Nationalizes Spanish-owned Airport Company. Available at: www.ndtv.com/article/world/bolivia-nationalizes-spanish-owned-airport-company-332673, accessed 10 June 10, 2013.

Oilprice.com (2013) INVESTOR WARNING: Bolivia Nationalizes Airport Management Company. Available at: http://oilprice.com/Geopolitics/South-America/INVESTOR-WARNING-Bolivia-Nationalizes-Airport-Management-Company.html, accessed 10 June 10, 2013.

Reuters (2013) Bolivia Nationalizes Spanish-owned Airports Operator. Available at: www.reuters.com/article/2013/02/18/us-bolivia-abertis-idUSBRE91H0DX20130218, accessed 10 June 10, 2013.

Questions

1. State the problem that Mary and her company face in Bolivia.
2. Identify the options available. Be sure to identify more than one.
3. Based on the options identified above, recommend a course of action. Be sure to provide a rationale and make a decision.

? discussion questions

1. Should developed country organizations such as the OECD set rules for ethical conduct for the rest of the world?

2. Given that companies such as Chiquita have a duty to protect their workers in foreign countries, is it wrong for them to make extortion payments to rebel groups to keep their workers safe?

3. Given that sanctions hurt the vulnerable in the target country, should they ever be used?

4. Do you believe that the Arab boycott of Israel has been an effective strategy? Why/Why not?

5. Explain why an assessment of political risk is an important consideration when entering foreign markets.

6. Discuss the various strategies that a multinational firm can use to help mitigate political risk in foreign markets.

7. Discuss the merits and demerits of the various approaches firms have to resolve cross-border disputes.

FURTHER READING

Czinkota, M., Knight, G., Liesch, P.W. and Steen, J. (2010) 'Terrorism and international business: A research agenda', *Journal of International Business Studies*, 41, 50: 826–43.

5

TRADE AND PROTECTIONISM

LEARNING OBJECTIVES

After reading this chapter you should be able to:

- Discuss the major drivers of international trade and investment

- Define the term 'protectionism' and discuss the major arguments used to support the practice

- Discuss the major forms of protectionism

- Define the term 'export promotion' and describe the various tools used by national governments to facilitate export growth

- Describe the role of the major transnational institutions involved in the regulation of global trade and investment.

INTRODUCTION

No country is completely self-sufficient in every product or service it consumes. International trade is important if the citizens of a country are to consume a wider range of products than is manufactured at home. Natural resource endowments, climatic conditions and technological constraints are among the many factors which may preclude self-sufficiency and make trade with other nations an imperative. The ability to engage in trade with other countries also allows nations to specialize and become more efficient at what they do. International trade in goods and services is also a valuable source of tax revenues for national governments, providing funds that may be used to finance social programs, debt service obligations and infrastructure development projects.

At the firm level, exporting may be a low-cost first step in entering new foreign markets. As will be discussed in Chapter 8, the approach carries minimal risk for the global marketer and may be an effective way of testing a new market before making a major financial commitment in an overseas production facility. The ability to import raw materials from foreign countries also gives the firm access to a wider range of inputs than is available in its home country. These foreign sources of raw materials may provide better quality inputs or perhaps cheaper inputs which can make the multinational firm more competitive in international markets.

As was noted in Chapter 3, countries around the world are engaged in negotiating free trade agreements. Whether it is membership in regional organizations such as the European Union, NAFTA or Mercosur, or participation in multilateral negotiations under the auspices of the World Trade Organization (WTO), governments have recognized the importance of trade liberalization. Significant progress has been made in the removal of barriers to international trade but **protectionism** still exists and has major implications for the global marketer. Protectionist measures adopted by foreign governments may effectively block the multinational firm's access to potentially lucrative new markets, increase the cost of doing business abroad and perhaps reduce overall revenue and profitability from overseas businesses. Protectionism is a major topic discussed in this chapter. The arguments in favor of protectionism are presented and the measures used by governments to restrict trade and investment are discussed.

The multilateral trading system is also examined in this chapter and the role of organizations such as the WTO in the regulation of global trade and investment is discussed. This chapter also considers some of the strategies used by national governments to promote exports and give their exporting firms a competitive advantage in international markets. Before these topics are covered, however, it is first necessary to examine the drivers of international trade. In other words, we must first understand what motivates countries to want to engage in international trade. This is the subject of the next section.

DRIVERS OF INTERNATIONAL TRADE

As noted above, no country is completely self-sufficient. All countries are dependent on international trade to some extent. Why is this? Why don't countries attempt to simply produce all the products and services demanded by their citizens? What factors determine which products are produced domestically and which are eventually imported from foreign countries? What determines the type and quality of products that a country is able to export? Why do countries such as China continue to enjoy sizeable trade surpluses, i.e. the difference in value between its exports and imports, while other countries record persistent trade deficits? Over the years, various scholars have attempted to develop theories and models that provide answers to these questions. These models have adopted both a firm-level and a country-level perspective in their attempts to understand the drivers of international trade. In this section, we will briefly examine some of these theories.[1]

MERCANTILISM

Mercantilism was the dominant economic philosophy from 1500 to 1750. Indeed, over that period mercantilist thinking guided the economic policies of many countries. Proponents of this doctrine held the view that the resources of the world were finite and, therefore, for one country to advance economically it meant that another country must lose out. International transactions between countries were envisioned as zero-sum games, i.e. for one country to win, the other party to the transaction must necessarily lose. Mercantilists were of the view that a country's wealth should be measured by its stocks of precious metals such as gold and silver and this thinking led to policies that emphasized the accumulation of these assets by the state. The accumulation of precious metals by individuals was of course not encouraged.

Proponents of mercantilism conceptualized the economy as consisting of three components: a manufacturing sector, an agricultural sector and foreign colonies controlled by the state. The role of the colonies was to provide a cheap source of raw materials and agricultural products such as sugar, as well as a ready market for manufactured products. Government policies were crafted that promoted exports and severely discouraged imports. In this way, the state

---

[1]   This section draws heavily from Czinkota, M., Ronkainen, I., Farrell, C. and McTavish, R. (2009) *Global Marketing: Foreign Entry, Market Development and Strategy Implementation*. Toronto: Nelson Education.

would record a positive balance of trade, i.e. a trade surplus. To discourage imports, the state resorted to the imposition of tariffs and quotas – two policy measures used by governments to restrict free trade. These are discussed in more detail later in this chapter. Exports, on the other hand, were heavily subsidised by the state to make them more attractive to foreign buyers. It should be noted that the only exception to the policy of import tariffs and quotas was raw materials that were being imported for further processing. Raw materials destined to enter a value-added manufacturing process were subject to low tariffs or may even be imported free of all duties.

The mercantilist doctrine had an impact well beyond international trade and investment. Domestic policy was also influenced by the philosophy. For example, it was of the utmost importance for the state to implement a low wage policy in order to ensure that its manufactured exports could be produced as cheaply as possible and its products could be price-competitive in export markets. Of course, at that time, labor, not technology, was regarded as the most important factor in production and a major contributor to the cost of goods produced. The state was therefore obliged to also implement policies that encouraged population growth and ensured a steady supply of cheap labor for its various manufacturing operations. Mercantilist doctrine found favor with many European countries, eventually becoming the dominant economic philosophy in Europe by the 17th century.

PHOTO 5.1

Interestingly, some scholars argue that mercantilism remains relevant even today and that the success of countries such as China owes much to this philosophy. Tax incentives provided to Chinese exporters and attempts to manage the country's exchange rate in order to subsidize manufacturers while penalizing domestic consumers are policies which are consistent with the mercantilist doctrine.[2] Indeed, liberal economic policies have largely been credited with causing the financial crisis that began in 2007, leading some analysts to predict a return to mercantilism even in advanced western countries.[3]

THE THEORY OF ABSOLUTE ADVANTAGE

As noted above, proponents of Mercantilism argued that international trade is a zero-sum game and it was, therefore, impossible for both parties to the transaction to benefit simultaneously. This view would be challenged by Adam Smith. Smith said in his **theory of absolute advantage**[4] that it was possible for two countries to engage in international trade and for both to derive gains from the exchange. To accomplish this, Smith argued that countries should specialize in the production of those products which it can produce more efficiently than its prospective trading partners. The country should then engage in international trade to secure all the other products needed by its citizens. It should be noted that Smith, and other Classical writers of his time, argued in favor of the labor theory of value which associated the value of a commodity with the amount of labor embodied in its manufacture. According to the theory of absolute advantage, therefore, countries need to specialize in those products that require the fewest units of labor to produce. A country should manufacture and export those products and import all others it wishes to consume. Each country should adopt a

2   Rodrik, D. (2013) The New Mercantilist Challenge. Available at: www.project-syndicate.org/commentary/the-return-of-mercantilism-by-dani-rodrik, accessed June 13, 2013.

3   Rodrik (2013) op cit.

4   Smith, A. (1976) An Inquiry into the Nature and Causes of the Wealth of Nations, in R. H. Campbell, A. S. Skinner and W. E. Todd (eds) *Liberty Classics*, vol. 11. New York: Oxford University Press.

similar pattern of concentrating on the production of those products which it could produce most efficiently, i.e. those products for which it has an absolute advantage, and engaging in trade for all others. By following this approach, all countries will benefit simultaneously, establishing that international trade is in fact **a positive sum game**.

THE THEORY OF COMPARATIVE ADVANTAGE

Following on from Smith's work on the theory of absolute advantage, David Ricardo would argue that it was possible for a country to benefit from international trade even when it was not the most efficient at producing the good being exchanged. In his seminal text, *The Principles of Political Economy and Taxation* (1817), Ricardo argued that a country could benefit from trade if it only had a **comparative advantage**. Such a comparative advantage would exist if the country was relatively more efficient in the production of one product than another, i.e. if there were a difference in the relative labor requirements for the production of the particular products. According to the theory of comparative advantage, countries need to examine their relative efficiencies in the production of various products and concentrate on those products requiring the fewest units of labor. A country would produce and export only that requiring the fewest resources and trade with other countries for all other products. Even if the country had an absolute advantage in the production of every product, it would still benefit from trade with other countries. Ricardo's work supports Adam Smith's finding that trade is not a zero-sum game, i.e. that the Mercantilist view is flawed. The theory of comparative advantage does, however, go further by proving that the benefits from trade are not dependent on the country having an absolute advantage.

THE HECKSCHER-OHLIN MODEL

The Heckscher-Ohlin model extends the analysis on comparative advantage by examining the impact of factor endowments and factor intensities on the gains from trade. The model is credited to Elie Heckscher and Bertil Ohlin, two Swedish economists. Key to understanding this model is the concept of factor endowments. Essentially, countries have different resource endowments. Populous developing countries such as India and China have relatively more labor than capital, while developed countries such as the USA and Germany have much smaller populations but relatively more capital. Also important to an understanding of the Heckscher-Ohlin model is the concept of factor intensities – products embody varying amounts of labor and capital. Semi-conductors used in sophisticated electronic equipment would utilize more capital than labor in their manufacture, while handmade carpets would require a greater input of labor to produce. Given these differences in factor endowments and factor intensities, it is reasonable to expect that a handmade carpet (a labor-intensive product) would be relatively cheaper to manufacture in a populous developing country such as India, while a semiconductor (a capital-intensive product) would be relatively cheaper to produce in a more advanced country such as Germany where capital is more abundant. According to the Heckscher-Ohlin model, it is these differences in factor endowments and factor intensities that produce the price differences between countries which drive international trade.

The major implication of the Heckscher-Ohlin model is that countries will import those products that use most intensively their least abundant factor of production, while they will export those products that use most intensively their most abundant factor of production.

One would expect, therefore, that a country such as India would be more export-competitive in products that require hand assembly and where manufacturing processes are not fully automated. Advanced countries such as Germany and the USA, on the other hand, would be expected to be most export-competitive in technology-intensive products. It should be noted, however, that empirical support for the Heckscher-Ohlin model has not been conclusive (see Box 5.1).

Box 5.1

Wassily Leontief provided an empirical test of the veracity of the Heckscher-Ohlin model. In 1953, Leontief used an Input–Output table, and US data from 1947, to model a scenario in which the USA simultaneously reduced its imports and exports by $1 million each. The analysis allowed Leontief to quantify the amount of capital (K) and labor (L) that would no longer be required to produce the $1 million in exports, and the amount of capital and labor that would be required to produce domestically those products that were no longer imported. The ratios of capital to labor $(K/L)x$ for exports and capital to labor for imports $(K/L)m$ could then be computed and compared. The metric $(K/L)m/(K/L)x$ is known as the Leontief statistic. The USA is an advanced capital-rich country. According to the Heckscher-Ohlin model, it would, therefore, be expected that the value computed for the Leontief statistic would be less than 1. The calculated value for the USA was in fact 1.3 – a surprising result. Numerous analysts have attempted to explain the so-called Leontief paradox. One explanation offered by economists is that countries have a preference for products that are produced with the factor that is most abundant in that country. In the literature, this is referred to as 'own intensity preference'. The USA and other advanced countries would demonstrate a preference for products produced with capital (as opposed to labor), leading to a reversal of the demand patterns expected by the Heckscher-Ohlin model. A higher preference for capital-intensive goods in developed countries such as the USA would bid up the price of those goods, making such advanced countries more competitive in labor-intensive products. On the other hand, countries with an abundance of labor would display a greater preference for labor-intensive products. The Leontief paradox raises a number of interesting questions for the strategy of multinational companies entering developing country markets.

THE PRODUCT CYCLE THEORY

The failure of the Heckscher-Ohlin model to explain international trade patterns led Raymond Vernon to propose the product cycle theory in 1966. This theory argues that advanced countries such as the USA would produce products which catered to other advanced countries, i.e. products which were labor saving and capital intensive. Vernon conceptualized the life cycle of a product as being divided into three stages (see Figure 5.1). In Stage 1, the product is produced only in an advanced country such as the USA. At this stage, the product is new and innovative. Firms responsible for the innovation are assumed to be focused on marketing the product in the advanced country with its high-income, sophisticated consumers. In this initial stage, the product is not marketed internationally.

In the second stage of the product cycle, firms in, say, the USA begin to export the product to other advanced countries such as Germany and Canada. At this stage, the product is mature and the emphasis is on the adoption of mass production techniques which allow firms to exploit economies of scale. In Stage 2, US firms may also begin to explore the possibilities of manufacturing the product in other advanced countries – maybe in Canada or Western Europe. If the economics are favorable for production in other advanced countries, exports from the USA begin to decline as foreign markets begin to receive supplies from non-US sources. There is also the possibility that product from non-American facilities could eventually begin to flow back into the USA.

In the third and final stage of the life cycle, the product is no longer considered to be innovative and manufacturing shifts to developing countries. At this stage, there is widespread consumer acceptance of the product and manufacturing processes are well established. The focus at this stage is on producing the product as cheaply as possible which makes low-wage developing countries particularly attractive. Driven by low labor costs, countries such as China, Vietnam and Mexico become major centers of production and advanced countries such as the USA, Canada and Germany become importers of what once was an innovative product.

FIGURE 5.1 Vernon's Product Life Cycle

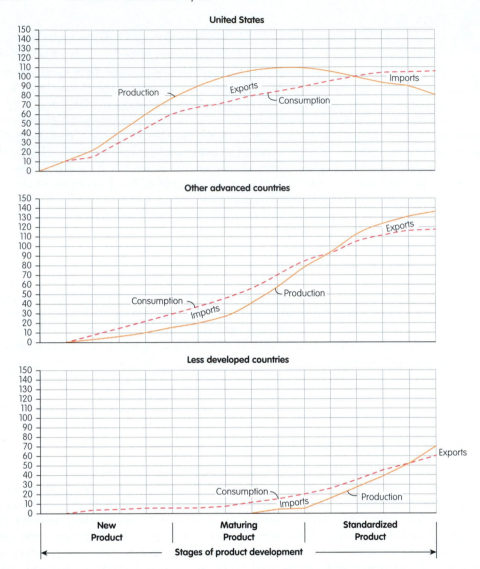

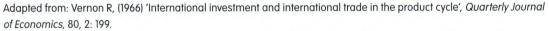

Adapted from: Vernon R, (1966) 'International investment and international trade in the product cycle', *Quarterly Journal of Economics*, 80, 2: 199.

The shifts in production from developed to developing countries that are integral to Vernon's life cycle theory suggest that comparative advantage is not static. Countries with a comparative advantage in one period may lose this advantage over time as the product matures and the ability to manufacture cheaply assumes more importance. In the early stages, production is localized in advanced countries with their sophisticated consumers and manufacturing technologies but moves to developing countries in the later stage as cost becomes a stronger driver. Unlike earlier theories, Vernon's product life cycle assumes that comparative advantage is dynamic, not static.

THE COUNTRY SIMILARITY THEORY

The country similarity theory proposed by Staffan Linder in 1961 attempts to understand international trade patterns by analyzing consumer demand. Theories discussed to this point, such as Heckscher-Ohlin and Vernon's product life cycle, have all emphasized the

FIGURE 5.2

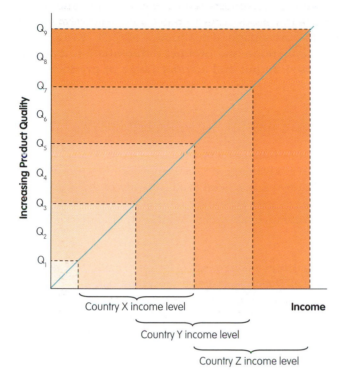

supply side of the international trade transaction. Linder's theory argues that the tastes and preferences of consumers would be a function of income levels. Countries with high per capita income levels will all exhibit a similar pattern of tastes and preferences, i.e. oriented towards expensive, high-quality, sophisticated products. Conversely, countries with lower per capita incomes would favor cheaper products of lower quality. The country similarity theory essentially argues that countries will trade most intensely with countries with similar levels of per capita income and less intensely with countries with dissimilar levels of per capita income (see Figure 5.2). It should be noted that this theory was proposed to explain the pattern of international trade in manufactured products, i.e. the focus was not on explaining trade in agricultural products.

Empirical support for the country similarity theory has been mixed. Based on the theory, one would expect that the greater the difference in per capita income levels between countries, the more dissimilar they would be and the less intensely they would trade. In other words, trade intensity and per capita income should be negatively correlated. While a number of studies have found a negative relationship, some researchers have dismissed these results as spurious, arguing that countries with similar levels of per capita income also tend to be geographically and culturally proximate. This geographic and cultural proximity may, according to some analysts, explain the negative correlation observed in supporting studies.

KRUGMAN'S MODEL OF INTERNATIONAL TRADE

Paul Krugman, a Nobel Laureate, and a number of other researchers have introduced models of international trade that incorporate concepts of monopolistic competition and product differentiation – characteristics which are not included in the trade theories discussed previously. Dubbed 'the new trade theory', these models relax the traditional assumptions of perfect competition and allow for monopolistic market structures where firms produce a differentiated product and brand loyalty is, therefore, possible. Krugman's model assumes that as countries engage in international trade, the overall size of the market expands, providing consumers with greater choice and spurring on firms in the trading countries to expand production to meet increased demand. Production costs per unit decline as firms take advantage of economies of scale. Krugman argues that by allowing for monopolistic competition and product differentiation, international trade leads to higher incomes, increased output and a wider range of products available to consumers in the trading countries.

THE DIAMOND OF NATIONAL ADVANTAGE

The Diamond of National Advantage, proposed by Harvard University's Michael Porter, builds on notions of comparative advantage by focusing on the factors that drive the competitiveness of nations. The framework has been used not only in the academic literature but also in numerous industry analyses undertaken by consultants on behalf of their corporate clients. According to Porter, competitive advantage in international markets is driven by four factors. These are:

1. Factor conditions, i.e. the country's endowment of factors of production, e.g. a highly skilled labor force, mineral deposits, petroleum reserves and arable agricultural land.
2. Demand conditions, i.e. a pool of knowledgeable and sophisticated consumers who can drive product innovation and spur domestic firms to achieve and maintain high-quality standards.
3. Supporting industries, i.e. a network of local firms providing professional services relevant to the company's domain of expertise.
4. Firm strategy, structure and rivalry which drive competitiveness among domestic firms, making them stronger and more effective participants in international markets.

Porter's model is dynamic. It assumes that countries are able to change their competitive position over time by focusing on one or more of the four factors above and their interrelationships. Unlike the product life cycle theory, for example, which assumes that developed countries, over time, lose their competitive advantage to low-wage countries, Porter's model argues that this is not the case. Porter's Diamond of National Advantage suggests that an effective business strategy, the benefit of supporting industry participants and the demands of sophisticated domestic consumers may well negate the impact of lower wage rates. Developed country firms are, therefore, able to maintain their competitive advantage over long periods despite the fact that other countries may have significantly lower labor costs. Porter's model has been used to explain the tendency for high technology firms to cluster in particular geographic locations such as Silicon Valley in California, USA.

MODELS OF INTERNATIONAL INVESTMENT

It is often necessary for firms to engage in foreign direct investment in order to reach consumers in international markets. In such situations, firms are confronted with a number of decisions with respect to the location of manufacturing operations and the optimal number of facilities needed to adequately serve the needs of their target markets. Invariably, these types of investment decisions result in benefits, such as increased employment and tax revenues, for one country at the expense of others. There are many examples. Hershey, the global confectionary manufacturer, made a decision to relocate its manufacturing operations in Ontario, Canada, to Mexico, putting some 600 people out of work.[5] Hershey had

---

5   Money.canoe.ca (2013) Ontario Chocolate Factory End Feared. Available at: http://money.canoe.ca/News/Sectors/Consumer/2007/02/17/pf-3639994.html, accessed June 13, 2013.

maintained a manufacturing presence in the Canadian province since 1962 but made the decision in order to reduce its costs and improve its competitive position in the market. Similarly, US-based Alcoa has abandoned aluminum production on the Italian island of Sardinia, putting several people out of work in an area already dealing with high rates of unemployment.[6] There are several theories which attempt to explain how firms make these types of investment decisions.

DUNNING'S OLI FRAMEWORK

Dunning's OLI framework has been proposed to explain how firms make foreign investment decisions.[7] This model draws on various strands of economic theory to argue that three factors drive the foreign investment decisions of multinational firms. The factors identified in Dunning's so-called eclectic model are as follows:

1. **Ownership advantages**: Firms that own manufacturing facilities in the foreign country have a competitive advantage over other firms which do not own such facilities. The ownership of assets in the foreign country gives the firm access to resources, such as cheap labor, as well as proximity to customers and other advantages that its foreign competitors do not enjoy. Foreign competitors that do not own production facilities in the target country will be forced to service their customers via other, less efficient, approaches. Lack of ownership puts these firms at a competitive disadvantage in international markets.
2. **Location advantages**: Dunning's model suggests that location advantages are also important. A firm's ability to shift its manufacturing operations to low-cost countries or to shift sales and profits to low-tax jurisdictions provides significant advantages over competitors that do not have such flexibility. Similarly, a firm's ability to operate in a country with a stable industrial relations climate or locate in a country willing to provide generous manufacturing incentives can also provide it with a major competitive advantage.
3. **Internalization advantages**: Dunning also argues that firms will only undertake foreign investment in a country if it is more profitable for the company to operate the overseas business on its own than other available options for entering the market. These options may include licensing the firm's technology to a firm in the foreign country or, depending on the nature of the business, establishing a network of international franchises. It may also include the execution of a management contract with some other entity to operate the business in the foreign market for a negotiated fee. Licensing and other approaches to entering foreign markets are discussed in Chapter 8. The point to be noted here is that engaging in foreign production on its own allows the firm to internalize its management skills, technology and capital assets which can be a major driver in the decision to undertake foreign investment.

TRANSACTIONS COST ANALYSIS

The foreign investment behavior of the firm may also be explained by appealing to transactions cost analysis. The focus here is on the individual transactions that firms make when entering and doing business in foreign countries. These transactions include purchasing raw materials, retaining the services of distributors and marketing the final product. There are costs associated with each transaction in which the firm is engaged

---

[6] Fuhrmans, D. (n.d.) Southern Europe Faces Vicious Cycle as Companies Retreat. Available at: http://online.wsj.com/article/SB10001424127887324712504578130962380845752.html, accessed June 11, 2013.

[7] Dunning, J. (1980) 'Toward an electric theory of international production: Some empirical tests', *Journal of International Business Studies*, Spring, 11: 9–31.

and these may be classified as: **search costs** (i.e. costs associated with finding suitable raw material suppliers, distributors and other intermediaries); **contracting costs** (i.e. costs associated with negotiating and drafting contracts which spell out the nature of the relationship between the firm, and its suppliers and market intermediaries); **monitoring costs** (i.e. costs of monitoring contractual agreements); and **enforcement costs** (i.e. costs of enforcing contractual agreements, should the need arise). Transaction costs are dependent on whether the firm opts to internalize or externalize the various functions it performs. The firm may choose to use its own internal resources to perform the function or it may decide to outsource it to a third-party firm. Transaction costs will vary dependent on which option the firm chooses. Transaction costs are also dependent on the foreign market in question and on the degree of cultural distance between home and host countries. Transaction costs, for example, are likely to be much higher for a US firm doing business in Saudi Arabia than they would be for the same US firm doing business in Canada, given language and other cultural similarities and common approaches to doing business between Canada and the USA.

According to transactions cost analysis, firms seek to minimize transaction costs in their efforts to expand and market their products globally. Firms will only opt to undertake investment in a foreign country if by so doing they are able to minimize their overall transaction costs. If other options such as outsourcing production and making use of external market intermediaries result in lower transaction costs for the firm, then the firm is unlikely to engage in foreign production.

PROTECTIONISM

The theoretical literature argues strongly in favor of free trade. The reality is, however, that governments around the world do adopt measures which restrict the free flow of goods and services as well as investment. Protectionist measures adopted by national governments may take several forms, such as the imposition of high tariffs on imported goods, the use of quotas to restrict the volume of goods coming into the country or the adoption of unreasonable quality standards on imported products. These and other protectionist measures are explained in this section. Before this is done, however, it is useful to examine the reasons governments engage in protectionism, despite the theoretical arguments in favor of free trade.

case study 5.1: Trade restrictions in Ecuador

In the wake of the global economic crisis that began in 2007, the government of Ecuador decided to impose severe restrictions on trade. Peruvian shampoo, Chilean grapes and US-made running shoes are now subject to import restrictions by the government in an attempt to prevent a collapse of the economy. The measures have put the above and other imported products out of the reach of local consumers. Some 627 products are affected by the restrictions in what has been described as the world's most protectionist response to the global financial crisis. To curb imports, the government has imposed import duties of 30–35 percent and measures to reduce import volumes by up to 35 percent. In addition, new surcharges come into effect on items such as shoes and textiles. These measures are expected to keep $1.5 billion from flowing out of the Ecuadorian economy and prevent significant job losses. Ecuador uses the US dollar as its domestic currency. According to President Rafael Correa: 'We can't continue to throw away the money from our oil, the money of our migrants, to buy imported perfumes and imported liquors.' He goes on to add: 'The poor don't consume perfumes, liquor and chocolates.'

Source

Valdivieso, J. and Bajak, F. (2009) Ecuador Erects Trade Barriers. Available at: http://finance.sympatico. msn.ca/investing/news/businessnews/article.aspx?cp-documentid=18231254, accessed March 1, 2009.

Discussion Questions

1. Do you believe that the protectionist measures adopted by the government of Ecuador will eventually spur economic growth?
2. Should the government of Ecuador continue to use the US dollar as its domestic currency?
3. Will the government's protectionist measures benefit the poor in the long run?

WHY PROTECTIONISM?

A number of reasons are typically used by national governments to justify their use of protectionist measures.

THE INFANT INDUSTRY ARGUMENT

Alexander Hamilton, the first US Secretary of the Treasury, is credited with the notion that certain nascent industries need to be protected by government if they are to eventually become internationally competitive. The so-called infant industry argument dates back to 1791 and suggests that if firms in these nascent industries are exposed to international competition too early in their development, they are unlikely to become major global players. Faced with intense global competition, these fledgling companies will be unable to survive and grow. It was, therefore, incumbent on the government to find ways to shield these companies from direct competition. The infant industry argument has been implemented by many countries around the world and provided the conceptual framework that guided many Latin American countries to adopt a policy of import substitution in the 1950s and 1960s.

THE EMPLOYMENT ARGUMENT

Job creation is a major policy objective of national governments in both developed and developing countries. Maintaining and indeed improving employment levels is also a major concern of political parties seeking voter support and is often a hot button issue during elections. It is, therefore, not uncommon for special interest groups, firms and individuals to petition governments for protection from foreign competition. If foreign products could be kept out of the domestic market, the argument suggests, then consumers will have little choice but to patronize local firms. This in turn will lead domestic firms to maintain or even increase their staffing levels. Imports displace domestic products on the local market which leads to a loss of manufacturing jobs. An excellent example of this is provided by the Canadian wine industry in the late 1980s. Prior to the execution of the Canada–US Free Trade Agreement (FTA) in 1988, representatives of the Canadian wine industry lobbied the federal government for protection from US grape imports. They argued that the FTA would lead to the loss of thousands of jobs in Canada's grape-growing regions, as the agreement would lead to a surge in imports of US grapes and a precipitous decline in demand for the locally grown fruit. Protection, they argued, would only need to be 'temporary' to allow the Canadian industry sufficient time to adjust to the new realities. Canadian grape growers had historically been protected by provincial government taxes imposed on US imports of cheaper and better quality grapes from California.[8]

---

[8]   CBC video archives at: http://archives.cbc.ca/IDC-1-69-1041-5825/life_society/canada_wine/clip4

THE NATIONAL SECURITY ARGUMENT

The terrorist attack on the World Trade Center on September 11, 2001, has heightened concerns about national security, not just in the USA where the attack took place but also in countries around the world. Governments have become increasingly skittish about goods, services and investment originating from certain countries. While some view the concerns expressed as legitimate, others argue that they simply provide an excuse for national governments to engage in protectionism. The US government, for example, expressed concerns about the US$18.5 billion bid from China National Offshore Oil Company (CNOOC) for Unocal, a major US oil company. US legislators favored a competing bid from Chevron, clearly troubled by the prospect of a former communist country controlling shipments of a strategic natural resource to the US market. The Canadian federal government would similarly block a bid of $7 billion from China Minmetals, a corporation owned by the Chinese government, for Noranda Inc., one of Canada's preeminent mining companies. Objections to the deal were largely centered on concerns that at some future time Canadian natural resources could be exported to China, even as the country faced shortages at home. This prospect did not sit well with Canadian law makers and the acquisition was not approved. The issue of national security has also surfaced in the telecommunications industry with Huawei, a Chinese multinational, facing accusations of cyber-espionage in the USA as well as in Europe. The company controls 25 percent of the telecoms equipment market in the EU but concerns have been expressed that the firm has close ties with the Chinese military and could feed sensitive intelligence data and communications back to China. In Australia, Huawei has been barred from bidding on a contract to supply that country's national fiber network because of such concerns, and other countries are considering similar restrictions.[9] For its part, Huawei denies the allegations and has deemed them to be motivated by protectionism.

FORMS OF PROTECTIONISM

Protectionism is a reality for the global marketing manager. As mentioned, governments have a variety of tools at their disposal to restrict trade and investment in an attempt to protect domestic industries and the jobs they provide.

TARIFFS

A tariff is essentially a tax imposed by a national government on a product that is traded internationally. Tariffs may be imposed on a product that is imported into a country (i.e. an import tariff), is exported from a country (i.e. an export tariff) or is being trans-shipped from one country to another (i.e. a transit tariff). Tariffs are a source of revenue for the governments that levy them. They are normally calculated as a percentage of the market value of the product traded (referred to as an **ad valorem tariff**) or they may be calculated as a specific dollar amount on each unit of the product that crosses the nation's borders (termed a **specific tariff**). In some cases, tariffs may have both percentage of market value and specific dollar amount components and are referred to as **compound tariffs**.

Tariffs may be imposed not only to generate revenues for the government but also to protect domestic industry. For example, if Germany were to impose a tariff on Chinese textile imports, the effect would be to raise the price of imported textiles in Germany and reduce the demand. This reduction in demand for imported textiles would provide an opportunity for textile manufacturers in Germany to sell more of their product in the domestic market.

---

9   BelfastTelegraph.co.uk (2013) China Telecoms Giant Huawei Could be Cyber-security Risk to UK. Available at: www.belfasttelegraph.co.uk/news/local-national/uk/china-telecoms-giant-huawei-could-be-cybersecurity-risk-to-uk-16251443.html, accessed June 13, 2013.

case study 5.2: USA's tire tariff for China

On September 26, 2009, the USA levied new tariffs on tires coming in from China. The US administration argued that tariffs were needed to protect US jobs. The complaint against Chinese manufactured tires was brought before the US International Trade Commission by the United Steelworkers' Union. The Commission sided with the USA, paving the way for the US government to levy tariffs over a three-year period on a declining scale of 35% in year 1, 30% in year 2 and 25% in year 3. China's exports of tires to the USA had increased from 14 million in 2004 to 48 million in 2008 and the USA had lost 5,000 jobs in the tire industry since 2004. Further, prior to the imposition of tariffs, US tire manufacturers had less than a 50 percent share of their domestic market.

The US government has not applied for an extension of the tariffs beyond the three-year schedule and has claimed that the action has resulted in the addition of 1,200 jobs to the US economy. Some analysts have, however, questioned the effectiveness of the tariffs, arguing that while the figure of 1,200 US jobs was reasonably accurate it was achieved at a high cost to the US economy. Indeed, the Petersen Institute for International Economics estimated that the cost to American consumers from higher prices that resulted from tariffs on the Chinese tires was in excess of $1 billion in 2011. The cost per manufacturing job saved was estimated as $900,000, but only a fraction of this figure actually reached the pockets of workers in the industry. The bulk of the money actually found its way into the coffers of the tire companies, both in the USA and abroad. The Institute goes on to argue that the increase in consumer expenditure on tires actually dampened spending in other areas and resulted in reduced employment in the retail sector. On balance, protectionism in the tire industry actually cost the USA 2,531 jobs when reduced employment in retail is offset against employment gains in tire manufacturing. Further, China retaliated against the imposition of tariffs on tires by imposing its own tariffs on chicken parts imported from the USA. This cost the US poultry industry $1 billion in lost sales.

Also interesting is the fact that companies such as Kumho Tires (China), a Chinese–South Korean joint venture, shifted part of its production to its facilities in South Korea in order to navigate around the US tariffs. The company's Chinese plants focused on supplying the European market, while its South Korean operation continued to serve the US market. With the expiration of the tariffs, the firm will once again shift its production of passenger car and light truck tires back to China.

Sources

CNTV (2012) US Decision on Chinese Tires Tariffs Stirs Debate, CCTV News – CNTV English. Available at: http://english.cntv.cn/program/china24/20120927/102144.shtml, accessed June 14, 2013.

Global Times (2012) US Tariffs on Chinese Exports of Tires Set to Expire, *People's Daily Online*. Available at: http://english.peopledaily.com.cn/102774/7957792.html, accessed June 14, 2013.

Hufbauer, G.C. and Lowry, S. (2012) US Tire Tariffs: Saving Few Jobs at High Cost. Petersen Institute for International Economics, Policy Brief No. PB12-9.

Koven, P. (2012) 'Trade spat with China has false pretenses', *Financial Post*, March 14, pp. 1–2.

Discussion Questions

1. Do you believe that the imposition of tariffs was in the long run in the best interests of the US tire industry? Why/why not?
2. With the expiration of the US tariffs on tires, do you believe that Chinese manufacturers will be able to recoup their share of the American market?

QUOTAS

A quota is a quantitative restriction on imports. Quotas limit the amount of a product that can be imported into a country over a specified period of time, such as a calendar year. Quotas are a form of **non-tariff barrier** (NTB), i.e. they are not tariffs but have the same impact in terms of restricting free trade and protecting domestic industries. Quotas restrict the availability of the foreign product in the domestic market and, therefore, provide an advantage to local producers. There are various forms of quotas.

Absolute quotas

An absolute quota establishes a strict limit on the volume of imports of a particular product that the government will allow to enter the country. In special circumstances, the government may decide to set the limit of allowable imports at zero. This is referred to as an embargo. National governments seldom use embargoes but Cuba's relationship with the USA does provide an example. For over 40 years, the USA has maintained an embargo against Cuba under the Foreign Assistance Act of 1961. Implemented in response to the Cuban missile crisis, the embargo prohibits US companies from engaging in trade with Cuban entities and also effectively prohibits US citizens from visiting the island. Food and medicine are the only exceptions to the trade restriction.

Tariff rate quotas (TRQs)

Under the Uruguay round of the General Agreement on Tariffs and Trade (GATT), a multilateral system of trade negotiations discussed later in this chapter, most countries have agreed to replace quotas with their tariff equivalents. Known as tariff rate quotas (TRQs), they establish a low tariff level on an initial quantity of the product being imported into the country. However, once this initial volume of imports is reached, the tariff rate imposed on additional quantities coming into the country escalates markedly. TRQs, therefore, have elements of both quotas and tariffs. Canada's system of supply management provides an example. Under this system, restrictions on imports of dairy and poultry products are implemented via tariff rate quotas in order to protect domestic producers of these commodities from foreign competition. The USA has similarly imposed TRQs on imports of agricultural products such as dairy, beef, peanuts and tobacco, and the EU also makes use of TRQs to limit imports of sugar from more competitive producers such as Australia, Thailand and Brazil.

Voluntary export restraints (VERs)

In some situations, a country may decide to impose a limit on the volume of its own exports shipped to another country. Such voluntary export restraints (VERs) establish limits on exports of particular products to either a fixed quantity or some pre-specified percentage of the overall foreign market. China, for example, has had tremendous success in exporting its textile products to the European Union and the USA. However, following the termination of the Agreement on Textiles and Clothing on January 1, 2005, China agreed to impose restrictions on its own exports entering the US and European markets. The move was in response to concerns that surging Chinese exports were causing harm to European and American clothing manufacturers and fears that the USA and the EU would soon impose their own quotas under WTO safeguard provisions in order to stem the tide of Chinese imports.

case study 5.3: Chinese export quotas

Quotas may also be implemented on exports of a product. While governments are usually interested in promoting exports, there are instances when quotas are instituted to maintain supplies of a product in the home country. This may be seen, for example, in the case of the market for rare earth minerals. The rare earth mineral industry consists of 17 metals such as neodymium and dysprosium which are produced in very small quantities but which are important components of many high technology products. Some 95 percent of rare earth minerals are produced in China which has imposed export quotas designed to discourage exports and spur the development of value-added industries in China. World production of these minerals amounts to only 125,000 tonnes per year and since the 1990s prices have been low due to a significant increase in Chinese output. The low-price environment has discouraged production of the minerals outside of China.

China implemented export quotas in 2009–2010 and the move has frustrated a number of countries which are dependent on Chinese production. The USA, the EU and Japan have filed

PHOTO 5.2

objections with the WTO as a result. Exports from China are limited to 30,000 tonnes per year. The restriction has, however, pushed up prices and begun to attract new non-Chinese suppliers to the market.

Source

Koven, P. (2012) 'Trade spat with China has false pretenses', *Financial Post*, March 14, pp. 1–2.

Discussion Questions

1. Based on your own research on the rare earth mineral market, do you believe that China will be successful in developing downstream, value-added industries based on these minerals?
2. Do you believe that the imposition of export quotas is an effective mechanism for China to control global supplies of these minerals?

EXCHANGE CONTROLS

Access to 'hard' currency is central to the consummation of most international trade transactions. Exporters based in the developed world, for example, are unlikely to accept payment in the local currency when transacting with importers in developing countries such as Venezuela or Thailand. The company's export prices are likely to be quoted in US dollars or euros and the expectation would be that payment would be received in one of those currencies. The importer needs to be able to convert local currency into one of these hard currencies if the transaction is to be completed. National governments can, therefore, control the volume of imports coming into the country by imposing exchange controls which limit the amount of foreign currency importers can purchase. Multinational companies with overseas subsidiaries are similarly impacted by exchange controls. Such companies rely on the free convertibility of the local currency in order to remit profits to the parent firm based in the home country.

National governments can also control the volume of imports coming into the country by setting a favorable exchange rate for exports and an unfavorable rate for imports. In this case, there are no restrictions on the amount of foreign exchange available to importers but their purchases of hard currency are subject to a premium. The unfavorable exchange rate, of course, makes imports more expensive on the local market and encourages some consumers to opt for domestic alternatives. In this way, the government acts to discourage imports.

Countries often invoke exchange controls when faced with economic or political crises. Venezuela, for example, opted to impose exchange controls in response to civil unrest in the country that threatened to disrupt the receipt of foreign exchange from oil exports. The Venezuelan government established the Commission of Foreign Exchange Administration (CADIVI) in 2003 and all firms and individuals wishing to purchase foreign exchange were obliged to register with that organization. CADIVI authorized purchases of foreign exchange based on the tariff code of the product being imported. Foreign exchange requests to import luxury goods from the developed world and those already produced by domestic firms the government wished to protect were simply denied.

RESTRICTED ACCESS TO LOCAL DISTRIBUTION

Governments may also be protectionist by restricting foreign firms' access to local consumers. If foreign companies are denied access to their target customers, or can only reach them at a very high cost, domestic competitors are effectively protected. Market entry may not be denied but the government may put in place regulations that make it difficult for the foreign firm to reach its desired customers and gain traction in the market. We see this, for example, in the case of Thailand's financial services industry. Thai regulations prohibit foreign financial institutions from opening more than four offices in the country and only one office is permitted in the capital city of Bangkok. Foreign banks are free to enter the country but government rules stymie their efforts to effectively service their target market.

The Japanese keiretsu similarly makes it difficult for foreign companies to compete. The keiretsu is a closely knit system of corporate and cultural relationships between Japanese banks, manufacturers, retailers and wholesalers. The businesses are essentially independent corporate entities but are linked by interlocking share ownership, common values and mutual interests. A keiretsu may be formed by firms in the same industry (a vertical keiretsu) or firms in a diverse range of industries (a horizontal keiretsu). A vertical keiretsu would link suppliers, manufacturers and distributors/retailers in the same industry and typically feature a dominant manufacturer such as Honda or Toyota. A major Japanese bank is usually at the center of a horizontal keiretsu. Japanese government policy, it should be noted, has historically been strongly supportive of the keiretsu form of business organization. Foreign firms experience great difficulty penetrating markets controlled by keiretsu partners and their efforts to acquire Japanese firms in certain industries are also likely to be frustrated. Examples of Japanese keiretsu groups include Mitsubishi, Mitsui and Sumitomo.

PRODUCT STANDARDS

National governments have a responsibility to protect the health and safety of their citizens. As a result, many countries impose quality standards on imported products and have procedures in place to enforce these standards. Canada, for example, with its bilingual population, mandates that food products entering the country be labelled in both English and French. Taiwan, meanwhile, enforces strict purity testing of all imported fruit juices and Malaysia requires that imported meat and poultry products be prepared in accordance with Islamic practice. While product standards are certainly beneficial in terms of ensuring the health and well-being of the population, they also provide an opportunity for governments to be protectionist by imposing draconian and unrealistic requirements.

LACK OF INTELLECTUAL PROPERTY (IP) PROTECTION

In some situations, multinational companies have invested heavily in research to develop the innovative products they market around the world. Such companies would obviously be hesitant to market their products in countries where the national government fails to accord foreign firms legal protection of their intellectual property. A government can, therefore, effectively discourage imports and protect local industries by its failure to guarantee that a firm's intellectual property rights will be legally protected.

INVESTMENT BARRIERS

Many countries impose restrictions on foreign ownership of certain industries. Financial services, broadcasting, telecommunications, defence contracting and air transportation are among the industries deemed by some governments to be off limits in terms of foreign ownership. We may consider the case of Dubai Ports World, a company headquartered in the United Arab Emirates, which attempted to purchase Peninsular and Oriental Steam Navigation Company (P&O) – a British company responsible for the management of a number of US seaports. Fears that the deal would pose a security risk to the USA led politicians to exert their influence to have the transaction blocked. The outcry would eventually result in Dubai Ports World yielding to the political pressures and selling its US interests in the port operations to American International Group (AIG).

GOVERNMENT EXPORT PROMOTION

Government export promotion may be defined as 'public policy measures which actually or potentially enhance exporting activity at the company, industry or national level'.[10] The fact that governments take an active role in promoting exports is not surprising, given the implications for increased employment and foreign exchange generation. Exporting carries with it a certain level of risk, particularly for smaller, less well established firms. Government export promotion programs seek to mitigate these risks and perhaps increase the probability of success for such firms. Government export promotion takes many forms.

PROVISION OF MARKET INTELLIGENCE

The availability of timely and accurate information on foreign markets is critical to success. Good market intelligence is, however, a major limiting factor in foreign market entry, particularly for small and medium-sized companies that often lack the resources needed to conduct even basic research. Without this information, companies are unable to adequately access the opportunities and risks that foreign markets present. Many governments believe that they have a role to play in alleviating this constraint and actively conduct research on select markets using the services of outside consultants. This research is freely shared with their domestic exporters. As an example, the Ontario Ministry of Agriculture and Food – a ministry within the provincial government of Ontario, Canada – has commissioned studies of the US, Mexican and Caribbean markets in an effort to assist agribusiness exporters in that province.

---

[10] Seringhaus, R. and Rosson, P. (1990) *Government Export Promotion: A Global Perspective*. London: Routledge. P.3.

EXPORT SUBSIDIES

Export subsidies reduce the cost of foreign market entry for the firm, making it more competitive in global markets. The elimination or reduction of corporate taxes on a firm's export revenues, duty-free importation of raw materials and equipment destined for the manufacture of export products and favorable interest rates to finance exports are all examples of export subsidies that may be implemented by national governments. Export subsidies distort international trade by providing some firms with advantages that their competitors do not enjoy, and as a result they often attract the attention of the WTO. For example, Brazil's aerospace subsidies to Embraer, a regional jet maker, have been judged to be illegal by the WTO.[11] Embraer was found to have received some US$4.5 billion in subsidies from Pro-Ex, the government's export finance program. These subsidies were in the form of lower interest rates to finance foreign sales of the company's regional jets. Interestingly, Bombardier, a Canadian company and one of Embraer's major competitors, has also been the recipient of export subsidies. These subsidies were provided to Bombardier through the Canadian government's Technology Partnership Canada (TPC) program. TPC is an agency of the Canadian government that provides funding for strategic research and development in areas such as aerospace and defense technologies.[12]

EXPORT FINANCING

Exporters, particularly small and medium-sized companies, may benefit significantly from assistance provided by their national governments in the form of direct loans, loan guarantees and credit insurance. As noted above, there are risks associated with all export transactions. In some instances, firms may not require direct financial support to be successful but would welcome interventions from their home government in the form of export credit insurance. The exporter may, for example, be dealing with the foreign importer for the first time and may have little information on that company's credit worthiness or financial health. Export credit insurance serves to shift the risk of loss from the exporter to a government agency, thereby facilitating the transaction. Without insurance, it is quite possible that the exporter would deem the risk to be too great and would opt not to pursue the sale. A number of governments provide export credit insurance and financing services to their domestic companies. In the USA, these services are provided through the Export-Import Bank which provides assistance to exporters in the form of direct loans and loan guarantees. The Canadian government provides similar services through a crown corporation – Export Development Canada. The Columbian Government Trade Bureau provides working capital to eligible exporters in Columbia and other countries have similar agencies. The Australian government provides these services through its Export Finance and Insurance Corporation, while British exporters receive support from the Exports Credit Guarantee Department. Exporters based in Hong Kong may be able to access export financing and export insurance services through the Hong Kong Export Credit Insurance Corporation. The topic of export financing is taken up again in Chapter 11 when we consider global pricing strategies.

FOREIGN TRADE ZONES

Home-country governments can encourage exports by the establishment of a foreign trade zone (FTZ). An FTZ is a defined geographic area within a country within which firms receive preferential treatment for their imports of raw materials and component parts and the exports

---

[11]   CBC News (1999) WTO Rules on Subsidy Dispute between Brazil and Canada, August 3. Available at: www.cbc.ca/story/business/national/1999/08/03/bombardier990803.html

[12]   See the TPC website for further details: http://tpc-ptc.ic.gc.ca/epic/internet/intpc-ptc.nsf/en/Home

of their final products. Firms operating within the confines of the FTZ are allowed to import, duty free, all the raw materials and components required to produce their final products. Once manufactured, the final products are exported, again without attracting any taxes levied by the home-country government. The finished products must be exported and tight controls are maintained to ensure that they do not enter the domestic market with potentially deleterious consequences for domestic producers. FTZs may be found in numerous countries around the world. Mexico, for example, has its *maquiladora* system – factories located within a foreign trade zone on the border with the USA. Maquiladoras may import raw materials and capital equipment with no duties payable to the Mexican government. There are roughly 3,000 maquiladoras in operation in Mexico which employ some 1.3 million people. Foreign trade zones operate in several other countries including China and Mauritius.

INTERNATIONAL TRADE INSTITUTIONS

Several transnational institutions are involved in the regulation of international trade and investment flows between nations.

THE WORLD TRADE ORGANIZATION

One key institution is the World Trade Organization (WTO) which was established in 1995 as the successor organization to the General Agreement on Tariffs and Trade (GATT). GATT was established in 1947 and became the de facto institution to handle world trade, following the failure of attempts to establish the International Trade Organization (ITO). At the UN Conference on Trade and Employment held in Havana, Cuba, several nations had agreed to establish the ITO which would have provided the basic rules that would govern international trade between member countries. The ITO, however, failed to win support from the US Congress and nations turned to the GATT for guidance on the regulation of international trade.

Under GATT, nations around the world have engaged in a series of trade negotiations aimed at reducing tariff and non-tariff barriers (see Table 5.1). Beginning in 1960, the various rounds of negotiations were assigned names. Through the successive rounds of negotiations and successful tariff reductions, membership steadily increased, from 23 nations in 1947 to 123 nations in 1994. The 1994 Uruguay round was the last under GATT as the WTO came into existence in 1995 and assumed responsibility for multilateral trade negotiations. The WTO is now responsible for all existing trade agreements negotiated under GATT and provides a forum for all multilateral trade negotiations. In addition, the organization is charged with resolving trade disputes and monitoring the trade policies of member countries.[13] As of 2012, there were 157 members of the WTO, including China which became a member in 2001 and Russia which joined in 2012.

It should be noted that the current round of trade negotiations under WTO was initiated in 2001 and is dubbed the Doha Round (after the city of Doha in Qatar where talks began). This round is focused specifically on lowering trade barriers and on revising trade rules. The liberalization of international trade in agricultural products is a key subject of this round of negotiations and is expected to have a significant impact on the economic prospects of developing countries. The round also specifically seeks to clarify and improve the existing rules dealing with the anti-dumping, subsidies and countervailing duties agreements.

THE WORLD BANK

The World Bank is one of two Bretton Woods institutions established in 1944 to assist in post-war economic recovery. At the 1944 Bretton Woods Summit in New Hampshire, 28 countries agreed

---

[13]   See www.wto.org/english/thewto_e/thewto_e.htm

TABLE 5.1   The Evolution of Multilateral Trade Negotiations

Round and location	No. of participants	Year	Comments
1 (Havana, Cuba)	23	1947	Establishment of GATT and tariff reductions
2 (Annecy, France)	38	1949	Further tariff reductions
3 (Torquay, UK)	38	1950	Further tariff reductions
4	–	–	This round of negotiations was skipped
5 Dillon Round (Geneva, Switzerland)		1960	Rounds of negotiations now given a name
6 Kennedy Round (Geneva, Switzerland)	60	1964–67	Expansion of tariff reductions and new trade rules established on anti-dumping measures
7 Tokyo Round (Tokyo, Japan)	102	1973–79	Significant tariff reductions and a series of agreements on non-tariff barriers. These were signed only by some participants and are known as the Tokyo codes. No agreement on agriculture reform or safeguard measures
8 (Uruguay Round)	123	1986–94	Last round of GATT. WTO created
9 (Doha Round)	159	2001–	First round conducted under the auspices of the WTO

Source: WTO (n.d.) The Multilateral Trading System: 50 Years of Achievement.

Available at: www.wto.org/english/thewto_e/minist_e/min98_e/slide_e/slideshow_index.htm

to establish this new institution to assist countries in Europe devastated by World War II. The institution's first loan was to France in the amount of $250 million in 1947. The World Bank is in fact a group of five organizations: the International Bank for Reconstruction and Development (IBRD) which lends to the governments of middle- and low-income countries; the International Development Association (IDA) which provides interest-free loans and grants to the governments of very poor countries; the International Finance Corporation (IFC) which provides loans and equity financing to private firms in developing countries; the Multilateral Investment Guarantee Agency (MIGA) which provides loan guarantees; and the International Centre for Settlement of Investment Disputes (ICSID) which is involved in the arbitration of cross-border investment disputes.

Box 5.2

A country's balance of payments summarizes its economic transactions with other countries with which it conducts business. It is essentially an accounting statement that records the country's monetary transactions over a specified period of time. These transactions are summarized in the current and capital accounts which are defined as follows:

- the Current Account records the country's imports and exports of goods and services, income and official transfers
- the Capital Account records the net change in the ownership of assets, i.e. the change in foreign ownership of domestic assets minus the change in the domestic ownership of foreign assets.

These two accounts taken together must sum to zero as double-entry accounting is the convention used in constructing a country's balance of payments. Each transaction is recorded by two entries of equal value – a credit (with a positive sign) and a debit (with a negative sign).

Over the years, the Bank has remained focused on leading recovery efforts around the world and is active in cases of natural disasters, humanitarian emergencies and post-conflict situations. For example, the Bank was a key player in efforts to assist Indonesia in the aftermath of the 2004 tsunami which claimed some 230,000 lives. The core of the Bank's activities is now poverty alleviation around the world, although economic reconstruction remains a key agenda item. In the wake of the global financial crisis that began in 2007, the World Bank committed roughly $60 billion in the fiscal year 2009 to assist countries reeling from its effects.

THE INTERNATIONAL MONETARY FUND

The International Monetary Fund (IMF) is also a Bretton Woods institution. Established in 1944, the IMF's mandate was to oversee the international monetary system, thereby ensuring exchange rate stability which would promote trade and prosperity. The need for an organization such as the IMF became painfully apparent during the Great Depression when countries around the world raised tariff barriers and devalued their currencies in an attempt to boost exports and spur economic growth. Competitive devaluations and restrictions on citizens' ability to hold foreign exchange did not have the desired effect and world trade declined sharply, exacerbating the economic hardships being experienced.

Twenty nine countries signed the articles of agreement to establish the IMF following the Bretton Woods Conference in 1944. These initial member countries agreed to peg their domestic currencies to the US dollar, and in the case of the USA to the price of gold. These pegs could only be adjusted with IMF agreement and only in cases of severe balance of payments disequilibrium. This so-called Bretton Woods system of fixed exchange rates would come to an end in 1973, following the US government's decision to suspend the convertibility of dollars into gold.

Apart from monitoring developments in the global financial system, the IMF also provides technical assistance to member countries as well as loans. The IMF has, however, come under criticism for its structural adjustment programs (SAPs) which impose conditions on borrowing countries. These so-called 'conditionalities' are designed to make the economies of borrowing countries more market oriented and trade driven and may include measures to reduce the size of the public sector, privatization of state enterprises and cuts to social programs. Concern has been expressed that these policy changes have a negative impact on the poor and the vulnerable in the society and do not contribute to poverty alleviation. Despite these concerns, however, the IMF has continued to provide financing to countries in economic crisis and has played an important role in attempts to stabilize countries of the EU during the sovereign debt crisis.

THE UNITED NATIONS

The United Nations is also a key organization involved in international trade. The United Nations Conference on Trade and Development (UNCTAD),[14] for example, works with the governments of developing countries to prepare their technical positions in preparation for

---

[14]   See the UNCTAD website at: www.unctad.org/Templates/Startpage.asp?intItemID=2068&lang=1

international trade negotiations with developed countries. Because these countries have limited resources, UNCTAD will provide assistance in the collection and analysis of trade data and in the formulation of a consistent negotiation position backed by rigorous economic analysis. In multilateral trade negotiations, the issues discussed are often complex and this assistance from UNCTAD is invaluable to poorer nations who may lack the technical skills and resources for data collection. The first meeting of UNCTAD was held in Geneva in 1964. The organization has a permanent secretariat and meetings are scheduled every four years. Currently, 192 states are members of UNCTAD, including Canada, Japan, Germany and the USA.

Established in 1964, the International Trade Center (ITC) is the international cooperation arm of UNCTAD and the WTO. The ITC's mandate is to assist developing countries and countries in transition to become more competitive in global markets, accelerate their economic development and consequently contribute to the achievement of the UN's Millennium Development Goals (MDGs).[15] Unlike the WTO and UNCTAD which operate at a macro level, the ITC's work is focused at the level of the individual firm. The organization is heavily engaged in the private sector in its target countries, working with small and medium-sized companies to assist them in promoting their exports and ensuring that they are well positioned to take advantage of international market opportunities.

SUMMARY

This chapter has examined the international trade environment. The point was made that trade allows countries to provide their citizens with a wider range of products and allows for greater specialization and efficiency in production. A number of theories were introduced to provide some understanding of what drives international trade and why free trade is a superior option for the world economy and for individual countries. Despite these theoretical arguments, however, countries still implement protectionist policies which restrict free trade and investment. A number of the reasons given for this approach were discussed in this chapter, including the need to protect infant industries as well as fears concerning national security. Various policy instruments to provide protection to domestic industry were also presented, along with examples of how they have been used by domestic governments.

While domestic governments have control over their national trade policy, most are signatories to international agreements which regulate the global trading environment. The role and function of the World Trade Organization were discussed in this context of trade regulation. The WTO, the successor organization to the GATT, administers the various multilateral trade agreements that attempt to bring order to the global trade environment and provide a forum for the settlement of trade disputes. Also discussed in the chapter were the Bretton Woods institutions, the World Bank and the IMF, both of which play a role in the regulation of international trade and investment flows. UNCTAD, an agency of the United Nations, also has a role to play in assisting developing countries in trade negotiations and is discussed in this context.

 Real World Challenges

Trina Solar Wrestles with EU Protectionism

Wayne Chen could remember the heady days in the solar panel industry as if they were yesterday. The Chinese government was pouring money into the sector and new firms were entering the industry almost daily. How

---

times have changed. Could this latest news out of Brussels of an almost 12% tariff on solar panel exports to the EU be the final nail in the coffin? As vice president of global marketing for Trina Solar Limited, Wayne knew just how important the European market was to his company's bottom line. The latest figures compiled by the accounting department showed the degree of dependence. In the last fiscal year, some 48% of the company's sales were generated in Europe, but with the glut of solar panels on the market the firm's profit margins stood at –25%. How could this have happened to Trina – one of the largest solar panel manufacturers in the country?

Suntech Power Holdings Co. was one of the first Chinese companies to enter the solar power industry. The company achieved significant success, becoming the world's largest manufacturer of solar panels and one of China's most successful companies. Buoyed by Suntech's success, the Chinese government made the solar panel industry one of its strategic priorities. The government provided generous incentives to encourage firms to enter the industry. Under one program, dubbed the Golden Sun and launched in 2009, the Chinese government covered half of solar developers' costs. Companies entered the industry at a rapid pace, attracted by the profit margins which could be as much as 33% per year. By 2011, however, the Chinese solar panel industry had stalled. Significant over-production and over-capacity drove prices down by as much as 40 percent. Suntech was forced into bankruptcy and dozens of smaller players had little choice but to exit the industry.

Between 2009 and 2011, production of Chinese solar panels had quadrupled and the European market was flooded. Imports of Chinese panels topped 21 billion euros in 2011, prompting the EU Trade Commission to step in, announcing a 12 percent tariff on imports of Chinese solar panels, cells and wafers. In announcing its decision, the EU gave China 60 days to correct the problem or risk having the tariff escalate to 47 percent. The Commission argued that Chinese products were being dumped on the European market and that the practice was having a deleterious impact on EU manufacturers. The subsidies provided by Beijing gave Chinese manufacturers an unfair price advantage in the EU market and the imposition of tariffs was the only way to redress the problem. The EU noted that a fair price for Chinese solar panels was some 88 percent higher than what they were being sold for. According to the Commission, some 20,000 jobs across Europe were in jeopardy as a result of the cheap Chinese imports.

PHOTO 5.3

Wayne was acutely aware that the solar panel industry in China was facing some tough times ahead. The USA had imposed tariffs last year and now there was this action from the Europeans. However, when he thought that the worst of the news was over, there was an announcement from the Chinese government that it was scaling back its subsidy program to the industry. Wayne had to move quickly if Trina was to survive. As he slumped in his chair, however, it was clear to him that coming up with a viable solution would not be easy.

Sources

Song, S. (2013 Is the Sun Setting on China's Solar Panel Boom? Available at: www.ibtimes.com/chinese-solar-panel-companies-faced-overcapacity-low-demand-eu-tariffs-are-facing-painful-future, accessed June 15, 2013.

Washington Post (2013) EU Imposes Anti-Dumping Tariffs on Chinese Solar Panel Imports in Escalating Trade Row. Available at: http://articles.washingtonpost.com/2013-06-04/world/39727242_1_eu-commission-chinese-solar-panels-trade-war, accessed June 15, 2013.

Questions

1. State the problem that Wayne and his company face.
2. Identify the options available. Be sure to identify more than one.
3. Based on the options identified above, recommend a course of action. Be sure to provide a rationale and make a decision.

? discussion questions

1. How would an isolated country such as North Korea benefit from establishing trade relationships with the rest of the world?

2. Given the theoretical arguments for free trade, why do governments resort to protectionism?

3. Should western governments allow the takeover of their domestic natural resource companies by Chinese state-owned enterprises?

4. Explain Vernon's concept of the international product life cycle. Does this theory adequately explain the competiveness of developing countries such as China in the area of manufacturing?

5. Identify three policy measures used by national governments to protect their domestic industries and explain how they work.

6. In 2006, the Canadian government banned the importation of spinach produced in the USA. The ban came as a result of an outbreak of E. Coli linked to spinach imported from the USA and after some 200 people had become sick, three of whom died. Would the actions of the Canadian government be viewed as protectionist? Why/why not?

6

RESEARCHING GLOBAL MARKETS

LEARNING OBJECTIVES

After reading this chapter you should be able to:

- Define the term 'international marketing research' and explain its importance

- Distinguish between domestic and international marketing research

- Discuss the various steps in conducting international marketing research.

INTRODUCTION

Global marketing involves risk. The multinational firm must commit resources in advance to establish production facilities in foreign markets, modify existing products for new international markets or develop entirely new products which can be marketed around the world. While the global marketing manager does not have a crystal ball, detailed information on the foreign target market may serve to offset some of the risks involved in these decisions. This information must, however, be current, objective and accurate if it is to contribute to improved decision making. Failure may often be traced to a lack of information and understanding of the international market. For example, in the 1970s KFC attempted to penetrate the Japanese market. The company opted for a drive-through model similar to what was being used successfully in the USA. The concept, however, would fail as very few Japanese at the time owned cars, a fact that KFC had neglected to consider in their market entry strategy. Had KFC invested some time in researching the Japanese market, the company may well have avoided this costly error. KFC would eventually reassess the market, close its drive-through locations and open restaurants in high traffic locations such as train stations. These would prove to be far more successful for the company.

Many global managers dismiss market research as being too costly or too time-consuming. However, as the KFC example above illustrates, failed market entry strategies may similarly be costly and time-consuming. It is important that the global marketer not assume a complete understanding of the foreign market but opt to validate her assumptions of market conditions. International market research will allow the global marketer to test assumptions of the foreign market and gain an in-depth and current understanding of its dynamics. KFC is a multinational organization with access to significant resources yet opted not to make an investment in market research for its initial launch in Japan. The same holds true for other multinationals. The lack of attention given to international marketing research is, however, even more prevalent in the case of small and medium-sized firms. Most small and medium-sized companies pursue international market opportunities based on little or no research but rather a reliance on anecdotal evidence and management's subjective assessments. Interestingly, these firms do seem to have an appreciation of the need to conduct domestic marketing research, even as they make foreign market decisions with little or no intelligence.[1]

International marketing research is designed to improve managerial decision making. Many large companies have dedicated in-house resources that may be deployed to assess foreign markets. The company may also rely on the services of a commercial marketing research firm such as New York-based The Nielsen Company, London-based Kantar or GfK SE which is based in Nuremberg, Germany. Whether the firm relies on in-house resources or pays a service provider fee, such research will be required to support various aspects of foreign market expansion from country selection, to an assessment of the competitive environment, to the formulation of marketing strategies in the foreign country. Key questions to be asked include: How do consumers in the foreign market make purchase decisions? How should we price our products in foreign markets? Do we really understand the distribution system overseas? How will government regulations impact our ability to operate in the foreign country? What type of competitive environment will we face if we enter new foreign markets? What advertising message should we use to appeal to consumers in our foreign target markets? International marketing research will allow the global marketer to get a handle on these and other questions that are central to a complete understanding of the foreign market. As illustrated in Case Study 6.1, marketing research gives the company confidence in its decisions, even when these may be controversial.

case study 6.1: Pepsi advertising

Pepsi's '**Live for Now**' advertising campaign features Nicki Minaj and Michael Jackson and has garnered both criticism and praise for its controversial tagline. Critics have suggested that it connotes 'no future' but Pepsi executives argue that extensive research conducted by the company indicates otherwise. The company's research conducted over a ten-month period in countries around the world was designed to determine whether there is a unique value system held by Pepsi loyalists that could be used to better position the brand globally. The research found that Pepsi's loyal consumers 'over-indexed' on the desire to make the most out of every moment. The company argues that this mindset distinguishes its brand from the competition. Pepsi used qualitative and quantitative analysis to better understand the value systems of its consumers around the world and determined that 'Now' did not come at the expense of the future. The company's research found that its customers were interested in living a life of exciting 'nows' – focused on the future but in the context of an exciting present. Based on unique consumer insights provided by the research undertaken, Pepsi has rolled out its ad campaign in key markets around the world and across all touchpoints, including the Internet and television.

PHOTO 6.1

[1] Czinkota, M., Ronkainen, I., Farrell, C. and McTavish, R. (2009) *Global Marketing: Foreign Entry, Market Development and Strategy Implementation*. Toronto: Nelson Education.

Source

Rooney, J. (2012) Pepsi's Brad Jakeman and Simon Lowden Explain Rationale Behind New 'Live For Now' Global Campaign. Available at: www.forbes.com/sites/jenniferrooney/2012/05/07/pepsis-brad-jakeman-and-simon-lowden-explain-rationale-behind-new-live-for-now-global-campaign/2/, accessed June 16, 2013.

Discussion Questions

1. Do you believe that Pepsi's global consumer research provides it with a unique brand position relative to its major rival, Coke?
2. Why would Pepsi loyalists in particular demonstrate such a strong affinity with the 'now'?

WHAT IS INTERNATIONAL MARKETING RESEARCH?

To better understand what international marketing research is all about, it is perhaps instructive to begin with a definition of marketing research. The American Marketing Association (AMA) defines market research as: 'The systematic gathering, recording, and analyzing of data with respect to a particular market, where market refers to a specific customer group in a specific geographic area.'[2] From this definition, we note that market research is a systematic process and involves the collection and analysis of data which lead to a better understanding of the consumers that comprise the market being investigated. International marketing research, on the other hand, may be defined as: 'Research that crosses international borders and involves respondents and researchers from different countries and cultures'.[3] This definition more explicitly recognizes that international marketing research crosses borders and takes into account differences in the culture of the researcher and the respondents involved. In fact, according to Craig and Douglas (2005), research that meets any of the criteria below would be considered international marketing research:

(a) Involves the collection and analysis of information and the development of inferences about consumers and businesses in two or more countries within the context of the same project.

(b) Involves the collection of information on a single country by an academic researcher or commercial marketing research firm from another country in order to understand the similarities and differences between the two countries.

(c) Involves the collection of information on immigrant populations in order to better understand how consumption patterns change when individuals from a foreign culture relocate to a new country and cultural context.

International marketing research is still very much concerned with the collection and analysis of information to improve management decision making, but clearly the focus is on providing a better understanding of the country and cultural contexts within which these decisions must be made.

As noted in the Introduction, international marketing research is important. When well executed international market research may provide the global marketer with a number of

---

[2] Marketingpower.com (2013) Dictionary. Available at: www.marketingpower.com/_layouts/Dictionary.aspx?dLetter=M, accessed June 16, 2013.

[3] Craig, C.S. and Douglas, S.P. (2005) *International Marketing Research*, 3rd edn. Chichester: John Wiley, p. 23.

FIGURE 6.1   Benefits of International Marketing Research

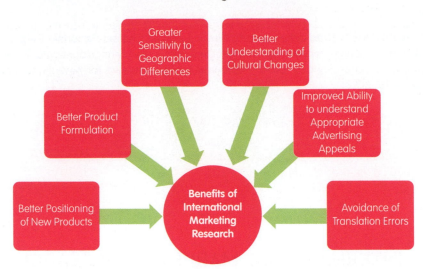

important benefits (see Figure 6.1).[4] First, international marketing research is important in assisting the firm to correctly position its products in foreign markets. For example, when PepsiCo entered the Chinese market with its Frito-lay brand of potato chips, consumer reaction was less than enthusiastic. The product did not sell well and the company noticed that sales were particularly disappointing in the summer months. The company's research subsequently revealed that fried foods, such as its potato chips, are associated with *yang* which is believed to generate body heat. In Chinese philosophy, *yang* is considered one of two forces that constitute the duality of the natural world. The other force is termed *yin*. Both *yin* and *yang* have physical manifestations such as light and dark, heat and cold or high and low. On understanding that its potato chips are associated with *yang*, it became clear to the company why sales would generally be low and even more depressed in the summer months. PepsiCo decided to reposition the product by introducing a new cool lemon variety which was sold in a pastel-colored package to reflect *yin*, which is associated with a cooling effect. The strongly lemon-scented chips are dotted with green specks of lime and mint and the package features blue skies and rolling fields of green grass. Malaysian pop star Angelica Lee, Hong King singer Aaron Kwok and NBA star Yao Ming were recruited to promote the product.[5] The chips were successfully repositioned in the minds of consumers and became the company's best-selling product in China.

Second, international marketing research allows the firm to avoid or correct product formulation errors. As will be seen in Chapter 9, companies must often make changes to their established products when they are to be marketed in foreign countries. These changes, however, should be informed by research. For example, prior to the launch of its oats-based baby foods in China, the HJ Heinz Company conducted research and discovered that Chinese consumers were not familiar with oats and were, therefore, likely to react negatively to its use in baby foods. To avoid potential problems, the company decided to reformulate its products using whitebait – a small fish that is a staple of the Chinese diet. The whitebait-oats formulation proved to be a hit with Chinese consumers and the product became an instant success. Without an understanding of the market that international

---

4   This section draws heavily on Craig and Douglas (2005) op cit.

5   Flannery, R. (2004) China Is a Big Prize. Available at: www.forbes.com/forbes/2004/0510/163_print.html, accessed January 17, 2012.

marketing research provided, it is unlikely that this US company's product would have been successful in the Chinese market.

The third area where the global marketer may benefit from international marketing research is geographic sensitivity. As is perhaps well known, India and Pakistan have had a longstanding dispute over the Jammu-Kashmir region. The region is claimed by both India and Pakistan and has been a flashpoint for conflict and violence between the two countries dating back some 60 years. However, when Microsoft launched Windows 95 in India its promotional material featured a color-coded map which did not show the disputed region as belonging to India. The Indian government reacted angrily, banning sales of the product. Had Microsoft conducted research on the market prior to the launch of the product, it is likely that this particular sensitivity would have been discovered and adjustments made to its collateral marketing materials. The company did eventually correct the problem when it introduced Windows 97 by removing the color-coding altogether.

A fourth benefit of international marketing research is the understanding it provides of ongoing cultural changes in prospective target markets. For instance, few global marketers foresaw the rapid changes that would take place in communist China and the demand that would be unleashed for western products. Few auto executives, for example, would have predicted that China would become the largest car market in the world with sales, according to consulting firm McKinsey, approaching 22 million passenger cars in 2020. Chinese commuters have traditionally relied on bicycles. Between 2005 and 2011, however, car sales in China increased by an average of 24 percent per year, with some Chinese cities now imposing limits on the number of cars allowed on their roads due to traffic congestion.[6] Global marketing research and advertising companies routinely undertake comparative analyses of markets around the world for their clients. Such efforts can help global marketers to spot trends in consumer preferences before they become well recognized by the competition.

The fifth area where international marketing research may benefit the global marketer is in the identification of appropriate advertising appeals. Coca-Cola, for example, was experiencing weak sales of its products in Brazil before discovering that the female kangaroo was the appropriate advertising device to win over consumers in that country. Coke launched ads featuring a female kangaroo and using the tag line: 'Mom knows everything'. In the ads, the kangaroo is featured wearing sunglasses and carrying cans of Coke in her pouch instead of a baby. Although there are no kangaroos in Brazil, the animal is seen by Brazilian women as being free-spirited and independent yet caring and nurturing. These characteristics resonate with women in the Latin American country, who account for 80 percent of Coke's roughly $4 billion in sales. The kangaroo concept was developed by Duailibi, Petit, Zaragoza, a Sao Paulo agency, and the marketing research cost Coke $800,000.

International marketing research may also benefit the global marketing firm by avoiding translation errors. We may see this, for example, in the case of the entry of Procter & Gamble (P&G) into Eastern Europe. P&G is a major US-based consumer products company which markets its brands in over 150 countries around the world. The firm's brand portfolio includes Gillette, Braun, Cover Girl, Tide, Scope and Oral-B. When entering Eastern Europe, P&G made a decision to translate its detergent labels into Polish and Czech, as a means of adapting its products to the local markets. Sales in those markets, however, were decidedly uninspiring and P&G was at a loss for a plausible explanation. The company opted to conduct some market research and discovered that consumers reacted negatively to the translated labels. Their view was that the translation was too perfect and this raised

---

6   AFP (2012) China Car Market to Grow 8% Annually: McKinsey. Available at: www.france24.com/en/20121121-china-car-market-grow-8-annually-mckinsey, accessed January 8, 2013.

concerns that P&G was attempting to pass itself off as an Eastern European company. Based on those results, the company readjusted its strategy by using imperfect Polish in its product labels to indicate that it was trying to fit in but was not yet fluent in the language. Sales eventually began to increase.

case study 6.2: Apple's Market Research

In a widely publicized interview with *Fortune* magazine, the late Steve Jobs, former CEO of Apple, is quoted as saying: 'We do no market research. We don't hire consultants … We just want to make great products'. Apple is well known for focusing on satisfying the needs of customers even before customers can articulate what those needs are. According to Jobs: 'It isn't the consumer's job to know what they want'. Instead, Apple's mandate was to develop great products and then let customers decide whether or not they satisfied an important need. The iPhone and iPad are both regarded as being highly innovative products. It is widely believed that research techniques such as focus groups, which may be used to allow prospective customers to brainstorm product ideas, had little place in the company's strategy.

PHOTO 6.2

However, in a patent infringement lawsuit against Samsung, documents filed in court revealed that Apple does in fact conduct some market research. This research is focused on understanding the buyer behavior of the company's current customers and what drives them to prefer Apple products. In a 2011 survey of iPhone users in multiple countries, the company found, for example, that for Chinese users the firm's brand and design were bigger drivers of the purchase decision than software and apps. In fact, 67 percent of Chinese consumers said they were motivated by physical features and design – a much higher percentage than in other countries such as Japan, the UK, France, Germany and South Korea. The company's research also indicated that trust in the brand was a deciding factor in the purchase decision among both US and Chinese consumers. It turns out that Apple considers its consumer surveys to be important trade secrets which could provide its competitors with an advantage if made public.

Sources

The Wall Street Journal (2012) Apple's Secrets Revealed at Trial. Available at: http://online.wsj.com/article/SB1 0000872396390044368750457756742184074545 2.html, accessed June 16, 2013.

WSJ.com (2012) Turns Out Apple Conducts Market Research After All. Available at: http://blogs.wsj.com/digits/2012/07/26/turns-out-apple-conducts-market-research-after-all/, accessed June 16, 2013.

Discussion Questions

1. Why do you think Chinese consumers are more motivated by the design and physical features of the Apple iPhone when compared to consumers in other countries such as Japan, the UK, France and Germany? How could the company use this insight?
2. How important is post-purchase consumer research to a technology company such as Apple?

DIFFERENCES BETWEEN DOMESTIC AND INTERNATIONAL MARKETING RESEARCH

Both domestic and international marketing research involve the collection and analysis of data used to inform managerial decision making. In fact, both utilize the same tools of analysis such as multiple regression, correlation analysis and analysis of variance. Further, both domestic and international marketing research may make use of the same data collection techniques such as focus groups and consumer surveys. The key difference between domestic and international research lies in the environment or context within which the tools and techniques are applied. As illustrated in Figure 6.2, there are four key aspects of the environment that impact the way standard marketing tools and techniques are applied:[7]

FIGURE 6.2   Contextual Differences in the International Application of Marketing Research Techniques

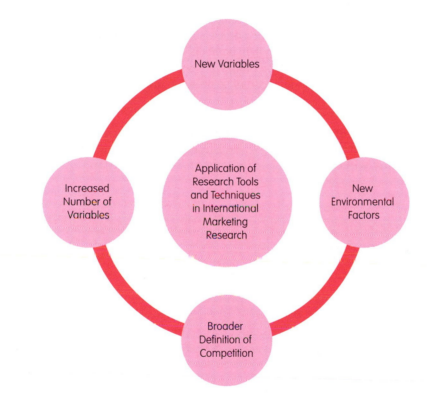

- **New variables**: In international marketing research, the researcher will be confronted with new variables that generally do not assume great importance in domestic research projects. In an international context, the researcher may have to consider variables such as tariff rates, quotas, international shipping charges and exchange rates that are not relevant in purely domestic research projects. These new variables add an additional layer of complexity to the international marketing research project.

[7]   Czinkota, M., Ronkainen, I., Farrell, C. and McTavish, R. (2009) *Global Marketing: Foreign Entry, Market Development and Strategy Implementation*. Toronto: Nelson Education, pp. 207–8.

- **New environmental factors**: The international marketing researcher is not able to ignore the culture, level of technological sophistication, socio-economic conditions and general level of economic development of the countries in which the research project is being conducted. As noted in Chapter 2, cultural differences have an important impact on consumer buying behavior and attitudes towards foreign products. It is, therefore, imperative that these be taken into account in any analysis of foreign target markets. Similarly, differences in the level of economic development of the countries under consideration must be factored into the analysis. KFC's entry into the Japanese market was discussed at the beginning of this chapter and illustrates the problems that may be encountered when the global marketer fails to objectively test the assumptions made about a country's level of economic development.

- **Increased number of variables**: International marketing research crosses borders and involves the collection and analysis of data from two or more countries. As the researcher adds new countries to the research project, the number of variables to be considered increases markedly. Data on each variable to be considered in the analysis must now be collected for every country included in the project, which increases the size and scope of the overall project.

- **Broader definition of competition**: Market researchers must understand the competitive environment within which the firm is to do business. In the case of international marketing research, the definition of competition may be much broader than is first realized. Consider, for example, the case of food processors and blenders, which are sold in developed countries primarily for their convenience and ability to save time in meal preparation. Food processor manufacturers such as Cuisinart, Braun and KitchenAid may well find that in marketing their products in developing countries they face competition not only from other manufacturers of food processors and blenders but also from cheap local labor. Failure to account for this broader definition of competition may lead to overly optimistic sales and market share forecasts.

The above suggests that international marketing research is much more complex and challenging than purely domestic research. While the tools and techniques used are the same, how they are applied will require deeper thought and consideration.

case study 6.3: Absolut in the USA

PHOTO 6.3

Absolut vodka is one of the top-selling vodka brands in the USA. When the brand was first launched in the USA, however, many scoffed at the idea of vodka made in Sweden. Vodka has traditionally been associated with Russia. In the late 1970s, Carillon Importers, a New York firm, was given the opportunity to import Absolut into the US market. The company invested $83,000 in researching the market but came away with decidedly negative results. Some respondents had never heard of Sweden while others confused it with Finland. None of the respondents polled saw Sweden as a vodka-producing country, suggesting that Absolut would be a difficult sell in the US market. Despite the negative results, Carillon Importers decided to proceed with the product launch. The brand was first introduced in Boston, then in New York, Chicago, Los Angeles, San Francisco and then across the rest of the USA. In the first year, the company sold only

10,000 cases. However, by 1985 Absolut would surpass its major Russian competitor and go on to become the best-selling vodka in the USA. Following success in Sweden and the USA, the brand would be introduced to countries across Europe, Asia and the Pacific Rim.

Source

Roston, E. (2007) Absolut Capitalism. Available at: www.absolutad.com/absolut_about/history/story, accessed January 20, 2013.

Discussion Question

1. What could account for the difference between the company's marketing research results and the success of Absolut vodka in the US market?

THE INTERNATIONAL MARKETING RESEARCH PROCESS

Conducting international marketing research is quite complex. The process may, however, be conceptualized as a series of steps or phases beginning with the definition of the problem and ending with the presentation of the research findings to senior management (see Figure 6.3). Given the complexity of the global environment, a systematic, step-by-step approach to the research process is recommended. The steps in the process are discussed below.

FIGURE 6.3   The Research Process

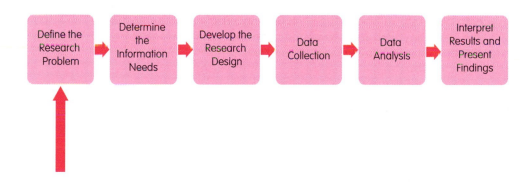

DEFINE THE PROBLEM

The first step in the international research process is the definition of the problem (Figure 6.4). It is, however, necessary to make a distinction between the business problem that the firm faces and the research problem. Business executives are generally comfortable articulating the business problems they face in foreign markets. They may allude to declining sales in Latin America or low margins in their markets in Eastern Europe. The international marketing researcher must, however, translate these business problems into research problems that are amenable to analysis. The firm's declining sales in Latin America, for example, may eventually lead to an investigation of the relationship between advertising expenditure and sales or the firm's pricing strategy and demand for its products. To produce results that truly inform managerial decision making, the international marketing researcher must invest the time to develop a series of research questions that succinctly define the problem the firm faces and identify the information that is needed to address the problem. Examples of questions the researcher may pose are:

- How would a 10 percent increase in retail prices impact our furniture sales in the US market?
- If we decreased our advertising expenditure by 20 percent what would be the impact on sales of our coffee machines in Brazil?
- Would our market share increase if we doubled the size of our sales force in Japan?
- What is the market potential for the next generation of our smartphones in India?

DETERMINE THE INFORMATION NEEDS

Having precisely defined the research problem, the next step in the process involves a determination of the specific information that must be collected to address it (see Figure 6.4). The information required will be determined by the nature of the problem to be resolved and whether the problem is of a **strategic** or **tactical** nature. Strategic decisions are high-level decisions which determine the long-term direction of the firm and involve the allocation of company resources across country markets and product categories. Such decisions are normally made at the corporate or regional subsidiary level within the company. Information required to support strategic decisions tends to be macro in nature and readily available from secondary sources such as World Bank publications and from national statistical agencies. GDP per capita, country debt levels and measures of political risk are among the metrics that may be required to inform strategic decisions. Tactical decisions, on the other hand, are more operational and usually require the use of primary information that the firm must collect itself specifically to address the problem. Tactical decisions may relate to issues such as what colors should be used on the company's new packaging or whether the company should reduce its prices to match those of the competition. More readily available secondary data are unlikely to be useful in answering such firm-specific research questions. To support such decisions, the firm may well have to conduct its own interviews of customers and members of the distribution channel in the target countries.

DEVELOP THE RESEARCH DESIGN

The third step in the process is development of the research design. In designing the research project, several issues need to be addressed. These range from selection of the unit of analysis to the choice of data collection and analysis techniques that will be used. Figure 6.5 summarizes the major considerations.

FIGURE 6.4   Determine Information Needs

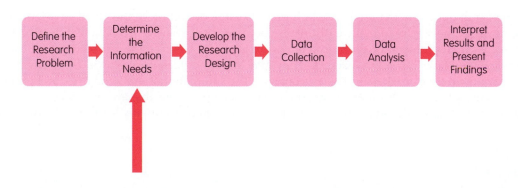

FIGURE 6.5   Develop Research Design

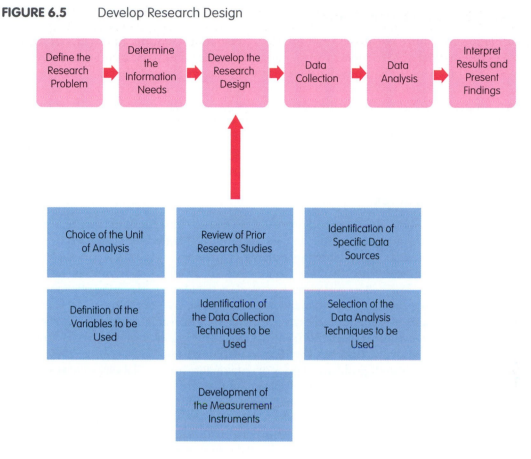

Choosing the unit of analysis

The international marketing researcher needs to make a decision on the level at which the research will be conducted. The unit of analysis may be a specific city within the target country, such as Frankfurt; the individual country – say, Germany; or the region of the world or a particular economic grouping to which the country belongs, such as the EU. The scope may also be global, encompassing most countries of the world. The broadest level of analysis is clearly global and this may be the appropriate unit depending on the nature of the research exercise. Firms in industries such as pharmaceutical drug manufacturing may well opt to conduct market research at the global level given the nature of their products. It should be noted, however, that while use of the world as the unit of analysis will allow for interesting country and regional comparisons, such research will certainly be more complex and costly to conduct in terms of both time and money. If appropriate, the researcher may elect to use a specific geographic region or trade bloc as the unit of analysis. Sub-Saharan Africa, NAFTA and the EU are examples. Adopting a specific region of the world as the unit of analysis does reduce the overall number of countries to consider, as well as the time and financial cost involved, but the researcher loses the ability to make comparisons with countries outside the chosen region. In the majority of international marketing research projects, the country is the unit of analysis selected. This greatly simplifies the research exercise by reducing the information requirements of the project. In special circumstances, the researcher may decide to use a specific city within the country as the unit of analysis. This may be appropriate, for example, if the demographic being targeted is highly concentrated in that city or the product being marketed is unlikely to be bought by individuals living in rural areas.

Reviewing prior research studies

Depending on the nature of the research problem to be addressed, the international marketing researcher may be able to identify prior research studies that have examined some or all aspects of the problem under consideration. Studies produced by academic researchers, for example, may contain information which can be used by the international marketing researcher to better conceptualize the relationship between the variables to be studied. Prior research studies may also contain valuable information on the country or region of interest to the firm which can provide useful background. A review of prior studies will allow the international marketing researcher to assess whether some or all aspects of the current research problem have already been satisfactorily addressed and whether there is a need for additional research.

Identifying data sources

Having decided on the unit of analysis and reviewed prior research studies, the international marketer's next task is to identify sources for the data that are to be collected. Data used in research projects may be classified as being either **secondary** or **primary**. Secondary data are data that were collected for purposes other than the firm's research project. Organizations such as the OECD, World Bank and IMF collect and publish secondary data for a wide range of countries and industrial sectors. These data are usually made available online free of charge or in some cases for a nominal fee. Social media and corporate websites are also valuable sources of secondary information for the international marketer (see Box 6.1). The use of secondary data sources is extremely cost-effective for the firm but the data available may not always be exactly what is required to address its research problems. Issues of data quality and availability may also surface in cases where the statistical agencies in developing countries are the sources being tapped. Lack of training and resources may result in data which are not accurate or are not produced in a timely manner. Primary data, in contrast, are data collected for the firm's specific research project. Such data are highly relevant to the research problems being addressed but are not available free of charge or at a nominal cost to the company. Primary data used in international marketing research projects are generally expensive to collect as they often involve overseas travel by consultants or company executives and the recruitment and training of enumerators and analysts.

 Box 6.1

In addition to traditional secondary data sources, the international marketer has available to him a vast amount of data generated by social media sites such as Facebook and Twitter, as well as by corporate websites and mobile device transactions. These data sources are important in understanding the behavior of the firm.

The term Big Data is commonly used to describe the vast amount of information generated every day from social media websites, company websites, mobile devices and various business transactions. While Big Data are a rich source of information for the international marketer they do present challenges for the firm in terms of storage, visualization and analysis. However with appropriate analytical tools and training, Big Data may be effectively mined to better understand customer preferences with respect to features that should be incorporated into products for new foreign markets as well as to inform the firm's strategies with respect to customer acquisition and retention.

Source

IDC (2011) Big Data Analytics: Future Architectures, Skills and Roadmaps for the CIO. Available at: www.sas.com/resources/asset/BigDataAnalytics-FutureArchitectures-Skills-RoadmapsfortheCIO.pdf

Variable definition

As the researcher develops the design of the project, the issue of variable definition will become important. Because international marketing research projects cross borders, variables may have very different meanings depending on the country and cultural context. This is not a significant problem in the case of purely domestic projects but is critically important when the project spans two or more cultures. In some parts of the world, for example, household appliances such as washing machines and blenders are considered luxury items, while in other countries they are viewed as mere conveniences. Even a term such as 'household' may have a different meaning depending on the cultural context. In Asia, extended families are quite common with three generations residing in the same home. In North America, however, such family arrangements are far less common. The use of the word 'household' in the firm's research may, therefore, evoke very different meanings among respondents in the two geographical regions. Variables need to be carefully defined at the outset of the project to ensure that misunderstandings do not occur and that the results obtained in the various target countries are in fact comparable.

Data collection techniques

The international marketing researcher has several options for data collection. The approach selected will be driven by a number of considerations, such as the budget available for the project and whether the exercise is purely exploratory or designed to yield definitive answers.

Observation is one approach that may be used to collect the data required for the firm's research project. This technique, as the name suggests, involves observing individuals going about their normal shopping activities. In a supermarket setting, for example, the researcher may observe shoppers in an actual store, noting which aisles receive the most traffic and how the store is navigated. The researcher is also able to obtain useful information by noting whether shoppers focus at eye level or stop to consider products located on the top and bottom shelves. A food manufacturing company will find such information useful in negotiating shelf space in overseas groceries. In some studies, shoppers are unaware that they are being observed. If observation is obtrusive, however, there is a possibility that the shopper may alter her behavior in response, negating to some extent the benefits of the exercise. Observation does not yield hard quantitative data but rather qualitative insights. The technique may be suitable in situations where little is known about the market and the research project is at a preliminary or exploratory stage. Firms would generally require more concrete data when committing significant resources to a new foreign market.

Focus groups are another option for data collection open to the researcher. With a focus group, the researcher brings together 7–10 knowledgeable individuals for a freewheeling discussion of a particular topic. Discussions may last for 2–4 hours and are guided by a trained moderator. The objective of the exercise is to stimulate the generation of ideas and creative ways of thinking about a research problem. Suggestions proposed by one individual may be challenged by others in the group and thereby create a dynamic that eventually leads to entirely new and innovative ideas. Focus groups may be used to test consumer reaction to the launch of a new product in a foreign market or to evaluate a change in market strategy for a product already being sold internationally. Because focus groups depend on open dialogue, they may have limited value in societies which do not place equal value on the opinions of men and women. In some Middle Eastern countries, for example, women may be reluctant to voice their opinions if these run counter to those expressed by the men participating in the group. In such situations, the researcher will have to decide whether mixed-sex focus groups are feasible or whether male and female participants should be separated. The sex of the moderator may also be an issue in such countries as a female moderator may not be received positively by male participants and may have difficulty guiding the discussion. Focus groups provide an opportunity for the project sponsor to directly observe the proceedings and hear first hand the opinions expressed about the company and its products. Professional marketing research firms may provide focus group rooms which are specially fitted with one-way mirrors to allow the project sponsors to observe the proceedings.

PHOTO 6.4

Interviews are an extremely effective mechanism for soliciting the information needed for international marketing research projects. Interviews are usually conducted face to face, by mail, telephone or online and typically involve participants responding to a series of questions. Face-to-face or personal interviews require that the interviewer physically meet with the respondent to conduct the interview. Generally, a structured questionnaire will be used for the interview, requiring participants to respond verbally to a list of prepared questions. Respondents' answers are recorded by the interviewer. A key advantage of personal interviews is the interviewer's ability to probe, i.e. to seek further clarification of the respondent. The information generated from personal interviews is, therefore, likely to be richer and more valuable to the international marketing researcher. In personal interviews, a skilled interviewer will also be able to assess respondents' non-verbal cues such as agitation or boredom and adjust her interviewing technique accordingly. Face-to-face interviews are, however, expensive and time-consuming. Interviewers must be trained and supervised and travel to meet with respondents is often required. In some countries, face-to-face interviews with women may only be possible if female interviewers are utilized. The international marketing researcher must be sensitive to such nuances of culture if the project is to be successful.

With mail surveys, travel is not required and the researcher is, therefore, able to reach a wider pool of potential respondents. With mail surveys, participants are required to read and respond directly to the questions asked and return the completed questionnaire to the researcher. It is usual to provide respondents with a stamped self-addressed envelope for this purpose. Unlike personal interviews, the researcher does not have the option of probing respondents to clarify or expand on the answers they have provided. The data generated are, therefore, not as rich. Mail surveys are generally cheaper to administer than face-to-face interviews but the response rate is usually much lower. Mail surveys are, of course, of limited value in countries with high levels of illiteracy and the researcher may have little choice but to conduct the interviews face to face or via telephone.

With telephone interviews, the interviewer will read the questions to the respondent and note the answers. With telephone surveys, the interviewer has the option of probing for additional information but does not have the option of using visual cues such as samples, pictures of the product, charts or graphs. Depending on the nature of the research project, this may be a serious limitation. Response rates for telephone surveys are usually fairly low and telephone service in some countries may be less than reliable, limiting the usefulness of the approach. As with personal interviews, it is also necessary to hire and properly train enumerators who, of course, should be fluent in the language in which the interviews are being conducted. Telephone surveys are, however, relatively inexpensive to administer. The same is true of Internet-based surveys. With this latter approach, the researcher uses an online questionnaire to solicit responses from participants. Respondents are generally sent an email which contains a link to the survey or they may encounter the link while visiting the company's website. As with mail surveys, the researcher does not have the ability to probe respondents to expand on their answers and use of the approach is certainly limited by the degree of Internet penetration in the country. Response rates to online surveys are generally low but the technology does allow for the use of rich media such as videos and animation which, depending on the project, may make this approach more attractive for the researcher. Box 6.2 offers some additional tips for conducting interviews in foreign countries.

Questionnaire development

Regardless of the survey technique that is being used, the researcher will usually be required to develop some type of a questionnaire or other measurement instrument. If using a questionnaire, the researcher must give considerable attention to its **format**. Questionnaires may

Box 6.2

Tips for conducting interviews in foreign countries:

- Your respondents may be confused or even insulted if your pronunciation of names, countries and cities is not accurate. Learn the proper pronunciation and do some practice before conducting the interview.

- Respondents need to know why you wish to interview them and how you plan to use the information. Let respondents know your objectives in conducting the research before you begin asking questions. Ask your questions in a clear and concise manner, avoiding the use of jargon, slang and technical terms. Remember that these may have a different meaning in other cultures or may not be understood at all.

- Don't attempt to become too personal with respondents too quickly. Let them decide when they are comfortable enough to engage in discussions of a more personal nature.

- Observe your interviewees' body language as this will offer important clues to how they are responding to your questions. Feelings such as boredom, suspicion or impatience are often manifested in an individual's body language. Note that body language is considered more significant in some cultures, such as Greece and Italy, than others.

- You may be conducting the interview in a language that is not the respondent's first language. In such situations, you will need to pace your speech in order to facilitate understanding.

- You should be aware that in some societies age, rank and title will be more important than in other societies. These views need to be respected. In some circumstances, you may need to present yourself as a peer or equal in order to obtain an audience.

Source

Adapted from Exportsource.ca (n.d.) Conducting Interviews in Foreign Markets. Available at: http://export-source.ca/gol/exportsource/site.nsf/en/es02793.html, accessed June 17, 2013.

Expand Your Knowledge

Ilieva, J., Baron, S. and Healey, N.M. (2002) 'Online surveys in marketing research: Pros and cons', *International Journal of Market Research*, 44, 3: 363–82.

This article examines the use of multimode strategies of data collection that may be useful in international marketing research. These strategies include the combined use of web-based, email and mail techniques and are proposed to circumvent the problem of low Internet penetration in some countries.

be **structured** or **unstructured**. Unstructured or open-ended questionnaires do not have predetermined answers from which respondents choose but require respondents to formulate their own answers to the questions posed. Unstructured questionnaires, therefore, provide respondents with considerable latitude to interpret the question and provide an answer. Structured questionnaires, on the other hand, provide respondents with a predetermined set of answers from which a choice is made. Unstructured questionnaires provide the researcher with richer and more in-depth information as respondents are able to elaborate on their answers. Responses to unstructured questionnaires are, however, more difficult to code and analyze. Also, in terms of format, the researcher needs to make a decision with respect to whether questions should be asked directly or indirectly. In Russia, for example, decades of communist rule have made individuals extremely suspicious of surveys. Also, some topics such as personal income may be considered too sensitive to be asked directly. In the case of questions regarding income, the researcher is well advised to present the respondent with a range of income levels from which she would select the one within which her income falls.

Box 6.3

In conducting global marketing research, it is important that the firm be provided with robust results. To accomplish this, the instruments used to collect the data must be both **valid** and **reliable**. Both of these concepts are important to the measurement of variables of interest. The measurement instruments used, such as multi-item scales, must be evaluated for both reliability and validity in the cultural context in which they are to be used. The term reliability means that if the instrument were to be used repeatedly to measure the same phenomenon, under the same conditions, similar results would be observed on each occasion. It is important to emphasize that conditions should be the same. An instrument that performs well in Asia may not perform satisfactorily in Eastern Europe or Africa.

Validity is a different concept. The researcher needs to be aware that there are various types of validity. Construct validity means that the phenomenon that the researcher sets out to measure (such as consumer attitudes towards counterfeit products or the degree of consumer ethnocentricity) has in fact been measured by the instrument used. Construct validity has several sub-types – convergent validity, discriminant validity and nomological validity. If the construct is measured in two different ways and the same result is obtained, then convergent validity has been established. For the global marketing researcher, convergent validity could be established by measuring the construct in two different ways in each of the countries being evaluated and testing the correlations between them. If the correlation coefficient is not significant, then convergent validity has not been established. If the correlations in two different countries are significantly different from zero and significantly different from each other, then the degree of convergent validity in the country with the lower correlation is suspect. Discriminant validity is also a sub-type of construct validity and refers to whether or not the specific concept is different from other concepts. Discriminant validity is established only if two concepts that theoretically should be unrelated are in fact found to be unrelated. In international marketing research, this means that the correlations should be insignificant in all the countries where the construct is measured. Nomological validity refers to whether the construct to be measured is related to some other external criterion. For example, in assessing the nomological validity of the GETSCALE in measuring the degree of consumer ethnocentrism, it was necessary to assess the correlation with external criteria such as ownership of foreign products. Of course, in using this approach in multi-country research projects, the external criteria must be available in each country and must have the same meaning.

Both reliability and validity are important. A measurement instrument can be reliable yet not valid, but it is impossible for an unreliable measurement instrument to be valid. Also, as noted previously, a measurement instrument that is shown to be reliable and valid in one culture may be unreliable and invalid in another culture, i.e. context matters.

Source

Craig, C.S. and Douglas, S.P. (2005) *International Marketing Research*, 3rd edn. Chichester: Wiley.

Apart from the questionnaire format, the researcher also needs to consider the *content* of the questions. The major consideration here is that the questions are not outside the respondent's range of experience. An employee at a supermarket responsible for restocking the shelves may not be the best individual to answer questions about the company's corporate strategies or financial strength. Such an employee, however, may be very well positioned to comment on the rate of inventory turnover of the major brands carried.

Question **wording** is also an important consideration. It is imperative that the wording of the questions is not ambiguous. Questions should be worded clearly and succinctly and leave little room for multiple interpretations. This is particularly important in the case of mail and Internet-based surveys where the researcher is not readily available to provide feedback and clarification. It is equally important that the international marketing researcher does not include **leading** questions, i.e. questions which contain embedded assumptions and lead the respondent in a particular direction.

In many international marketing projects, there will be a need to translate the questionnaire before it can be used in the foreign country. In this regard, the best approach to use is termed **translation-back-translation**, which was discussed in Chapter 2. With this method, the original text is translated from, say, English to Mandarin by one professional translator. The text, now in Mandarin, is then translated back into English by a different professional translator. The two English versions of the questionnaire are then compared and any differences noted. Significant differences in the two English versions point to problems with the translation which need to be resolved.

In order to alert the researcher to potential problems with the format of the questionnaire, it is recommended that a **pre-test** be conducted. With a pre-test, the questionnaire is administered to a sub-sample of respondents in advance of conducting the actual survey. Responses are analyzed to determine whether or not questions were correctly interpreted and if there were problems with the content or wording. It is advisable that the respondents selected for the pre-test be drawn from the pool of individuals to be surveyed and that the method of contact be the same as that to be used in the actual survey. In other words, if the survey is to be conducted via telephone then this should be the contact method used in the pre-test. Also, individuals selected for the pre-test should be excluded from the population of respondents to be contacted for the actual survey.

Sampling methodology

It is unlikely that the researcher will be able to interview each and every individual in the population of potential respondents. Time and budget constraints will usually preclude this. There may be thousands of consumers of the firm's products located in dozens of countries or there may be hundreds of retailers or other channel members scattered across several continents. It is, therefore, important for the researcher to select a **sample** of respondents from the total population. The process begins with the development of a **sampling frame,** i.e. a listing of all the potential respondents to the survey. In international marketing research, this often presents a problem. In some countries, even basic sampling frames such as telephone directories may be unavailable or too out of date to be useful. However, depending on the unit of analysis and the nature of the project, development of a sampling frame may not be a major constraint. Government ministries may have current lists of agricultural producers or industrial manufacturers in the country, disaggregated by region within the country. Lists of small and medium-sized businesses may similarly be available along with trade and industry associations. Having developed the sampling frame, the researcher must next select a representative sample of respondents from the list. In order to ensure that various sub-groups such as women or older consumers are represented, it may be necessary to first stratify the population before the sample is drawn. In drawing the sample, the researcher may use either **probability-based** or **non-probability-based** techniques. With probability-based sampling, the chance of any individual being included in the sample is known in advance, whereas with non-probability-based sampling this is not the case. If the researcher is unable to construct an appropriate sampling frame, there may be little choice but to utilize non-probability sampling techniques. The researcher must also make a decision with respect to the **size** of the sample. There is a trade-off involved. The larger the sample selected, the more closely it will represent the total population. However, the larger the sample chosen, the greater will be the cost of data collection and analysis. One may argue that a relatively small sample would be acceptable for research projects that are purely exploratory and not designed to support major investments on the part of the company. On the other hand, the researcher may opt for a larger sample (and more accurate results) if the firm is to commit significant financial resources based on the findings of the study. Statistical formulas to determine the sample size are available but these generally require knowledge of the population variance. However, this parameter is usually not known, leading researchers to simply utilize the amount of the available budget and the cost per interview to determine the size of the sample to be used.

Select data analysis technique

The international marketing researcher has available a number of analytical techniques that may be brought to bear on the research problem under consideration. The choice of analytical technique will be driven by a number of considerations such as the nature of the research problem the study is attempting to address, as well as the type and quality of the data collected. Some of the more common analytical approaches used include cross-tabulation, t-tests, cluster analysis, multiple regression and factor analysis. In many situations, the company would be interested in predicting the future direction of the foreign market. This would require the researcher to use available data to make forward-looking statements with respect to the overall growth of the market or the company's future sales and market share. Several techniques such as lead-lag analysis are available to accomplish this.

DATA COLLECTION

Having completed the research design, the next step in the process is the actual collection of the data (see Figure 6.6). A key consideration here, of course, is ensuring that the data collected are of high quality. Enumerators need to be adequately trained and supervised, and the researcher is well advised to undertake a **realism check** to ensure that the data being collected are in fact consistent with what is known about the market. If, for example, channel checks reveal rapid movement of imported wines through retail outlets, yet only a few consumers interviewed indicate that they consume imported wine, that should be sufficient reason for the researcher to stop and re-evaluate the data collection process (and perhaps aspects of the research design).

FIGURE 6.6   Data Collection

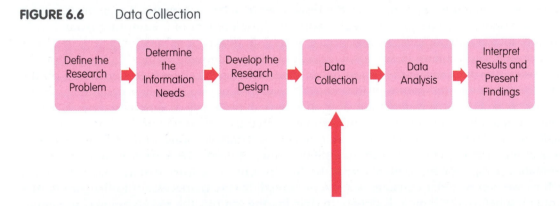

DATA ANALYSIS

Having completed the collection of good quality data, the researcher must next focus on the analysis (Figure 6.7). Decisions would already have been made on the particular analytical technique(s) to be used. There is little point in using sophisticated analytical techniques on poor quality data. The analytical approach used should, therefore, be consistent with the type and quality of the data collected and the overall objectives of the study.

FIGURE 6.7   Data Analysis

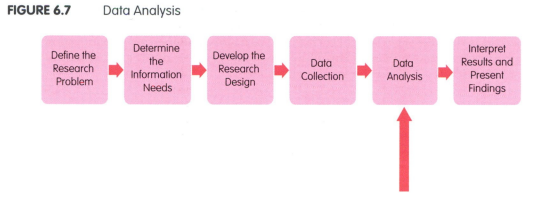

INTERPRET RESULTS AND PRESENT RESEARCH FINDINGS

The objective of international marketing research is to provide management with insights which will assist in making sound decisions. Having completed the research exercise, the international market researcher must also interpret the results and present the findings to senior management (Figure 6.8). While it is important to demonstrate that the research methodology was sound, it is equally important that the researcher be able to tease out the managerial implications of the findings and illustrate what they mean for the company. Ideally, the research should lead to the identification of two or three options for management to consider. If firm recommendations are made, then these need to be fully supported by the findings of the research project. The presentation should also demonstrate how it addressed each of the original research objectives and should identify any follow-up actions deemed to be appropriate.

FIGURE 6.8   Interpret Results and Present Findings

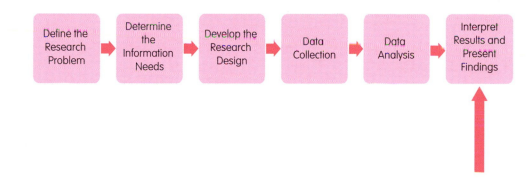

SUMMARY

This chapter has examined the international marketing research process. The term international marketing research was defined and how it differs from domestic marketing research was discussed. The point was made that the tools and techniques used in international marketing research and domestic marketing research are the same but that the environment or context within which they are applied is different. International marketing research is generally more complex because of these environmental differences. Despite this complexity, it was argued that it is imperative that firms invest in research prior to entering foreign markets. It was also pointed out that research should guide the firm's decisions in foreign markets, including those decisions related to product formulation, positioning, labelling and promotion. Failure to undertake the necessary research may lead to costly errors for the firm.

The importance of taking a systematic approach to international marketing research was also noted, and the chapter outlined a step-by-step process that may be followed by the international marketing researcher. This process begins with the clear identification of the research problem and proceeds through data collection, analysis and presentation of the research findings to the company's management.

? discussion questions

1. Define the term 'international marketing research' and explain how it differs from domestic marketing research.

2. How is international marketing research beneficial to the global marketer? Provide at least two examples to support your answer.

3. What is a focus group? What challenges may the international marketing researcher face when using focus groups in the Middle East?

4. What is translation-back-translation and why is it important in conducting international marketing research?

5. In conducting a survey of Russian consumers, an international marketing researcher included the following question: 'What was your income last year?' The response rate to this question was less than 3 percent. What could be the problem with the wording of that question and how would you ask it differently?

6. In conducting research in Australia for a US manufacturer of home appliances, a researcher opted to use a structured mail questionnaire. The first question on the questionnaire was: 'How often do you use your vacuum cleaner?' What do you see as the major problem with the wording of this question?

FURTHER READING

Craig, C.S. and Douglas, S.P. (2005) *International Marketing Research*, 3rd edn. Chichester: John Wiley & Sons.

This text provides an excellent treatment of the international marketing research process. It has become the de facto standard for courses in international marketing research.

Kumar, V. (2000) *International Marketing Research*. Upper Saddle River, NJ: Prentice-Hall.

This text covers the international marketing research process but in addition contains a number of chapters dealing with regional markets such as Asia-Pacific, the Middle East, Latin America and Europe.

Stevens, J. (2002) *Applied Multivariate Statistics for the Social Sciences*, 4th edn. Malwah, NJ: Lawrence Erlbaum.

This text provides a thorough foundation in the various analytical techniques normally encountered in international marketing research.

SELECTING FOREIGN MARKETS

INTRODUCTION

Companies of all sizes need to expand abroad in order to capitalize on growth opportunities which may exist beyond the confines of their national borders. Firms may face a limited domestic market for their products that results from a relatively small population size and/or low income levels. In some cases, the nature of the firm's products may dictate that it look beyond its domestic market for future sales and profits. Technology-intensive consumer electronic products, for example, fall into this category and require that the firm pursue international market opportunities. A firm may also opt to pursue an international market expansion strategy as an approach to combating a threat from a foreign competitor entering its domestic market. Whatever the motivation, once the firm has made a decision to expand abroad the need to answer a number of salient questions becomes apparent. Which foreign markets should be targeted? Should the firm enter a number of international markets simultaneously or gradually over time? Does the firm have the technical and managerial skills to be successful in the foreign markets selected? Does the firm have the marketing skill and brand positioning to be successful in the foreign markets selected?

Many companies have considerable experience in pursuing foreign markets. Major multinational companies such as Microsoft, Coca-Cola, General Electric, Royal Dutch Shell and Vodaphone Group have significant worldwide operations and considerable experience in operating in various countries. There are, however, a number of small and medium-sized firms with very limited or no exposure to international markets. These firms face a steep learning curve as they begin the market expansion process. Regardless of size, however, all firms would benefit from a thoughtful and systematic approach to selecting foreign markets.

Box 7.1

Firms may follow two broad internationalization strategies. The first is referred to as a **waterfall** strategy. With this approach, the company begins the internationalization process by establishing operations in a nearby country which is culturally similar and at the same level of economic development. Having understood this new market, the firm next moves to another developed country market before tackling more risky and culturally dissimilar markets. This approach gives the firm's management adequate time to learn the nuances of each market and become comfortable before tackling more challenging markets. The alternative is a **sprinkle**r strategy in which the firm enters a number of decidedly different markets at the same time or over a short period of time. Country selection is based on market potential and not psychic distance. With this approach, the firm's management does not have sufficient time to learn the intricacies of each market but must adjust to several new environments simultaneously. This is far more taxing on the resources of the firm but may be the preferred strategy if the firm has an innovative product and needs to maintain its first-mover advantage in markets around the world.

Source

Johansson, J. (2003) 'Global marketing: Research on foreign entry, local marketing, and global management', in B. Weitz and R. Wensley (eds) *Handbook of Marketing*. Thousand Oaks, CA: SAGE.

INTERNATIONALIZATION

The process by which firms become more engaged in international markets is referred to as **internationalization**. This process may be undertaken quickly with the firm pursuing operations in several different countries simultaneously or over a short period of time, or the process may be more gradual (see Box 7.1). Further, internationalization involves varying degrees of financial and other resource commitments to foreign markets. In going abroad, the firm must select a **mode of entry**, i.e. an institutional arrangement by which the firm will enter the foreign market. Modes of entry may vary from exporting, which requires little by way of resource commitment, to foreign direct investment which necessitates a much higher commitment level. These approaches are discussed in more detail in Chapter 8. Mode of entry is closely related to other aspects of the internationalization process such as country selection, which is discussed below.

MOTIVATION

One may identify two basic reasons for firm internationalization.[1] Firms may be **proactive**, i.e. they internationalize because they want to take advantage of opportunities existing outside their geographic boundaries. The company may, for example, have new products or technologies which appeal to a wide base of potential customers in countries around the world and the firm may wish to capitalize on this demand. Managerial urge is also a consideration, i.e. the management of the company is aggressive and has a strong desire to build a global operation. In some cases, internationalization may be motivated by the firm's drive to achieve greater profitability, either by tapping into new markets or by reducing

---

[1]   Czinkota, M., Ronkainen, I., Farrell, C. and McTavish, R. (2009) *Global Marketing: Foreign Entry, Market Development and Strategy Implementation*. Toronto: Nelson Education.

costs. The drive to tap into new markets is seen in the case of SAB Miller's $12.6 billion acquisition of Foster's. SAB Miller is the second largest player in the global beer industry but had a relatively weak position in Australia's high-margin premium beer segment. Foster's, an Australian brewery, controlled almost a 50 percent share of the total volume of beer consumed in Australia and offered SAB Miller an opportunity to tap into this premium segment of the Australian market. Although the Australian beer market is mature, the premium segment still offered relatively high growth rates and long-term potential.[2] Expansion into new foreign markets may also allow a manufacturing firm to engage in longer production runs, thereby achieving greater economies of scale and becoming more cost-competitive. In the above situations, the common thread is that the firm expands into new markets because it wants to and not because it has to.

In some cases, however, the firm may be **reactive**, i.e. it internationalizes because it has little choice. Companies which face mature or declining markets at home may be in such a position. Failure to expand abroad literally threatens the very survival of the organization. Companies may also be forced to internationalize as a means of countering a competitive threat from a foreign rival. The entry of a foreign competitor into a firm's domestic market may require that the firm expand abroad and take on the competitor on its own home turf. In this case, internationalization becomes a strategic move to counter a competitive threat, but one which would not have been made had the threat not materialized. Firms may also be forced to seek out markets abroad as their flagship products enter the maturity stage of the product life cycle. Internationalization in this case is seen as a strategy to squeeze incremental sales out of brands which have performed well in the domestic market but now face declining sales at home, perhaps due to the emergence of me-too products, shifts in consumer tastes and preferences or some other factor. By

FIGURE 7.1

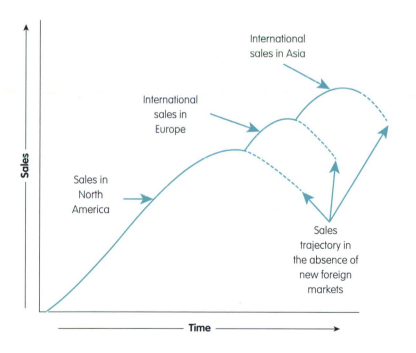

2   Euromonitor (2011) SABMiller Agrees Takeover Deal with Foster's. Analyst Insight from Euromonitor International. Available at: http://blog.euromonitor.com/2011/09/sabmiller-agrees-takeover-deal-with-fosters.html, accessed June 18, 2013.

introducing the product to a series of new foreign markets, the firm is able to maintain a growth trajectory (see Figure 7.1).

case study 7.1: Russian vodka

Russian vodka manufacturers are facing a major challenge. Sales of the spirit have been declining at home and manufacturers are facing intense global competition from a number of regional and international producers such as Diageo, Nemiroff and Ukraine's Soyuz-Victan. When measured by volume of consumption, the Russian vodka market is huge. In 2005, Russians consumed 1.8 billion liters of vodka but this volume is down significantly from previous years. Russians typically consume some 2 billion liters of vodka annually. In 2011, only 1.7 billion liters were consumed so the trend is decidedly negative for the domestic market. Faced with a weak home market, Russian vodka manufactures have begun to aggressively pursue new markets in North America and Western Europe. Breaking into these developed country markets is, however, likely to be difficult. Russian vodka producers have historically done well in markets within the Commonwealth of Independent States (CIS) and Israel. These markets are familiar. The new target markets in North America and Western Europe, while large and growing, are also far more competitive. Russian producers will have to identify and capitalize on the unique selling points of their products. Notions of heritage and a reputation for quality are characteristics that could be exploited. Parliament Vodka, for example, appeals to such features by drawing attention to its 18th-century production process that uses milk to remove unwanted particles, followed by a multistage purification procedure. While producing a better quality product, the process is complicated and expensive and, as a result, is not widely used in the industry. Other vodka manufacturers are attempting to exploit cultural associations in order to build market share in these new markets. Legend of Kremlin, for example, is produced in limited quantities and marketed in hand-decorated bottles by an offshoot of President Putin's administration. Russia is the spiritual home of vodka and manufacturers have the option of capitalizing on this perception in their efforts to win over western consumers.

Source

Adapted from Woodard, R. (2006) Russians Go West in Search of Vodka Gold. Available at: www.euromonitor.com/Articles.aspx?folder=Russians_go_west_in_search_of_vodka_gold&print=true, accessed July 29, 2006.

Discussion Questions

1. Are Russian vodka manufacturers correct to set their sights on North America and Western Europe in the face of declining sales and competition in their home market?
2. In targeting North American and European markets, should Russian vodka manufacturers position their products on quality and cultural associations?
3. If Russian vodka manufacturers are able to build market share in North America and Western Europe, what is the likely strategic response from the major international companies such as Diageo?

In some situations, poor production planning may force firms to consider foreign markets. As a result of overproduction, the firm may find itself with excess inventory which it is unable to move in the domestic market. In such a situation, overseas sales become a way for the company to bring supply and demand back into balance.

Proactive and reactive motivations may not completely explain the internationalization motives of all firms. Some firms have been described as being **born global**, i.e. they operate in a range of foreign countries almost from inception. Born-global firms are typically small, technology-driven companies whose firm-specific advantages are their innovative products. Because their products are innovative and revolutionary, these firms are highly motivated to exploit their first-mover advantage in markets around the world. Concern that competitors may soon follow with alternative technologies drives these firms towards rapid internationalization. Born-global firms also rely heavily on their network of alliances and affiliates around the world to enter a number of disparate foreign markets at the same time.[3]

Expand Your Knowledge

Knight, G. and Cavusgil, S.T. (1996) 'The born global firm: A challenge to traditional internationalization theory', in S. Cavusgil and T. Madsen (eds) *Advances in International Marketing*, Vol. 8. Greenwich, CT: JAI Press, pp. 11–26.

This is a classic article on born-global firms.

THEORIES OF INTERNATIONALIZATION

Several theories have been advanced to explain the internationalization behavior of the firm. These theories have attempted to explain the rationale for firm internationalization, as well as the pattern of internationalization.

THE UPPSALA MODEL

One theory of internationalization, termed the Uppsala or U model, posits that the firm's experiential knowledge is the major driver of its pattern of internationalization.[4] A lack of knowledge of foreign markets, in essence, inhibits the firm's internationalization and results in an incremental approach being adopted. According to this theory, the firm will first expand to a psychically close market and, having become familiar with that market, will target slightly more 'distant' markets.[5] One would, therefore, expect the firm to first expand to neighboring countries which are similar to its home country before tackling markets further afield. The Uppsala model also suggests that firms will deepen their commitment to foreign markets as they internationalize. As illustrated in Figure 7.2, firms will progress from exporting to the establishment of a foreign sales subsidiary, then on to foreign assembly and finally foreign production. These modes of entry are discussed in more detail in Chapter 8. Each of the five stages represents a greater level of commitment to the foreign market. Exporting requires the least commitment of financial and other firm

[3] Johansson, J.K. (2003) 'Global marketing: Research on foreign entry – Local marketing, global management', in B. Weitz and R. Wensley (eds) *Handbook of Marketing*. London: SAGE.

[4] Johanson, J. and Vahlne, J.-E. (1990) 'The mechanism of internationalization', *International Marketing Review*, 4: 11–24.

[5] Ellis, P. (2008) 'Does psychic distance moderate the market size–entry sequence relationship?', *Journal of International Business Studies*, 39, 3: 351–69.

FIGURE 7.2   Stages in the Process of Internationalization

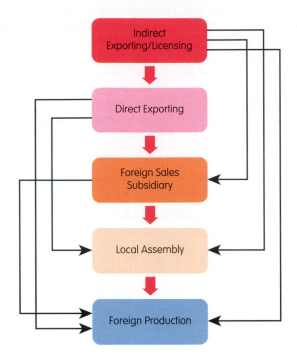

resources, while foreign production requires a significant degree of commitment on the part of the firm.

The Uppsala model has been criticized for its linear approach to the internationalization process.[6] There is evidence that firms may leapfrog or skip stages, moving, for example, from direct exporting to foreign production, bypassing the intermediate steps of establishing a foreign sales subsidiary and local assembly. The model has also been criticized for seeming to ignore so-called 'born-globals', i.e. firms discussed above which internationalize soon after their birth and at a more rapid pace than would be suggested by the theory. In some cases, firms have also been observed to enter foreign markets in a pattern that does not appear to be driven by psychic distance. Research has also shown that firms may progress through some of the stages but then exit the market altogether, only to re-enter using a lower commitment entry mode. This again does not accord well with the U model.

DUNNING'S OLI FRAMEWORK

Another theory of internationalization which is often cited is Dunning's OLI framework.[7] This theory, which was discussed in Chapter 5, argues that firms expand abroad to capitalize on ownership, location and internalization advantages. Ownership of foreign assets will confer on the firm a competitive advantage in the foreign market which is not enjoyed by competing firms that do not own such assets. The firm is, therefore, driven to expand abroad and attempt to own and control such strategic assets. Firms may also pursue investments outside their geographic borders in order to secure location advantages. These location advantages may be in terms of tax or other investment incentives offered

---

[6]   Johanson, J. and Vahlne, J.-K. (2009) 'The Uppsala internationalization process model revisited: From liability of foreignness to liability of outsidership', *Journal of International Business Studies*, 40: 1411–31.

[7]   Dunning, J.H. (2003) 'Some antecedents of internalization theory', *Journal of International Business Studies*, 34: 108–15.

by the government of the host country or a more favorable industrial relations climate for the firm's operations. Of course, low wages and other cheap local inputs may also confer location-specific advantages on the firm. According to the OLI framework, a company may also expand abroad if such expansion allows it to internalize its **firm-specific advantages** such as a new technology. In other words, the firm has a choice of either operating directly in the foreign market to exploit its own technology or other competitive advantage, or licensing that technology to a firm in the foreign market. By operating in the foreign country directly, the firm internalizes the benefits of its technology. According to transactions cost economics, the firm will choose this option only if it minimizes total transactions cost. If not, the firm will license its technology or make use of third-party, contract manufacturing services to enter the market.

THE 'SPRINGBOARD' OR 'LATECOMER' PERSPECTIVE

The Uppsala and OLI models presented above were advanced to better understand the internationalization behavior of firms from more developed countries. They do not, however, adequately explain the behavior of emerging market multinational firms (Parmentola, 2011).[8] Multinational firms from countries such as China and Brazil are not observed, for example, to pursue a gradualist approach to foreign market expansion. They do not first move to countries which are psychically close before expanding to more distant countries. The Uppsala model does not fit well the pattern of internationalization of these companies. In many cases, these firms also don't have superior technologies or world-class brands, as would MNCs from the developed world, and have little by way of firm-specific advantages to internalize. The OLI framework, therefore, does not do a particularly good job of explaining the internationalization pattern of these companies.

The springboard or latecomer perspective has been specifically proposed to explain the behavior of multinational companies from emerging markets.[9] This theory argues that emerging market firms internalize in order to overcome limitations inherent in their home-country environment, such as small market size, institutional immaturity or a relatively unsophisticated consumer base. These firms accomplish this by aggressively acquiring strategic assets from MNCs in developed countries. The internationalization strategies of multinationals from emerging markets will be discussed in greater detail in Chapter 14.

FOREIGN MARKET SELECTION

Expansion into foreign markets requires that the firm assess the market potential of a number of countries. Due to resource constraints, it is impossible for a company to operate in all countries of the world simultaneously. Further, not all countries possess the market characteristics which make for profitable operation. Firms must, of necessity, make decisions regarding which countries to target and which to avoid. Indeed, even large multinational companies such as McDonald's and Coca-Cola do not attempt to operate in every country in the world (Rugman and Verbeke, 2004).[10] The global marketing manager must, therefore, make decisions with respect to country selection. To accomplish this task, it is advisable to

---

[8] Parmentola, A. (2011) 'The internationalization strategy of new Chinese multinationals: Determinants and evolution', *International Journal of Management*, 28, 1: 369–95.

[9] Luo, Y. and Tung, R. (2007) 'International expansion of emerging market enterprises: A springboard perspective', *Journal of International Business Studies*, 38, 4: 481–98.

[10] Rugman, A. and Verbeke, A. (2004) 'A perspective on regional and global strategies of multinational enterprises', *Journal of International Business Studies*, 35, 1: 3–18.

adopt a step-by-step, systematic approach. Such an approach involves the establishment of long-term objectives for what the firm is attempting to accomplish in the market, as well as thorough research on a broad selection of potential target countries. The global marketing manager must be able to justify the selection of one country over other potential candidates which are ultimately not selected for entry. It is also important that the firm examine its own resources and capabilities to ensure a proper fit with the country selected. While a systematic approach to country selection may be expected to yield superior results, companies tend to rely on more intuitive ad hoc approaches (Papadopoulos et al., 2011).[11]

It should be emphasized that country market selection is an extremely important decision for the firm.[12] Pursuing international markets is expensive and the financial consequences of poor country selection may be severely negative for the company. There is also the opportunity cost associated with resources that could have been better deployed in consolidating the firm's market position at home, or in penetrating foreign markets that are a better fit for the company. In the case of firms that are new to international marketing, there may also be a psychological cost if poor country selection leads to failure of the foreign market expansion effort. The company's managers may become turned off international marketing altogether with the attendant lost market opportunities. Country market selection may also be expected to have ripple effects throughout the entire organization from production planning to finance and human resource management. The firm will have to adapt its business practices in these and other areas to the new countries in which it will operate. Poor country selection will have implications for all of these areas of the firm's operation.

Distance is a major driver of the country selection process. Cultural distance or, more broadly, psychic distance is clearly an important consideration, as discussed above. If a firm's business model has been successful in its home country, the model is likely to also prove successful when used in a psychically close host country. Much of what the firm has learned at home will still be relevant in the new environment. The smaller the cultural distance between the home and host countries, the more likely it is that the firm will be successful in the new environment.

STEPS IN COUNTRY SELECTION

As illustrated in Figure 7.3, there are four steps in the country selection process. The first step in the process is termed **macro segmentation**. The objective at this stage is to develop and apply segmentation criteria which allow the marketing manager to screen a large number of potential candidate countries. With over 200 countries in the world, this first step is designed to quickly weed out a significant number of countries from further consideration.

The global marketing manager may, for example, be focused on penetrating the Latin American market. Given that there are over 20 countries in this region, it may not be feasible or desirable for the company to establish a presence in all of them. The global marketing manager may, however, develop macro-segmentation criteria to group member countries into defined clusters. Of course, the criteria selected must be actionable and measureable to be useful and the segments formed must be homogeneous within and heterogeneous between. A commitment to democratic government may be one such criterion, allowing the firm to screen out those countries, such as Cuba and Venezuela, with left-leaning governments.

The next step in the process is preliminary or **fine-grained screening**. This second step involves a further screening of those Latin American countries with democratic governments. At this stage, the global marketing manager develops a second set of criteria to further reduce

---

[11]   Papadopoulos, N., Malhotra, S. and Martin, O. (2011) 'International market selection and assessment', in T.J. Wilkinson (ed.) *International Business in the 21st Century*, Vol. 1. Westport, CT: Praeger, Chapter 10.

[12]   Papadopoulos et al. (2011) op cit.

FIGURE 7.3   Steps in the Country Selection Process

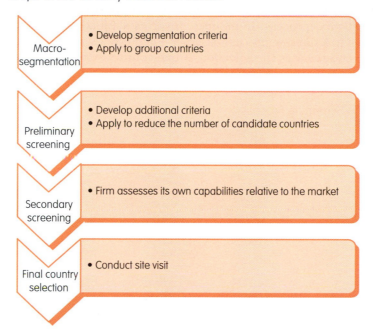

Macro-segmentation
- Develop segmentation criteria
- Apply to group countries

Preliminary screening
- Develop additional criteria
- Apply to reduce the number of candidate countries

Secondary screening
- Firm assesses its own capabilities relative to the market

Final country selection
- Conduct site visit

the number of candidate countries to a more manageable number. Criteria at this stage may include economic growth rates, population or income per capita. The use of economic growth rates, for example, may lead to a screening in of countries such as Argentina, Peru and Chile but the screening out of countries such as Belize. In essence, countries with above-average growth rates, as measured by GDP per capita, are screened in and those below the average screened out. Depending on the nature of the product, population size may be the key decision-making criterion at this stage, with the firm targeting those countries with the greatest populations. This would lead to countries such as Brazil and Mexico being screened in but less populous countries such as Costa Rica and Uruguay being screened out. Similarly, if high income is a key consideration, then more emphasis may be placed on income per capita as the screening criterion. Cluster analysis, which was mentioned in the preceding chapter, may be a useful tool for this exercise if the firm is considering a large number of candidate countries. Fine-grained screening should result in the selection of 2–3 countries for deeper consideration.

The third step in the country selection process is **secondary screening**. At this stage, the firm attempts to assess whether its capabilities fit with the country markets identified in Step 2. Firm capabilities may need to be assessed in a number of areas such as marketing ability, product quality and innovation, financial strength, brand image and the firm's strengths in the areas of product support and customer service. If, for example, consumers in the markets under consideration are sophisticated and demanding but the firm's products are not world class, there may be little point in attempting to enter those markets. In this step, the global marketing manager is attempting to match the characteristics of the country with the capabilities of the company. This step will further reduce the number of countries under consideration.

The fourth step in the process is **final country selection**. Up to this point, the global marketing manager has relied on secondary data in developing a shortlist of candidate countries. In the fourth step, the global marketing manager is advised to corroborate these data by conducting a site visit to the one or two countries that remain on the shortlist. A site visit will provide an opportunity for the company to meet with channel intermediaries, assess local competitors first hand and speak to government regulators as well as industry association representatives. This step in the process is the most costly but is only performed on a small number of countries. A final decision to enter a country should not be made until a site visit has been conducted and the results are deemed to be supportive of the firm's strategy.

The country selection process, in essence, involves subjecting countries in a region or grouping of interest to a filtering process based on established screening criteria, as illustrated in Figure 7.4. The end result is the selection of one country which the firm targets.

FIGURE 7.4   The Screening Process

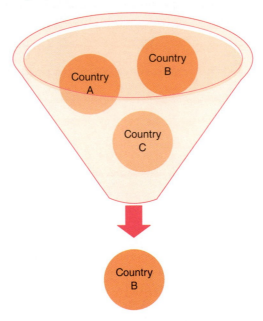

INTERNATIONAL CONSUMER SEGMENTATION

The selection of foreign markets is often more complicated than choosing a single target country. In some situations, there may be consumers who, because of their similarities, comprise a single segment but who reside in different countries. Consumers in cross-national segments may have more in common with their counterparts in other countries than they do with citizens of their own countries. Papadopoulos, Malhotra and Martin (2011) point to examples where formerly contiguous countries have been divided by artificial geo-political boundaries due to wars or other reasons, or where individuals may live in different countries but share a common set of psychographic or other characteristics. As an example, Goth youth, irrespective of country of residence, share more in common with each other than with other youth from their own countries. The above suggests that the country may not necessarily be the most appropriate unit of analysis but that micro-segmentation approaches involving the use of psychographic or behavioral dimensions would also provide useful insights.

Following this reasoning, researchers have proposed a two-stage model that combines country-level screening with screening at the consumer level (Figure 7.5). The model has been applied to the European market. In stage 1, market attractiveness was measured using market size and each country's level of economic development. In stage 2 of the model, the focus is on micro segmentation, i.e. on finding clusters of consumers across Europe who share a fairly common set of values. Consumer behavior is related to values so the clusters formed will be useful in the development of marketing strategies for the European market. Inglehart's value system measures society's shift from survival to self-expression values and from traditional to secular-rational values. This system was used in the micro-segmentation stage to identify clusters of European consumers with similar values.

FIGURE 7.5   A Two-stage Model of International Market Selection

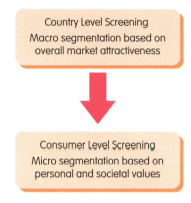

Source: Adapted from Gaston-Breton, C. and Martin, O. M. (2011) International market selection and segmentation: a two-stage model, *International Marketing Review*, 28, 3: 267–90.

Macro segmentation identified three clusters of countries based on overall market attractiveness. In the first cluster were France, Germany, Italy, Spain and the UK – five large and developed economies. In the second cluster were eight countries: Austria, Belgium, Denmark, Finland, Luxembourg, Ireland, Sweden and the Netherlands, which scored well in terms of market development but were found to be less attractive based on market size. The third cluster consisted of 14 countries that were less attractive both in terms of market size and development. Considering the most attractive cluster, the researchers used micro segmentation to further subdivide the top five countries based on values. It was found that France, Italy and Spain could be grouped together based on their value systems and that Germany and the UK formed their own individual micro clusters, representing the high and low ends of the value scales.

FIGURE 7.6   Macro-segmentation: Countries' factor scores

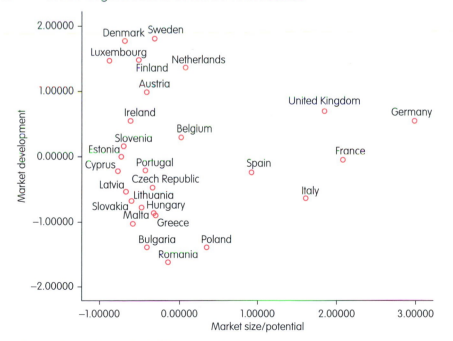

Source: Gaston-Breton, C. and Martin, O. M. (2011) International Market selection and segmentation: a two-stage model, *International Marketing Review*, 28, 3: 277

FIGURE 7.7   Value orientation of the first cluster of most attractive European countries

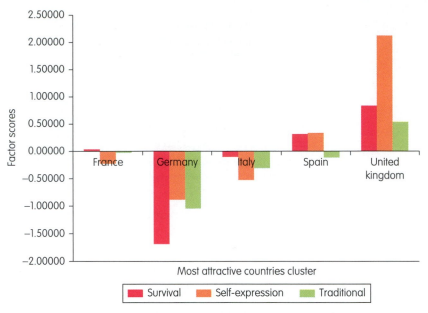

Source: Gaston-Breton, C. and Martin, O. M. (2011) International Market selection and segmentation: a two-stage model, *International Marketing Review*, 28, 3: 281

Spotlight on Research 7.1   International Market Selection

Alexander, Rhodes and Myers (2011) take up the issue of international market selection in an article published in *International Marketing Review*. The authors focus their attention on retailing companies given their important role in the marketing and distribution of goods internationally. They note that while the extant literature is well developed, addressing issues such as the reasons for retail internationalization, little attention has been paid to international market selection. The authors seek to shed light on the relationship between international retail organizations and the foreign markets which they opt to penetrate. They point out that much of the international retailing literature has relied on general observations of retailers' actions, and they conclude that retail managers expand their operations into geographically and culturally similar markets before tackling more challenging ones. Some researchers have, however, argued that the truth may not be quite so simple. Work by Godley and Fletcher (2000), for example, points to the importance of purchasing power in the host country as a major driver of retail internationalization. This view is supported by Gripsrud and Benito (2005) who argue that, unlike manufacturing, international retail activity is driven more by demand factors than by the need to exploit location-based advantages. From their assessment of the literature, Alexander et al. (2011) argue that there is a need to reconcile the issue of cultural versus geographic influences on international retail expansion. There is also a need to better understand the importance of host-country market growth and home-country market size on international expansion activities and market selection decisions.

Hypotheses

Alexander, Rhodes and Myers (2011) test the following hypotheses:

H1. The level of international retail activity will be greater than the largest size of the home and host markets, though moderated by a measure of distance between those markets.

H2. The retail structural development of the home market will positively affect the level of international retail activity based in that market.

H3. The retail structural development of the host market will negatively affect the level of international retail activity based in that market.

H4. Purchasing power within a host market will positively influence international retailers' market selection decisions.

H5. Euro membership by both home and host economies will positively affect international retailers' investment in the host country.

H6. Shared language skills in the home and host markets will positively affect market selection decisions.

H7. Cultural affinity between the home and host markets will positively influence international retailers' market selection decisions.

Method

In this research, the authors consider Eastern European markets as the host markets and choose the markets of Western Europe as the home markets. Data are drawn from 13 Western European countries and ten Eastern European countries with international retailing activity. Data are cross-sectional for the period 2002–2003 and are sourced from existing Mintel databases of European retail activity, national statistics offices, the European Commission's published data and Hofstede (1980). Distance between markets are calculated as the distance between country capitals, using Apple maps. The authors utilize a gravity model in hypothesis testing. In order to test H1, a gravity measure is constructed (Grav11) as the product of home- and host-country GDP divided by the distance between the country capitals. Three other gravity measures were constructed but were rejected in favor of Grav11. Other independent variables are: Home-country retail businesses (Hmrbu); Home-country retail businesses per capita (Hmrbupc); Host-country retail businesses (Hsrbu); Host-country retail businesses per capita (Hsrbupc); Host-country retail sales per capita (Hsrspc); Euro membership – value 1 if both home and host countries are members or imminent members of the euro, else 0 (Euro); Home language – (the sum of) the percentage of the population that speaks each of the European languages (Hlang); Host language – (the sum of) the percentage of the population that speaks each of the European languages (Slang); and a single 'traditional' measure derived from the sum of the squared cultural distances (Hofst). The dependent variable is the number of operations established in each host country by firms from each home country (Operat).

The model is specified as follows:

$$Operat_{ij} = \alpha + \beta_1 Grav11 + \beta_2 Hmrbupc + \beta_3 Hmrbu + \beta_4 Hsrbupc + \beta_5 Hsrbu + \beta_6 Hsrspc + \beta_7 Euro + \beta_8 Hlang + \beta_9 Slang + \varepsilon_{ij}$$

Results

The authors find support for three of the hypotheses. H1 is supported as there is a positive relationship between Grav11 (i.e. home and host GDP are multiplied and then divided by the distance between markets) and the level of international retail activity between markets ($\beta = 0.228$, $\rho < 0.01$). Hypothesis H2 is also supported by the regression results. A greater number of home retail businesses (Hmrbu) has a positive impact on international retail activity ($\beta = 0.0000054$, $\rho < 0.01$), while a greater level of home retail businesses per capita has a negative impact on international retail activity ($\beta = -0.283$, $\rho < 0.01$). The authors argue that more developed retail markets will possess a lower number of retail businesses per capita, but also the larger the total number of retail businesses in the home country, the greater the potential source of international retail activity. The more developed the structure of the home market, the more international retail activity is generated from that market. The results do not support H3. The number of retail establishments in the host country does not have an impact on internationalization. H4 is, however, supported as the results indicate that retail sales per capita in the host country have a positive effect on the number of businesses in a host market ($\beta = 0.00141$, $\rho < 0.05$). Retailers clearly want to operate in markets with higher levels of spend per customer. In terms of

(Continued)

(Continued)

exchange rate stability, H5 is not supported by the regression results. The removal of exchange rate uncertainty (by the home and host countries sharing the same currency) does not seem to have any impact on the level of international retail activity. The coefficient on the dummy variable Euro is not significant. Shared language (Hlang and Slang) is also not significant and, therefore, H6 is not supported by the results of the above model. The authors do recognize, however, that, while important, language is only one element of culture. In order to better understand the impact of cultural similarity, a second model was developed and estimated using Hofstede's measures of cultural distance (Hofst) in addition to Hlang and Slang. When measured as the sum of squared distances, the cultural distance variable is found to be significant ($\beta = -0.00027$, $\rho < 0.05$).

Implications

According to the authors, the results presented above suggest that GDP creates the necessary organizational development and competition that push retailers to enter international markets. At the same time, retail spend per capita in the host country acts as a pulling force, drawing retailers into specific foreign markets. It is the combination of market structure and market visibility (retail spend) that drives firms to internationalize (see Figure 7.8). The authors go on to suggest that retail managers do not have the freedom of action implied in the marketing literature and that their actions are constrained by structural conditions in the market.

FIGURE 7.8   Controplual model

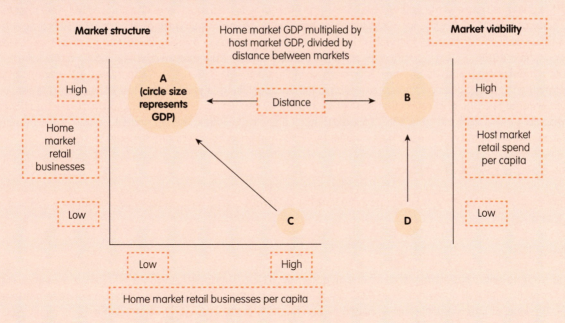

Sources

Alexander, N., Rhodes, M. and Myers, H. (2011) 'A gravitational model of international retail market selection', *International Marketing Review*, 28, 2: 183–200.

Godley, A. and Fletcher, S. (2000) 'Foreign entry into British retailing, 1850–1994', *International Marketing Review*, 17, 4/5: 392–400.

Gripsrud, G. and Benito, G. (2005) 'Internationalization in retailing: Modeling the pattern of foreign market entry', *Journal of Business Research*, 58, 12: 1672–80.

Hofstede, G. (1980) *Culture's Consequences: International Differences in Work Related Values*. Thousand Oaks, CA: SAGE.

Discussion Questions

Read the complete article by Alexander et al. (2011) and answer the following questions:

1. Do you believe the results of this research would change if one considered retailers from more culturally dissimilar markets? Using US retailers entering markets in Asia, how would you alter the research design to test your hypothesis?
2. Characteristics such as firm size, international experience and resource capability are ignored in this research. Do you believe that these firm-level factors are important drivers of retail internationalization? Why/why not? How would you test your hypothesis empirically?

SUMMARY

This chapter has examined the process of foreign market selection. The chapter first provided a discussion of the process of internationalization, including an examination of the multinational company's motivations for foreign market expansion. The point was made that firms are driven by either proactive or reactive motivations, i.e. internationalizing because they want to or because they have to. The steps in the process of internationalization were also presented, beginning with low commitment entry modes such as exporting and transitioning up to deeper commitment options such as foreign production. Various researchers have attempted to explain the process and pattern of internationalization and a number of their theories are presented in this chapter. These include Dunning's OLI framework and the Uppsala or U model that are most applicable to developed country multinationals. Also presented was the springboard model that its proponents argue is more applicable to multinationals from emerging countries such as China and India.

Chapter 7 also examined the issue of country selection. It was argued that even large multinational companies do not operate in all foreign countries simultaneously, nor would they necessarily want to, given the relative unattractiveness of some markets. The point was also made that the cost to the firm for incorrect country selection may be high and that companies are, therefore, well advised to utilize a systematic process. Such an approach was outlined in this chapter and involves use of a series of screening criteria to arrive at the selection of a final target country. It was also argued that the individual country may not be the most appropriate unit of analysis when selecting foreign markets, as the global marketing manager may wish to pursue international market segments that cut across geographic boundaries. An alternative two-stage model was, therefore, presented that involves screening at the country and customer levels. This latter approach allows the global marketer to arrive not only at a set of preferred country markets but also at customer segments that are consistent with the firm's marketing strategy.

 Real World Challenges

J Crew Targets Countries in Europe

Steve Johnson was quite proud of himself. As vice president for international marketing for J Crew, Steve had come in for quite a bit of praise at the company's flash pop-up in London. The temporary store had created the buzz he had hoped for and locating the pop-up on the campus of Central Saint Martin's – one of London's most prestigious art schools – was acknowledged as a stroke of genius. Steve felt confident

(Continued)

(Continued)

about his choice of the UK as the first country targeted in the firm's planned European expansion. He was, however, much less confident about the next European country to be targeted. With the recession sweeping across Europe, Steve had until now sidestepped Europe altogether and had instead launched in Asia, opening stores in Beijing and Hong Kong in association with Lane Crawford, a luxury department store. He had also orchestrated the opening of a store in Canada, located in the trendy Yorkdale Shopping Centre in Toronto.

J Crew is a US specialty retailer of fashionable men's, women's and children's clothing and accessories. The company was founded in 1983 and launched its first catalog in that year. The company would open its first retail outlet in New York some six years later and would take its first international steps with the opening of its Canadian store in 2011. In 2012, the firm launched its e-commerce website and began marketing its products in over 100 countries. Despite financial struggles in the early years, J Crew has managed to establish a credible reputation in the US market. The firm has partnered with top designers and counts First Lady Michelle Obama among its high-profile customers.

In light of his success with the London launch, Steve was invited to the company's board meeting to lay out his plans for international expansion. As he prepared for the meeting, Steve thought to himself, 'Why do we really need to expand abroad? What's really pushing us?' The USA still provided a lot of opportunities for expansion and the company was finally gaining some traction at home. J Crew was now associated with quality, luxury clothing at an affordable price. It was true that a number of J Crew's competitors were expanding internationally. For example, US brands such as Forever 21, Victoria's Secret and Abercrombie & Fitch were all establishing their presence in Europe. Steve had to admit that this was probably a strong motivation for foreign market expansion but he also knew that the process had to be managed correctly. After all, it wasn't that long ago that he had to recommend to his board of directors that J Crew withdraw from the Japanese market. The company simply wasn't ready for international expansion. At the height of the Japanese expansion program, J Crew operated some 69 stores. The stores were closed as they ran into financial trouble, and by 2009 the company had exited the Japanese market altogether. As one company spokesperson noted: 'It's not just a matter of going out and opening a store. You have to have the right real estate, the right partners and an organization to take on the work. We did not have the critical mass or the team to do that.'

Steve hoped that the UK market would be different. Although UK consumers are frugal, there were segments of that market willing to pay for quality and this is where J Crew would have to be positioned. The success in the UK of premium brands such as Whistles and Reiss gave Steve some comfort that its initial foray into Europe would be successful. He saw London as a testing ground before taking J Crew into continental Europe. Steve was committed to a gradual and very cautious approach to international expansion. It would, therefore, be an understatement to say that he was taken by surprise at the board meeting when a majority of the company's directors began calling for an aggressive expansion strategy. The board was not interested in pursuing Steve's gradual strategy; it wanted to see J Crew stores up and running in all major cities across Western Europe in the next 12 months. As he walked back to his office, Steve knew that he faced some tough decisions.

Sources

Cotterill, S. (2012) International Marketing: 'Hello, World', J Crew says, Via the Web, *Internet Retailer*. Available at: www.internetretailer.com/2012/06/27/hello-world-jcrew-says-web, accessed June 19, 2013.

Euromonitor.com (2013) Will Slow and Steady International Expansion Win the Race for J Crew? Analyst Insight from Euromonitor International. Available at: http://blog.euromonitor.com/2013/06/will-slow-and-steady-international-expansion-win-the-race-for-j-crew.html, accessed June 19, 2013.

Faulkner, R. (2011) J Crew Eyes International Expansion. Available at: www.drapersonline.com/news/j-crew-eyes-international-expansion/5027930, accessed June 19, 2013.

Jcrew.com (2013) About J Crew. Available at: www.jcrew.com/help/about_jcrew.jsp, accessed June 19, 2013.

Sgn-group.com (2011) J Crew Heads Overseas | SGN Group. Available at: http://sgn-group.com/fashion-news/j-crew-heads-overseas, accessed June 19, 2013.

Questions

1. State the problem that Steve Johnson faces.
2. Identify the options available to Steve. Be sure to identify more than one.
3. Based on the options identified above, recommend a course of action. Be sure to provide a rationale and make a decision.

? discussion questions

1. Motivation to internationalize may be described as proactive or reactive. Distinguish between these two, providing real-world examples to illustrate the differences.

2. Which of the theories discussed in this chapter best describes the internationalization process of emerging market multinational firms? What are the key features of this theory?

3. In foreign market expansion, the global marketing manager must make decisions with respect to which countries to target and which to avoid. List and discuss the four steps involved in country selection.

FURTHER READING

Dunning, J.H. (2003) 'Some antecedents of internalization theory', *Journal of International Business Studies*, 34: 108–15.

Ellis, P. (2008) 'Does psychic distance moderate the market size-entry sequence relationship?', *Journal of International Business Studies*, 39, 3: 351–69.

Johanson, J. and Vahlne, J.K. (2009) 'The Uppsala internationalization process model revisited: From liability of foreignness to liability of outsidership', *Journal of International Business Studies*, 40: 1411–31.

Luo, Y. and Tung, R. (2007) 'International expansion of emerging market enterprises: A springboard perspective', *Journal of International Business Studies*, 38, 4: 481–98.

ENTERING FOREIGN MARKETS

INTRODUCTION

Chapter 7 examined the issue of country selection. The global marketing manager, however, also has to contend with a related matter, i.e. how the firm should enter the foreign markets selected. Once the specific country market has been selected, the global marketer will be confronted with a series of related decisions such as: How will the firm expand abroad, via exporting or some other strategy? If it does expand abroad, how much control will it have over its products and marketing efforts? Can the firm afford to expand abroad? What would be the most cost-effective approach for it given the company's budget? How much risk will be involved in the approach selected for international market penetration? The global marketing manager has a number of options available in deciding how best to enter foreign markets. As we will note in this chapter, each approach is unique in terms of the associated risks, the degree of control afforded the global marketing firm and the costs involved in implementation. These approaches also represent differing levels of commitment to the foreign markets entered. The global marketing manager must understand the characteristics, advantages and disadvantages of each approach in order to make an informed decision. This is the focus of the present chapter.

ENTRY MODE SELECTION

Having identified a country deemed suitable for market entry, the next choice the global manager must make is the mode of entry. The term 'entry mode' was defined in the preceding chapter as the institutional arrangements firms employ to enter foreign markets. Mode of entry selection is an important aspect of the process of internationalization and a key determinant of its success. The global marketing manager has a number of options available, ranging from exporting to foreign direct investment. To some extent, the mode of entry decision is determined by the internationalization objectives of the firm. If the company, for example, is merely interested in exploring foreign markets, it is more likely to adopt a low commitment mode of entry such as exporting. On the other hand, if the firm is focused on developing a low-cost manufacturing capability to service its foreign markets, this implies the adoption of a high commitment entry mode, i.e. foreign direct investment. In general, entry modes may be categorized as **export modes**, **intermediate modes** or **hierarchical modes**. Export modes are low risk and low return and provide limited control for the exporting firm. Intermediate modes include international joint ventures and strategic alliances and involve a sharing of the risks and rewards of market entry commensurate with the share of ownership of each partner. Hierarchical entry modes involve the establishment of a wholly-owned subsidiary in the target country and provide the global marketer with complete control of the operation but also exposure to a higher level of risk.

EXPORTING

Exporting involves the manufacture of a product in one country and its sale in one or more foreign countries. The manufacturing firm typically retains the services of a market intermediary such as a distributor in the target country who assumes responsibility for the sale of the product in exchange for a commission. In some cases, the distributor will take title to the product, while in other cases the product remains the property of the manufacturer until sold to a retailer or final consumer. Exporting may be classified as being either **direct** or **indirect**. In the case of direct exporting, the manufacturing firm deals directly with an intermediary in the foreign market. With indirect exporting, the manufacturer transacts with an intermediary in its own home country and this intermediary in turn contracts with a distributor in the foreign market (see Figure 8.1). With indirect exporting, the manufacturer is not really engaged in a global marketing transaction as there is no direct contact with the foreign market. In essence, it is a domestic transaction.

Exporting carries several advantages for the firm. First, the process of exporting requires little by way of managerial skill or knowledge of the foreign market. The process is relatively straightforward and, because the foreign end of the transaction is handled by a local distributor, the manufacturer does not require in-depth knowledge of host-country import documentation or even a very sophisticated understanding of the foreign market. Exporting also carries with it minimal risk for the firm. Distribution agreements may be cancelled at any time with the requisite notice in advance, allowing the firm to quickly disengage from the foreign country if the

FIGURE 8.1   Direct and Indirect Exporting

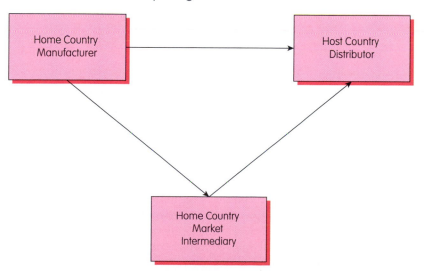

need arises. No employment contracts or long-term lease agreements need to be entered into. Further, relative to other modes of entry, exporting does not involve significant costs to the firm.

case study 8.1: GV snowshoes

GV Snowshoes was established in 1959 and is currently the world's only manufacturer of traditional, aluminum-framed and composite snowshoes. The company's mission is to give its customers the freedom to move through nature, gliding over fluffy white snow and traversing terrain that would otherwise be inaccessible wearing mere boots. An aboriginal company, GV Snowshoes makes an extensive line of both

PHOTO 8.1

traditionally crafted snowshoes and high-tech designs to meet the needs of both novices and experts. In 1982, the company consolidated the snowshoe manufacturing industry via a number of strategic acquisitions. According to the company's director of sales and marketing, exporting became a natural extension of the firm's strategy. The company, which is based in Quebec, Canada and maintains a staff of 50, has been exporting to the USA for over 20 years but has begun to tackle markets further afield, such as Finland, Switzerland, Germany and France. According to the company's director of marketing, the firm's export strategy is simple: 'We are a manufacturer, so the more we sell, the more we produce. We try to broaden our market so that we can manufacture snowshoes year-round even though our products

are designed for winter activities.' He goes on to add: 'Never give up. The rewards and experience you gain dealing with other countries are so great. Not only do you increase your volume of sales, the image and reputation of your company improves as well. But the most important reward is the personal knowledge and experience that you receive from each different country. It helps you understand different points of view that make you stronger to approach any other challenge.' It is clear that this company appreciates the advantages of exporting as a strategy for growth.

Source

GV Snowshoes (2006) Exporting Winter Fun. Available at: www.exportsource.ca/gol/exportsource/site.nsf/en/es02792.html, accessed November 11, 2006.

Discussion Question

1. Is exporting the appropriate mode of entry for GV Snowshoes? Why/why not?

Given the low risks associated with exporting, one would expect that returns will also be low relative to other entry mode options. This is in fact the case. Overall profitability will be lower than would be achieved had the firm opted, for example, to pursue foreign direct investment. The issue of control also needs to be considered. With this entry mode, the manufacturing firm exercises little control over how the product is positioned and sold in the foreign market. This may be an important consideration, particularly in the case of products with significant brand equity. Distributors may not always act in the best interest of the brand and may market the product through inappropriate channels or without adequate support. Also, as noted above, little knowledge of the foreign market is required to use exporting successfully as an entry mode. This, however, may also prove to be a disadvantage for the firm over the long term as there is little opportunity to develop a deep understanding of the foreign market. Should the firm wish to establish a deeper commitment to the foreign market, there will be little experiential knowledge to guide the decision.

case study 8.2: Gray's Pepper Products

Gray's Pepper Products has only 24 employees but is committed to the export market. Based in Jamaica, the firm manufactures and exports a line of its condiments – Gray's Hot Pepper Sauce, Gray's Spicy Sauce and Gray's Extra Hot Habanero Pepper Sauce – to Canada and the USA. Founded 30 years ago, the company now operates a modern, fully automated manufacturing facility with a capacity to process some one million peppers annually. This is a far cry from the early days when the founder of the company processed and bottled the peppers by hand. Gray's works with exclusive distributors in New Jersey and Toronto and has experienced increased export sales to North America which the company credits to these distributor relationships. The company notes, however, that visitors to the island of Jamaica are also another export channel. Tourists from North America and Europe have the opportunity to sample the company's products in the various hotels and resorts on the island. On their return home, they often contact the company to make arrangements to secure their own stash of the firm's fiery products.

Source

Jamaica Gleaner (2006) Gray's Pepper Products Ltd – A Pioneer in Export – Bringing Spice to Taste Buds across the Globe. Available at: www.jamaica-gleaner.com/gleaner/20060512/business/business4.html, accessed May 12, 2006.

PHOTO 8.2

Discussion Questions

1. How important is exclusivity in the distribution relationship to a company such as Gray's Pepper Products?
2. Does the company's reliance on distributors create any risks for the firm?

Types of intermediaries

Intermediaries are essential to the success of the exporting firm. Intermediaries may provide the firm with market intelligence and have typically established customer relationships in the target countries of interest to the firm. Intermediaries are generally also familiar with customs and import regulations in the countries they service and can essentially assume responsibility for those aspects of the export transaction. The exporting firm has a number of options available when selecting an intermediary. Manufacturers interested in indirect exporting may find themselves approached by an **export buying agent**. These agents are resident in the country of the manufacturer but work on behalf of a foreign buyer. An export buying agent essentially acts to source products in its country of residence for a foreign buyer and is paid a commission by the foreign purchaser. Alternatively, the manufacturer may use the services of an **export-import broker**. The role of a broker is simply to bring buyer and seller together. Brokers are specialist firms and have deep expertise in a relatively narrow range of product categories. They may be expected to have good knowledge of the market and the major players in the industry but take no part in the actual handling of the physical product. Brokers are paid a commission by the principal, which may be either the buyer or the seller.

An **export management company** (EMC) may provide the firm with a more comprehensive option for penetrating export markets. EMCs are domestic firms which act on behalf of a number of non-competing exporters. EMCs are generally small firms and have considerable expertise in the product categories they handle. Operationally, these intermediaries may either take title to the products they handle and market them internationally for their own account or they may act as agents. If purchasing for its own account, the EMC will negotiate with the manufacturer on a transaction by transaction basis and no exclusivity is implied in the relationship. The EMC does not have its own sales territory and the manufacturer is free to use other channels to gain access to the foreign market. In this arrangement, the EMC takes on the risks associated with the export transaction but has the potential to achieve greater profitability, compared to acting as an agent of the manufacturer. The manufacturer, on the other hand, is relieved of the trading risks and is paid for its products without having to be concerned about the vagaries of the foreign market. The lack of opportunity to develop foreign market expertise when using an EMC may, however, prove to be a disadvantage for the manufacturer in the medium to long term.

If acting as an agent of the manufacturer, the EMC will most likely have a formal contract which provides for exclusivity. As agents, EMCs can dramatically simplify the export transaction for the manufacturing firm. These firms have knowledge of the foreign market and documentation procedures, and because they deal with a number of companies they can spread their costs over a number of clients, products and transactions. As a result, EMCs may provide the manufacturer with a cost-effective option for entering foreign markets. Of course, the EMC's large number of clients may also prove to be problematic for the manufacturer. The EMC may, for example, find that it does not have sufficient time to devote to the manufacturer's products in addition to servicing its other clients. It should also be recognized that EMCs are paid a commission on sales and so may be tempted to take on too many clients and too many products in an attempt to increase their own revenues. They may also be tempted to devote their time to those products that sell well in the foreign market and may be reluctant to invest the time to develop the market for the manufacturer's other products.

The manufacturer may also utilize the services of a **trading company** in its efforts to penetrate foreign markets. Trading companies have a long history dating back to colonial times. Chartered trading companies were formed in the 16th to 18th centuries by imperial rulers committed to expanding their wealth and power. Firms such as the Hudson's Bay Company and the English and Dutch East India Companies are examples of these early trading companies. Today it is in Japan that the concept of the trading company has been most developed. The *Sōgō shōsha* (or general trading companies) of Japan include firms such as Mitsubishi, Sumitomo Corporation, Mitsui, Toyota Tsusho and C. Itoh which are well known around the world. These companies are involved in general commerce and their scope of activities includes manufacturing, exporting, importing and **countertrade** (or barter) as well as shipping, financing and insurance. These trading firms have the ability to find buyers in foreign markets and negotiate distribution arrangements for other companies. Trade financing and foreign exchange transactions are also within their scope of activities.

Firms that export directly to a foreign country have the option of using a distributor or importer in that country. **Distributors** are independent firms based in the foreign country and are not affiliated with the manufacturer. They purchase products from the manufacturer and take responsibility for marketing them in the target foreign country. Distributors are the sole importers of the manufacturer's products in their country and because they take title have substantial latitude in terms of how these products are marketed and promoted in their market. In some cases, distributors may operate as part of an integrated channel that includes ownership of wholesale and retail establishments. **Agents** are also based in the foreign target country and provide representation for the manufacturing firm. These intermediaries do not take title to the products they handle. They market products to wholesalers and retailers in the target country but these are shipped by the manufacturer directly to the overseas customer. For their service in securing the sale, agents are paid a commission by the manufacturer.

LICENSING AND FRANCHISING

In order to penetrate international markets, other options open to the global marketer are **licensing** and **franchising**. These are both classified as intermediate entry modes as they allow for a sharing of the risks (and benefits) of foreign market expansion. With licensing, the firm (the **licensor**) grants the right to use its intellectual property to another firm (the **licensee**) in exchange for financial compensation referred to as a **royalty**. The licensing fee or royalty may be calculated as a fixed price per unit sold by the licensee or a percentage of sales (i.e. a **running royalty**). In other cases, the licensee may be required to guarantee the licensor a

minimum royalty or the parties may negotiate a **lump sum royalty** payment on execution of the licensing agreement or some other milestone. Combinations of these payment options are, of course, also possible. The intellectual property involved in licensing transactions may include patents, trademarks, copyright materials, technical drawings or business models. International licensing agreements provide the licensee with the right to work the acquired intellectual property within a defined geographical territory.

case study 8.3: May the Force be with Disney

In 2012, the Walt Disney Company announced its purchase of Lucasfilm, the maker of *Star Wars* and other commercial hits such as the Indiana Jones films for $4.05 billion. Disney will pay 50 percent of the purchase price in cash and will issue 40 million shares to close the deal. The transaction will give Disney control over *Star Wars*, one of the most successful family entertainment brands of all time, along with Lucasfilm's gaming division, Industrial Light & Magic (a special effects company) and Skywalker Sound (a post-production studio). With the acquisition, Disney also announced plans to release a new episode of *Star Wars* every 2–3 years beginning with Episode 7 in 2015. Given the strength of the *Star Wars* brand, Lucasfilm has become a major licensor of content with over $200 million of licensing and merchandising revenue in 2012. Disney plans to capitalize on this opportunity by integrating *Star Wars* content across all of its entertainment platforms and by pursuing international markets more aggressively. Currently, the majority of Lucasfilm's licensing deals are for toys and 50

PHOTO 8.3

percent of sales are in the USA, leaving a largely untapped international market. The international sales that are made are through middlemen who take a significant share of the profits. Disney has the opportunity to expand licensing deals beyond toys and market products directly through its own international divisions – an approach which should markedly increase profitability.

It is expected that the Asia-Pacific region will be a major focus for the company's international expansion efforts. According to Euromonitor, the world's top ten markets with the highest penetration of licensed toys and games include seven in the Asia-Pacific region. South Korea, Singapore and Thailand are the top three markets, with Japan and Australia also being important in terms of the penetration of licensed toys. Licensing is extremely important in the toy industry. When backed by some sort of media push, licensed toys carry a higher price tag than non-licensed toys and the share of licensed toys in total toy sales has been increasing over time. Interestingly Hasbro, the world's second largest toy manufacturer, holds the license for *Star Wars* toys until 2020 and would be expected to benefit significantly from the Disney–Lucasfilm transaction.

Sources

Block, A. (2012) Robert Iger to Wall Street: Disney Bought Lucasfilm for 'Star Wars'. Available at: www.hollywoodreporter.com/news/robert-iger-wall-street-disney-384543, accessed February 2, 2013.

Tansel, U. (2012) Mickey Gets the Force, *Euromonitor*. Available at: http://blog.euromonitor.com/2012/11/mickey-gets-the-force.html, accessed February 1, 2013.

Discussion Questions

1. What factors should Disney consider in deciding whether to distribute licensed *Star Wars* content internationally through its own channels, e.g. Disney stores, or maintain the involvement of third-party distributors in foreign markets?
2. A strategic focus for Disney is the digital delivery of its licensed content. Do you believe that this acquisition supports that strategy? Why/why not?

Licensing provides advantages and disadvantages for both the licensor and licensee. In the case of the licensor, this mode of entry provides an inexpensive way to penetrate foreign markets. There are no capital requirements as it is the responsibility of the licensee to work the technology or other intellectual property in the foreign jurisdiction. The licensor is not required to establish manufacturing facilities, hire workers or promote the product in the international market. These costs are for the licensee's account. Further, to successfully use this mode of entry, the licensor does not require a deep understanding of the foreign market. It is the licensee that is responsible for ensuring that the product gets into the hands of foreign customers and must, therefore, possess knowledge of buying behavior and the structure and operation of the market. Depending on the country being targeted, licensing may also be an effective strategy for circumventing the protectionist policies of host-country governments. The licensor is immune from protectionist measures directed against foreign firms as it does not operate in the foreign jurisdiction. The licensee is a local firm and, therefore, not subject to these government policies. While licensing offers several advantages to the licensor, there are also disadvantages. One of the most important is, of course, the lack of opportunity for the licensor to learn about and to understand the foreign market. This may prove to be a major disadvantage at the end of the licensing agreement, should the licensor wish to continue operating in the foreign market. Another potential disadvantage for the licensor is the possibility that the sharing of technical know-how with the foreign licensee may result in the creation of a major competitor at the end of the licensing agreement. This may be addressed to some extent with non-compete clauses but these have a finite period of enforcement. This is a risk that the licensor will have to face in such agreements.

From the standpoint of the licensee, the benefits of licensing agreements revolve around access to proven technology. There is no need for the licensee to invest in research and development projects with uncertain outcomes and requiring substantial financial commitments. Also, licensing the technology provides the licensee with speed to market and the ability to leapfrog the local competition. The licensee will also receive ongoing technical support from the licensor which is clearly a major benefit of the licensing agreement. From the standpoint of the licensee, however, there is a risk that the licensor may not provide its latest or most innovative technical solutions. In other words, the licensor may attempt to farm out its old technologies to companies in the developing world – technologies which are soon to be (or have already become) obsolete in more advanced countries. This becomes a matter of negotiation between the prospective licensing partners.

Negotiating licensing agreements

There are several issues to be addressed in the negotiation of licensing agreements. The scope of the agreement needs to be properly delineated, including a clear understanding of precisely what technologies are included and the geographic jurisdiction within which they may be worked. There will also need to be consideration of the use and disclosure of technical information, as well as of the length of time that the agreement will remain in force. Also important in these negotiations will be the issue of compensation payments.

From the standpoint of the licensor, there are several costs that should be covered in any licensing agreement. First, there are **transfer costs**, i.e. the cost of transferring the technology to a company in a foreign jurisdiction. There are also **R&D costs** which the licensor incurred in the development of the innovation, and third there are **opportunity costs**. The latter relate to the opportunities lost to work the technology in some other manner such as exporting the product to the foreign country or the licensor establishing its own manufacturing facility in the foreign jurisdiction. Licensors would ask that the above three costs be factored into the structure of negotiated royalty payments. In reality, however, licensees are often reluctant to compensate for R&D costs, arguing that these represent sunk costs and should not be included in the negotiations.

Franchising

Franchising is similar to licensing in that one company (the **franchisor**) grants another (the **franchisee**) the right to use its intellectual property in a specified jurisdiction over a defined time period. In the case of franchising, however, the intellectual property in question is the franchisor's business model. Such arrangements are common in the fast food industry, as well as in other areas such as hotel accommodation and car rentals. With franchising agreements, the franchisor will provide the franchisee with details of the business operation which allows the franchisee to simply duplicate the system in a foreign country. The business model transferred will contain details such as: store design and layout; menus and ingredient specifications; market research; and the legal right to use the franchisor's trademarks. As with licensing, the franchisor is paid a **management fee** (or 'royalty') in exchange for its intellectual property and incurs no capital costs in entering the foreign market. The franchisee benefits from having access to a proven business model and ongoing technical support from the franchisor. Product or process improvements developed by the franchisor will generally be passed on to its franchisee network. Table 8.1 shows the top 10 global franchise operations, all of which are from the USA. The top non-US franchises are also shown in Table 8.1.

TABLE 8.1   Top Global Franchises, 2012

Franchise	2012 Rank	Country of origin	Industry/Category
SUBWAY	1	USA	Food Franchises
McDonald's	2	USA	Food Franchises
KFC	3	USA	Food Franchises
7-Eleven	4	USA	Convenience Store Franchises
Burger King	5	USA	Food Franchises
Pizza Hut	6	USA	Food Franchises
Wyndham Hotel Group	7	USA	Hotel Franchises
Ace Hardware Corporation	8	USA	Home Improvement Franchises
Dunkin' Donuts	9	USA	Food Franchises
Hertz	10	USA	Car Rental Franchises
Highest ranked non-US franchises			
InterContinental Hotel Group	13	UK	Hotel Franchises
Kumon	18	Japan	Child Education Franchises
Tim Hortons	20	Canada	Food Franchises
Dia	25	Spain	Food Franchises
Europcar	28	France	Car Rental Franchises
Yogen Fruz	38	Canada	Food Franchises

(Continued)

TABLE 8.1   (Continued)

Franchise	2012 Rank	Country of origin	Industry/Category
Yves Rocher	40	France	Retail Franchises
Cartridge World	46	Australia	Computer Franchises
ActionCOACH	50	Australia	Business Consulting Services
H&R Block	52	Canada	Accounting & Financial Franchises
Naturhouse	62	Spain	Food Franchises
WSI	68	Canada	Internet Franchises
Almeida Viajes	73	Spain	Travel Franchises
The Pita Pit	80	Canada	Food Franchises
Coffee News	91	Canada	Advertising & Marketing Franchises
Pirtek	95	Australia	Maintenance Services

Source: Franchise Direct (2012) Top 100 Global Franchises 2012: Overview. Available at: www.franchisedirect.com/top100globalfranchises/top100globalfranchises2012overview/158/1433/, accessed January 30, 2013.

International franchise operations may be set up as either direct or indirect systems. With direct systems, the franchisor transacts directly with franchisees in the foreign market and controls their operation. With indirect systems, the franchisor transacts with a **master franchisee** in the foreign jurisdiction. This master franchisee in turn is responsible for the recruitment, coordination and control of individual franchisees in its territory (see Figure 8.2).

FIGURE 8.2   Direct and Master Franchising Systems

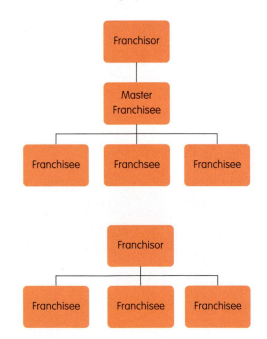

case study 8.4: Subway takes the UK

Subway has eclipsed McDonald's as the largest fast food chain in the UK. In 2010, the franchise chain had 1,400 stores in the UK – more than McDonald's and any of the other fast food restaurant chains. In 2000, Subway had only 25 outlets in the UK. Subway's success in the UK is the result of a deliberate strategy. When the company started in 1965, it was focused exclusively on the North American market. The firm soon realized, however, that it was missing out on a huge international market opportunity in countries such as the UK with a population of 60 million, most of whom had never had a Subway sandwich. The company entered the UK market in 1996 with its first outlet in Brighton and by 2006 had opened 600 outlets. By that year, the company had more outlets in the UK and Ireland than KFC, Burger King and Pizza Hut. Subway's success is due to a number of factors, such as the perception that it offers healthier menu options, an extensive choice of breads and fillings and its strategy of opening outlets in non-traditional locations such as car dealerships, appliance stores and churches. Success, however, is also due in large part to its low-cost franchise model which the company rolled out in the USA in 1974. UK outlets are not company owned but rather international franchises owned by individual entrepreneurs. Investors pay a fee to operate a Subway franchise and are provided with marketing and technical support from the parent company. Subway operates a decentralized franchise system in which development agents purchase the rights to a territory and take responsibility for finding suitable sites and qualified franchisees. The capital cost of owning a Subway franchise is kept deliberately low but the company does take a relatively high royalty payment. In the UK, franchisees are also organized into a purchasing consortium to increase their bargaining power with suppliers and receive better prices. All Subway restaurants must be laid out the same way but franchise owners have flexibility in terms of opening hours, staff recruitment and local promotions.

Sources

Hawkes, S. (2011) Super Sub. Available at: www.thesun.co.uk/sol/homepage/features/3457391/Sandwich-giant-overtakes-McDonalds.html, accessed January 26, 2013.

Jargon, J. (2012) Subway Runs Past McDonald's Chain. Available at: http://online.wsj.com/article/SB100014240 52748703386704576186432177464052.html?mod=e2tw, accessed January 26, 2013.

Mangan, L. (2005) On a Roll. Available at: www.guardian.co.uk/news/2005/jul/18/food.britishidentity, accessed January 31, 2013.

PHOTO 8.4

Discussion Questions

1. Given the current economic climate in Europe, will Subway have to make any changes to its business model in order to continue its growth trajectory in that region?
2. In expanding into the UK, why would Subway opt to use franchising as its preferred mode of entry?

FOREIGN SALES SUBSIDIARY

Having gained some experience as an exporter, the global marketer may consider establishing a sales presence in the country. This would require the firm to recruit and train a local sales force dedicated to handling its products in the foreign market. This hierarchical mode of entry brings the firm one step closer to its foreign customers. Foreign sales subsidiaries are wholly owned by the parent firm which bears all of the risk of failure. They are incorporated and operate under the laws of the host country in which they are located and not the home country of the parent. Generally, foreign sales subsidiaries have complete control over the sales function in their specific jurisdiction. While they receive marketing support from head office, they generally do not drive the overall strategic marketing decisions of the parent company.

Foreign sales subsidiaries provide the multinational company with greater control over the sales function in the foreign country. With a dedicated sales team on the ground, the firm will have the opportunity to work closely with channel members and receive feedback directly from foreign customers. This more in-depth market knowledge will come at a cost to the firm which will incur ongoing charges for training, compensation and office and support services. Unlike **domestic sales representatives** who travel between the parent company's home country and the foreign country to generate sales and take orders, foreign sales subsidiaries represent a deeper level of commitment to the foreign market. Given this greater commitment, foreign sales subsidiaries are likely to be perceived more favorably by host-country governments and the retail trade in the foreign country.

FOREIGN DIRECT INVESTMENT

Foreign direct investment (FDI) is a hierarchical entry mode and involves the investment of financial capital in a foreign jurisdiction either to acquire new assets or expand the company's stake in assets in which it already has an interest. Investment in plant and equipment as well as real estate and infrastructure characterizes FDI flows. Given the nature of the assets involved and the size of the investment, FDI often implies a long-term commitment to the foreign country. Unlike other modes of entry such as exporting, FDI decisions are much more difficult to unwind should the firm wish to exit the foreign market. Clearly, the decision to undertake FDI requires thorough research and confidence in the country. The FDI Confidence Index measures the impact of political, economic and regulatory changes in a country and the implications they have for business confidence (see Box 8.1). As shown in Figure 8.3, in 2012, business leaders around the world were bullish on China, India and Brazil, as well as on the USA, Germany and Australia.

Firms engage in FDI for a number of reasons. These are generally viewed as being **market related** if the investment is driven by the need to seek new foreign markets. FDI may be undertaken if the firm believes that there are larger and more attractive market opportunities in foreign countries or if the firm already operates abroad but wishes to expand its market share. In some cases, the company may wish to deepen its relationship with its foreign customers by establishing a physical presence in the foreign country.

Box 8.1

The FDI Confidence Index is produced by A.T. Kearney's Global Business Policy Council and has been published since 1998. The index is based on a proprietary survey of C-level business executives and regional heads of major corporations in 27 countries and representing 17 industrial sectors. In essence, the survey measures the likelihood of investment in a particular country over the next three-year period. The index is computed based on non-source-country responses, i.e. it excludes responses from respondents from the country being assessed. The responses from Australian executives, for example, are not used in computing the index value for Australia. The higher the value of the index, the more attractive is the target country from an investment standpoint. According to A.T. Kearney, there is a strong correlation between country ranking and the share of FDI going to the most attractive country targets.

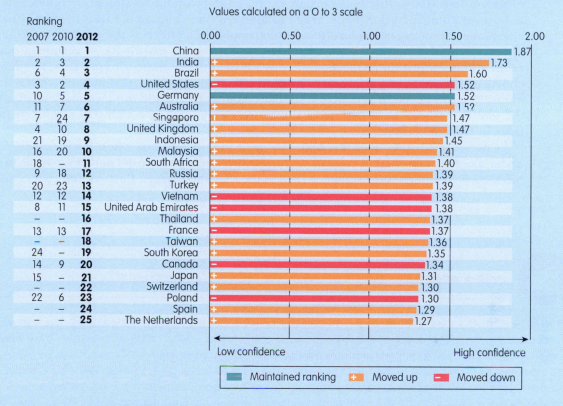

FIGURE 8.3   FDI Confidence Index, 2012

Source: Kearney, A. T. (2012) Cautious Investors Feed a Tentative Recovery. Available: http://www.atkearney.com/gbpc/foreign-direct-investment-confidence-index/full-report/-/asset_publisher/PHesJ9DLURrR/content/cautious-investors-feed-a-tentative-recovery/10192, accessed January 28, 2013.

Protectionism was discussed in Chapter 5. Companies may pursue FDI as a means of circumventing protectionist measures adopted by host-country governments and which are directed at foreign companies. For example, tariff barriers or quota restrictions which may inhibit exports by foreign firms do not apply to companies that have established a manufacturing presence in the country. The impact of protectionism on FDI may be seen in the case of Wenzhou Kazakhstan Sequoia Shoes Company – a Chinese shoe manufacturer active in Africa. Initially, this company exported its shoes to Nigeria and other African countries. However, in 2004, the Nigerian government imposed a ban on shoe imports to protect its domestic industry. Wenzhou saw millions of dollars worth of shoes seized by Nigerian customs. With support from a number of Nigerian government ministers, the company would eventually retrieve its impounded shoes. However, in order to prevent a reoccurrence Wenzhou decided to establish a manufacturing plant in Nigeria and become a 'local' company. Kazakhstan Sequoia Nigeria Atlantic Industrial Company was formed as a result and now employs 600 workers, operates four assembly lines and has an annual output of two million shoes.[1]

---

[1]   Wei-lin, L. and Staff Reporter (2011) Zhejiang Shoemaker Finds his Feet in Africa. Available at: www.wantchinatimes.com/news-subclass-cnt.aspx?id=20110323000015&cid=1502, accessed March 3, 2013.

FDI may also be beneficial to the global marketing company as a means of navigating host-country government regulations. By acquiring a company in the host country or establishing a partnership with a local firm in the host country, the global marketer is able to secure knowledge that is important to obtaining favorable treatment by politicians and government bureaucrats. Another **trade-related** reason to engage in FDI is the ability to take advantage of country of origin effects. Country of origin effects is the positive (or negative) stereotyping of a country. Some countries are known for excellence in certain products, such as Italy for leather products; Germany for high performance, luxury cars; Belgium for chocolate products; etc. If country of origin effects are positive, this may provide a strong motivation to engage in production in that country. The 'made in …' product label allows the global marketer to benefit from the country's reputation, which will ultimately boost sales in foreign markets.

As noted in Chapter 1 of this text, the need to contain costs often leads companies to undertake FDI. Lower labor costs in countries such as China have led numerous firms to shift production from high-wage countries such as the USA and Canada. **Cost-related** factors driving

case study 8.5: Chinese vs. US production

The USA is seeing a slow return of the manufacturing jobs that were lost to China and other low-wage countries. In the last few years, a number of American firms in a wide range of industries have begun a 'reshoring' of jobs once outsourced to Asian countries. Companies such as Chesapeake Bay Candle and Peerless AV have begun to manufacture some product lines in the USA. Chesapeake Bay Candle, for example, used to ship its scented candles from China and then from Vietnam to the US market but in 2011 decided to open a state-of-the-art manufacturing facility near to its headquarters in Maryland, USA. The company cited rising wage rates in China and increased shipping costs as major factors in the decision to move back to the USA. The firm has also established a research and development facility in its new US factory to allow it to respond more quickly to consumer demands and new trends. Peerless AV made the decision to reshore jobs back to the USA for a different reason. The company manufactures brackets and stands for televisions and screens, including the large video walls found at music and sporting events. In 2002, the company decided to move from steel to aluminum construction of its brackets in response to customer demands for better-looking products to support the now thinner screens being produced. Peerless was unable to find an American firm able to supply suitable extrusions and castings at the right price. The company was, however, able to find a Chinese supplier and moved production there. Several years later, the company found copies of its product appearing in markets around the world and realized that production in China had come at the cost of having its intellectual property compromised. While counterfeit production was a major consideration, the company also cited rising shipping costs and difficulty in reacting to design changes as factors in the decision. Peerless maintains a factory in China from which it supplies the Chinese market and the rest of Asia. The company now manufactures 95 percent of its products in the USA instead of 65 percent and has seen a commensurate change in the composition of its workforce. The firm used to employ 250 workers in the USA and 400 in China but now employs 350 in the USA with robots performing the hot and dirty jobs such as pouring molten aluminum and laser cutting steel. The new manufacturing arrangement makes the company much faster in responding to orders for custom products but also speeds up the delivery of more standardized products as well. With new televisions appearing at a much faster rate, what used to be a 10-year product life cycle for the firm's standard products has been reduced to 18 months, making speed and responsiveness important elements in the company's strategy.

Source

Wadcock, I. (2012) 'The boomerang effect: As Chinese wages rise some production is moving back to the rich world', *The Economist*. Available at: www.economist.com/node/21552898, accessed September 25, 2012.

Discussion Questions

1. Do you believe this 'reshoring' trend will continue, with more and more manufacturing jobs being returned to developed, high-wage countries such as the USA?
2. Is it important for high-wage developed countries to have a strong manufacturing sector or should they focus on services and technology?

FDI also include the availability of cheap natural resources. When natural resources in a foreign country are cheap but bulky and expensive to transport, it makes economic sense for the firm to manufacture close to the source of raw material supplies and export the finished higher valued final product. Interestingly, Apple has recently announced its intention to begin assembling a line of Mac notebooks in the USA. The process is referred to as '**reshoring**' and involves the movement of manufacturing operations from low-wage countries such as China to more advanced economies such as the USA.[2] The trend has been sparked by a number of factors that include a sharp increase in Chinese wage rates, quality problems experienced with overseas manufacturing arrangements and intellectual property concerns, as well as political pressures to return manufacturing jobs to the USA. Apple has been joined in the trend by companies such as General Electric, Michigan Ladder and several others (see Case Study 8.5).

Companies may also engage in FDI for **customer-related** reasons. The fact that a major customer opts to expand its operations to a foreign country may be sufficient motivation for its supplier to follow suit. This is essentially a strategic move designed to preempt the possibility that the customer will establish new supplier relationships in the host country. Also, in many cases governments will offer incentives to attract FDI. **Government incentives** to induce private foreign firms to invest in the country may range from tax breaks to grants for the acquisition of plant and equipment or the training of local workers. Industries such as auto manufacturing which make significant contributions to employment have benefited a great deal from such government incentives.

Ownership structure

When engaging in FDI, firms have the option of full or partial ownership of the foreign assets. Full ownership would require the multinational firm to have 100 percent (or close) of the shares in the foreign entity. Partial ownership would require that the multinational company own substantially less than 100 percent of the shares in the foreign enterprise. There are several factors to be considered in the multinational company's decision to opt for full or partial ownership. **Control** is certain to be a consideration. The multinational firm needs to determine how important control over the activities of the foreign company is to its overall strategy in the country. The higher the degree of ownership, the greater is the level of control that can be exercised over the foreign operation. Control may be extremely

---

[2] MIT Technology Review (2013) Apple and the Trend of Reshoring Manufacturing Jobs. Available at: www.technologyreview.com/news/509326/made-in-america-again/, accessed June 24, 2013.

important to the multinational firm if the overseas operation is expected to be a major contributor to overall corporate profitability or there is a need to protect technology assets or brand reputation. The **reaction of the host-country government** to foreign ownership is a second consideration. Full (100 percent) ownership may be problematic for some foreign governments, particularly if the operation is in sensitive industries such as natural resources, financial services or telecommunications.

The specific ownership structure selected will carry with it a set of advantages and disadvantages. For example, firms may undertake an **international joint venture** (IJV) in which two or more firms invest funds to create a new entity operative in the foreign country. Collaboration between the investment partners is viewed as a long-term arrangement, with each partner sharing the profits and risks of the new venture. Participation in an IJV offers several advantages for the global marketer. It is clearly an effective mechanism for reducing the risks associated with foreign market expansion as these risks are shared with an equity partner.

case study 8.6: Fonterra in New Zealand

Fonterra has chosen international joint ventures as its primary mode of entry into foreign markets. Fonterra is a New Zealand-based dairy cooperative which is owned by over 11,000 farmers. Taken together, these dairy farms represent almost 90 percent of the total New Zealand milk supply. The company is global although more than half of its NZ$16,726 million in revenue comes from the local New Zealand market. The firm has some €9 billion in assets and annual profits of €505m. Fonterra processes 14 billion liters of milk annually in New Zealand and an additional 6.5 billion liters in other markets around the world. The cooperative has sales in the USA, Western Europe and Asia, including Japan and Indonesia which it cites as

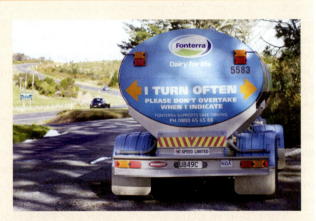

PHOTO 8.5

its key markets. Unlike its major rivals such as Kerry Foods, Fonterra has opted not to rely on acquisitions when entering foreign markets. The cooperative has instead pursued international joint ventures which have enabled the firm to expand into markets in South and North America and South Africa. Joint ventures have, for example, been established with Nestlé, Dairy Farmers of America, Clover Industries and Royal FrieslandCampina. The joint venture with RoyalFriesland Campina, a Dutch dairy cooperative, has resulted in the formation of the world's largest supplier of lactose excipients (pharmacologically inactive substances that act as carriers for the active ingredients in a pharmaceutical drug) used in medical inhalers. The joint venture controls 90 percent of this specialized, high margin, business. In 2003, Fonterra created a joint venture with Nestlé to form Dairy Partners Americas. This joint venture targets the Latin American market and the alliance now operates 14 manufacturing sites in the region and has some 4,000 employees. In this case, Fonterra provided expertise in milk procurement and processing to complement Nestlé's strengths in product development, branding and distribution. Fonterra has also partnered with Clover, South Africa's largest dairy company, to penetrate the African market. Using Clover's strengths in Africa, the joint venture now markets dairy ingredients and food service products throughout the Sub-Saharan region.

Sources

Fonterra Company website: www.fonterra.com/global/en/About/Our+Partners

Leslie, B. (2012) Fonterra Plans for European Expansion. Available at: www.farmersjournal.ie/site/farming-Fonterra-plans-for-European-expansion-12581.html, accessed February 9, 2013.

Madden, J. (2012) Joint Ventures Help Fonterra's Global Expansion. Available at: http://blog.euromonitor.com/2010/12/joint-ventures-help-fonterras-global-expansion.html, accessed February 4, 2013.

Discussion Questions

1. Why do you believe Fonterra has been successful in its use of international joint ventures in penetrating foreign markets?
2. What criteria should Fonterra use in selecting international joint venture partners?

In many cases, one of the equity partners in an IJV is a company located in the host country. Such a structure brings additional benefits in terms of knowledge of the host country's economic and political environments as well as its nuances of culture. Indeed, in some countries, market access would be virtually impossible without a local partner.

IJVs do, however, suffer from a number of disadvantages. As may be expected, there is the potential for conflict between the equity partners. This is compounded by the cross-border nature of these transactions, with executives from different cultural backgrounds involved in making key decisions. Conflicts may arise over the sharing of profits, the strategic direction of the new venture and control over various aspects of its operations. If these are not resolved in a timely manner, the result could be dissolution of the partnership. The executives chosen to manage the new enterprise are in most instances selected from the ranks of the parent companies. This practice raises the issue of divided loyalties. In critical decision-making situations, will these executives perform in the best interests of the new venture or of the parent companies? The sharing of sensitive information between the equity partners may also be a challenge until trust has been well established. If there is significant cultural distance between the partners, it may take some time for this trust to emerge.

Expand Your Knowledge

Chen, S-F.S. and Hennart, J-F. (2004) 'A hostage theory of joint ventures: Why do Japanese investors choose partial over full acquisitions to enter the USA?', *Journal of Business Research*, 57: 1126–34.

This article uses hostage theory to explain why foreign firms will opt to take only a partial stake in a local target. The authors argue that partial ownership allows for better *ex ante* screening of the target as well as better *ex post* enforcements of contracts.

Given the disadvantages above, the global manager may opt not to share ownership but to undertake a **Greenfield investment** or **cross-border acquisition** of a target in the foreign country. With a Greenfield investment, the company invests the funds required to create a new enterprise in the foreign country. The new enterprise is wholly owned and controlled by the firm making the investment. This approach requires the investing firm to cover all the costs associated with the new plant and equipment, as well as with the recruitment and training of workers and management. The firm is also liable for all associated production and marketing costs and must navigate the political environment of the host country on its own. The company does, however, have complete control over all decisions. With cross-border acquisitions (CBAs), the multinational company acquires an existing firm which is already operating in the host country. All of the assets of the target are transferred to the acquiring company including existing product lines, brands, technology, customer lists and manufacturing facilities. Unlike Greenfield investment, the multinational company does not have the option of installing state-of-the-art equipment at the outset but may be saddled with outdated equipment which may need to be refurbished or replaced. With a CBA, the acquiring firm also assumes all of the liabilities of the target. CBAs do, however, allow the acquiring company to quickly move into the target market without the time lags associated with the construction of new facilities.

RULES FOR ENTRY MODE

The major modes of entry have been described above. Each mode of entry has its own risk–reward profile, as shown in Figure 8.4. At one extreme, exporting involves relatively little risk for the firm but also carries little by way of profit potential. At the other extreme is foreign direct investment which carries considerably more risk but is also potentially much more lucrative.

While an understanding of the risk–reward profile is important, in practical terms firms tend to adopt one or more rules to guide their entry mode selection. A firm may, for example, use the same entry mode every time it enters a foreign market. If expansion usually takes place by acquiring a target in the host country, then the firm will continue to use this approach regardless of the country or the specifics of the situation, such as the size of the target firm or industry. This has been referred to as the **naïve** rule. Some firms focus on the risk of foreign market expansion and automatically select the entry mode which minimizes the company's exposure to these risks. Referred to as the **pragmatic** rule, this approach is designed to always protect the firm from the downside risks when expanding into new markets. In selecting an entry mode, firms may also follow the **strategy** rule. With this approach, all entry mode options are on the table and the firm undertakes a systematic evaluation of each with respect to benefits and costs. The objective is to select the mode of entry that maximizes the net contribution from the foreign market transaction.

FIGURE 8.4   Risk-Reward Profile

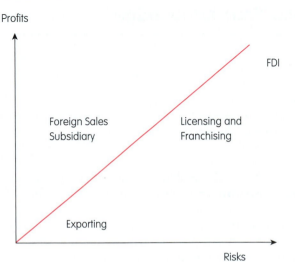

Spotlight on Research 8.1 Choice of Entry Mode

Chiao, Lo and Yu (2010) examine the issue of entry mode selection. Using transactions cost theory and the resource-based view of the firm as their theoretical base, the authors seek to better understand the entry mode choices made by Taiwanese manufacturing firms. They consider two choices – international joint ventures and the establishment of a wholly-owned subsidiary – and also look at the moderating influence of perceived institutional distance. In this article, the authors investigate the strategies of firms from Taiwan entering the Chinese market, arguing that entry mode research has not focused much attention on multinationals from developing countries entering other developing countries. They also point out that previous studies which have used transaction cost theory, the resource-based view or institutional variables in analyzing entry mode choice have yielded inconsistent results.

FIGURE 8.5   Conceptual Model

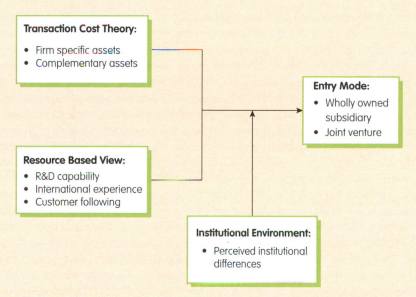

Hypotheses

The authors' conceptual model is illustrated in Figure 8.5. Guided by transactions cost theory, the authors consider both firm-specific and complementary assets, while the resource-based view of the firm leads the researchers to examine the firms' R&D capabilities, international experience and their need to follow major customers. With respect to the institutional environment, the authors focus on the perceived distance between the firms' home and host countries. Chiao, Lo and Yu (2010) seek to test the following hypotheses:

H1. The more firm-specific assets held by a foreign firm, the more likely the firm will enter a host market by means of a wholly-owned subsidiary.

H2. The more valuable the complementary assets held by a local firm, the more likely a foreign firm will choose a joint venture as a means by which to enter a host market.

H3. The greater the R&D capabilities held by a foreign firm, the more likely the firm will enter a host market by means of a wholly-owned subsidiary.

(Continued)

(Continued)

H4. The more international experience a foreign firm has, the more likely the firm will enter a host market by means of a wholly-owned subsidiary.

H5. If an investor (supplier) follows an established customer in investing in a host country, the likelihood increases that the investor (supplier) will set up a wholly-owned subsidiary in the host market.

H6. Perceived institutional differences (PEDs) between a firm's home country and its potential host country moderate the relationship between transaction cost and its choice of entry into a host market.

H7. A foreign firm's perception of institutional differences between its home country and a host country moderates the relationship between resource-based factors and a firm's choice of entry mode into the host market.

Method

The authors use logistic regression to test the hypotheses above. Their analysis is based on data collected by the Taiwanese government as part of a 2003 national survey of the FDI activities of that country's manufacturing firms. Of the 819 firms included in the sample, 60 percent were small and medium-sized firms with 40 percent categorized as large companies. In terms of industry classification, 37 percent of firms in the sample were in the information and electronics industry, about 30 percent were in the metal and machinery industry, 17 percent were in the chemicals and plastics industry and 17 percent were in the food, textiles and other industry. In the analysis, subsidiaries were classified as being wholly owned or joint ventures, depending on the percentage of equity controlled by the parent company. The dependent variable is, therefore, binary with a value of 1 for a wholly-owned subsidiary, and 0 otherwise. The authors consider technology as the only firm-specific asset and it too is operationalized as a binary variable. If the subsidiary's central technological asset was provided by the parent company, it is coded as 1; otherwise it is coded as 0. For complementary assets, the authors consider the local supply of four factors of production: labor, capital, technology and raw materials and components. Respondents were asked to rate the contributions of the parent company to the supply of each factors as follows: mainly from the parent company; roughly equal contributions; and mainly from local sources. Factor analysis was used to reduce these items to a single factor for inclusion in the regression model. The parent's R&D capability was measured as the ratio of R&D expenses to total operating revenues, while the need to follow customers was measured as a binary variable coded '1' if the parent company was following a customer by investing in the host country and '0' otherwise.

Four metrics were used to measure international experience – the ratio of foreign sales to total sales, the ratio of foreign assets to total assets, the ratio of foreign fixed assets to total fixed assets, and the ratio of foreign employees to total employees. A 10-point scale was used to assess each metric and factor analysis was again used to reduce the items to a single measure for use in the logistics regression.

Perceived institutional difference is used as a moderating variable and is measured according to how difficult the multinational perceives operations in the host country to be, with respect to factors such as turbulence in political and economic conditions; inefficiency in government administration; differing social and business customs; requirements for local sourcing of components and raw materials; restrictions on the products or components manufactured; restrictions on foreign ownership; and requirements for technology transfer. In addition, the researchers control for both firm size and industry of operation.

Results

The authors find support for H1. Companies with more firm-specific assets tend to enter the host country by means of a wholly-owned subsidiary ($\beta = 1.374$, $\rho < 0.01$). H2 is also supported as the results indicate that firms that require more complementary assets tend to enter the host country via joint ventures ($\beta = 20.120$, $\rho < 0.05$). All of the resource-based view variables are also seen to be significant and have the expected signs, indicating support for H3, H4 and H5. The researchers, however, find only partial support for H6 and H7.

The results suggest that firms with large perceived institutional differences tend to enter the host country by means of wholly-owned subsidiaries ($\beta = 0.230$, $\rho < 0.01$). The interaction effects of perceived institutional differences and complementary assets ($\beta = 0.179$, $\rho < 0.05$) and international experience ($\beta = 0.133$, $\rho < 0.1$) were both found to be significant. The interaction effects of perceived institutional differences and the transaction cost economics variable (firm-specific assets), as well as the resource-based view variables – R&D capability and the need to follow customers – were, however, not significant. To further investigate the moderating role of perceived institutional differences, the authors divided the sample into two groups – firms that score lower than average on this variable and those that score higher than average. They find that when the perception of institutional difference is low, firms which need complementary assets tend to enter the host market via joint ventures ($\beta = 20.072$, $\rho < 0.05$), whereas firms which are following a customer tend to enter markets via wholly-owned subsidiaries ($\beta = 0.306$, $\rho < 0.1$).

Implications

This article speaks to the importance of institutional factors when firms make entry mode choices. The work demonstrates empirically that multinationals that possess more firm-specific assets, less need for complementary assets, greater parental R&D capability, more international experience and the tendency to follow their customers are more likely to enter foreign markets by means of wholly-owned subsidiaries. The study also demonstrates that perceptions of institutional differences between home and host countries moderate the relationship between the transactions cost variables and entry mode choice. The research further suggests that, depending on the level of perceived institutional difference, transaction cost variables and resource-based variables impact entry mode choices differently.

Source

Chiao, Y.C., Lo, F.Y. and Yu, C.M. (2010) 'Choosing between wholly-owned subsidiaries and joint ventures of MNCs from an emerging market', *International Marketing Review*, 27, 3: 338–65.

Discussion Questions

Read the complete paper and answer the following questions:

1. This study considers multinationals from Taiwan entering the Chinese market. Do you believe the results are generalizable to other home and host developing-country markets? Which of the authors' hypotheses (if any) are likely to hold if the home country is Asian and the host country is Latin American?
2. This study considers only two entry mode choices – wholly-owned subsidiaries and joint ventures. How would the results of this study change if non-equity entry mode choices were included in the analysis? Justify your answer.

SUMMARY

This chapter has examined the choice of entry mode when entering foreign markets. Building on the material presented in Chapter 7 on country selection, this chapter has discussed the major approaches to foreign market penetration open to the global marketing manager. The advantages and disadvantages of exporting, licensing, foreign sales subsidiaries and foreign direct investment were presented in order to provide the global marketing manager with the basis for entry mode selection. It was emphasized that each entry mode is associated with a particular risk–reward profile and that low-risk approaches such as exporting also carry little potential for significant profits. Higher profits are attainable but only by assuming a higher level of risk and commitment to the foreign market. It was also argued that the global marketing manager should consider issues of control and speed to market when selecting an entry mode.

Real World Challenges

Coca-Cola's Acquisition in the Chinese Juice Market

The news came as a complete shock to Muhtar Kent – Coca-Cola's Chief Executive Officer. The email clearly stated that the Chinese government had rejected his company's $2.3 billion bid to acquire Huiyuan Juice Group Ltd, China's largest juice manufacturer. How could this be, Muhtar thought? This acquisition would have allowed Coca-Cola to roughly double its market share in China's rapidly growing fruit juice market and achieve savings on raw material costs including packaging and fruit. The deal would have given the company better access to the Chinese market where it is competing head-to-head with PepsiCo. Both Coca-Cola and PepsiCo are trying to diversify beyond the market for soda by acquiring local beverage companies with products that appeal to local tastes and preferences. PepsiCo, for example, had recently invested $1.3 billion in a 75.5 percent stake in OAO Lebedyansky – Russia's largest juice manufacturer.

Both Coca-Cola and PepsiCo were active players in the Chinese market of 1.3 billion consumers. Atlanta-based Coca-Cola controlled almost 53 percent of the Chinese soda market, while PepsiCo had a 33 percent share of this market. In fact, Coca-Cola had big plans for the Chinese market. The company planned to invest $2 billion in China over the next three years in plant and distribution infrastructure, including $90 million already invested in a technology center in Shanghai. The fruit juice market in China is forecast to grow 16 percent a year – roughly double the growth rate of the soda market. Although Huiyuan did have some local rivals, it was a very well known brand in China. The firm was established in 1992 and sold 220 fruit and vegetable juices as well as nectars. The majority of these were sold under its own brand name. Most of Huiyuan's sales were in China but the company also had a small presence in the USA and in Southeast Asia.

Muhtar tried to calm himself and come up with a rationale for the deal's rejection. The email from China's Ministry of Commerce stated that there was a concern that if the deal were approved, Coca-Cola would use its dominant market position to raise prices and limit choice for Chinese consumers. But how? As far as Muhtar knew, Coca-Cola's share of the Chinese fruit and vegetable juice market was only 12 percent and Huiyuan controlled 8 percent. A meager 20 percent combined was hardly market dominance, thought Muhtar. He was convinced that allowing a Chinese and a US company, each controlling less than 25 percent of the market, to combine should not be considered anti-competitive. Maybe the Chinese government was looking at other data. Huiyuan did control 33 percent of China's market for pure fruit juices. Maybe that was the concern.

Sources

www.bloomberg.com/apps/news?pid=20601080&sid=aaJRBs7TNaXw&refer=asia

www.bloomberg.com/apps/news?pid=21070001&sid=aTAERrjwuus4

Questions

1. State the problem that Coca-Cola faces in the Chinese juice market.
2. Identify the options available to Coca-Cola now that the acquisition has been rejected.
3. Based on the options identified above, recommend one course of action for the company. Be sure to provide a rationale.

> ### ? discussion questions
>
> 1. From the standpoint of the licensor, what are the major advantages and disadvantages of licensing as a mode of entry?
>
> 2. For a small start-up company with limited financial resources but cutting-edge technology, what mode of entry would you recommend if the company wishes to expand rapidly into a number of foreign markets within a short period of time? Be sure to provide a justification for your recommendation.
>
> 3. Each mode of entry has its own risk–reward profile. What mode of entry carries the highest risk but also has the greatest profit potential? What mode of entry carries the least risk but has the lowest profit potential?

FURTHER READING

Ghemawat, P. (2001) 'Distance still matters: The hard reality of global expansion', *Harvard Business Review*, 79, 8: 137–47.

Hennart, J.F. and Reddy, S. (1997) 'The choice between mergers/acquisitions and joint ventures: The case of Japanese investors in the United States', *Strategic Management Journal*, 18, 1: 1–12.

Kogut, B. and Singh, H. (1988) 'The effect of national culture on the choice on entry mode', *Journal of International Business Studies*, 19, 3: 411–32.

Reuer, J., Shenkar, O. and Ragozzino, R. (2004) 'Mitigating risk in international mergers and acquisitions: The role of contingent payouts', *Journal of International Business Studies*, 35: 19–32.

Root, F.R. (1983) *Foreign Market Entry Strategies*. New York: AMACOM.

Yiu, D. and Makino, S. (2002) 'The choice between joint venture and wholly-owned subsidiary: An institutional perspective', *Organization Science*, 13, 6: 667.

GLOBAL PRODUCTS AND SERVICES

LEARNING OBJECTIVES

After reading this chapter you should be able to:

- Explain the key differences between products and services

- Discuss the merits and demerits of standardization versus adaptation

- Distinguish between adaptation and localization

- Discuss the drivers of product adaptation

- Explain the brand value chain

- Discuss strategies for transferring brand names and meanings across national borders

- Discuss brand changeover strategies

- Discuss the process of global new product development

- Discuss the role of the Internet in new product development

- Identify the key issues involved in deciding the locus of new product development

- Discuss the significance of counterfeit production in the implementation of global marketing strategies.

INTRODUCTION

Products and services are central to the marketing strategies of the global marketing firm as they serve to distinguish the company from its competitors in the marketplace. The extent to which these offerings resonate with consumers will have a substantial impact on the firm's overall success in international markets. Appealing to consumers in various foreign countries is, however, a difficult task. Cultural differences between countries, and differences in local tastes and preferences, as well as entrenched local competitors with brand-loyal customers, create significant difficulties for the global marketing manager. As part of an effective strategy, companies may need to adapt their products to various local markets or develop entirely new products for these markets. For example, microwaves are set to become a billion-dollar industry in Brazil. Sales are already in the region of $836 million with some 20 million households owning these appliances. It is expected that by 2017 that number will double to 40 million households, with companies such as Whirlpool, Electrolux and Panasonic competing for market share. In order to compete in this market, LG opted to adapt the traditional product by manufacturing a smaller microwave targeted at single Brazilians living alone. By adapting its product to this rapidly growing segment of the market, LG was able to secure a 9 percent share of the overall market.[1]

Decisions will also have to be made with respect to where – head office or overseas subsidiary – product development and adaptations take place. The global marketing manager also needs to recognize that products may be at different stages in the product life cycle in various countries and may also be used very differently in these markets. These issues need to be factored into the firm's global product strategy. Also, when entering foreign markets, the global marketing firm needs to be concerned with issues such as counterfeit production. Protecting the company's intellectual property is likely to be a challenge in a number of foreign markets and the firm will require effective strategies to counteract the negative impact of counterfeit production on its sales and brand reputation.

THE NATURE OF PRODUCTS AND SERVICES

The American Marketing Association defines a product as a bundle of attributes (i.e. features, functions, benefits and uses) capable of exchange or use. A product may be an idea, a physical good, a service or some combination of these. Products exist for the purpose of exchange and the satisfaction of individual and organizational needs and may be a mix of tangible and intangible elements. Generally, the term 'product' is used when referring to the tangible element, while the term 'service' is reserved for the intangible element. One may also think of a product as a combination of a core or physical component, such as a car and an augmented component, like the manufacturer's warranty. The essential idea, however, is that firms attempt to bundle unique combinations of attributes in order to satisfy the needs of consumers.

As noted above, the term service is usually reserved for the intangible. Services have a number of unique characteristics that serve to distinguish them from physical products. The first is, of course, the fact that they are **intangible**. A spa treatment, a haircut or even attendance at a global marketing lecture does not leave the individual with anything that is tangible. It is the experience that matters. In some cases, the firm may attempt to enhance the experience by bundling the service with something physical, such as providing the customer with a coupon for a 10 percent discount on her next spa treatment. Often, it is the bundling of the service with a physical product that creates a unique value proposition for the firm (see Case Study 9.1).

Services are also **perishable** and cannot be stored or inventoried. If a barber is waiting for his 2pm appointment and the person does not show, that time is lost forever. Haircuts cannot be stored and delivered at some future time and the revenue from that missed appointment is also lost. Services are described as being **heterogeneous**, i.e. the quality of the service is very much dependent on the person who provides it. Barbers, massage therapists, doctors and university professors differ in terms of their skills and abilities and these differences will be reflected in the quality of the services they provide. Maintaining service quality is often a significant challenge for the firm and will be even more so when services are provided in different cultural contexts. The ability to communicate with and relate to consumers is central to effective service delivery and, therefore, service providers need to be attuned to the cultural nuances of the host country.

Simultaneity is another characteristic of services, i.e. consumption and production take place at the same time. For example, an individual receives his haircut at the same time as the barber produces it. Further, customers tend to be heavily involved in the production of

---

[1]   Blog.euromonitor.com (2013) Microwaves in Brazil Are Becoming a Billion Dollar Business: Are You in the Game? Analyst Insight from Euromonitor International. Available at: http://blog.euromonitor.com/2013/01/microwaves-in-brazil-are-becoming-a-billion-dollar-business-are-you-in-the-game.html, accessed June 26, 2013.

case study 9.1: Premium Skincare

For companies such as The Organic Pharmacy in London, UK, the bundling of products and services is expected to allow the firm to provide customers with a more compelling value proposition. The company operates in the premium skincare industry. The firm partnered with geneOnyx to provide the first in-store DNA skincare test to its customers. Based on a simple saliva test, The Organic Pharmacy generates tailored skincare recommendations that are unique to each customer. The anti-aging service costs £295 for a one-hour consultation and includes a skincare prescription. In the UK, the premium anti-aging industry grew at 8 percent in 2011, despite a generally weak economy, and is expected to remain robust into 2016. In the UK, consumers are looking for products that emphasize their individuality and unique needs. In fact, sales of premium anti-aging products in the UK are expected to outpace sales across Western Europe, including Germany and France. The strong growth in this segment of the market has attracted other players. Murad, for example, has begun to offer its customers complementary skin analysis using its YouthCam skin analysis system, along with its anti-aging products. Harrods' beauty hall has put in place the Ioma Beauty Diag machine, which provides detailed skincare recommendations from a series of images of the skin to identify problems.

MyChelle Dermaceuticals is also a player with its Visia Complexion Analysis System, which is available in whole food market outlets in the USA and the UK.

Source

Tyrimou, N. (2013) Bespoke Services to Boost Premium Skin Care. Available at: http://blog.euromonitor.com/2013/01/bespoke-services-to-boost-premium-skin-care.html, accessed February 11, 2013.

Discussion Questions

1. Do you believe that bundling skin analysis services with anti-aging products provides companies in this industry with a competitive advantage?
2. Why do you believe that sales of anti-aging products in the UK have outpaced the rest of Western Europe?
3. The Organic Pharmacy intends to roll out its DNA skincare tests globally. How successful do you believe it will be in regions such as Latin America and Asia?

services. They often have to be physically present and participative in the delivery of the service, and in some cases may themselves be responsible for its delivery, such as when purchasing tickets for a movie at a self-serve kiosk. Because producers and consumers generally have to be physically present, the market for services tends to be local.

STANDARDIZATION VERSUS ADAPTATION

When entering foreign markets, the multinational firm must make a decision to either standardize its products or adapt them in some way to suit the requirements of the host country. Standardization involves marketing the product as it is in foreign markets. Product features are the same in the home and the host countries. This approach offers the firm a number of important advantages. First, the multinational firm will be in a position to capitalize on the economies of scale associated with longer production runs and the attendant decrease in per unit costs. Production lines are set up to manufacture one product and no time is lost in equipment changeovers to handle variations. As a result, the firm will be able to drive down its manufacturing costs and price more aggressively in the foreign market. Further, product modifications may be costly for the firm and the decision to market a standardized product will obviate the need for the firm to incur these additional costs. Standardization does, however, have its limitations. Because a product is standardized, it most likely will not appeal completely to all customers in every country. Such products are said to be **off-target** and may, therefore, not enter the consideration set of some consumers. Further, customers seeking uniqueness will likely not purchase a standardized product, resulting in lost sales for the company. It is also the case that standardized products which are sold around the world will be vulnerable to local brands in some countries. Brands developed specifically for the local market may embody more of the characteristics desired by consumers in that country. As a result, standardized foreign brands may experience some difficulty in competing with these well-entrenched local brands.

★ Box 9.1

A distinction should be made between product **adaptation** and product **localization**. Product localization involves making changes to the product that are required for the unit to function or be saleable in the foreign country. Unless the firm makes these changes, the product will not enter the consumer's consideration set. Localization may be required if, for example, there are differences in the configuration of electrical outlets in the home and host countries or differences in voltage requirements. In other instances, there may be government regulations that drive product changes and determine whether it can legally be sold in the country. Localization may also be termed **mandatory adaptation**. Adaptation, on the other hand, refers to changes which are made to the product in order to better match consumer tastes and preferences. Also referred to as **discretionary adaptation**, these changes provide consumers with a reason to purchase the foreign product over the domestic alternatives.

If the decision is made to adapt the product, the firm has a number of options depending on whether it is addressing a homogeneous or heterogeneous consumer segment (see Figure 9.1). The multinational firm may, for example, opt to develop a series of products for each foreign market in which it has an interest. Such a **multi-domestic** strategy assumes customer heterogeneity, i.e. it recognizes that customers in the various country markets have distinct needs which cannot be satisfied by one standardized product. While this strategy allows the firm to cater specifically to the needs of its international customers, the approach is not likely to be cost-effective. Research will be needed to understand the needs of customers in each country market and new products designed to meet those specific needs. The strategy will also prove challenging operationally as manufacturing becomes more complex given that a wider variety of product features would need to be accommodated. A multi-domestic strategy does, however, allow the firm to cater more precisely to local customers and compete more effectively with established local brands.

A multi-domestic strategy assumes customer heterogeneity but is likely to present a series of implementation challenges for the firm. Another alternative is for the company to pursue a strategy of **mass customization**. With this approach, products are designed on a global platform that may be adjusted to use conditions in a variety of country markets. This is essentially the 'glocalization' strategy discussed in Chapter 1, in which products incorporate both global and local features. For example, Vaillant is the second largest manufacturer of heating and ventilation systems in Europe. The company's products are available in over 75 countries around the world and the firm maintains a sales presence in over 20. Because building codes and customer needs differ across countries, attempting to satisfy these diverse requirements would necessitate the production of hundreds of models. Instead,

FIGURE 9.1   Product Adaptation Alternatives

PHOTO 9.1

Vailliant manufactures all its products with a number of common components, such as the burners and control units, and would then add country-specific adaptations for each market. This reduces the cost of customization while not severely limiting customer choice.

If homogeneous customer segments can be identified for the firm's products, then a **global product strategy** may well make sense for the company. Customers in essence have the same needs and are seeking the same product benefits irrespective of the fact that they reside in different countries. Global products attempt to reflect the needs of individuals around the world who fit the profile of the firm's ideal customer.

DRIVERS OF ADAPTATION

Several factors drive the need for product adaptation. These range from the nature of the product itself to the characteristics of the market. As illustrated in Figure 9.2, these may be categorized as country-level drivers, industry/firm-level drivers and product-level drivers (Waheeduzzaman, 2002).[2] These factors may act individually or in concert to trigger the need for adaptation of the firm's products. Country- and industry-level variables are, of course, outside the firm's control while product-level variables are to some extent within the company's control.

COUNTRY-LEVEL DRIVERS

Companies often face a regulatory environment that is quite different from that which exists in their home markets. Governments may impose restrictions on foreign products that demand adaptation if they are to be sold in the host country. Canada is officially a bilingual country even though only 21 percent of the population is Francophone. English is the language spoken by the vast majority of Canadians and is also the language of business. Despite this fact, all foreign products entering Canada must legally be labeled in both English and

---

[2]   Waheeduzzaman, A.N.M. (2002) 'Five lines of inquiry in standardization adaptation research', *American Marketing Association Conference Proceedings*, 13: 380.

French. **Government regulations**, therefore, are an important driver of product adaptation. Modifications such as bilingual product labeling are considered to be mandatory adaptations and would be required by all foreign firms that wish to market their products legally in the host country.

Also, at the country level, **culture** often serves as a major driver of product adaptation decisions. Take, for example, the case of Alfajr Watch & Clock Company which claims to be the first to manufacture a Swiss watch to service the needs of the Muslim community. The timepiece shows Muslim prayer times and the Qibla direction, i.e. the direction of Mecca, for cities around the world. Consumers need only select their city from a list and the watch will automatically set prayer times for that city and act as a Qibla locator. To ensure accuracy with respect to local prayer times, the watch automatically refers to the prayer times calendar or *Taqweem* for the particular country. Alfajr is a Saudi Arabian firm but manufactures its watches in Switzerland.[3] Another company, Splashgear, manufactures and markets full-body swimsuits for Muslim women. The firm's products are made from a synthetic combination of polyester, nylon and Lycra which gives the swimsuits flexibility without them sticking to the body. The swimsuits are made in a number of colors, including hot pink, and one of the company's tag lines is: 'Nothing in the Quran says men and women can't swim together.'[4] Culture is clearly a major country-level driver of firms' product adaptation decisions.

FIGURE 9.2   Drivers of Product Adaptation

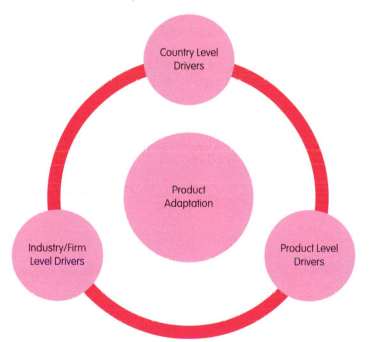

In considering the need for product adaptation, firms must also be cognizant of a country's **level of economic development**. In some situations, a firm may need to market a rather basic model of its product in low-income countries where affordability is a major constraint. By removing product features, the firm is able to produce and market the product at a price point that is more attractive to low-income consumers. The process is known as **backward**

3   Arabnews.com (2012) Alfajr Launches First Swiss Watch with Prayer Times. Available at: www.arabnews.com/alfajr-launches-first-swiss-watch-prayer-times, accessed June 27, 2013.

4   Washingtonpost.com (2005) Muslim Women Enjoying Special Swimsuits. Available at: www.washingtonpost.com/wp-dyn/content/article/2007/02/18/AR2007021800741.html, accessed June 27, 2013.

innovation and is practiced by companies such as Whirlpool which markets a low-end washing machine in countries such as India. The host country's level of economic development will also have an impact on package sizes and the number of units included in each package. In order to make consumer discretionary products such as shampoos and razors affordable, the firm may reduce the size of the package or the number of units in each package. Shampoo may be sold by the sachet instead of in a standard-size bottle and razor blades may be marketed by the piece. These are in essence discretionary product adaptations designed to encourage trial of the product and eventually build market share in environments where the level of economic development is lower than in the firm's home country.

case study 9.2: Al Quds Jeans

Al Quds manufactures and markets jeans targeted at the Muslim community. The company is based in Northern Italy and manufactures its jeans at a plant in Karachi, Pakistan, that employs some 10,000 people. The name Al Quds is Arabic for Jerusalem, and, according to the company, the name was chosen because the city is equally sacred to Muslims, Christians and Jews. Jeans manufactured by the company are innovative and target a segment of the market that is not well served. The company's jeans fit high on the waist and are loosely fitting around the legs to facilitate repeated bending during prayers. The jeans also feature a number of pockets to store various items that must be taken off during prayer and are manufactured with green seams as that is the sacred color of Islam. The founder of the company said that he was inspired to develop the product after seeing a newspaper article with a number of Muslims wearing jeans and bent over during prayers. He soon recognized that there were no jeans on the market which were targeted at this segment. The company now markets its products to the over 1 million Muslims living in Italy. The firm also plans to target the over 25 million Muslims across Europe, as well as those in the Middle East and North America.

Sources

Sanminiatelli, M. (2006) Italian Company Designs Jeans for Muslims. Available at: http://money.canoe.ca/News/TopPhoto/2006/03/21/1498649.html, accessed October 7, 2006.

Sawfnews.com (2006) Muslim Jeans for Worshippers Cause a Stir in Pakistan. Available at: www.sawfnews.com/muslim-jeans-for-worshippers-cause-a-stir-in-pakistan/, accessed June 27, 2013.

Discussion Questions

1. Given the modifications made to this product, do you believe that there is a market outside the Muslim community? Why/why not?
2. Do the modifications made to this product address a real need in the marketplace or will Al Quds jeans be a passing fad?

In some situations, it is the **geographical characteristics** of the host country that drives the firm to adapt its products. This may be illustrated by reference to the case of Nestlé, the Swiss food company, and the changes that were required to market its chocolate products in tropical countries. In such countries, the availability of refrigerated display cases may be a challenge for retailers. Without these, chocolate products would quickly melt in the tropical heat, making them unattractive to prospective consumers and damaging the reputation of the brand. In marketing its Kit-Kat brand, and to counteract this problem, Nestlé opted to reduce the fat content of the product. Reducing the fat content of the chocolate raises its melting point, thereby allowing the product to survive for longer periods of time without refrigerated storage.

INDUSTRY/FIRM-LEVEL DRIVERS

The multinational firm also has to consider a number of firm-level and industry factors that may have a bearing on the decision to adapt its products to foreign markets. At the firm level, the issue of **resource availability** is certainly of paramount importance. Does the company in fact have the resources needed to adapt its products to those foreign markets in which it wishes to conduct business? Product adaptations may be costly or relatively inexpensive. At one extreme, the company may have to completely redesign or reformulate its existing products with the attendant research and development costs. In other instances, however, the only changes actually required are cosmetic, such as new product labeling and package designs. Indeed, it may be that to be marketable in a foreign country no substantive changes to the product are actually required, only a change in the product's positioning. The key point here, however, is that some costs are likely to be incurred by the company once the decision to adapt the product is made. It is, therefore, important that the company determines whether the additional expenditures are justified given the incremental increases in revenue and profits that should follow from adapting the product to new foreign markets. Assuming that the economics of adaptation are positive, the firm also has to determine whether it has the human resources needed to successfully implement the process.

The multinational firm does not operate in a vacuum. The firm's products are marketed in foreign countries against those of local competitors, as well as those of other multinational companies with an interest in the market. When benchmarked against the offerings of local and foreign competitors, the multinational firm's products should embody as many of the features, and ideally more of the features, desired by customers in the foreign country. If they do not, the multinational firm's products will be at a distinct competitive disadvantage in the market. **Competitive pressures** are, therefore, an important driver of the need to adapt to the foreign market.

Position in the **product life cycle** also has a role to play in driving the need for adaptation. As is well known, the product life cycle traces the evolution of a product's sales or profits over time and through the four stages of introduction, growth, maturity and decline. Generally, a product is introduced into a market and slowly gains traction with sales and profits building as consumers become more aware of its features and benefits. The product is considered to be innovative and there are few competing products on the market. The product next enters the growth phase where sales/profits ramp up as it becomes more widely adopted by consumers. Additional competitors enter the market attracted by the high returns being experienced. In the maturity phase, the rate of increase in sales/profit growth slows and there are a substantial number of competitors in the market. The product is no longer considered new or innovative and firms intensify their efforts to differentiate their offerings in order to maintain their market share. Eventually, however, the product enters the decline phase with sales and profits falling in absolute terms. Firms begin to exit the market at this point in the face of declining margins and stiff competition. Some firms may drastically reduce prices in order to maintain market share or attempt to add new product features to draw in new customers and re-launch the product.

The product life cycle may be viewed from the perspective of an individual brand, a product category or even an entire industry. It should also be noted that the same product may be at different phases of the product life cycle in different countries (Figure 9.3). For example, a product may be in the decline phase in the advanced country responsible for the innovation but in the growth or maturity stage in less developed countries. As a result, the multinational firm may be adding features to its products sold in less developed countries in order to take advantage of growth opportunities or to differentiate its offerings from those of its competitors, while making no new modifications to products destined for sale in developed countries.

FIGURE 9.3

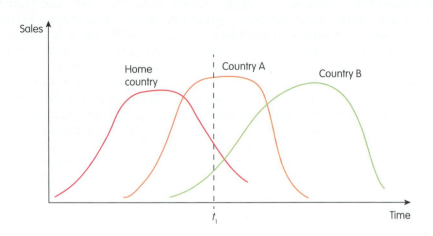

PRODUCT-LEVEL DRIVERS

The nature of the product also has a bearing on the need for adaptation. The notion of **cultural grounding** is important in this regard. Non-durable consumer products which are used in the home, such as food, tend to be more culture-bound than industrial or technology-intensive products[5] (see Figure 9.4). For the latter type of products, little or no adaptation is generally required and the firm may well be successful in marketing a standardized product in the foreign country. Multinational firms involved in marketing food and other nondurable consumer products, however, are likely to face considerably more pressure from consumers to adapt their products to the foreign culture. One notable

FIGURE 9.4   The Influence of Cultural Grounding on Product Adaptation

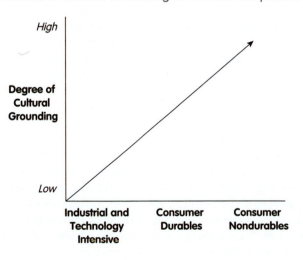

---

5   Quelch, J.A. and Hoff, E.J. (1986) 'Customizing global marketing', *Harvard Business Review*, May–June: 59–68.

example is Woodman's Sea Products of Trinity Bay, Newfoundland, Canada. This company has made significant inroads into the Japanese market for snow crabs but has had to undertake a number of adaptations. For the Japanese market, the firm first boils the crabs and then freezes them – a process which results in a less salty tasting product, which is more acceptable to the Japanese palate. The company also carefully selects the crabs destined for the Japanese market, shipping only those with a bright red color as this is what consumers in Japan look for when shopping for crabs.

PHOTO 9.2

Source: http://geo.international.gc.ca/asia/main/newsletter/ciap-2006-09-en.asp

In some instances, the global marketer may need to adapt the product because of how it is used in the foreign country. **Use conditions** may well be very different from those in the firm's home country. Consumers may be drawn to the product for reasons that differ from its intended use, creating an opportunity for the firm to modify and extend the brand.

THE ECONOMICS OF ADAPTATION

The factors driving product adaptation decisions have been discussed above. A key issue that remains, however, is the extent of the changes that should be made by the firm. A simple conceptual framework may assist the global marketing manager in thinking about this problem. As illustrated in Figure 9.5, as the firm moves from producing a fully adapted product to one that is fully standardized, its manufacturing costs will steadily decrease. As the product becomes more standardized, however, it also becomes increasingly off-target, i.e. it fails to appeal fully to the needs of any one group of customers. This results in a loss of sales among consumers in a number of country markets where there is a preference for a more customized and unique product. The cost of lost sales and the cost of manufacturing may be combined to determine the extent of adaptation a firm should undertake. This is represented by the lowest point on the combined cost curve.

FIGURE 9.5   The Economics of Product Adaptation

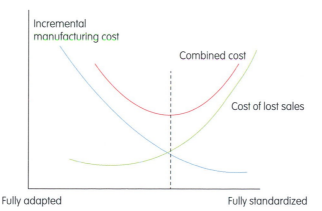

Source: Johansson, J.K. (2003) *Global Marketing: Foreign Entry, Local Marketing, and Global Management.* New York: McGraw-Hill/Irwin.

GLOBAL BRAND STRATEGIES

The multinational firm is generally marketing a number of product brands in the countries in which it operates. Some of these brands may be local, some regional and others global. The number of brands marketed may be the result of a deliberate strategy of new product development on the part of the firm, or it may be the result of merger and acquisition activities over a number of years in which both complementary and competing brands enter the firm's portfolio. Management of the company's brand portfolio is a major consideration for the global marketing firm.

According to the American Marketing Association, a brand may be defined as a name, logo, term, sign, symbol or some combination of these that serves to identify the goods and services of one seller or group of sellers and to differentiate them from those of competitors. A strong brand offers the firm a number of important advantages in the marketplace (Keller, 2003).[6] Research has shown that brand names tend to be positively associated with perceptions of product quality and purchase rates. Familiarity with a brand has also been shown to increase consumer confidence and positively influence purchase intentions. Several studies have further demonstrated that brand leaders are able to command higher prices in the marketplace and that this takes place at the expense of less well-established brands. A brand's dominant position in the marketplace also makes it less vulnerable to price competition from less well-respected brands and consumers tend to have a more positive evaluation of the advertising appeals of dominant brands. A number of positive channel-related effects have also been found to be associated with leading brands. For example, stores are more likely to feature leading brands when they wish to convey an image of high quality and, of course, these brands have a much less difficult task of securing shelf space and channel acceptance than their less well-known competitors.

MEASURING BRAND EQUITY

Table 9.1 ranks the top 12 global brands. Coca-Cola is the global leader with a brand valuation of almost $78 billion, closely followed by Apple at $77 billion. Clearly, brands are valuable assets for the firms that own them. The value of a brand to the firm is referred to as its **brand equity** and is derived from perceptions held by consumers that well-known brands have important positive attributes and that consumers derive desirable results from their use. In essence, products that carry a well-known brand name are expected to generate more money for the firm than products that are not as well branded. Firms, of course, seek to manage their brand portfolio so as to maximize brand equity. It is, therefore, important for the global marketing manager to understand how brands create value and how brand equity can be effectively measured. Keller and Lehman (2003) outline a framework for understanding the process of brand value creation[7] (Figure 9.6). The framework, referred to as the **brand value chain**, is based on the premise that ultimately it is the consumer that is responsible for value creation. The process of value creation begins when the firm makes the decision to invest in a marketing program. These investments may be in terms of advertising and promotion, product-related research and development, public relations, personal selling or support to channel intermediaries. The objective of these investments is to positively influence the mindset of the consumer towards the brand.

The positive mindset that is created by investments made in the firm's marketing program relates to the consumer's attitudes, perceptions, beliefs, experiences and feelings towards the brand. According to the literature, the consumer mindset has a number of dimensions:

- brand awareness, i.e. the extent to which consumers are able to recognize the brand and identify the associated products and services
- brand association, i.e. the strength and favorability of perceived attributes and benefits consumers associate with the brand

---

6 Keller, K.L. (2003) 'Branding and brand equity', in B. Weitz and R. Wensley (eds) *Handbook of Marketing*. London: SAGE.

7 Keller, K.L. and Lehmann, D.R. (2003) 'How do brands create value?', *Marketing Management*, May/June: 27–31.

TABLE 9.1   Top Global Brands, 2012

Rank	Name of company	Brand value ($m)
1	Coca-Cola	77,839
2	Apple	76,568
3	IBM	75,532
4	Google	69,726
5	Microsoft	57,853
6	GE	43,682
7	McDonald's	40,062
8	Intel	39,385
9	Samsung	32,893
10	Toyota	30,280
11	Mercedes-Benz	30,097
12	BMW	29,052

Source: Interbrand (2012) *Best Global Brands: The Definitive Guide to the 100 Best Global Brands.*

FIGURE 9.6   The Brand Value Chain

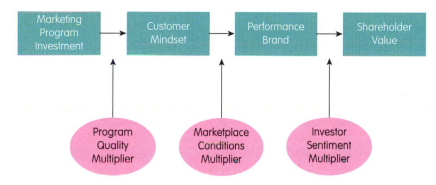

Source: Adapted from Keller and Lehman (2003)

- brand attitudes, i.e. consumers' assessment of the overall quality and satisfaction they generate from the brand
- brand attachment, i.e. loyalty to the brand
- brand activity, i.e. the extent to which consumers seek out additional information about the brand, speak to other consumers and attend brand-specific events.

A positive consumer mindset results in certain performance outcomes in terms of, for example, the quantity of the product purchased, the market share and the price consumers are willing to pay. Performance outcomes also relate to the potential for successful brand extensions and overall brand profitability. Eventually, the investment community begins to pay attention to this superior performance which is reflected in such metrics as the company's share price, market capitalization and price/earnings ratio.

The brand value chain also assumes the existence of a number of multipliers or linking variables that determine how value created at one stage is transferred to the other (see Figure 9.6). The program quality multiplier takes into account the qualitative aspects of the marketing program (as opposed to the amount invested) in terms of its clarity, relevance, distinctiveness and consistency. These factors serve to enhance the impact of the investments made in marketing programs. The marketplace conditions multiplier refers to factors such as channel support for the brand, the reaction of competitors and the number of profitable consumers that are attracted to the company's brand. Increased channel support for the brand would be expected to have a positive impact on value creation, as does the inability of competitors to respond aggressively to the firm's marketing program. The ability to attract a large number of profitable consumers also has a positive impact on the value creation process. As illustrated in Figure 9.6, Keller and Lehman (2003) also argue in favor of an investor sentiment multiplier which takes into account a number of external factors such as the dynamics of the financial markets, e.g. the level of interest rates, as well as the growth potential for the brand and the industry. Also considered in this multiplier is the importance of the brand to the firm's portfolio and any risks to which the brand and its category are exposed.

GLOBAL BRANDING

Building a global brand is an expensive and complex undertaking. In some cases, brands developed for the home country must be marketed in foreign countries, while in other cases the firm may opt to develop brands which are positioned from the outset as being global. According to Usunier and Shaner (2012), transferring brands across borders presents the multinational firm with a number of challenges as brand names and brand meaning often do not travel well.[8]

TRANSFERRING BRAND NAMES

To be successful, international brand names should:

- have a consistent pronunciation across all languages
- have a positive meaning that fits the intended product attributes and positioning
- be simple enough for target market customers to be able to spell the name when they hear it and pronounce it when they see it.

For the above to be accomplished, the writing and spelling system should be familiar to the target country customer but, as noted by Usunier and Shaner (2012), this is problematic in a country such as China where the Roman alphabet is unfamiliar or in Japan where it is viewed as foreign and is not well received. The problem is compounded by names that contain long sequences of consonants or vowels, as these are not found in some languages such as Chinese and Japanese and create an impediment to linguistic transferability. Consumers who are unable to pronounce a foreign brand name will usually change the pronunciation by dropping letters or putting the emphasis on different syllables. Simple brand names have been found to be more easily transferrable across international borders than more difficult names.

TRANSFERRING BRAND MEANING

When brands are marketed in foreign countries, new meanings may emerge which may be at variance with the brand's original meaning. These new meanings may be negative, as in the oft-quoted example of Kellogg's having to change the name of its *Bran Buds* cereal in Sweden where the name was interpreted as 'grilled farmer' or the case of the Chevrolet *Nova*

---

[8] Usunier, J.-C. and Shaner, J. (2012) 'International branding: Creating global brand equity through language', in T.C. Melewar and S. Gupta (eds) *Strategic International Marketing: An Advanced Perspective*. London: Palgrave Macmillan, pp. 5–22.

which, when translated into Spanish, suggests that the car does not work. In some instances, the brand's source meaning is completely lost because consumers in the target country simply don't understand the name. For example, in non-English-speaking countries the brand name *Tide* is pronounced 'teed' which hardly evokes an image of powerful waves washing clothes that this popular detergent is supposed to conjure up. Connotative meaning is also often lost when brands cross borders because consumers in the target country don't understand the use of rhetorical elements in the source language. *Fédor*, for example, is marketed as an orange juice 'made of gold' (*fait d'or*). However, only French speakers would understand the meaning, assuming that they appreciated the play on words (Usunier and Shaner, 2012).

ALTERNATIVE APPROACHES TO BRAND TRANSFERABILITY

Researchers have identified a number of approaches to transferring brand names across national and linguistic borders. The first is **translation**. With translation, the firm attempts to find words in the target country language that correspond to the exact words used in the source country language. As illustrated above, in the Kellogg's *Bran Buds* example, this does not always produce satisfactory results. Simple translation of the brand name often fails to convey brand meaning and is usually not the best option for the firm. **Transliteration** is another option open to the firm in which an attempt is made to reconstitute the connotative meaning of the brand name in the target country language. This may involve the use of different words. For example, Gillette's *Silkience* shampoo is marketed as *Soyance* in France and *Sientel* in Italy. A third option for the firm is **transparency** or the use of blank names. Blank names have no meaning when first introduced into the market but acquire meaning over time as consumers are exposed to the product and its advertising and promotional appeals. Brand names may be source blank and/or target blank, depending on whether they have meaning in the source and/or target countries. Sony, for example, is source blank as the word has no meaning in Japanese and is also target blank in most countries. Tide, on the other hand, is not source blank as it has a meaning in the USA but is target blank in most other countries. The use of transparent names with no strong linguistic or cultural associations is perhaps the best option for the firm.

BRAND CHANGEOVER STRATEGIES

A key issue in brand management is the introduction of a new global brand to markets in which the firm already markets a local brand. The mechanics of brand changeover present a few options for the global marketer.[9] If the local brand is well known, the global marketer may opt to pursue what is described as a **fade-in/fade-out** strategy in which the global brand is associated or linked with the local brand for a specified period of time, after which the local brand is dropped. Essentially, there is a transition phase that allows consumers to adjust to the global brand. During this transition, the global and local brands may be linked in a number of ways. For example, one brand may be used to introduce the other (i.e. endorsement branding) or both brands may be presented side by side during the transition phase (i.e. double branding). For example, Mars, the US food company, used the tagline 'Pedigree by Pal' when it introduced Pedigree (its global brand of dog food) as a replacement for Pal (its local brand). Similarly, when Whirlpool acquired Phillips' white goods division, both names appeared on its appliances for a period of time. The Phillips name was eventually dropped.

A second brand changeover strategy open to the multinational firm is **summary axing**, in which the local brand is simply dropped and the global brand simultaneously introduced. Mars again provides an example. In the mid-1980s, the company simply pulled its Treets brand

---

[9] This section draws heavily on Johansson, J.K. (2003) *Global Marketing: Foreign Entry, Local Marketing, and Global Management*. New York: McGraw-Hill/Irwin.

off the European market and introduced M&Ms using the same 'Melts in your mouth, not in your hand' tagline that had been used to promote the Treets brand. It should be emphasized that this latter approach may anger customers who are loyal to the local brand and may create public relations difficulties for the firm. Mars in fact did suffer a backlash from its adult consumers and saw sales and profits decline. A third option for the firm is to **forewarn.** With this strategy, the company informs consumers in advance that their local brand will soon be known by its new global name. Learning the lesson from the Treets debacle, Mars used extensive forewarning to replace its local Raider brand with its global Twix brand. The company's television commercials advised customers that 'Now Raider becomes Twix, for it is Twix everywhere in the world'.

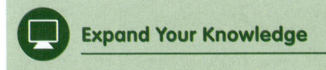

Expand Your Knowledge

Townsend, J.D., Yeniyurt, S. and Talay, M.B. (2009) 'Getting to global: An evolutionary perspective of brand expansion in international markets', *Journal of International Business Studies*, 40: 539–58.

This article explores brand globalization from an evolutionary perspective. The authors suggest that firms may accelerate the brand globalization process by entering the three major continents in the early stages of international expansion.

NEW PRODUCT DEVELOPMENT

New products are the lifeblood of the global marketing firm. While the firm may attempt to extend the life of its brands, new product innovations are required to keep the company uppermost in the minds of consumers and resist competitive pressures. The development of new products is important to the success of the firm in international markets and should be an ongoing process for the company. Of course, for new global products to be brought to market, they must meet the company's criteria for market, technical and financial feasibility. As illustrated in Figure 9.7, new product development includes a number of tradeoffs between satisfying customer needs, time to market and cost. Other things being equal, a new product

FIGURE 9.7   Tradeoff in New Product Development

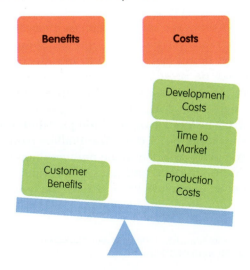

will be more profitable for the global firm if it provides greater product benefits than the alternatives available to the consumer and can be brought to market quickly with relatively low development and production costs (Dahan and Hauser, 2003).[10] To ensure a satisfactory outcome, the global marketing firm is, therefore, well advised to adopt a systematic approach to the development of new products.

The process of new product development may be conceptualized as a sequence of related steps, as outlined in Figure 9.8. It is also referred to as a **stage gate process** because at each stage members of the product development team are required to provide adequate justification for moving on to the next stage. Of course, the firm may have several of these processes taking place concurrently in order to ensure that a continuous flow of new and innovative products come to market as needed. The process begins with **idea creation** and culminates with the global launch of the new product. Ideas for new products may be the result of the firm's research and development efforts but may also be generated by sources external to the company such as suppliers, retailers or consumers. In fact, the best new product ideas may be generated by those external to the company. In general, company employees view the market through the lens of their own products and may have a difficult time thinking 'outside the box'. **Lead users** are consumers with strong product needs and a vested interest in devising solutions that address those needs. These users are generally ahead of their time in thinking about the needs the product should be addressing and are an excellent source of new product ideas.

FIGURE 9.8   Process of Global Product Development

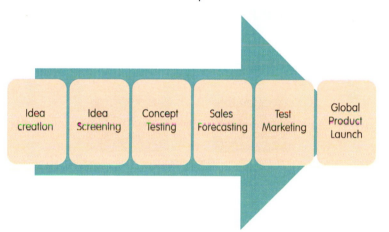

Not all new ideas that come to the attention of the company should, however, be pursued. The second step in the process is, therefore, to screen new ideas based on a set of well-developed criteria. **Idea screening** should be undertaken using three broad sets of criteria: market, financial and technical. Technical criteria relate to the key question: can the product be made? If the current state of technical knowledge does not allow the firm to manufacture the product, it may be necessary to partner with another firm, acquire new technical skills or abandon the product idea altogether. Market criteria include such considerations as the size of the addressable market for the new product and its potential growth rate, while financial criteria relate to whether or not the new product can be profitably manufactured and marketed.

From the pool of new product possibilities, the firm will focus on two or three for further analysis and development. The third step in the process is **concept testing**.

---

10   Dahan, E. and Hauser, J.R. (2003) 'Product development: Managing a dispersed process', in B. Weitz and R. Wensley (eds) *Handbook of Marketing*. London: SAGE, pp. 179–222.

At this stage, the firm seeks to gain early insights into how the new product will likely be received by prospective customers. Will consumers view the new product as adding value? Does the new product incorporate features that consumers believe are the most important? To gauge consumer reaction, the firm may produce a prototype of the new product and conduct a series of focus groups in the international markets of interest. This process will allow the company to receive feedback from prospective customers on areas in which the product may be improved or even whether they see any value added from its introduction to the market. Focus group research will also provide some early indications of how consumers intend to use the product and the likelihood of purchase. Listening to the voice of the customer is an iterative process, as illustrated in Figure 9.9. The firm may in fact have to re-conceptualize the product several times in response to feedback from consumers.

FIGURE 9.9   Voice of the Customer

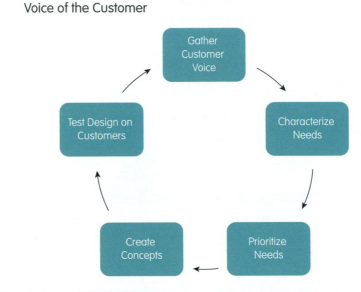

Source: Adapted from Dahan and Hauser (2003)

Box 9.2

The **Kano model** is used to map the needs of customers to product benefits in the concept testing stage of global product development. According to the shape of the features to satisfaction curve, customer needs are categorized as: 'Must Have', 'More the Better' or 'Delighter' (see Figure 9.10). Must-have needs are met by current technologies and consumers have come to expect these features to be included in the product. In fact, they may show significant dissatisfaction if they are not incorporated into the new product. Competing products routinely include these features. Needs may also be classified as 'more the better' if the technology or innovation simply serves to increase the level by which the need is met. This increase in satisfaction usually occurs with diminishing returns. Needs classified as 'delighter' are those which consumers do not expect to have satisfied or may not even be consciously aware exist. Companies that are able to incorporate such features into their products will trigger a sharp escalation in consumer satisfaction and eventual brand loyalty. The Kano model is dynamic. Companies should expect that today's delighter needs will become tomorrow's must haves.

FIGURE 9.10   The Kano model

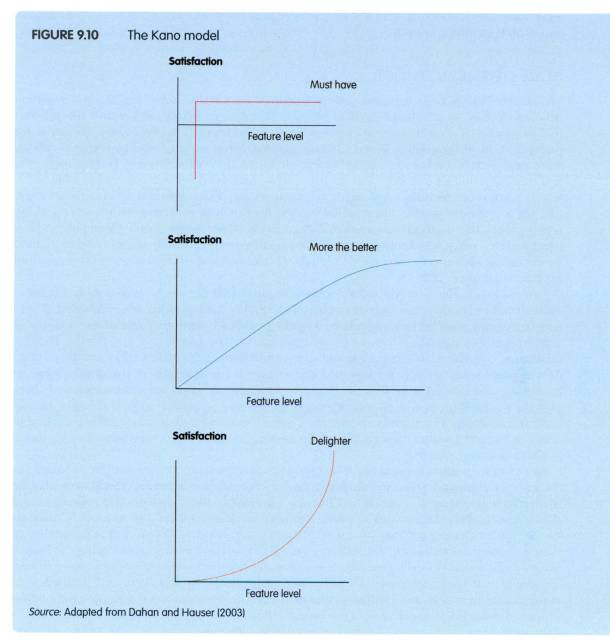

Source: Adapted from Dahan and Hauser (2003)

For those new product ideas that survive the concept testing stage, the fourth step in the process is the development of **sales forecasts**. The key consideration here is to determine how many units the company can reasonably expect to sell over the life cycle of the product. If the product is new to the world, it may be necessary to develop a forecast using a suitable proxy variable to predict the sales performance of the new product under consideration. In other situations, the firm may use lead-lag analysis to forecast sales or employ the technique of forecasting by analogy. Assuming satisfactory projected sales, the next step in the product development process is **test marketing**. A limited number of units of the product are produced and introduced to a few test markets around the world. The selection of test sites and the timing of the product introduction need to be carefully considered to allow the company to accurately gauge the commercial potential of the product. Assuming a favorable consumer response, the firm proceeds to the next step of full commercialization and **global product launch**.

ROLE OF THE INTERNET

The Internet can play an important role at various stages of the global product development process. It may be a valuable tool to allow companies to better understand the product features most desired by their customers. In the development of its i-Zone, a system for printing mini photographs, Polaroid Corp. used a private online site to solicit feedback from prospective customers on the various features they valued most. Interestingly, the features most highly valued were not the ones envisioned by the company's engineers, which were more technical and costly to manufacture. The Internet may also be an effective source of new product ideas, allowing the firm to spot emerging trends ahead of the competition. This strategy was used by Betfair, a UK-based online gaming company, which observed that eBay was successful in addressing the needs of hobby traders and so created an exchange platform to cater to individuals with an interest in betting on various sporting events (Muammer, 2003).[11]

In most cases, global product development requires that the company assembly a team of specialists in various areas such as engineering, quality management and marketing. These specialists may well be located in the company's offices in various parts of the country or scattered across subsidiary offices around the world. The Internet is an effective tool for facilitating collaboration across time and space and ensuring that all members of the product development team are actively involved and engaged. For example, in the development of its fighter jets, Boeing uses Internet-based technologies to coordinate meetings and allow customers, developers and project managers to see and comment on new designs. In this case, the company's customers may be the US Air Force and Britain's Royal Navy, located in Washington and London respectively, while developers and project managers may be based in California and Seattle.[12]

As the new product approaches the commercialization stage, testing will be required. In the case of computer software, this may be conveniently done online. Customers may be invited to beta-test new products and provide feedback to the company. The process allows the firm to correct deficiencies in programming and design before the product is released to the public. Companies may also use this process to test the design and functionality of their website prior to launch. The Internet may also prove to be invaluable during the launch stage of the product development process. For example, it may be used effectively to create global customer awareness of the firm's new products, as was done with BlackBerry's launch of its new Z-10 and Q-10 smartphones. The company provided a significant amount of information online in advance of the launch, allowing consumers to evaluate the product's new and improved features. A series of email messages, for example, was sent to existing BlackBerry users providing photos and descriptions of the new product. Once the product is launched, the Internet is, of course, also effective at providing ongoing customer support and technical assistance.

THE LOCUS OF NEW PRODUCT DEVELOPMENT

The global marketing firm must also make a decision with respect to where new products will be developed and financed. For most multinationals, the bulk of research and development work takes place at head office with innovations rolled out to foreign market

---

[11]   Muammer, O. (2003) 'Using the Internet in new product development', *Research Technology Management*, 46, 1: 10–15.

[12]   Muammer (2003) op cit.

subsidiaries as they become available. In some cases, however, companies may derive benefits from having new product development activities located in the overseas subsidiaries with the resultant innovations shared with head office. For example, Campbell's, the US food company, established an R&D center in Hong Kong with a mandate to adapt the company's products to the Chinese market. However, given the interest in ethnic foods across North America and Europe, this mandate has since been expanded with the center now responsible for transferring innovations developed for the Asian market to the US parent and subsidiaries in the West.[13]

The decision regarding where to locate new product development is driven by a number of factors. One may, for example, point to the need to access specific technical skills in a particular country as being an important driver. Proximity to leading universities or industry clusters may well provide the firm with engineering and scientific skills which would be difficult to access elsewhere. Also important may be access to demanding consumers with discerning tastes and a passion for quality. Locating new product development activities close to such consumers may provide the company with an invaluable testing ground for new designs and technologies. A number of the major auto companies, for example, have located their design centers in California to allow them access to a pool of trend-setting consumers.

In terms of organization, it should be noted that global product development historically emphasized co-location of cross-functional teams in order to facilitate collaboration among marketing, engineering, supply chain and manufacturing specialists.[14] Today co-location is becoming less important and companies are moving towards a more distributed networked organizational structure facilitated by advanced communication technologies. Members of the same product development team, which may include outside consultants and technical specialists, may be located in multiple countries but are connected digitally. Sophisticated computer design tools and high bandwidth networks allow firms to draw on specialist resources wherever they may be located around the globe.

Eppinger and Chitkara (2006) outline ten key factors for the successful deployment of global product development strategies:

1. The company's senior executives must make global product development a strategic priority for the firm. This commitment includes making the investments required to ensure success. Many companies appoint an executive with overall responsibility for the global product development strategy. This individual's mandate would include the establishment of global design centers, facilitating the distribution of work across the various product development teams and ensuring that teams have the resources and tools needed to accomplish their tasks.

2. The company must develop a methodology for ensuring process modularity. The product development process must be broken down into clear steps which allow work packages to be assigned to specific teams.

3. Product modularity is also important to the success of the global product development strategy. With product modularity, complete sub-systems may be assigned to specific teams located in different countries. The authors note that without such modularity more intense collaboration across design interfaces would be necessary.

4. It is important not to outsource elements of global product development that comprise the core competence of the firm. Such a decision may well leave the firm captive to a supplier or may create a potential competitor.

5. With a distributed product development infrastructure, protection of the firm's intellectual property becomes more important. A number of teams located in various countries, including outside contractors, may have access to critical data. A modular approach to product development may serve to protect the firm's intellectual property by limiting access to proprietary information on the complete system.

---

[13] Czinkota, M., Ronkainen, I., Farrell, C. and McTavish, R. (2009) *Global Marketing: Foreign Entry, Market Development and Strategy Implementation*. Toronto: Nelson Education.

[14] Eppinger, S.D. and Chitkara, A.R. (2006) 'The new practice of global product development', *MIT Sloan Review*, Summer.

6. The company must ensure that all product development teams, wherever located, have access to the same source data. Technical specification and elements of design may be adjusted as the project develops. These changes must be made available to members of the global product development teams involved.

7. The company must pay attention to providing the requisite infrastructural support to the network of teams involved in the product development process. Power and network outages in countries such as India and China may severely hamper productivity and work flow.

8. Governance structures and strong project management are required to effectively implement a global product development strategy. The firm must ensure that the requisite management skills and controls are in place to ensure that complex processes are kept on track.

9. For global product development to be effectively utilized, the firm also needs to build a collaborative culture within the organization. The firm will have to find ways to promote collaboration across individuals and teams from different national cultures, who operate in various time zones and may even be employed by different companies (in the case of subcontractors). Under these conditions, policies and standards must be consistent and transparent to all teams and team members involved in the project. The authors suggest that the deployment of head-office managers to remote project locations to train overseas team members and act as a liaison with headquarters may be an effective strategy. Trust between teams needs to be developed but is only likely to occur over time.

10. The effective implementation of a global product development strategy will require organizational change. Individuals will be required to assume new roles and reporting relationships, as well as to develop new skills and behaviors. These changes may prove challenging for the organization but must be managed effectively if the strategy is to be successful.

COUNTERFEIT PRODUCTION

At some point, the global marketing manager may have to address the problem of counterfeit production. Counterfeit products are 'knock-offs' or fakes and are defined as any product 'bearing an unauthorized representation of a trademark, patented invention, or copyrighted work that is legally protected in the country where it is marketed'.[15] In a 2007 study, the European Commission estimated that the total value of counterfeit products crossing national borders was $250 billion. Roughly 7–10 percent of all products sold worldwide were fakes, according to this organization. Other agencies have put the value of counterfeit products even higher. When national counterfeit markets and pirated digital materials such as movies and music are considered, the International Chamber of Commerce estimated the counterfeit market to be worth roughly $650 billion in 2008. These numbers are significant and in fact exceed the size of the market for other illegal activities such as weapons smuggling and human trafficking. They also put the counterfeit industry on a par with the market for illegal drugs.[16]

Several reasons may be advanced for the proliferation of counterfeit products around the world. Chief among them is the fact that the penalties for counterfeiting are far less severe than for drug smuggling and the margins from this illegal activity are also very generous. There is, therefore, little by way of a deterrent to individuals wanting to enter the industry. It should be noted that China is the main source of counterfeit products, although the practice is also rampant in other countries such as India, Taiwan, Korea and Brazil. While not a major source of counterfeit products, Canada is an important trans-shipment point for entry into the USA.

According to the OECD,[17] counterfeit production has a number of undesirable effects. At the level of the multinational firm, the practice:

---

15   Czinkota et al. (2009) op cit., p. 314.

16   Hargreaves, S. (2012) Counterfeit Goods Becoming More Dangerous. CNN Money. Available at: http://money.cnn.com/2012/09/27/news/economy/counterfeit-goods/index.html, accessed February 22, 2013.

17   Organization for Economic Cooperation and Development (OECD) (2007) The Economic Impact of Counterfeiting and Piracy. Available at: www.oecd.org/industry/ind/38707619.pdf, accessed February 25, 2013.

- leads to lost sales as authentic products are crowded out of the market by fake products. Sales volume and market share will be reduced for the owner of the intellectual property as some consumers unwittingly purchase the fake products. The multinational firm's sales activity will also be reduced because other consumers knowingly purchase the pirated product. In either instance, the owner of the intellectual property suffers the consequences of declining sales volume

- results in lost goodwill for the owner of the intellectual property. When the fake product does not perform as expected, consumers who unwittingly purchased the product may opt to blame the manufacturer of the genuine product. Further, the proliferation of counterfeited luxury brands may reduce the desirability of the genuine product and again damage the brand's value in the marketplace

PHOTO 9.3

- results in lost royalties for the owner of the intellectual property
- increases the firm's cost of operation as resources must be allocated to monitoring and policing the market for pirated products. These costs do not improve product quality or the functional benefits consumers derive from consumption of the product

- dampens the incentive for innovation. Firms may be reluctant to invest in research and development in an environment in which their intellectual property is not protected.

Any product may be counterfeited. While the practice may have originated in brand-name consumer products such as Rolex watches, Louis Vuitton handbags and Nike running shoes, it is no longer confined to these types of products. Indeed, manufacturers must now question the authenticity of the parts and other inputs used in production. Aircraft manufacturers, for example, have raised concerns about the counterfeit production of landing gears used in their products and counterfeit cockpit displays have been discovered in military aircraft deployed in Afghanistan. These displays provide pilots with diagnostic data including engine status, fuel usage, geographic location and warning messages. The defective parts were eventually traced to Hong Dark Electronic Trade in Shenzhen, China.[18] A US Senate investigation found that the problem of counterfeit parts on military aircraft was quite pervasive and that China was the source of 70 percent of the defective products.

The practice of counterfeit production has also spread to pharmaceutical drugs and pesticides. Counterfeit production now raises serious health and safety concerns for authorities around the world. For example, counterfeit teething powder in Nigeria, fake cough syrup in Panama and counterfeit baby formula in China have all led to the deaths of children. Each year fake drugs are estimated to kill upwards of 100,000 people worldwide. Viagra has become the most counterfeited pharmaceutical drug. The drug, manufactured by Pfizer Inc. and used to treat erectile dysfunction, generated revenues in excess of $1 billion in 2011. The company has been fighting off counterfeiters since the drug was first launched in 1998. The Internet provides customers with a discreet and low-cost option to acquire the medication but it comes with substantial risks. While a counterfeit Viagra tablet may be purchased online for as little as $1 with the authentic medication retailing for $15, the fake drug may be extremely injurious to health. Pfizer has discovered chalk, brick dust, paint and even pesticides in the bogus product, with one batch of pills originating in China and sold in South Korea containing the remains of human fetuses.[19]

The company has attempted to combat the problem by launching an awareness program, as well as by the use of technology. Awareness campaigns have been focused on teaching consumers and healthcare professionals what they should look for in recognizing the fake

[18] Capaccio, T. (2011) China Counterfeit Parts in US Military Aircraft. *Bloomberg*. Available at: www.bloomberg. com/news/2011-11-07/counterfeit-parts-from-china-found-on-raytheon-boeing-systems.html, accessed February 25, 2013.

[19] Gillette, F. (2013) Inside Pfizer's Fight Against Counterfeit Drugs. *Bloomberg Businessweek*. Available at: www. businessweek.com/printer/articles/91868-inside-pfizers-fight-against-counterfeit-drugs, accessed February 15, 2013.

pills. The company notes, for example, that the counterfeit products are thinner, have a more pronounced edge, are lighter blue in color and when cut blue particles are often seen in the white core. The company has also deployed radio frequency identification (RFID) technology in its attempts to address the problem. With this approach, a high frequency electronic tag which contains a unique product identification number is placed on each bottle of Viagra as it moves through the packaging line. These data are stored on Pfizer's secure servers and may be accessed by authorized pharmacists and wholesalers in order to verify the authenticity of the products they handle.

PHOTO 9.4

As noted above, counterfeit production results in a number of undesirable effects for the multinational firm that owns the intellectual property. At a more macro level, the practice also produces a number of negative consequences:[20]

- Counterfeiting is illegal and provides a source of funds for organized criminal networks. The proceeds may in fact be used to finance other illegal and immoral activities which have a deleterious impact on society as a whole.
- Counterfeiting stifles innovation and economic growth. The practice creates a disincentive to research and development and the problem is particularly acute in those industries driven by investment in science and technology, such as pharmaceutical drugs.
- Counterfeiting shifts jobs from the manufacture of genuine products to fakes. However, wages in factories producing counterfeit products are usually lower and working conditions poorer as the operations are clandestine and not subject to government health and safety legislation.
- Counterfeit production may be costly to the environment as fakes are confiscated and destroyed by authorities. There is evidence that some fake products, such as pesticides, have caused serious environmental damage.

case study 9.3: Canada Goose clothing

Canada Goose is a Canadian company that manufactures a line of high quality winter outerwear. The company's parkas are recognized around the world for the quality of their craftsmanship. Products are hand stitched and use coyote fur around the hoods and some Hutterite down as part of the insulation system. The firm has also developed an innovative Thermal Experience Index (TEI) that helps customers find the degree of warmth they seek in a parka. As online shopping has become more pervasive, so also has counterfeiting of the company's products. Counterfeit manufacturers based in China produce the firm's products in large quantities and sell them to online retailers who operate rogue websites. These websites may in fact pose as Canada Goose, complete with the company's logo and a contact address in a major western city such as Toronto, New York or London. To combat the problem, the company has taken several steps.

Based on the notion that consumer education is an important strategy, Canada Goose has redesigned its website to include a section on counterfeiting. Visitors to the site are invited to enter a URL to determine whether a particular retailer is an authorized reseller of the company's products. The site also contains information on how consumers can recognize counterfeit Canada Goose products. The company has also modified its products by placing holograms in the seams which feature images that can be seen from different angles and are expensive and complicated for counterfeiters to reproduce. In addition, the company has retained the services of brand protection agencies in London and Boston, and these firms scan the Internet several times per day to identify rogue websites and counterfeit products sold on legitimate websites such as eBay, Kijiji and Craig's List.

---

20   OECD (2007) op cit.

For the company, these and other actions have become normal business practice as it attempts to protect its brand in a global marketplace. The company notes, however, that this has increased its cost of doing business by six figures per year.

Source

Cox, D. (2012) Canada Goose vs. Counterfeiters The Canadian Press: Canada Goose wins $105K in Swedish Counterfeit Case. Available at: www.cbc.ca/news/canada/north/story/2012/10/23/north-canada-goose-wins-counterfeit-case.html

Discussion Questions

1. What other strategies could Canada Goose employ to combat counterfeit production of its products?
2. In 2012, Canada Goose won an intellectual property infringement case in Sweden in which the firm was awarded damages totaling 701,000 Swedish kronor. The verdict also saw two Swedish nationals receive jail sentences for manufacturing and marketing fake Canada Goose products from 2009 to 2012. Do you believe this case will prove to be a deterrent to other would-be counterfeiters?

 Spotlight on Research 9.1   Consumer Ethnocentrism

Bian and Moutinho (2011) examined the demand side of counterfeiting by analyzing the impact of self-assessed product knowledge, product involvement and consumers' perceived brand image of counterfeit branded products (CBPs) on consumer purchase intentions. The authors make the point that much of the literature on counterfeit products has focused on the supply side, while the limited number of demand-side studies have only examined factors such as price benefits, psychographic and demographic variables, social influences and product features. The authors emphasize that the scope of their research is limited to non-deceptive counterfeiting, i.e. situations in which the individual knowingly purchases the counterfeit good and is not tricked or deceived into making the purchase.

Hypotheses

The authors tested the following hypotheses:

H1. The level of consumers' favorableness to the brand personality of a CBP has a positive relationship to the purchase intention of a CBP.

H2. Consumers' perceptions of product attributes have a positive influence on the purchase intention of a CBP.

H3. Consumers' perceptions of benefits have a positive influence on the purchase intention of a CBP.

H4. There is a negative relationship between product involvement and consumers' perceived brand image of a CBP.

H5. There is a negative relationship between product involvement and consumer purchase intention of a CBP.

H6. There is a negative relationship between product knowledge and consumers' perceived brand image of a CBP.

(Continued)

(Continued)

H7. There is a negative relationship between product knowledge and consumer purchase intention of a CBP.

H8. The relationship between product involvement and purchase intention of a CBP is mediated by consumers' perceived brand image of a CBP.

H9. The relationship between product knowledge and purchase intention of a CBP is mediated by consumers' perceived brand image of a CBP.

H10. When product involvement is high, the positive effect of perceived brand image (product attributes, benefits/consequences and brand personality) on consumer purchase intention of a CBP is stronger than when product involvement is low.

The authors' conceptual model is depicted below.

Method

The authors use counterfeit Rolex watches in their study which was conducted in Glasgow, UK. This choice was rationalized by the fact that Rolex is a well-established and familiar luxury brand and is also one of the most counterfeited brands. Further, the UK is considered one of the main recipients of counterfeit products, and, according to the authors, counterfeits are widely available in Glasgow. An intercept survey was conducted at four supermarkets in which every tenth individual was stopped and asked to complete a structured questionnaire; 430 shoppers were stopped, resulting in 321 useable responses. All the constructs used in the study were measured using a five-point Likert scale (1 = strongly disagree, 5 = strongly agree). With the exception of brand image, the constructs were sourced from previous studies. The Revised Personal Involvement Inventory proposed by McQuarrie and Munson (1992) was used to measure product involvement, Smith and Park's (1992) knowledge scale was used to measure product knowledge, and purchase intentions were measured using a five-item scale developed by Spears and Singh (2004). The authors devised their own construct to measure the concept of brand image. A series of focus groups was conducted which resulted in 28 items that represented the brand image of counterfeit Rolex watches. Principal Component Analysis was used to reduce these to seven factors (all eigen values are greater than one). These factors showed a three-component structure – brand personality (excitement and competence), product attributes (general and functional) and benefits/consequences (satisfaction, image and function). The authors' hypotheses were tested using hierarchical regression analyses with both direct and mediated effects being tested simultaneously.

Results

H1 suggests that brand personality will be positively related to purchase intentions. The results of the analysis, however, show only partial support for this hypothesis as only one dimension of brand personality is seen to significantly influence consumer purchase intention of counterfeit Rolex watches (competence: $\beta = 0.342$, $\rho < 0.01$; excitement: $\beta = 0.064$, $\rho > 0.05$). H2 suggests that consumers who willingly purchase a CBP are more likely to possess more positive product attribute perceptions of a CBP. Once again, the regression results show only partial support. Functional product attribute is found to be a positive and statistically significant predictor of purchase intentions ($\beta = 0.12$, $\rho < 0.01$) but not of general product attribute ($\beta = 0.08$, $\rho > 0.05$). In terms of benefits, H3 suggests that consumers' perceptions of benefits have a positive influence on the purchase intention of a CBP. Partial support is once again found. Satisfaction is found to be a statistically significant predictor of purchase intentions ($\beta = 0.13$, $\rho < 0.01$) while functional benefit and image benefit are not. The more consumers believe they will derive some satisfaction from purchasing the counterfeit Rolex, the more likely they are to consummate the purchase. Consumers, it would appear, don't expect that the counterfeit Rolex will impress anyone or even that it will work particularly well.

Accordingly, in regard to H4, there should be a negative relationship between product involvement and consumers' perceived brand image of a CBP. This hypothesis is not supported by the empirical analysis, i.e. consumers' perception of the brand image of a counterfeit Rolex does not vary with the level of product involvement. Similarly, there is no support for the hypothesized negative relationship (H5) between product involvement and intention to purchase. Product involvement has no significant impact on consumers' intention to purchase a counterfeit Rolex ($\beta = 0:08$, $\rho > 0:05$). In terms of product knowledge, there is only partial support for H6. The authors hypothesized that there would be a negative relationship between product knowledge and consumers' perception of brand image. They find, however, that product knowledge is only negatively associated with one element of image – product attribute ($\beta = -0.110$, $\rho < 0:05$). There is no relationship to brand personality and perceived benefits. Consumers with superior knowledge of timepieces are more likely to consider a counterfeit Rolex as a low-grade product in terms of its general product attributes, such as the quality of materials and workmanship.

H7 is also rejected. The authors do not find a statistically significant relationship between product knowledge and consumer purchase intention ($\beta = 0:086$, $\rho > 0:05$). Product knowledge is also not found to be a significant mediator of the relationship between brand image and purchase intention (H9). The authors correctly point out that there is no need to test the mediating effect of product involvement (H8) as the conditions which demonstrate a mediating effect are not observed. Product involvement is not related to either brand image or consumers' intention to purchase a counterfeit Rolex.

Further, given that there is no statistically significant relationship between low product involvement and brand image factors, H10 is also rejected. Purchase intentions do not vary depending on the level of product involvement. The latter is not an effective moderator of the relationship between brand image and purchase intentions.

Implications

Based on the results of their analysis, the authors argue that:

1. Companies should reconsider devoting resources to improving consumers' product knowledge with the expectation that this would curb their demand for counterfeit products. More knowledgeable consumers are not less likely to purchase a counterfeit product and do not have less favorable perceptions of counterfeit brands compared to less knowledgeable consumers.

FIGURE 9.11   Conceptual Model

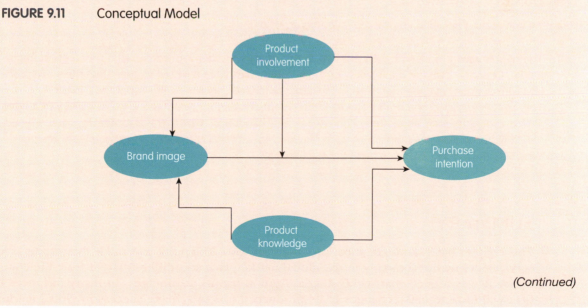

(Continued)

(Continued)

2. Marketers of branded products should similarly not devote resources to improving product involvement with the expectation that this would reduce the demand for CBPs.
3. Companies interested in combating counterfeit production should, however, develop marketing campaigns to stress brand personality differences between branded and counterfeit branded products. The authors suggest that 'highlighting the negative personality of the typical users, brand endorsers, company employees and CEO of the companies of CBPs, as these people are regarded as the directly influential factors on consumer perceived brand personality' may be an effective strategy.
4. Marketers of branded products should integrate their anti-counterfeiting and corporate social responsibility programs to create a genuine, green and long-lasting image for their products. Functional benefits were not seen to be related to purchase intentions in this research, suggesting that consumers perceive CBPs as disposable. This perception could be linked to concern for the environment, prompting consumers to reduce their CBP purchases.

Sources

Bian, X. and Moutinho, L. (2011) 'The role of brand image, product involvement, and knowledge in explaining consumer purchase behaviour of counterfeits: Direct and indirect effects', *European Journal of Marketing*, 45, 1/2: 191–216.

McQuarrie, E.F. and Munson, J.M. (1992) 'A revised product involvement inventory: Improved usability and validity', *Advances in Consumer Research*, 19, 1: 108–15.

Smith, D.C. and Park, C.W. (1992) 'The effects of brand extensions on market share and advertising efficiency', *Journal of Marketing Research*, 29, 3: 296–313.

Spears, N. and Singh, S. (2004) 'Measuring attitude toward the brand and purchase intentions', *Journal of Current Issues and Research in Advertising*, 26, 2: 53–66.

Discussion Questions

Read the complete article and answer the following questions:

1. The hypotheses proposed by the authors of this study were derived from existing theoretical frameworks. Does the fact that the majority of these hypotheses were rejected suggest that there is a problem with our current understanding of consumer purchase decisions with respect to CBPs?
2. This study examined one brand (Rolex) in one product category (watches). Do you believe that more visible products such as clothes, sunglasses and handbags, which are also heavily counterfeited, would have resulted in a more convincing relationship between brand image and purchase intentions? Why/why not? How would you test your hypothesis?

SUMMARY

This chapter has examined global product strategies. The point was made that products and services define the company in the global marketplace and differentiate it from the competition. It was argued that while standardization has its advantages, in many instances the firm will have to make changes to its products if it is to achieve success in global markets. A distinction was made between discretionary and non-discretionary adaptation, and the drivers of adaptation were also identified and discussed. The chapter also focused on the management of global brands. It was emphasized that brands have value in the marketplace and it is, therefore, important that they be effectively managed. To achieve this, it is important that the firm understand how brand equity is created, and this chapter has, therefore, presented a model of brand value creation.

New products are extremely important if the firm is to stay ahead of the competition in the global marketplace. The process of new product development was described in this chapter, beginning with idea generation and proceeding to the global launch of the product. The issue of counterfeit production was also addressed in the chapter. The magnitude and scope of the problem were discussed, along with the potential deleterious impacts the practice may have at both the firm and country levels. Strategies used by specific firms to combat the problem were shown to illustrate potential approaches to overcoming the challenge.

? discussion questions

1. Distinguish between the terms 'product adaptation' and 'product standardization'.

2. Explain the term 'mass customization' and provide an example of how a firm may use this strategy when entering foreign markets.

3. What role (if any) does cultural grounding play in a firm's decision to adapt its products for foreign markets?

4. What is meant by the term 'backward innovation' and why is the concept useful in designing the firm's global product strategy?

5. What role does the product life cycle play in a firm's decision to adapt its products for international markets?

6. What impacts do counterfeit products have on the multinational firm that manufactures the genuine product and owns the intellectual property?

7. What is the Kano model and what insights does it provide in listening to the voice of the customer?

 ## Real World Challenges

BlackBerry launch a smartphone in China

Jeff knew that this would not be his typical international product launch. As BlackBerry's (formerly Research in Motion) VP of Global Marketing, he had received a 'green light' to proceed with the launch of the company's smartphone in the Chinese market. With a population of over 1 billion and a growing middle class, this launch would appear to be a 'no-brainer' for this globally oriented Canadian company. BlackBerry had recently signed an exclusive service agreement with China Mobile Ltd to provide wireless service to the company's smartphone users in China. This was supposed to pave the way for an aggressive entrance into this potentially lucrative market. What concerned Jeff, however, was not the mechanics of launching the company's products – after all, he had done that several times in a number of countries – but the report on his desk by Marbridge Consulting which indicated that in 2005 China sold 15 million counterfeit phones compared with 60 million handsets marketed through authorized dealers. In other words, roughly 20 percent of the smartphones in China were knock-offs (or had been smuggled into the country).

(Continued)

(Continued)

The Marbridge report also noted that an unlicensed factory in China requires only 1 million yuan ($125,000) to get into the business of producing knock-offs. Further, these factories can get product to market fairly quickly by simply by-passing government testing of their product. Unlicensed handset factories in China also do not pay taxes and provide no customer service – which means that they can keep costs low and sell phones for a fraction of the cost in North America. From his research, Jeff knew that knock-off handsets and used phones have been undercutting the margins of most of the phone manufacturers in China and forcing them into the red. John Ure, a researcher at the University of Hong Kong, recently indicated that it is virtually impossible to police the black market in China. While smuggling is a capital offense in China, operators of unlicensed factories merely receive a slap on the wrist from a government with a poor track record of enforcing intellectual property rights. The end result is that these unlicensed handset factories continue to grow in size and scale, putting additional pressure on foreign smartphone manufacturers.

Jeff knew that these knock-off factories in China would not be successful if they did not have customers. Chinese consumers are obviously price sensitive and are apparently willing to overlook issues of poor customer service and a product that may well not meet even local quality standards. According to Mike Davies, an analyst with Gartner, 'Manufacturers will have an ongoing problem in China if customers continue to buy things based on price, not quality'. Jeff also had to question just how lucrative the Chinese market really was. A number of investment banks and law firms had already supplied BlackBerries to their employees in China using services provided in Hong Kong. How much up-side remained in the corporate market was a question that Jeff had to wrestle with.

Questions

1. State the problem that Jeff faces in launching BlackBerry's handsets in China.
2. Identify the options available to BlackBerry. Be sure to identify more than one.
3. Based on the options identified above, recommend a course of action for the company. Be sure to provide a rationale and make a decision.

FURTHER READING

Chabowski, B.R., Samiee, S. and Huit, C.T.M. (2013) 'A bibliometric analysis of the global branding literature and a research agenda', *Journal of International Business Studies*, 44: 622–34.
Keller, K.L. and Lehmann, D.R. (2003) 'How do brands create value?', *Marketing Management*, 12, 3: 26.
Powers, T.L. and Loyka, J.J. (2007) 'Market, industry, and company influences on global product standardization', *International Marketing Review*, 24, 6: 678–94.
Van Gelder, S. (2004) 'Global brand strategy', *Journal of Brand Management*, 12, 1: 39–48.

GLOBAL DISTRIBUTION STRATEGIES

LEARNING OBJECTIVES

After reading this chapter you should be able to:

- Define the term 'marketing channel' and explain the differences and similarities between domestic and international marketing channels

- Identify and discuss the various options open to the firm for the global distribution of its products and services

- Define the term channel design

- Discuss the key considerations in the design of a global distribution channel

- Discuss the role of international market intermediaries and their selection

- Discuss the key issues involved in the management of an international marketing channel

- Discuss the key issues involved in international logistics management

- Define the term parallel distribution and discuss its implications for global marketing strategy

- Discuss the opportunities and challenges of global retailing.

INTRODUCTION

To achieve a firm's foreign market expansion objectives, the global marketing manager must get the company's products into the hands of consumers in the foreign country. This presents a number of unique challenges that are not confronted by firms engaged in purely domestic marketing transactions. The distribution of the company's products across national borders is a much more complex undertaking, involving far more intermediaries, unfamiliar channel relationships and at times confusing import regulations. Differences in culture and level of economic development in the target country also have to be factored into the firm's global distribution strategy, as these add an additional layer of complexity.

The global marketing manager will need to design a **marketing channel** to reach the final consumer in the foreign market, bearing in mind factors such as the nature of the firm's products, competition and cost. The global marketer will also need to identify intermediaries in the target country, negotiate distribution agreements and manage the resultant relationships. Market power and conflict within the international marketing channel are also issues that will require attention if the firm is to be successful in reaching its target customers. In some cases, problems may also arise with respect to the unauthorized distribution of the firm's products in the foreign country. These situations will necessitate that the firm quickly implement strategies to combat the problem or risk alienating its authorized distributors and angering its customers.

MARKETING CHANNELS DEFINED

A marketing channel is defined as a sequence of firms or individuals involved in making a product available to final consumers or industrial buyers. International marketing channels are distinguished by the fact that they cross national borders. These channels may be simple, involving only a few intermediaries, or they may be quite complex (see Figures 10.1 and 10.2). To some extent, the complexity of the marketing channel will be

FIGURE 10.1   Simple Global Distribution Channel

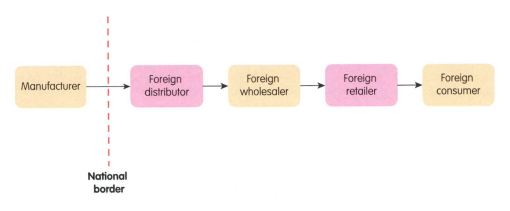

FIGURE 10.2   Complex Global Distribution Channel

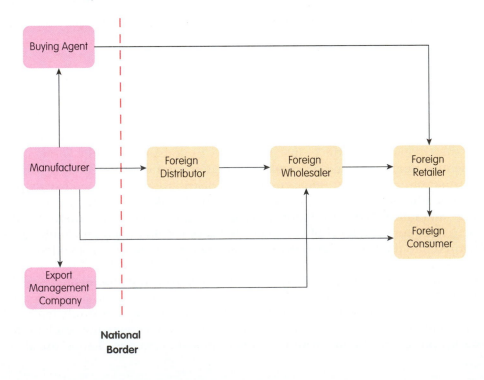

FIGURE 10.3   Options for Global Distribution

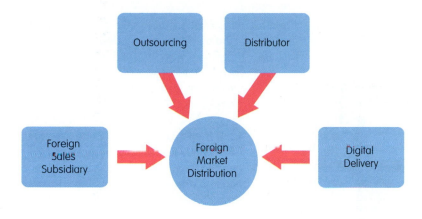

determined by the nature of the product. Industrial products tend to have relatively short distribution channels compared to consumer-oriented products. In general, the global marketing manager has a number of options to make the firm's products available to foreign customers (Figure 10.3). The firm may establish a foreign sales subsidiary in the target country staffed with sales professionals dedicated to handling its products. This option gives the company an ongoing physical presence in the country but may require that the firm recruit and train local staff and maintain office facilities. The company may also retain the services of a distributor in the target country. As noted in an earlier chapter, distributors are independent firms which purchase product from the manufacturer and take responsibility for making it available to the end user. A third option is for the firm to outsource the entire distribution system to a third-party firm (see Case Study 10.1), while a fourth option, depending on the nature of the product, is digital delivery.

It should be noted that marketing channels involve not only the movement of the physical product from the manufacturer to the end consumer but also the flow of information and title. As the product moves through the channel, information will also need to be shared with intermediaries at each stage. Such information may include data on price, quality, storage and use instructions as well as country of origin. Ownership of the product will also be transferred between intermediaries as the product moves through the channel from manufacturer to end user. Marketing channels must, therefore, be viewed as more than a flow of physical products.

case study 10.1: Global food production

Global manufacturers of perishable foods face significant challenges. Not only do they face the typical problems of moving goods with a short shelf life through the supply chain, but they also source products from diverse offshore locations to service customers in various countries around the world. Perishable food products require special handling in transit and in storage in order to preserve the integrity of the product at the point of sale. Given the perishable nature of their products and the diverse locations of their customers, manufacturers have moved to consider decentralized distribution systems, low inventory strategies and distribution arrangements that put the product closer to the end user. Suppliers of refrigerated and temperature-controlled logistics solutions have responded with innovative options that allow manufacturers to outsource services such as freeze-blasting, variable

(Continued)

(Continued)

temperature storage, integrated rail movement and LTL consolidation. One could consider the case of Canada's McCain Foods – a $1.6 billion potato product and snack food manufacturer headquartered in Florenceville, New Brunswick, and with significant operations in the USA. The firm employs 20,000 people and is the world's largest

manufacturer of frozen potato products. Major customers include Wendy's and McDonald's. In serving the American market, McCain Foods has partnered with AmeriCold Logistics to outsource cold storage and distribution at 12 of the logistics provider's facilities across the USA. AmeriCold is a third-party logistics (3PL) provider that operates refrigerated and temperature-controlled warehouses. Under the terms of the partnership agreement, AmeriCold handles product from all four of McCain's potato plants and from five of the company's six snack food plants. This means that AmeriCold is responsible for some 1.7 billion pounds of inbound receipts and accounts for 60 percent of McCain's outsourced logistics spend. The partnership makes sense in the context of McCain's global marketing strategy, given that some of the com-

PHOTO 10.1

pany's customer contracts are short term. Under these circumstances, construction of dedicated cold-storage facilities would be both risky and uneconomic. Outsourcing to AmeriCold gives McCain the flexibility to respond to consumer demand, tap into the 3PL's expertise and operate a more efficient supply chain.

Sources

O'Reilly, J. (2006) Cold Comfort. Available at: www.inboundlogistics.com/articles/features/0806_feature02.shtml, accessed November 12, 2006.

Czinkota, M., Ronkainen, I., Farrell, C. and McTavish, R. (2009) *Global Marketing: Foreign Entry, Market Development and Strategy Implementation*. Toronto: Nelson Education.

Discussion Questions

1. For food manufacturers, what factors should be considered in the decision to partner with a third-party logistics provider?
2. What risks (if any) do you see in the McCain Foods–AmeriCold relationship?

CHANNEL DESIGN

A key consideration for the firm in reaching foreign customers is the design of the international marketing channel. Channel design must consider two key factors – **channel length** and **channel width**. Channel length refers to the number of different types of intermediaries included in the channel. A channel that includes only the manufacturer, a foreign distributor, a foreign retailer and the end user is considered shorter than a channel that also includes a foreign wholesaler and maybe an export management company based in the manufacturer's home country. Channel width, on the other hand, refers to the number of intermediaries of each type included in the channel. A channel that included, say, 10 wholesalers and 15 retailers would be considered wider than a channel with one of each type of intermediary.

In determining the design of the international marketing channel, the firm should consider a number of factors. As illustrated in Figure 10.4, 11 factors are generally regarded as critical to the design of international channels. Referred to as the 11Cs framework, the first three of the factors are exogenous to the firm while the remaining eight are within the firm's control. They are discussed below.

FIGURE 10.4   The 11 Cs of International Channel Design

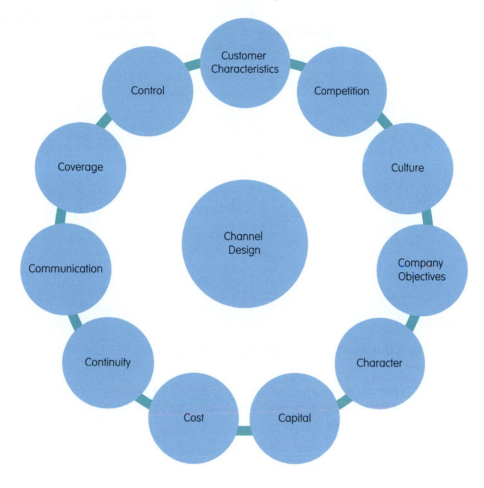

CUSTOMER CHARACTERISTICS

The characteristics of the final consumer are clearly important in channel design. The firm needs to understand the demographic and psychographic characteristics of its target customers if it is to be successful in reaching them. What is the age distribution of our customers? Where do they live? Are they rural or urban? What is their average income? What is the gender distribution of our target customers? Are they more likely to shop in upscale malls or discount outlets? While beyond the firm's control, it is essential that the global marketing manager understand the profile of the target market and use this knowledge in the design of an effective international distribution channel.

COMPETITION

Invariably, the firm will face competition in the foreign market. There may be a number of local and foreign companies vying for the same customers. These competitors may already have long-term relationships with the major distributors in the country, making it extremely difficult and costly for the firm to reach its target market. Table 10.1, for example, shows the length of exclusive distribution relationships for some of the major food brands sold in the Caribbean market. As illustrated, Kellogg's has worked with the same distributor in Jamaica for over 70 years, while Cadbury has had the same distributor in the Trinidad market for 30 years. If major distributors have long-term exclusive relationships with competing manufacturers, they may be extremely reluctant to take on the firm's products. The firm will, therefore, be left with more

TABLE 10.1   Exclusive Distribution Relationships of Global Food Brands in the Caribbean

Global brand	Target country	Length of exclusive distribution relationship (in years)
Kellogg's	Jamaica	79
Heinz	Jamaica	40
Frito-Lay	Bahamas	30
Quaker	Bahamas	12
Hershey	Trinidad	8
Kerrygold	Trinidad	38
Lipton	Trinidad	15
Gerber	Bahamas	15
Cadbury	Trinidad	30
Carnation	Trinidad	30
Maple Leaf Foods	Jamaica	10

Source: Adapted from Ontario Ministry of Agriculture and Food (2002).

costly alternatives, such as establishing its own foreign sales subsidiary or entering into contractual arrangements with a less well-established distributor that may not have the requisite retail contacts, network and experience.

CULTURE

In this context, 'culture' refers to **distribution culture**. Distribution channels have their own unique culture that is the product of the nature of the relationships that have evolved between the intermediaries. The culture of the international marketing channel may make it extremely difficult for the firm to reach its target market. This is clearly seen in the case of the Japanese *keritsu*. The *keritsu* is a close-knit set of relationships between intermediaries in the Japanese distribution system characterized by interlocking directorates and ownership structures. It is not uncommon, for example, to have major retailers owned by distributors which may also own the major transportation companies. Wholesalers may have representation on the board of directors of the retailers as well as the major distributors. These relationships are complex and difficult for western companies to understand and they make reaching the Japanese consumer an extremely challenging proposition.

COMPANY OBJECTIVES

The design of the international marketing channel must allow the company to meet its strategic objectives. In expanding into new foreign markets, the firm should have established clear targets for what it wants to accomplish in terms of market share and overall profitability. The channel design must ensure that these targets are achievable. An international marketing channel, for example, that does not allow the firm to reach its most preferred customers will likely result in the company not meeting its sales and profit expectations. Similarly, a channel design that includes retailers that are inconsistent with the company's brand image will likely hurt the firm's attempts to build market share in the foreign country.

CHARACTER

The character or nature of the product is a crucial consideration in the design of the international marketing channel. For example, if the firm's products are highly perishable, an excessively long channel will likely be detrimental to product quality and the firm's brand image in the marketplace. Non-perishable items, on the other hand, tend to be supported by relatively longer channels.

CAPITAL

Capital, or the cost involved in establishing the international marketing channel, is also of importance to the firm. A channel design may be effective at reaching the company's target market but may be too costly to establish. It should be noted that the fixed costs involved in channel design need to be recovered and may well have to be passed on to the consumer in the form of higher prices. However, this may not be in the best long-term interest of the company in a highly competitive international environment.

COST

Cost is related to capital and refers to the ongoing expenses of operating the marketing channel once established. The manufacturer may, for example, be required to cover expenses related to in-store advertising and promotions, or the firm may have to cover costs related to product training or financial incentives for sales personnel employed by the distributor. In other instances, the company may have to cover costs to secure shelf space from the retailer, and in other cases the firm may be charged a stocking fee. These ongoing costs need to be factored into the firm's decision to adopt a particular channel design.

COVERAGE

The global marketing manager must also consider the issue of market coverage. This factor relates to how readily accessible the firm's products are to prospective foreign customers. Depending on the nature of the product, the firm may have to design a channel that provides for **intensive coverage**, i.e. widespread availability. Food products and small convenience items, for example, demand intensive distribution. These products are relatively low priced and are used regularly by a wide cross-section of the population. Widespread availability across a variety of retail outlets is essential for the commercial success of such products. Other products may require that the firm provide for **selective coverage** in which availability is limited to a few retail outlets. Discretionary consumer items such as jewelry, for example, benefit from selective distribution. In some cases, the firm may opt for **exclusive coverage** in which its products are sold through one retailer in the target market. Manufacturers of high-end performance luxury cars, for example, may utilize this form of coverage, believing that it is more in keeping with the image of their products.

CONTROL

The use of market intermediaries will result in the firm losing some degree of control over its products. Depending on the nature of the product, this may not be a major issue. In the case of highly branded consumer items, for example, control may be a critical consideration in the design of the channel. The firm will want to market the product through a channel that is supportive of the product's brand image. This is seen, for example, in the case of

Prada, the Italian luxury fashion house which is famous for its handbags and footwear. The company traditionally used a wholesale model in which its products were marketed through third-party retail outlets. However, as world economies struggled with the financial crisis that began in 2007, it became clear to the company that its wholesale model was no longer working. Third-party retailers desperate to generate sales began to heavily discount the company's luxury brands. This was not consistent with the image the company wished to project and the firm has begun to place more emphasis on its own retail store network.[1] In the case of commodity type items, however, the issue of control is not likely to be a major concern for the firm.

CONTINUITY

The global marketing manager must ensure that the channel design implemented will allow the firm to maintain a continuous presence in the foreign target market. Companies which establish a foreign market presence only to withdraw after a short period of time are likely to face considerable challenges in re-entering that market. Loss of distribution in the target market may well have a very negative impact on consumer sentiment, which may have long-lasting effects.

COMMUNICATION

Effective management of international distribution relationships requires ongoing communication between the firm and its market intermediaries. This inter-organizational communication will, however, be complicated by a variety of factors such as cultural distance between the parties. Language differences, both verbal and non-verbal, may well make communication between the firm and its intermediaries a challenging proposition. Differences in approaches to conducting business are also likely to present hurdles to effective communication. Geographic distance between the manufacturer's home country and the target market may also present obstacles, although this is much less likely to be a problem now, given current electronic and video-conferencing technologies.

THE ROLE OF FOREIGN MARKET INTERMEDIARIES

As noted above, the firm may opt to reach its foreign customers via digital delivery. For many types of products, however, this is not a viable option and the company must set about the task of designing a formal international marketing channel to move physical products to the final consumer. Once the design is in place, the company should then consider which specific intermediaries to recruit and how to manage the channel relationships.

SELECTION OF FOREIGN MARKET INTERMEDIARIES

The process of selecting a foreign market intermediary is an extremely important one. The process should begin with a clear articulation of what the company hopes to accomplish in the foreign market in terms of, for example, sales volume, market share and geographic coverage. It is also necessary for the global marketing manager to have some appreciation of foreign market conditions and of what a distributor can realistically be expected to accomplish. This analysis would allow the manager to better understand the type of distributor that would be most effective in the target country. The next task is to identify and

---

[1] Walker, R. (2012) Prada's Growth Model Shows the Way Forward. Available at: http://blog.euromonitor.com/2012/05/pradas-growth-model-shows-the-way-forward.html, accessed March 5, 2013.

FIGURE 10.5   Screening Criteria

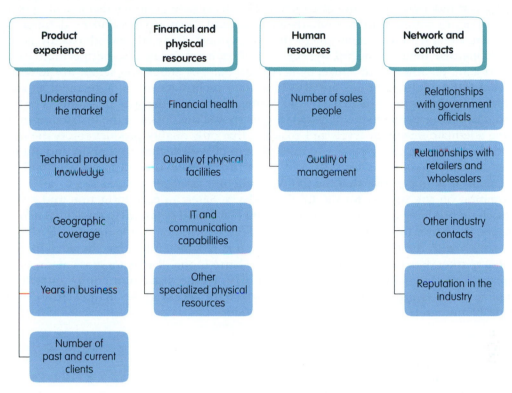

shortlist a number of potential candidate intermediaries. The global marketing manager may identify prospective distributors at trade shows relevant to the company's industry or by consulting directories of distributors compiled by host-country governments or relevant industry associations. The global marketing manager may also find it useful to consult with retailers, transportation companies and other firms in the trade. Face-to-face discussions with prospective distributors and objective evaluation are essential. In screening prospective distributors, the global marketer should use well-defined criteria in the selection process. At a minimum, these should include the criteria listed in Figure 10.5. A background check of the most promising distribution partners, including a credit check, is also useful as part of the screening process.

DISTRIBUTION AGREEMENTS

In some instances, the global marketer may find that the most suitable distributors are already handling the products of competitors and are, therefore, not available. The more experienced distributors may, for example, have handled major international brands for decades and are understandably reluctant to entertain switching to a product line that is new to the country. If the screening process is successful, however, and a suitable distributor is found, it would be necessary to draw up a contractual agreement. In general, it is recommended that distributor agreements should initially be short term (1–2 years) or contain a termination clause. This will provide the parties with a way out of the relationship if it is not working. The global manager may also wish to consider a six-month trial period with some minimum purchase requirements in the case of a new and inexperienced distributor.

The distributor agreement must also clearly specify the distributor's geographic territory. If geographic boundaries are not well defined, problems may arise as the company rolls out its expansion strategy nationally and regionally. The company's existing distributors may assume rights to territory if boundaries are not well defined in their contracts. It is also recommended that the firm reserve the right to service particularly important clients directly and independent of the distributor.[2] The distributor contract also needs to be clear with respect to compensation. Commission rates and discounts need to be defined in the agreement along with the timing and method of payment. To avoid misunderstandings which could jeopardize the relationship, the currency of payment should also be specified. Payment in US dollars or other 'hard' currency is typical, but this should be stated in the contract. Payment terms and conditions are also important inclusions in the agreement as are any additional expenses to be incurred by the parties. Of course, the specific products or brands covered by the agreement should be detailed as should the duties of the distributor in maintaining adequate inventory levels and ensuring that only quality product enters the market.

The distributor may also have responsibilities to provide technical support and after-sales service to customers in its territory and these functions also need to be specified in the agreement. It is imperative that the global marketing manager have access to all available information on the market for the firm's products. Sales, price information and customer feedback on product quality are some of the data that would be useful to the global marketing manager. It cannot be assumed, however, that the distributor will automatically share this information with the manufacturer. As a result, it is recommended that the need to provide relevant market data be included as an explicit clause in the distributor agreement. It is also suggested that the method of communication between the distributor and manufacturer be formalized as it is important that the distributor have access to the manufacturer in order that problems can be addressed in a timely manner.

CHANNEL MANAGEMENT

Foreign market intermediaries and manufacturers are independent entities located in different countries and pursuing their own objectives. More than likely there will be significant differences between the parties in their approach to conducting business and their methods of communication. In order for the relationship between manufacturer and intermediary to be successful, it is imperative that both parties commit to a set of shared objectives and be willing to work together to achieve them. Ongoing channel management will be required if the relationship is to remain on track and achieve performance expectations. Several aspects of channel management need to be considered.

LEADERSHIP, POWER AND MOTIVATION

Generally, the manufacturer is the entity that provides strategic leadership in the marketing channel. According to Anderson and Coughlan (2003),[3] the **channel leader** is the entity that brings other channel members together and has a strong voice in managing channel activities and behaviors. The channel leader has **power** in the relationship, i.e. the ability to alter the behavior of other channel members and urge them to take actions that they otherwise would not. The channel management literature recognizes five bases of power in a relationship: reward, coercive, expertise, legitimate and referent power (French and Raven, 1959).[4] The channel leader may opt to use one or more of these, depending on the nature of the relationship and the cultural context. The use of referent power has been found to have a strong

---

[2]   Czinkota, M., Ronkainen, I., Farrell, C. and McTavish, R. (2009) *Global Marketing: Foreign Entry, Market Development and Strategy Implementation*. Toronto: Nelson Education

[3]   Anderson, E. and Coughlan, A.T. (2003) 'Channel management: Structure, governance, and relationship management', in B. Weitz and R. Wensley (eds) *Handbook of Marketing*. London: SAGE, pp. 223–47.

[4]   French, J.R. and Raven, B. (1959) 'The bases of social power', in D. Cartwright (ed.) *Studies in Social Power*. Ann Arbor, MI: University of Michigan Press, pp. 150–67.

positive influence on attitudes of intermediaries, while the use of coercive power leads to the development of negative attitudes and conflict in the channel relationship.[5] Chinese channel leaders, for example, tend to rely on non-coercive power in their relationships.

The channel leader (or **channel captain**) will be responsible for motivating channel intermediaries to achieve performance expectations. As noted above, intermediaries are independent corporate entities and pursue their own objectives which may be at variance with those of the manufacturer. In essence, the marketing channel is a decentralized (as opposed to an integrated) system where the parties do not share a common objective. This is the classic **principal–agent** problem in which the principal (manufacturer) hires an agent (distributor) to act on its behalf. The manufacturer has an objective of maximizing profits over its own product lines, while the distributor seeks to maximize profits over all product lines, including the product lines of other manufacturers. Further, the principal does not observe the efforts of the agent and these efforts cannot be inferred directly from the market results achieved. As a result of these conditions, agents may not necessarily put forward their best effort unless an appropriate incentive structure is put in place. In essence, incentives are required to align the objectives of the distributor with those of the manufacturer. These incentives may be financial and/or psychological. For example, distributors will be strongly motivated by the earning potential of the company's products. The provision of generous margins will certainly motivate the distributor to commit the time and effort necessary to effectively market the company's products. Regular communication, praise and support from the manufacturer will also serve to motivate the distributor to achieve superior results.

MONITORING AND CONTROL

It is imperative that the global marketing manager establish procedures for ongoing monitoring and control of the channel relationship. These actions are required to ensure that the product flows through the channel effectively and reaches the end user in good condition and in a timely manner. Monitoring and control are required despite careful screening and selection of intermediaries and despite the use of contracts and incentives. It is recommended that the global marketing manager establish performance targets for channel members that include metrics such as market share, sales volume, inventory turnover, number of new accounts and the introduction of new products. The global manager may wish to institute a system of periodic reporting and site visits in order to effectively monitor and control intermediary performance. Face-to-face meetings are usually helpful in the process. It should be recognized, however, that a failure to meet performance expectations may be beyond the control of the intermediary. The entry of a strong international competitor into the market or a sudden downturn in the economy may hurt the intermediary's efforts to meet its targets. These types of exogenous factors should, of course, be factored into the assessment of performance.

It should be recognized that there is also a cultural dimension to the issue of monitoring and control. It is known that Chinese channel members place considerable emphasis on trust in their channel relationships which reduces the need for monitoring and control.[6] Two types of trust are discussed in the channel management literature. **Goodwill trust** speaks to a moral obligation and responsibility to demonstrate concern for the interests of other members of the marketing channel. **Competence trust**, on the other hand, refers to a belief that channel partners have the requisite expertise to achieve the objectives established for the relationship. Goodwill and competence trust contribute positively to the stability of the channel relationship. The global manager should note that trust in channel relationships takes

5   Farrell, C. and Lin, X. (2010) 'The evolution and governance of marketing channels in the People's Republic of China', in C. Lu Wang (ed.) *Handbook of Contemporary Marketing in China*. Hauppauge, NY: Nova Science Publishers.

6   Liu, Y., Li, Y., Tao, L. and Wang, Y. (2008) 'Relationship stability, trust and relational risk in marketing channels: Evidence from China', *Industrial Marketing Management*, 37: 432–46.

time to develop, but once it is developed trust leads to **relational stability** where channel members have a consistently favorable view of each other and the benefits of the relationship clearly outweigh the cost of discontinuation.[7]

CONFLICT

Efforts by the global marketing manager to engender trust in the channel relationship may not be successful and **conflict** may ensue. In a conflict situation, channel members perceive each other as opponents instead of partners working towards a common goal. Clearly, conflict, if left unchecked, will undermine the performance of the distribution relationship and may eventually lead to its dissolution. Researchers have suggested that the level of channel conflict is a function of the importance of the issue that sparks the disagreement, the frequency with which these disagreements take place and their intensity (Brown and Day, 1981).[8] Major issues such as distributor compensation that surface frequently and on which the parties are far apart will lead to conflict in the relationship. As noted above, the exercise of coercive power tends to generate conflict in the channel relationship. The exercise of other bases of power, however, tends to minimize conflict in the channel.

TERMINATION

If the performance of the intermediary is poor or there is excessive conflict in the relationship which undermines the performance of the system as a whole, the global marketing manager may have little choice but to terminate the relationship. It may also be necessary to terminate the distributor relationship if the company makes a decision to establish a foreign sales subsidiary or to withdraw completely from the country. Termination provisions should be carefully detailed in the distributor agreement and must be consistent with local laws. Once the decision to terminate is made, it is important to inform the distributor and formulate a plan for the smooth transition of accounts. In a North American context, termination of a distributor agreement is a relatively straightforward matter. The company merely informs the intermediary and provides whatever notice is stipulated in the agreement. In other countries, however, the matter is far less straightforward and termination can be both costly and complex. In such situations, the firm is well advised to seek competent legal advice.

INTERNATIONAL LOGISTICS MANAGEMENT

In addition to the selection and management of market intermediaries, the global marketing firm must also be concerned with ensuring the smooth and efficient movement of the company's products to the final consumer. This is the area of **international logistics**. According to David and Stewart (2010), the term 'international logistics' may be defined as the process of planning, implementing and controlling the flow and storage of goods, services and related information from a point of origin to a point of consumption located in a different country.[9] The process encompasses **materials management**, or the movement of raw materials and parts into the firm, and **physical distribution**, or the movement of the firm's finished products to the final consumer. Both phases of the international logistics process need to be well coordinated if the firm is to achieve its objectives in the overseas market.

---

[7]   Liu et al. (2008) op cit.

[8]   Brown, J.R. and Day, R.L. (1981) 'Measures of manifest conflict in distribution channels', *Journal of Marketing Research*, 18: 263–74.

[9]   David, P. and Stewart, R. (2010) *International Logistics: The Management of International Trade Operations*, 3rd edn. Andover, Hampshire: Cengage Learning.

While there are similarities between domestic and international logistics, there are also a number of important differences:[10]

- The **environment** within which the global marketing manager operates is quite different from the environment in the firm's home country. Language and other elements of host-country culture may well be considerably different from those of the firm's home country, as may the level of economic development and the state of the country's infrastructure.
- The global marketing manager also has to deal with vastly more **complex decisions** that stem from differences in import documentation and rules, as well as available modes of transportation, longer transit times and different (and unfamiliar) carriers.
- There is also the issue of the **number of intermediaries** involved in the movement of the product across national borders. Government regulators, banks, insurance companies, freight forwarders and others may be involved in the process, each with their own forms, documents and procedures.
- As already mentioned, the global marketing manager is dealing with longer transit times and greater shipping distances. These factors increase the **risks** involved in the international movement of goods, making packaging and insurance considerations that much more important, but also that much more complex.
- The international movement of products also requires a careful analysis of the **risks of nonpayment**, given that the parties involved are located in different countries and are operating in different legal jurisdictions. The issue of **currency fluctuations** is also not to be overlooked. Exchange rate movements are not a concern in domestic logistics management but are of paramount importance in an international context.
- The global marketing manager has to deal with **terms of trade** that are more complex than those used in the domestic movement of physical products. These terms of trade specify alternatives for the transfer of ownership and title as the product moves from the point of origin to the final consumer. Terms of trade are discussed in the following chapter.

DISTRIBUTION ACTIVITIES

The international movement of products involves a number of activities which have to be performed well in order to satisfy consumer demand in the foreign market.

Transportation

The transportation function is important as it will determine not only when the product reaches the final consumer but also its condition. The international logistics manager must consider the transportation infrastructure and the availability of various modes of transportation. **Transportation infrastructure** refers to the various privately and state-owned elements that are deployed to facilitate the transportation function. These include port facilities, airport runaways, railway networks, road systems, warehouse facilities, etc. In developed countries, the global marketing manager will more than likely have access to a well-developed transportation infrastructure. However, the same may not be true in the context of developing countries. The international logistics function may be severely hampered by weak port facilities, making inbound transportation a challenge, or the internal road network may be underdeveloped, making efficient access to the final consumer extremely difficult. Deficiencies in the target country's transportation infrastructure need to be determined well in advance of actual market entry and strategies developed to mitigate the impacts. The availability of alternative **modes of transportation** is also a major consideration for the global marketer. Four distinct modes of transportation are available to the firm: water, rail, air and road. It is important that the firm understands the characteristics of each mode and has a set of criteria available to evaluate them.

---

[10] David and Stewart (2010) op cit.

SELECTION CRITERIA

In terms of the selection of a transportation mode, **transit time** is obviously an important consideration. The period of time from the departure of the carrier to its arrival at its destination may vary substantially depending on the mode of transportation selected. For example, a transit time of several hours by air may translate into several days if ocean transportation is selected. This may have serious implications if the product is highly perishable or the firm needs to address an acute shortage of the product in the foreign target market. **Reliability** is also a consideration in selecting an appropriate mode of transportation. The firm needs to have some assurance that the shipment will arrive at its destination on schedule. Delays of a few days may prove to be quite problematic in the case of some products and components. Just-in-time production systems, for example, depend on components arriving at the factory just when they are needed. In such situations, a delay in delivery may disrupt production and have a cascading effect on the rest of the distribution channel. Of course, the global marketer must also consider the relative **cost** of the various modes of transportation available. It will generally cost the firm more to ship the product by air compared to sending by water or road. Higher valued perishable items are usually better candidates for airfreight. Items which are dense, i.e. have a high weight to volume ratio, are also more suitable for transportation by air compared to bulky, heavier items.

ALTERNATIVE MODES

As noted above, the global marketing manager has a choice of four transportation modes. Each has its own set of characteristics which need to be carefully considered in making a decision.

Water: Transportation by water provides the firm with a low-cost shipping alternative for bulky, heavy, low-cost items. This option is usually selected if speed and reliability are not major considerations. Water transportation is heavily subject to the vagaries of the weather and indeed some waterways may be completely impassable during the winter months. When deciding on the use of water transportation, the global marketing manager must also consider the port facilities in the destination country, including such issues as water depth, bridge clearances and the availability of cranes to facilitate the loading and unloading of cargo. Many countries are land-locked and, therefore, water transportation will have to be combined with some other mode of transportation in order to get the product into the hands of the final consumer. It does not provide an end-to-end transportation solution.

Air: As noted earlier, airfreight provides a faster but more expensive alternative to water transportation. This mode of transportation is usually reserved for higher valued items for which on-time delivery is critical. Products with a high weight to volume ratio are usually good candidates for air transportation. Most countries are accessible by air and have adequate airport facilities.

Road: In some cases, it may be possible to ship products between countries using ground transportation. Road transportation is best used for relatively short hauls of high valued products. This mode can provide a door-to-door solution for the company, allowing delivery directly to the customer's premises. Not dependent on a fixed departure schedule, this mode of transportation also offers the global marketing manager considerable flexibility. In some developing countries, however, roadways may not be well maintained and this may present a challenge.

Rail: Trains are effective for hauling bulky cargo such as coal and grain over long distances. Trains adhere to fixed departure schedules and so this mode of transport does not offer the global marketing manager significant flexibility.

DOCUMENTATION

Shipping products across international borders requires that the global marketing manager be familiar with the documentation requirements of the target country. In the case of simple export transactions, the most important document is the **bill of lading**. This document represents a receipt for the goods shipped and is the basic contract between the shipper and the carrier. The bill of lading also provides evidence of title to the goods being transported. Also important is the **insurance certificate**, which provides evidence that the products to be transported are covered against loss or damage while in transit. The international logistics manager may also have to furnish **a shipper's export declaration**, which confirms that the goods may be legally exported, and, in the case of products that may be injurious, a **shipper's declaration for dangerous goods** is usually also required.

In addition to the above, the firm is required to produce a **commercial invoice** which is essentially a bill for the products that the company has sold to its foreign customer. The importing country may also require a **certificate of origin** which states the country in which the products were manufactured. This latter document is important in the proper calculation of tariff rates. As noted in an earlier chapter, membership of certain trade groupings provides for duty-free entry into member countries. The certificate of origin establishes eligibility for duty-free entry. Some countries may also require presentation of a **consular invoice** that is provided by the consular office in the importing country and allows the national statistical office to track and compile trade data. Depending on the country and the nature of the product, an **import license** and a **foreign exchange license** may also be required for the products to enter. Governments may impose restrictions on the importation of certain products or the quantity that may be imported, while others may ration the purchase of hard currencies in an attempt to correct macroeconomic imbalances. Import and foreign exchange licenses allow governments to maintain control of imports and hard currency outflows. The **letter of credit** is the final document usually required in the international shipment of goods across national borders. The letter of credit is a method of payment and is issued by the importer's bank at the request of the importer. It is an effective method of mitigating the risk of non-payment in international transactions and is discussed more fully in the following chapter.

FACILITATION

Most companies, particularly small and medium-sized firms, do not attempt to master the documentation and import requirements of the countries they target. In most cases, firms rely on **freight forwarders** to assist with these functions. In essence, freight forwarders are multi-modal transportation specialists with expertise in selecting the lowest cost and most appropriate method of transportation for particular product types. In carrying out their functions, these organizations can, among other things, do the following:

- recommend the optimal (economical/timely/safe) routing for the product and book space with a carrier
- advise on or arrange the appropriate packaging, marking and labeling
- arrange transportation insurance
- arrange storage of the product and give advice on warehousing facilities, rates and procedures
- find alternative ways of moving the goods in the event of an emergency.

Because of the economies of scale, freight forwarders can also offer transportation consolidation services that can be less costly than those the exporting firm could arrange directly with the transportation company. The freight forwarder can consolidate the shipment with other small shipments from several clients into a larger, more economical load if the exporter has insufficient volumes to fill an ocean container or highway truck. At the destination, the freight forwarder or agent will unload and deliver the 'de-consolidated' shipment to the destination in the target country.[11]

---

[11] Team Canada (2005) *Step-by-Step Guide to Exporting*, 3rd edn. Ottawa: Minister of Public Works and Government Services Canada.

In light of these benefits, it is easy to see why companies might be better off using the services of an experienced freight forwarder rather than developing an in-house transportation management unit. Now, while freight forwarders act on behalf of the exporter, customs brokers act on behalf of the importer. Brokers act for the importer to clear the imported goods through customs and ship them to their destination.

PACKAGING

The global marketing manager must pay particular attention to the packaging of the product for international shipment. Packaging serves three important functions.[12] First, packaging offers protection to the product in transit. Protection is required from mechanical damage such as would occur if the product is dropped, squeezed or violently shaken. Cracks, dents, breaks and nicks may be the result of such actions. Packaging also protects the product from sea water damage during ocean transportation or simply from exposure to rain or snow. Proper packaging is also a significant deterrent against theft and pilferage. The second important function of packaging is to facilitate the proper handling of the product while in transit. With proper packaging, the stevedores will be able to safely move the product without having to resort to improvised systems that may cause significant damage to the cargo. In packaging the product, the global marketing manager should consider factors such as the weight and dimension restrictions of the equipment used to handle cargo in the destination country. Different countries will have their own specific standards and regulations. The third function of packaging relates to its customer service function. While it is important that the product be well protected and is delivered to the final consumer in good condition, it is also important that the package be easy to open without recourse to special tools and that the customer be able to do so without damaging the product. Further, the packaging used should reflect the image of the brand. Consumers will perceive a well-designed and constructed package as a sign that the company manufactures a quality product.

INVENTORY MANAGEMENT

It is important for the global marketer to maintain an adequate level of inventory in order to ensure that product is available to consumers in a timely manner. Inability to supply the product may anger consumers and cause them to switch to competing brands. Once these customers are lost, they may be difficult to regain. While stock-outs need to be avoided, it also needs to be recognized that there are costs associated with maintaining inventory levels. These costs include storage, insurance, breakage, pilferage, taxes, depreciation and financing charges which the firm needs to cover from its operating revenues. Customer satisfaction must be balanced against the need to minimize inventory holding costs.

Two factors drive the decision on inventory level.[13] The first is **order cycle time** or the time that elapses between placement of the order and its delivery to the final consumer. The longer the order cycle time, the higher the inventory level that the firm should hold. Companies can, of course, adopt strategies to speed up order cycle times, including use of faster modes of transportation, warehousing product closer to the final consumer, adoption of electronic ordering technologies, etc. Any approach that serves to bring down order cycle times will allow for a reduction in the level of inventories held. The second factor driving inventory level is **customer-service level** or the ability of the firm to fulfill customer orders within a specified period of time. Choice of customer-service level, such as to fill 80 percent of orders received within three days, drives the need to hold inventory. The higher the customer-service level, the greater the level of inventory the firm must hold in order to meet the

---

[12]   This section draws heavily from David and Stewart (2010) op cit.

[13]   Hollensen, S. (2011) *Global Marketing: A Decision Oriented Approach*, 5th edn. Englewood Cliffs, NJ: Prentice Hall.

standard. Given the costs involved in holding inventory, firms should strive for an appropriate level of customer service and not the maximum level of customer service.

WAREHOUSING

In many cases, the global marketer must also consider the issue of warehousing in the host country. This may be required, for example, if the firm is committed to a high level of customer service and wants to ensure that product is on hand in the target market. Warehousing product in the host country obviates the need for the company to continuously ship supplies from its manufacturing facilities in the home country.

PARALLEL DISTRIBUTION

As noted above, it is recommended that distribution agreements specify a territory for which the intermediary will be responsible. Performance metrics such as sales volumes and market share are then developed based in part on this defined geographic coverage. In some instances, performance evaluation and overall channel management are complicated by **parallel distribution** or the sale of authentic (non-counterfeit) products through market intermediaries other than those authorized by the manufacturer. Also referred to as the **gray trade** or the **gray market,** the products involved are genuine, trademarked brands and are only distinguished by how they have reached the final consumer or end user. In essence, unauthorized intermediaries intervene in a selective or exclusive marketing channel to take business away from the manufacturer's authorized distributors. Unlike counterfeiting, the distribution of gray traded products is not illegal (unless, of course, the products are obtained illegally or pose a health and safety risk to the population).

A gray market may develop in any number of products from inexpensive watches to heavy earth-moving equipment. Japanese Kubota tractors, for example, are sold in several countries through unauthorized distributors. These countries include the USA. This is a problem because Kubota tractors are designed and manufactured specifically for the Japanese market and do not have important safety features required of tractors sold in the USA. The tractors are genuine but were not meant to be sold outside of Japan and, as a result, US purchasers of these tractors may experience some difficulty in finding replacement parts.[14]

CONDITIONS

Several conditions must exist for parallel distribution to develop. The first is **wide price differences** between country markets. Gray markets develop when manufacturers set significantly different prices between markets. The firm may, for example, set a lower price in an emerging market compared to a developed country market. This creates an arbitrage opportunity that can be exploited by gray traders. The same may occur if an intermediary in one country has an oversupply of the product and discounts it heavily in an attempt to recover its investment. Whatever the reason for the price discrepancy, gray traders will purchase the product in the lower priced country and market it in the higher priced country at a profit. Because profits are the motive that underlies parallel distribution, the second condition for gray markets to exist is **inexpensive logistics**. If the transaction costs involved in importing the product are excessive, the parallel importer's profits will be undermined and a gray market is unlikely to develop. The third condition for parallel distribution is **limited availability** of the product. If there is no shortage of the product (or a particular model or version) in the foreign market, parallel distribution is unlikely to occur.

---

[14]   See www.kubota.com/priorproduct/GrayMarketFindOut.aspx and www.orangetractortalks.com/2008/09/discov ered-its-gray-market/

IMPLICATIONS FOR THE FIRM AND ITS CHANNEL PARTNERS

Because gray marketed products are genuine, the global marketer does generate revenue from gray market activity. The product is merely finding its way to the final consumer or end user via an alternative distribution channel. This does not mean, however, that there are no implications for the global marketer. Parallel distribution invariably leads to **strained relationships** between the manufacturer and its authorized distributors as it reduces their sales and profitability. Authorized distributors now face intra-brand competition and may blame the manufacturer for the problem and for not doing enough to correct it. The gray trade may also lead to an **erosion of brand equity** should the products sold not perform as expected. Although gray market products are genuine, they may not have been designed for the particular foreign markets in which they are sold. Product accessories may be the wrong configuration and safety features legally required in the foreign country may not have been included. Consumers purchasing such products will be understandably upset and there may be a backlash against the manufacturer and its channel partners.

PHOTO 10.2

Many manufacturers refuse to honor warranties if the product was not purchased through an authorized intermediary. This position may upset some consumers, leading to the manufacturer having to defend itself against **legal action**. Parallel distribution may also complicate the implementation of the firm's global marketing strategy. **Sales forecasting**, for example, becomes more difficult in foreign markets subject to random spikes in gray product imports. There may also be implications for pricing in markets with substantial gray market activity.

ARGUMENTS IN FAVOR OF THE GRAY TRADE

As discussed above, parallel distribution has a number of negative implications for the firm and its channel partners. However, gray market importation is not illegal and there are those who argue that firms involved in the practice have every right to do so in a free enterprise economy. In fact, researchers have argued that gray marketing provides an informal way of segmenting the market with authorized intermediaries offering a higher price, high service option and gray traders offering consumers a lower price, low service option. Gray marketing drives down prices for consumers but this comes at a cost in terms of lower levels of service. There is also the argument that gray traders actually expand the total sales of the product by drawing in consumers attracted by the lower-priced alternative and who would not have considered patronizing the authorized distributor (Anderson and Coughlan, 2003).[15] Some have even argued that parallel distribution creates employment for those engaged in this form of price arbitrage.

CHANNEL ACTIONS AGAINST THE GRAY TRADE

Global marketing firms generally do not subscribe to the arguments made by proponents of the gray trade and have implemented a number of strategies to combat the practice:[16]

---

[15]   Anderson and Coughlan (2003) op cit.

[16]   Johansson, J.K. (2003) *Global Marketing: Foreign Entry, Local Marketing, and Global Management*. New York: McGraw-Hill/Irwin.

- **Supply interference** is one approach in which the company appeals to its authorized channel members to screen more diligently the orders they receive and not fill those obviously destined for unauthorized sale in foreign markets. A retailer of Rolex watches, for example, may wish to ask a few questions of a customer wishing to purchase several hundred timepieces.
- **Dealer interference** is another option open to the global marketer. With this option, the focus is on the country of importation. The company identifies the source of gray marketed products and visits the outlet with a view to convincing the importer to discontinue the practice. In some instances, it may be possible to convert the gray trader into an authorized distributor with its own territory.
- **Demand interference** is a third strategic option open to the global marketer. With demand interference, the emphasis is on educating the consumer about the problems associated with the purchase of product through unauthorized intermediaries. The basic idea is that if consumers can be made aware of the potential pitfalls of purchasing gray marketed products, they would cease to patronize unauthorized dealers. As previously discussed, these pitfalls include a lack of warranty protection, difficulty locating replacement parts and product accessories that are incompatible with the product purchased.
- **Strategic attack** is yet another option open to the global marketer. This is again a demand-side solution. With this strategic approach, the firm attempts to create stronger reasons for the consumer to patronize the authorized distributor at the expense of the gray trader. The manufacturer may, for example, provide its authorized distributors with better pricing terms, allowing these savings to be passed on to the consumer. The manufacturer may also offer extended warranty protection to consumers purchasing the product through an authorized reseller. The provision of these incentives is expected to lead consumers to make a deliberate choice in favor of the authorized dealer.

The strategic approaches presented above are, of course, not mutually exclusive and may be used in combination to combat the problem.

 ## Spotlight on Research 10.1   Attitudes Towards Gray Market Products

Huang, Lee and Ho (2004) examine consumer attitudes towards gray market products. The authors argue that demand-side strategies for dealing with parallel distribution have lagged supply-side approaches. They suggest that focusing on the demand side may, however, be more effective. They argue that the implementation of demand-side strategies requires a deep understanding of consumer attitudes to gray market products, but that this is an area that has not attracted a great deal of attention in the literature. In this article, the authors seek to develop a scale to measure consumer attitudes towards gray market products and analyze the factors that affect these attitudes.

Hypotheses

The authors test the following hypotheses:

H1. Consumers' price consciousness positively affects their preference for gray market goods.

H2. A consumer who more strongly maintains the price–quality inference has a more negative attitude toward gray market goods.

H3. Consumers' risk averseness negatively affects consumer attitude toward gray market goods.

H4. For products with a higher consumer involvement, consumers' attitude and purchase intention toward gray market goods are positively related.

The conceptual model is illustrated in Figure 10.6.

(Continued)

(Continued)

FIGURE 10.6   Conceptual Model

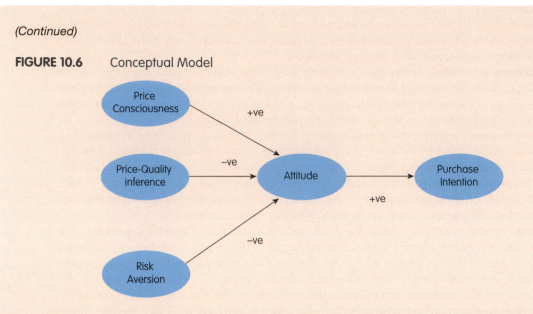

Method

The authors utilize the price-consciousness and price–quality inference construct measures proposed by Lichtenstein et al. (1993), as well as the risk-averseness construct advanced by Burton et al. (1998). A three-item scale developed by Dodds et al. (1991) is used to measure purchase intention. All three constructs were measured using a seven-point Likert-type scale. Empirical work was conducted in Taiwan and three product categories were examined – beverages, watches and mobile phones. These products are used by everyone, appear frequently in the gray market and are associated with different levels of consumer involvement. The scale created by Zaichkowsky (1985) and revised by McQuarrie and Munson (1991) was adopted in pretests to measure levels of consumer involvement. These pretests were conducted on 120 undergraduate marketing students who were assigned to three groups and tasked with answering a number of questions designed to measure product involvement. The researchers found that the involvement score for beverages was lower than that for watches and that for watches was lower than that for mobile phones. The results were statistically significant.

Exploratory factor analysis followed by a series of focus groups was used to develop the measurement items that would constitute the attitude construct. A total of 13 items were identified. A second-stage survey of working Taiwanese adults pursuing Bachelor's degrees at night, along with further principal component analyses, was used to refine the construct.

The measurement items used in the four constructs are detailed below:

Consumer attitude toward gray market goods

- Generally speaking, buying gray market goods is a better choice.
- I never consider gray market goods when choosing merchandise (–).
- Considering price, I prefer gray market goods.
- I like shopping for gray market goods.
- Buying gray market goods generally benefits the consumer.
- There's nothing wrong with purchasing gray market goods.

Price consciousness

- I am not willing to go to the extra effort to find lower prices (–).
- The money saved by searching for lower prices is usually not worth the time and effort (–).
- I would never shop at more than one store to find lower prices (–).
- The time it takes to find lower prices is usually not worth the effort (–).

Price–quality inference

- Generally speaking, the higher the price of a product, the higher the quality.
- The price of a product is a good indicator of its quality.
- You always have to pay a bit more for the best.

Risk averseness

- I don't like to take risks.
- Compared to most people I know, I like to 'live life on the edge' (–).
- I have no desire to take unnecessary chances on things.
- Compared to most people I know, I like to gamble on things (–).

Purchase intention

- I would purchase _____.
- I would consider buying _____.
- The probability that I would consider buying _____ is _____.

All measures show good internal consistency with Cronbach alpha values above 0.7. The only exception is the risk-aversion construct with an alpha of 0.66 which is just above the minimal acceptable value of 0.65. The reliability measures of all four constructs are good, ranging from 0.70 to 0.95. The authors also establish the validity of the constructs. In this research, structural equation modeling is used in hypothesis testing. The model is estimated separately for the three focal products – beverages, watches and mobile phones. In all three cases, model fit was found to be acceptable (GFI = 0.90, AGFI = 0.86 or above).

Results

Initial estimation revealed that the price-consciousness construct was not statistically significant and, therefore, H1 is not supported for any of the product categories. Given this result, the authors opted to drop this variable and re-estimate the model. The overall fit of the reduced model was found to be acceptable (GFI = 0.92 or above, AGFI = 0.89 or above). The authors find that price–quality inference negatively and significantly affects consumer attitude, indicating support for H2 across all product categories. Consumers who believe that quality can be inferred from a product's price tend to have a more negative view of gray market products. Similarly, the authors find support for H2. Risk aversion negatively and significantly affects consumer attitudes towards gray products.

In terms of H4, the researchers find support in the cases of watches and mobile phones but not for beverages. The effect of consumer attitude on purchase intentions is not significant in the case of the latter product, although there is a positive and statistically significant relationship in the cases of watches and mobile phones.

Implications

Based on the results, the authors of this study argue as follows:

1. The price–quality construct is negatively and significantly related to consumer attitude towards gray market products. In their marketing campaigns, managers of international brands should, therefore, reinforce consumers' perceptions of quality in their authorized channels. Consumers who purchase gray market products are price sensitive. Quality is, however, still an important consideration in shaping attitudes towards gray market products and can be used by the managers of international brands to maintain competitiveness against gray market importers.
2. Given that risk aversion negatively impacts attitudes towards gray market products, brand owners should actively promote authorized dealers and the guarantees and service quality they provide. By steering customers in the direction of these authorized distributors, brand owners may reduce the impact of gray traders in the marketplace.

(Continued)

(Continued)

Sources

Burton, S., Lichtenstein, D.R., Netemeyer, R.G. and Garretson, J.A. (1998) 'A scale for measuring attitude toward private label products and an examination of its psychological and behavioral correlates', *Academy of Marketing Science*, 26, 4: 293–306.

Dodds, W.B., Monroe, K.B. and Grewal, D. (1991) 'Effects of price, brand, and store information on buyers' product evaluations', *Journal of Marketing Research*, 28, 3: 307–19.

Huang, J.H., Lee, B.C.Y. and Ho, S.H. (2004) 'Consumer attitude toward gray market goods', *International Marketing Review*, 21, 6: 598–614.

Lichtenstein, D.R., Ridgway, N.M. and Netemeyer, R.G. (1993) 'Price perceptions and consumer shopping behavior: A field study', *Journal of Marketing Research*, 30, May: 234–45.

McQuarrie, E.F. and Munson, J.M. (1991) 'A revised product involvement inventory: Improved usability and validity', *Advances in Consumer Research*, 19: 108–15.

Zaichkowsky, J.L. (1985) 'Measuring the involvement construct', *Journal of Consumer Research*, 12, Dec.: 341–52.

Discussion Questions

Read the full article by Huang, Lee and Ho (2004) and answer the following questions:

1. This study was conducted in Taiwan, a country with a high dependence on international trade and where gray market products are widely available and familiar to consumers. Would you hypothesize that a country's dependence on trade will impact the results of this study? Why/why not? How would you test your hypothesis empirically?
2. The authors of this study do not find a statistically significant relationship between price consciousness and attitude towards gray market products. They suggest that *inter alia* this may be because the relationship is moderated by other factors such as product cost as a percentage of income. How would you alter the authors' research design to investigate this possibility?

GLOBAL RETAILING

A number of retailers have embarked upon a strategy of internationalization. Well-known names such as McDonalds, Wal-Mart, Carrefour and the Body Shop are active in numerous countries around the world. Compared to manufacturing companies, retailers have been slow to internationalize. However, rising consumer incomes overseas and tariff reductions have sparked interest in pursuing foreign market expansion, particularly in high-growth emerging markets. At the same time, developed country markets have not exhibited significant growth and in some cases have experienced long periods of decline. This factor has also propelled many retailers to seek out growth opportunities outside their national borders. In addition, developed country consumers have become increasingly comfortable with online shopping and this has also served to make the domestic retail environment more challenging. While many retailers have developed transactional websites to market their products, there is an increasing risk of cannibalizing sales from their physical stores.[17]

---

[17] Lahouasnia, L. (2012) The Internationalization of Retailing: Success, Failure and the Importance of Adapting to the Market, *Euromonitor International*. Available at: www.diy.com/diy/jsp/corporate/content/about/index.jsp

Internationalization is by no means a simple matter for a retailer. Some product categories such as food require that considerable adaptations be made in order to cater to the tastes and preferences of the host-country consumer. This makes foreign market expansion much more complicated. For example, 7-Eleven, a major global retailer, has had to modify its product offerings in response to consumer preferences in different countries. The company retails 'Super Big Gulp' soft drinks in the USA but dumplings in China.[18] Similarly, Tesco Plc, one of the world's top ten grocery retailers, sells sliced pigs' ears, chicken feet, ducks' heads and soft shell turtles in its Dachengdong store located outside central Beijing.[19] These product offerings are unlikely to appeal to consumers in most developed country markets. On the other hand, non-grocery items such as consumer electronics, clothing and furniture have more universal appeal and retailers in these product categories have a much less daunting task catering to foreign customers. Apparel retailers such as H&M, Zara and Gap carry basically the same merchandise across all their stores, irrespective of the country.[20] In some other cases, however, the retail concept itself may not resonate with the foreign consumer and the retailer may fail to gain traction in the market. The home improvement market in China is a prime example.

Despite the adjustments required, many retailers have made the judgment that internationalization is a requirement for survival and that major opportunities exist in emerging markets. This may well be the case. For example, Stockholm has the highest density of H&M stores in the world with some 25 stores in a 30 sq. km area, serving a population of only 872,000. Beijing, on the other hand, with a population of over 20 million has a number of completely underserved neighborhoods. Further, store expansion in Stockholm is likely to lead to declining sales per square metre and this decline is likely to be exacerbated by a well-developed culture of Internet retailing. In contrast, online shopping is not as well developed in Beijing and so consumers are almost completely reliant on physical stores.[21] For retailers such as H&M, emerging market store expansion is likely to generate better results than a continued focus on mature developed country markets.

case study 10.2: B&Q in China

With a large population, rapidly growing economy and expanding real estate market, China presents an attractive opportunity for western home improvement retailers. B&Q is one of the leading home improvement and garden center retailers in Europe and one of the largest in the world. Owned by Kingfisher PLC, the firm has 350 stores in the UK, nine stores in Ireland and more than 60 stores in other countries around the world. B&Q has had a presence in the Chinese market for over a decade, opening its first store in 1999. The company has, however, only been able to generate a small profit from its Chinese operation, and, despite two acquisitions, has seen its sales per square feet fall significantly.

It has become obvious that internationalization is not as straightforward as the company expected. B&Q's business model is predicated on the 'do-it-yourself' concept which is quite familiar to consumers in Western

(Continued)

18 Lahouasnia (2012) op cit.

19 Steiner, R. (2010) City Focus: Kingfisher Looks at China Takeaway, *This is Money*. Available at: www.thisismoney.co.uk/money/markets/article-1695957/City-Focus-Kingfisher-looks-at-China-takeaway.html, accessed March 9, 2013.

20 Lahouasnia (2012) op cit.

21 Lahouasnia (2012) op cit.

(Continued)

PHOTO 10.3

Europe and North America. Chinese consumers, however, are not familiar with the concept and much prefer to hire migrant laborers to do the work for them. The big box retail concept was clearly inappropriate for the Chinese market and the stores should have focused on giving consumers a good look at the finished project possibilities as opposed to the tools needed to execute the project. Smaller, more service-oriented stores with a narrower range of products would probably have been more profitable for the company.

B&Q has had to close a number of its stores in China and sublet space to avoid heavy losses. Interestingly, Kingfisher faced similar problems in Hong Kong, South Korea and Taiwan and was forced to completely exit those markets. For the home improvement business, internationalization is not a simple proposition.

Sources

Adapted from Lahouasnia, L. (2012) The Internationalization of Retailing: Success, Failure and the Importance of Adapting to the Market, *Euromonitor International*. Available at: www.diy.com/diy/jsp/corporate/content/about/index.jsp

Steiner, R. (2010) City Focus: Kingfisher Looks at China Takeaway, *This is Money*. Available at: www.thisis-money.co.uk/money/markets/article-1695957/City-Focus-Kingfisher-looks-at-China-takeaway.html, accessed March 9, 2013.

Discussion Questions

1. Should B&Q completely wind up its operations in China? Why/Why not?
2. Do you agree that the company should have focused on smaller, more service-oriented stores with a narrower range of products?

Interestingly, it is not only China with its population of 1.3 billion that is attracting the attention of major retailers. In 2010, Wal-Mart bought a majority stake in Massmart Holdings Ltd, one of South Africa's leading retailers. Massmart operates nine wholesale and retail chains, and one buying group comprised of 330 stores and 633 buying group members. The firm is active in 12 countries in Sub-Saharan Africa and owns brands such as Game, Makro, Dion Wired, Builder's Warehouse and Builder's Express. This strategic acquisition is expected to serve as an entry point to the rest of southern Africa over the next several decades and the move has caught the attention of other major international retailers which have traditionally been focused on Asia and Latin America. Massmart's expansive footprint across Sub-Saharan Africa was certainly a major factor in Wal-Mart's acquisition. However, other South African retailers have also recognized the long-term potential of the region and have moved to capitalize on the opportunities. Companies such as Woolworths Holdings Ltd, Pick 'n' Pay Stores Ltd and Shoprite Holdings Ltd, for example, have begun to expand into neighboring countries from their home base in South Africa.[22]

---

[22] Bra, C. (2012) Retailers' Strategies in Sub-Saharan Africa. Available at: http://blog.euromonitor.com/2012/03/retailers-strategies-in-sub-saharan-africa.html, accessed March 5, 2013.

SUMMARY

This chapter has examined global distribution strategies. The concept of the international distribution channel was defined and the point was made that this channel may be simple or relatively complex. It was also pointed out that the global marketing manager must carefully consider a number of factors in designing an international marketing channel and that getting the design right is extremely important to successful foreign market expansion. This chapter has also considered the role of foreign market intermediaries and the process that should be followed to screen and select them.

A number of issues involved in the management of the international marketing channel once it is operational have also been discussed in this chapter. Power, conflict, the motivation of intermediaries, control and trust are some of the channel management issues that the firm needs to consider. Also presented above was a discussion of international logistics management and its related activities, such as transportation, warehousing, documentation, packaging and inventory management. The challenge of dealing with parallel distribution was also examined in this chapter. The point was made that while the practice is not illegal, it does present problems for the global marketing firm. Chief among these is the strained relationship with authorized distributors that is likely to result as gray traded products reduce their market share and profitability. A number of strategies for curbing the practice were then presented. The chapter concluded with a discussion of global retailing and some of the issues that may confront retailers that make the decision to expand abroad.

 Real World Challenges

The Gray Market for Nikon Cameras

Bridget stared out the window of her 10th floor office. She knew that sooner or later she would have to address the issue of parallel distribution. Her company, NKT Singapore Ltd, had successfully negotiated a three-year contract with Nikon Corporation of Japan to serve as the sole importer of Nikon cameras into the Singaporean market. Under the terms of the contract, NKT Singapore was authorized to import Nikon's products and provide service, support and software downloads for its cameras. NKT was responsible for paying all applicable taxes and duties on imported Nikon cameras and ensuring that the products were certified for use in Singapore. NKT was also responsible for ensuring that customers received the requisite manuals and power cables with their purchases. With the Nikon contract executed, NKT had put in place an extensive network of local dealers and distributors across the country to ensure national coverage. Each reseller had been provided with an exclusive sales territory. The NKT agreement with Nikon had been in place for six months and while sales had been Okay they had not been spectacular.

PHOTO 10.4

The first sign of trouble in the marketing channel occurred one Monday morning in April when Bridget received an angry voicemail from one of NKT's distributors. A customer had brought in a Nikon camera for repair. The product, however, was clearly different from those NKT imported. The camera was a genuine Nikon but the manual was written in Arabic and none of the cables and lenses matched those sold in Singapore. That single voicemail message was just the beginning as Bridget soon faced a flood of dealer and customer complaints. In fact, her marketing staff reported

(Continued)

(Continued)

to her that someone had started a blog and that hundreds of customers were complaining about poor customer service and the company not honoring its warranty commitments. Dealers and distributors were very concerned about their own corporate reputations and held the view that they were not responsible for the problems customers faced. They were also frustrated by the fact that the gray market Nikon cameras were being sold at a 35 percent discount to the retail price charged by authorized resellers.

As president of NKT, Bridget had a significant amount of power in the organization but she was not sure that providing service and support to gray market products was the sensible course of action. Bridget decided to schedule a conference call with Nikon's CEO and the VP of Global Marketing. She knew that NKT could not solve this problem on its own and needed the help of the manufacturer. As she jotted down notes for the conference call, she wondered why Nikon would even care about this issue. The manufacturer's sales were not being affected and Singapore was a relatively small market for this global company. Even if they were willing to help, Bridget had to decide what to ask for and how the solution would be financed. She even contemplated whether she should contact her company's lawyers and attempt to get out of the contract with Nikon.

Source

Adapted from http://support.nikontech.com/app/answers/detail/a_id/331

Discussion questions

1. State the problem that Bridget faces.
2. Identify the options available to NKT.
3. Based on the options identified above, recommend a course of action for the company. Be sure to provide a rationale.

? discussion questions

1. As a manufacturer, what factors would you consider in the selection of a distributor for entry into the Chinese food market?

2. What is 'distribution culture' and what role does it play in the design of international marketing channels?

3. Distinguish between goodwill and competence trust. What role does trust play in the management of international marketing channels?

4. What is the principal–agent problem and how does it apply in the context of international channel management? How can the problem be addressed by the multinational company?

5. What is parallel distribution and under what conditions is it likely to occur?

6. What strategies can the multinational firm adopt to address the issue of parallel distribution?

7. What are the implications of parallel distribution for the firm and its channel partners?

FURTHER READING

French, J.R. and Raven, B. (1959) 'The bases of social power', in D. Cartwright (ed.) *Studies in Social Power*. Ann Arbor, MI: University of Michigan Press, pp. 150–67.

Liu, Y., Li, Y., Tao, L. and Wang, Y. (2008) 'Relationship stability, trust and relational risk in marketing channels: Evidence from China', *Industrial Marketing Management*, 37: 432–46.

GLOBAL PRICING STRATEGIES

11

LEARNING OBJECTIVES

After reading this chapter you should be able to:

- Discuss the factors involved in the setting of global prices

- Discuss the pricing strategies open to the multinational firm

- Define the term 'transfer pricing' and discuss how the concept may be used by the global marketing firm

- Discuss the transfer pricing options open to the global marketing firm

- Discuss the challenges involved in the implementation of a transfer pricing strategy

- Discuss international terms of sale

- Explain the international payment options available to the multinational company

- Discuss strategies available to the firm for the management of foreign exchange risks

- Discuss the export financing options available to the global marketing firm

- Define the term dumping and discuss its implications for the implementation of global marketing strategy

- Discuss non-price options available to the global marketing firm.

INTRODUCTION

The pricing decisions made by firms have a direct bearing on their ability to generate sales and build market share in global markets. The multinational firm does not, however, have complete latitude to set any price that would allow it to reach its profit objectives. The firm in fact faces a number of constraints. As will be seen later in this chapter, the nature of demand for the firm's product places limits on the price that the firm may charge. While consumers may be willing to pay relatively high prices for well-made, quality branded products, this may not be the case for lesser known brands. Basic economic theory also tells us that the **price elasticity of demand,** or the responsiveness of quantity demanded to changes in price, will also have a bearing on what the firm is able to charge for its products. Further, given that the company's products compete against others in the marketplace, the pricing strategies of the firm's competitors may also alter the firm's pricing behavior.

The global marketing firm may also face a host of government restrictions and constraints on its pricing strategy. For example, in some countries governments may impose controls on the prices charged for certain products. This is seen, for example, in the case of Venezuela which maintains price controls on food staples such as rice as a means of combating food price inflation which disproportionately impacts the poor in society. As a legal requirement, these price controls must be respected by the foreign company. As noted in an earlier chapter, Cargill Inc. ran afoul of these regulations in Venezuela with serious consequences for the firm. In Canada, prescription drug prices are also controlled but in a less direct manner. In that country, the Patented Medicine Prices Review Board (PMPRB) monitors prescription drug prices with a view to ensuring that they are not excessive. In addition, individual Canadian provinces maintain a list of prescription medicines that are eligible for reimbursement under provincial health care programs. Multinational drug companies have a pecuniary interest in ensuring that their prices are competitive lest their brands be dropped from the approved list.[1] Governments in many countries also have regulations against two or more firms colluding to fix the prices they charge their customers. Again, these are legal requirements and the global marketer is well advised to adhere to them.

Of course, the firm also needs to price its products in global markets in a way that allows it to generate an acceptable return on investment and is consistent with the product's brand image. In some situations, a buyer's inability to access foreign exchange may complicate the firm's pricing strategy and force it to consider non-price payment options. Complexity is also introduced into pricing decisions when the firm has to consider issues of intra-corporate pricing and the degree of autonomy that should be granted to foreign subsidiaries in the setting of prices. These and other pricing issues are discussed in this chapter.

SETTING GLOBAL PRICES

The global marketer must consider a number of factors in setting global prices. Some of these factors are internal to the company and it, therefore, has some measure of control over them. Other factors, however, are exogenous to the multinational company and have to be taken as given in setting international prices.[2] These internal and external factors are listed in Figure 11.1 and discussed below.

FIGURE 11.1   Factors Influencing the Setting of International Prices

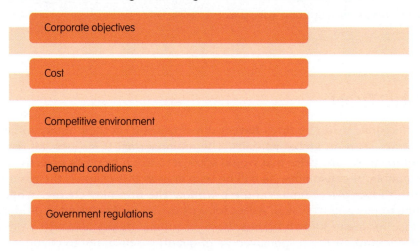

Corporate objectives

Cost

Competitive environment

Demand conditions

Government regulations

---

[1] Czinkota, M., Ronkainen, I., Farrell, C. and McTavish, R. (2009) *Global Marketing: Foreign Entry, Market Development and Strategy Implementation.* Toronto: Nelson Education

[2] Monroe, K.B. (2003) *Pricing: Making Profitable Decisions.* New York: McGraw-Hill, p. 12.

CORPORATE OBJECTIVES

The company's global pricing strategy must be consistent with its overall corporate objectives. These objectives may include, for example:

- establishing the company as a market share leader in specific international markets
- establishing the firm as a low-cost leader around the world
- positioning the firm as a global high-end luxury brand manufacturer.

The firm's global pricing strategy must be crafted to support these objectives. Of course, prices set must also ensure that the firm is able to achieve the target return on investment established for its overseas operations. In this regard, the firm's time horizon is also a consideration. If the foreign market is viewed as a long-term strategic interest for the company, this may be reflected in a pricing policy that aims to slowly build market share over a long period of time. The firm, in other instances, may be driven by a short-term profit opportunity and would be more likely to price aggressively to quickly achieve its objectives and exit the foreign market.

COSTS

Companies cannot continue in business over the long term unless they are able to cover both fixed and variable costs. Cost, in essence, acts as a floor below which the firm cannot price its products and expect to remain in business. While firms may deliberately price below cost in order to move excess inventory or to secure a competitive edge in a particular market, these are short-term tactics and not long-term strategies. The practice of **dumping**, or selling below cost of production, is discussed later in this chapter. It should also be remembered that the price that a manufacturer sets for its products becomes a cost for intermediaries in the marketing channel. In fact, the price set by each intermediary becomes a cost for the next intermediary in the marketing channel. The result is that, depending on the length of the channel, the price charged to the foreign consumer may be substantially higher than the price set in the manufacturer's home country. This phenomenon is known as **price escalation**. Table 11.1 presents a number of scenarios to illustrate the impact of channel length and logistical costs on the final price paid by the consumer. In our example, the addition of a foreign wholesaler and distributor to the domestic marketing channel results in a 119 percent increase in the price paid by the final consumer. Addition of a foreign distributor adds 59 percent to the cost

TABLE 11.1   A Hypothetical Example of Price Escalation

	Case #1: Domestic channel $M \rightarrow W_d \rightarrow R_d \rightarrow C_d$	Case #2: Foreign channel with direct sales to the foreign wholesaler $M \rightarrow W_f \rightarrow R_f \rightarrow C_f$	Case #3: Foreign channel with distributor $M \rightarrow D_f \rightarrow W_f \rightarrow R_f \rightarrow C_f$
Manufacturer's net price	20	20	20
+ Insurance and shipping costs (15 percent)	0	3.00	3.00
+ Tariffs (20 percent of CIF value)	0	4.60	4.60
Distributor's cost = CIF value + tariffs	0	0	27.60

(Continued)

TABLE 11.1 (Continued)

	Case #1: Domestic channel $M{\rightarrow}W_d{\rightarrow}R_d{\rightarrow}C_d$	Case #2: Foreign channel with direct sales to the foreign wholesaler $M{\rightarrow}W_f{\rightarrow}R_f{\rightarrow}C_f$	Case #3: Foreign channel with distributor $M{\rightarrow}D_f{\rightarrow}W_f{\rightarrow}R_f{\rightarrow}C_f$
Distributor's margin (25 percent) + VAT (16 percent of distributor's cost and margin)	0	0	27.60 6.90 5.52 ——— 40.02
Wholesaler's cost	20	27.60	40.02
Wholesaler's margin (33.3 percent) + VAT (16 percent of margin)	6.66	9.19	13.33 2.13 ——— 15.46
Wholesaler's price (= retailer's cost)	26.66	36.79	55.48
Retailer's margin (50 percent) + VAT (16% of margin)	13.33	18.40	27.74 4.44 ——— 32.18
Retailer's price to consumer	39.99	55.19	87.66
% price escalation over domestic (Case #1)	–	38	119
% price escalation over direct sales to W_f (Case #2)	–	–	59

Notes:
M = Manufacturer
D = Distributor
W = Wholesaler
R = Retailer
C = Consumer
Subscript 'f' = Foreign
Subscript 'd' = Domestic

Source: Adapted from Czinkota, M., Ronkainen, I., Farrell, C. and McTavish, R. (2009) *Global Marketing: Foreign Entry, Market Development and Strategy Implementation.* Toronto: Nelson Education.

of the final product relative to the channel with only a foreign wholesaler. In setting prices, manufacturers need to be aware of the impact of price escalation on the price that consumers will ultimately pay and the implications for competitiveness at the retail level.

There are a number of approaches that may be employed to address the problem of price escalation. The manufacturer could:

- reorganize, i.e. shorten, the marketing channel. By removing intermediaries, the firm also removes costs and reduces the final price to the consumer. This option should, of course, be carefully considered as all channel functions still need to be efficiently performed.
- undertake production in the foreign market. This strategy will remove costs associated with overseas shipping, tariffs and distributor margins and again reduce the final price to the consumer.

- undertake product modifications to make it less expensive in the foreign market. Backward innovation could significantly reduce final product prices by eliminating expensive add-on features that consumers may not need.
- lower the manufacturer's price. The manufacturer may wish to consider lowering the price that it charges for the product, in addition to perhaps exerting some pressure on intermediaries to reduce their own profit margins. Pressuring intermediaries to reduce their margins may be possible, depending on the extent of power the manufacturer wields in the channel. Of course, if the manufacturer demonstrates a willingness to reduce its own profit margin, the request may be better received by channel intermediaries. Major global retailers such as Wal-Mart with a strategy of everyday low prices (EDLP) may be the channel partner exerting the pressure to contain margins and keep consumer prices down, and not the manufacturer.

DEMAND CONDITIONS

The nature of demand for the firm's product also has an impact on its pricing strategy. If demand for the firm's product is inelastic, price changes will have little impact on the quantity demanded by consumers, and the firm will have substantially more pricing power in the marketplace. If demand for the company's product is elastic, however, even small changes in price will have a disproportionately large impact on the quantity demanded. Firms in such situations will be unable to raise prices without suffering a significant drop in sales.

The global marketer also needs to consider the price–quality relationship when setting product prices. Price acts as a signal of quality when consumers are unable to evaluate the merits of the product in any other way because of a lack of information (Roslin, 2012).[3] Consumers tend to associate quality with relatively higher prices and this perception will impact the price they are willing to pay for the firm's products. High-end luxury brands will command a higher price than their less well branded competitors in part because of the perceived quality associated with high-end brands. It should be noted that the price–quality association is to some extent dependent on culture. Research has shown that the association is stronger in some cultures than in others. For example, in the case of nondurable products such as food, beverages and household items, the price–quality association has been found to be quite low among consumers in Belgium, France, the Netherlands, Germany and the USA. Consumers in these countries place far more emphasis on other factors such as style, taste, vendor location and store loyalty when assessing the quality of nondurable products. In Asia, however, the price–quality association is much stronger. Consumers in Southeast Asia associate high prices with status and quality, and in fact use the price–quality relationship as a risk-reduction mechanism when making product choices.[4]

In making their judgments, consumers also make use **of reference prices**. Consumers compare observed (actual) prices with reference prices. Reference prices may be internal (or temporal) or external (or contextual). Internal reference prices are mental prices that the consumer uses to assess an observed price. Internal reference prices may be, for example, the last price paid by the consumer, the average price charged for similar products or what the consumer believes is a 'fair' price for the product. The internal reference price may also be the consumer's **reservation price**, or the upper amount she is willing to pay for the product or even the lowest amount she is willing to pay. External reference prices, on the other hand, are prices posted by the merchant at the point of sale as the regular price of the product.[5] Reference prices stimulate the consumer's perception of where the product is positioned relative to competing brands.[6]

---

[3] Roslin, R.M. (2012) 'Setting prices for global markets: Global insights and perspectives', in T.C. Melewar and S. Gupta (eds) *Strategic International Marketing: An Advanced Perspective*. London: Palgrave Macmillan.

[4] Roslin (2012) op cit.

[5] Ofir, C. and Winer, R. (2003) 'Pricing: Economic and behavioral models', in B. Weitz and R. Wensley (eds) *Handbook of Marketing*. London: SAGE.

[6] Roslin (2012) op cit.

Further, as was discussed in the previous chapter, getting the firm's products to the final consumer in a foreign country involves a chain of intermediaries. It was also pointed out that financial considerations are important in terms of motivating channel members to effectively handle the firm's products. The global marketing manager needs to bear this in mind in setting global prices. The manufacturer's selling price impacts the distributor's, and ultimately the retailer's, profit margins and must, therefore, be set carefully to allow each to generate an acceptable return. Manufacturer prices that do not allow for adequate profits for channel intermediaries will undermine the relationship between the channel partners and eventually lead to retention issues.

COMPETITIVE ENVIRONMENT

The ability of the firm to set prices in international markets will be heavily influenced by the competitive environment. Cost may serve as a floor below which prices cannot fall in the long run and demand may serve as a ceiling beyond which the firm cannot set its prices. The competitive environment, on the other hand, determines where between these two extremes prices are actually likely to settle.[7] In markets with several strong competitors, any price increase by the firm may result in reduced sales as consumers switch to other brands. In some cases, it may be prudent for the company not to compete on price but instead to compete on non-price elements such as product quality, after-sales service or credit terms.

GOVERNMENT REGULATIONS

Quite apart from the factors noted above, governments exert an important influence on the ability of the multinational company to price its products. For example, in many countries it is against the law for firms to collude on the price that their customers should be charged. Referred to as **price fixing**, companies in the industry in essence circumvent the free market and force consumers to pay an artificially determined price. For example, in the wake of the terrorist attacks on September 11, 2001, airlines were mandated by governments to adopt additional security measures. At the same time, airlines experienced a marked drop in passenger traffic as consumers opted to stay at home or utilize other means of transportation. Faced with additional security costs and reduced revenues, a number of airlines opted to collude on the prices set for cargo transportation. This decision would eventually lead to charges of price fixing being leveled against a large number of major players in the airline industry, including American Airlines, United Airlines, Lufthansa, Air France, British Airways, Cargolux and Air Canada.[8]

In some instances, governments may impose **price controls** on certain products. These set the maximum price that the company can charge and are usually implemented to ensure access by the poorer segments of society, or for purely political reasons.

case study 11.1: Venezuelan price controls

In an effort to contain inflation, the Venezuelan government has expanded its list of price-controlled products. The revised list now includes products such as toilet paper, shampoo, deodorant and pasteurized fruit juice. The government of Venezuela has a long history of imposing price controls designed to combat severe inflationary pressures in the economy. In February 2012, annual inflation stood at almost 26 percent. The new price controls announced require that businesses reduce their prices on 19 product categories, with the reductions ranging from 4 to 25 percent

---

[7] Czinkota et al. (2009) op cit.

[8] 'Air Canada in inquiry over cargo price-fixing', *Financial Post*, February 15, 2006; 'Cargo carriers', *Financial Post*, February 16, 2006.

depending on the product. In total, 616 individual new items are now subject to price controls under the country's Law on Fair Costs and Prices. This law is designed to not only combat inflation but also to discourage price speculation and ensure that Venezuelan citizens have access to basic products. The National Superintendency of Fair Costs and Prices (Sundecop) is the government agency responsible for monitoring compliance with the country's price control regulations. Sundecop has explained that the 19 new products were selected because of their importance in the budgets of average Venezuelans and were based on a study which found that from 2007 to 2011 these products had increased in price by some 400 percent, which was well above the national rate of inflation. In addition to deploying officers to monitor compliance, Sundecop has also launched a consumer awareness campaign to educate Venezuelan citizens and encourage them to assist the government in the monitoring process. The monitoring and compliance program will first focus on large supermarkets and pharmacy chains but will be extended to smaller retail outlets. Companies found to be in violation of the law face closure or fines of $5,400 (15 times the minimum wage).

Sources

Business Week (2012) Venezuela Expands Price Controls to New Products. Available at: www.businessweek.com/ap/2012-04/D9TT0UVG1.htm, accessed March 20, 2013.

Robertson, E. (2012) Regulated Prices for 19 Household Products Come into Effect. Available at: http://venezuelanalysis.com/news/6905, accessed March 20, 2013.

Discussion Questions

1. Do you believe that Venezuela's Law on Fair Costs and Prices can be effective at combating inflation?
2. What effect do you believe Venezuela's price control law has on foreign direct investment?

MULTINATIONAL PRICING STRATEGIES

The global marketer has a number of options available when pricing products in international markets. As noted above, the specific strategy adopted depends heavily on a number of factors, such as demand conditions, the competitive environment, government regulations, etc.

BASICS OF INTERNATIONAL PRICING

Market skimming: If the firm's objective is to achieve the highest level of profits possible in the shortest time frame, a market skimming strategy may be a useful approach. The strategy works if the product is new, innovative and in high demand. With this option, the firm establishes a very high price with the launch of the product on the international market. Consumers who wish to be among the first to own the product will be attracted despite the high price charged. The firm in essence is able to 'skim off' the less price-sensitive consumers. Over time, however, the firm reduces the price to attract more price-sensitive consumer segments and to fight off competitors who have entered the market.

Penetration pricing: With penetration pricing, the firm enters the international market with an extremely low price. The objective is to capture a large share of the market. Unlike skimming, which seeks to maximize contribution margins, penetration pricing focuses on market share. To be successful, the global marketer must have access to a large pool of price-sensitive consumers and must be able to control production and distribution costs in order to achieve and maintain profitability. The ability to achieve economies of scale in production and distribution as the firm expands its share of the market is essential to the success of this strategy. Penetration pricing may well be an effective long-term strategy for the company as the low prices are likely to discourage competitors from entering the market. The approach may also be useful when marketing to low-income consumers at the bottom of the pyramid.

Market pricing: In highly competitive markets, in which consumers have access to a range of essentially similar products and brands, market pricing may be an appropriate strategy. With this approach, the firm launches the product on the international market at a price that is on a par with what competitors are charging. To successfully implement this strategy, the firm needs to have a good understanding of the production and marketing costs involved in order to determine whether entry is feasible using this pricing approach. Basing the entry decision on the market price will eventually lead to problems for the firm if it is unable to generate a satisfactory return.

Cost-plus pricing: Rather than adopt the price charged by other firms in the market, the global marketer could instead focus on its cost. Cost-plus pricing is relatively straightforward and requires that the firm take into account all of the fixed and variable costs associated with getting the product into the hands of its foreign customers. Manufacturing, R&D, distribution and logistics costs, as well as the firm's profit margin, are combined to arrive at the product's selling price. All domestic and foreign market costs are fully allocated to the product. While this approach locks in the firm's profits, in practice it may result in prices that are too high for the firm to be competitive in international markets. Alternatively, the firm may opt to use a **marginal cost approach** in which only the incremental costs of producing and marketing the product in the international market are considered. R&D expenditures and all domestic fixed and variable costs are excluded from the calculation.[9] The result will be product prices that allow the firm to be far more competitive in foreign markets.

Demand-oriented pricing: Rather than focus on cost, the global marketing manager could also emphasize the price elasticity of demand in arriving at a foreign market price. Generally, price and quantity demanded are inversely related. The higher the price set for the product, the lower will be the quantity demanded. In demand-oriented pricing, the global marketer estimates the sales volumes at different price levels in order to determine the price that maximizes overall profit contribution. An illustration is provided in Table 11.2. From the example, the firm would appear to be better off with a selling price of $1,500 (Alternative #3), even though this is not the price that maximizes total sales revenue.

TABLE 11.2   Example of Demand-oriented Pricing

	Alternative #1	Alternative #2	Alternative #3
Retail price ($)	1,000	1,200	1,500
Unit sales ($)	500	450	300
Total revenue ($)	500,000	540,000	450,00
Total variable costs ($)	450,000	441,000	330,000
Manufacturing costs @ $300/unit	150,000	135,000	90,000
Marketing costs @ $200/unit	100,000	90,000	60,000
Distributor's margin @ 30 percent of sales	150,000	162,000	135,000
Entry costs @ 10 percent of sales	50,000	54,000	45,000
Contribution ($)	50,000	99,000	120,000

Source: Adapted from Roslin, R.M. (2012) 'Setting prices for global markets: Global insights and perspectives', in T.C. Melewar and S. Gupta (eds) *Strategic International Marketing: An Advanced Perspective.* London: Palgrave Macmillan.

---

[9]   Czinkota et al. (2009) op cit.

SUBSIDIARY COORDINATION

Multinational companies differ in terms of the degree of autonomy granted to subsidiaries in the pricing decision (see Figure 11.2). Some firms follow what is described as a **polycentric pricing strategy** in which subsidiaries have full control over their pricing decisions and there is little or no head-office involvement. Subsidiary managers are authorized to set prices in accordance with market conditions in their countries and without taking into account the pricing decisions made by their counterparts in other countries. While this strategy leads to prices that are responsive to consumer demand and competitive conditions, it does create an arbitrage opportunity. Gray traders, for example, may be able to take advantage of the price discrepancy between country markets with the negative consequences described in the preceding chapter.

Other multinational companies opt to follow a **geocentric pricing strategy** in which the parent company establishes a floor price below which subsidiaries are not allowed to sell the product. Subsidiary managers are, however, free to add a country mark-up to reflect the unique market conditions in their countries. This does provide for prices that are reasonably responsive to market conditions but the strategy does not eliminate the possibility of price arbitrage. A third alternative open to the firm is an **ethnocentric pricing strategy**. With this approach, the parent company sets one worldwide price which all subsidiary managers are obliged to follow. The possibility of price arbitrage is eliminated but the prices charged at the country level are no longer responsive to local market conditions.

FIGURE 11.2   Multinational Pricing Options

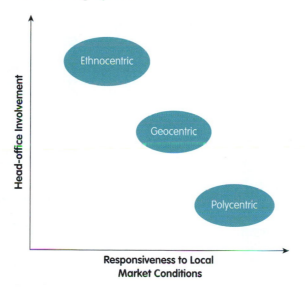

TRANSFER PRICING

The pricing strategies discussed above relate to the final product price charged to the consumer in the various foreign countries in which the firm does business. Multinational firms also need to make decisions with respect to how prices are established internally within the corporation. This brings us to consider the issue of **transfer pricing** or the pricing of products sold to members of the same corporate family. A parent company may, for example, provide raw materials or semi-finished products to its subsidiaries around the world. These products need to be fairly valued for accounting and tax purposes and internal prices must, therefore, be determined.

The multinational company may use several approaches to setting transfer prices and the approach used will be governed by a number of factors:

- global tax implications
- competitiveness
- motivation of subsidiary managers.

In terms of tax implications, it should be recognized that transfer prices may be used to minimize the company's tax burden by shifting profits to jurisdictions with the lowest corporate tax rates. Consider a manufacturing parent company in a low tax jurisdiction and a foreign sales subsidiary in a high tax jurisdiction. The parent could set a high transfer price in order to reduce subsidiary profitability and the firm's overall tax burden. This is illustrated in Figure 11.3 for a hypothetical manufacturer of washing machines. The parent company located in the low tax jurisdiction has a cost of production of $200 and transfers the washing machine to its foreign sales subsidiary at a price of $350. This becomes the subsidiary's cost to which is added transportation, shipping and promotion costs of $50. The subsidiary sells the washing machine for $400 in the foreign market, generating no profits and paying no taxes. The parent company's gross margin is $150 but because it operates in a low tax jurisdiction (15 percent) the total tax burden will be $22.50/unit. Had the washing machine been transferred to the subsidiary at $250, the subsidiary would have paid $45/unit in taxes and the parent $7.50/unit for a total corporate tax bill of $52.50/unit. This simplified example illustrates the power of transfer pricing in minimizing a company's global tax burden.

The price competitiveness of subsidiaries may also be improved if the parent company lowers the price at which inputs are transferred and allows the subsidiary to pass these savings on to its customers. A lower transfer price reduces the subsidiary's cost of production

FIGURE 11.3   Use of Transfer Prices to Shift Taxes

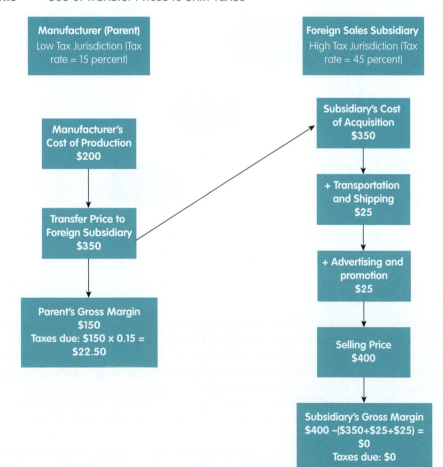

and improves price competitiveness. In markets with particularly strong and entrenched local competitors, this approach may offer significant benefits. In setting transfer prices, the parent company may also wish to consider the issue of motivation. Transfer prices may be set so as to increase or decrease subsidiary profitability. Given that year-end bonuses for subsidiary managers and key staff are based on profitability, the firm's internal pricing mechanism may also be used as a tool to reward and motivate employees. This tool must, however, be used judiciously, given the impact it is likely to have on managers in other countries.

TRANSFER PRICING METHODS

There are several methods that may be used to arrive at a transfer price. Multinational firms may, for example, use a **cost-based** approach in which the input is transferred from parent to subsidiary at a price that equals the parent's cost of acquisition. No mark-ups or discounts are applied in this intra-corporate pricing method. In other words, if an input is acquired by the parent for $1,000, it is transferred to the subsidiary for precisely that amount. The cost-based approach reduces input costs for the subsidiary, as there are no mark-ups involved, and increases its overall profitability. The supplying unit within the parent company is usually not supportive of this method as it earns no profit on the transaction. If the division is a profit center, this approach can create tensions within the company. As a compromise, some firms utilize a **cost-plus** method in which the supplying unit is allowed to add a percentage mark-up to the price at which the product is transferred. This allows the supplying unit to record a reasonable profit on the transaction.

The multinational firm also has the option of using a **negotiated** transfer pricing policy in which the supplying unit and purchasing unit arrive at a mutually agreeable transfer price through internal negotiations. If the two units are unable to arrive at a price through negotiation, then one is imposed on the parties by corporate headquarters. Another method that may be used to establish intra-corporate prices is the **arms-length** approach. Here, the multinational firm transfers the input to its subsidiary at the same price that it would have charged an unrelated third party. Members of the same corporate family receive no special treatment over unrelated third-party companies. The arms-length method is the approach generally favored by government regulators.

CHALLENGES

Transfer pricing presents a number of challenges for the multinational firm. The first relates to the measurement of subsidiary performance. The company needs to carefully consider what impact transfer pricing will have on how the performance of its subsidiaries is measured. The second challenge that may arise in the use of the various transfer pricing methods is the closer government scrutiny that may result. Tax authorities routinely audit the accounts of multinational firms and will impose penalties if not fully satisfied with their intra-corporate pricing practices. A 2005 survey of company executives noted that there were a number of triggers which may lead to a transfer pricing audit. These include increased audit and enforcement targets by fiscal authorities. Changes to transfer prices or size of transactions reported by multinational companies were also identified as important triggers.[10]

TERMS OF SALE

In import and export transactions, it is essential that there be a clear understanding of the responsibilities of both the exporter and importer and where in the process title changes hands. To facilitate this understanding, prices are quoted using a set of standardized **terms**

---

[10] Ernst and Young (2005) 2005–2006 Global Transfer Pricing Surveys: Global Transfer Pricing Trends, Practices, and Analysis. November. Available at: http://resources.rybinski.eu/resources/sendFile:db7fcc1c-be5

of sale referred to as International Commerce Terms (or simply **INCOTERMS**).[11] INCOTERMS were developed by the International Chamber of Commerce in 1936 and have undergone a series of revisions over the years. At the time of writing, the 2010 version was the most recent set of INCOTERM rules. There are a total of 11 rules (down from 13 in the 2000 version), seven of which cover any mode of transportation and four of which are specific to sea and inland waterway transportation (see Figure 11.4). These terms may also be grouped according to the responsibilities of the exporter and the importer. With the 'E-terms', the seller's only responsibility is to make the goods available to the buyer at the seller's facilities. With the 'F-terms', the seller is responsible for delivering the products to a carrier which the buyer has selected. 'C-terms' require that the seller assume responsibilities for transportation but not the risk of loss or damage once the goods have been shipped. Finally, the 'D-terms' require that the seller assume all costs and risks associated with delivery of the goods to the buyer's premises or other destination specified by the buyer. Table 11.3 illustrates the pattern of responsibility for both the exporter and importer.

FIGURE 11.4   INCOTERM 2010

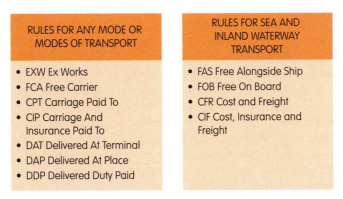

RULES FOR ANY MODE OR MODES OF TRANSPORT	RULES FOR SEA AND INLAND WATERWAY TRANSPORT
• EXW Ex Works • FCA Free Carrier • CPT Carriage Paid To • CIP Carriage And Insurance Paid To • DAT Delivered At Terminal • DAP Delivered At Place • DDP Delivered Duty Paid	• FAS Free Alongside Ship • FOB Free On Board • CFR Cost and Freight • CIF Cost, Insurance and Freight

Source: International Chamber of Commerce, http://www.iccwbo.org/products-and-services/trade-facilitation/incoterms-2010/the-incoterms-rules/

TABLE 11.3   Responsibility of the Exporter and Importer under INCOTERM Rules

Activity	EXW	FCA	FAS	FOB	CFR	CIF	CPT	CIP	DAT	DAP	DDP
Packing for Export	X	X	X	X	X	X	X	X	X	X	X
Export Clearance	I	X	X	X	X	X	X	X	X	X	X
Pre-carriage Loading	I	X	X	X	X	X	X	X	X	X	X
Pre-carriage	I	*	X	X	X	X	X	X	X	X	X
Main Carriage Loading	I	I	I	X	X	X	X	X	*	X	X
Main Carriage	I	I	I	I	X	X	X	X	*	X	X
Insurance						X		X			
Main Carriage Unloading	I	I	I	I	*	*	X	X	*	X	X

---

[11]   This section draws heavily from David, P. and Stewart, R. (2010) *International Logistics: The Management of International Trade Operations*, 3rd edn. Mason, OH: Cengage Learning–Atomic Dog.

Activity	EXW	FCA	FAS	FOB	CFR	CIF	CPT	CIP	DAT	DAP	DDP
On Carriage	I	I	I	I	I	I	X	X	I	X	X
On Carriage Unloading	I	I	I	I	I	I	I	I	I	I	X
Import Clearance	I	I	I	I	I	I	I	I	I	I	X
Pay Import Duty	I	I	I	I	I	I	I	I	I	I	X

Note: The responsibility of the exporter is denoted by an "X", the responsibility of the importer by an "I" and by a "*" if responsibility depends on the point of delivery. If the responsibility for an activity is undetermined the cell is left blank.

Source: Adapted from David, P., *International Logistics: The Management of International Trade Operations*, 4th edition. Berea, O: Cicero Books. ISBN 978-0-9894906-0-3.

Ex-Works (EXW): In an EXW transaction, the seller's only responsibility is to make the product available to the buyer at the seller's premises. The product, of course, must be packaged for export but it is the responsibility of the buyer to arrange transportation from the seller's facilities and to load the product onto a vehicle for transportation. The exporter and importer are required to agree on a mutually acceptable time/date for delivery. This INCOTERM rule is most beneficial for the exporter but puts the importer in the rather difficult position of having to collect the product in a foreign country.

Free Carrier (FCA): In an FCA transaction, the exporter is required to deliver the product to a carrier specified by the importer. With this INCOTERM rule, the exporter is still responsible for packaging the product for export but now has additional responsibilities for loading the product into a carrier's container, as well as for loading the container onto the carrier's truck. If a port of exportation is named, then the exporter is responsible for the cost associated with transporting the product to that point. The price quoted will include the above tasks but all other costs will be for the importer's account. The importer is responsible for contracting with a carrier and arranging clearance of the cargo in the importing country. This rule is used specifically for multimodal transportation of containerized cargo and replaces several other 'F-terms' such as FOR (free on rail), FOT (free on truck) and FOB-Airport (free on board – airport).

Free Alongside Ship (FAS): The FAS rule is specific to sea and inland waterway transportation. The exporter is responsible for packing the product for export, transporting it to the designated port and unloading it alongside the carrier's vessel. It should be noted that in many instances delivery is not actually alongside the ship but to a holding area at the port with subsequent transportation to the ship. The price quoted by the exporter will include the costs of performing these tasks. The importer is responsible for all costs associated with uploading the cargo onto the vessel and ocean transportation. The importer is also responsible for the cost of unloading the cargo in the destination country and clearing the shipment through customs.

Free on Board (FOB): The FOB rule is also specific to ocean and inland waterway transportation. With this INCOTERM rule, the exporter is once again responsible for packaging the merchandise for export and transporting it to the designated port. The exporter is also responsible for uploading the merchandise onto the carrier's vessel. The importer is then responsible for the cost of ocean transportation, as well as unloading the cargo and customs clearance in the destination country.

Cost and Freight (CFR): With the CFR rule, the exporter is responsible for packing the merchandise for export and transporting it to the port. The exporter is also responsible for unloading the cargo at the port and uploading it to the carrier's vessel. The price quoted by the exporter will include the above tasks and also the cost of transportation to the named port of debarkation. At some destinations, the contract with the carrier will also include the cost of unloading the cargo in the importing country. If it does not, then the importer will be responsible for those costs. With CFR transactions, responsibility for the shipment is transferred from exporter to importer at the port of departure. Risk of loss or damage is transferred to the buyer at that point even though it is the seller that contracts for ocean transportation. The CFR rule is specific to ocean and waterway transportation.

Cost, Insurance and Freight (CIF): The CIF rule is also specific to ocean and inland waterway transportation. Here, the exporter is responsible for packing the goods for export, transportation to the port of exportation, unloading at the port and subsequent uploading to the vessel for overseas transportation. The price quoted by the exporter will include the above costs as well as insurance and the cost of ocean transportation to the port of debarkation. The importer is responsible for customs clearance in the importing country and subsequent inland transportation to its premises in the country of importation.

Carriage Paid to (CPT): This INCOTERM rule applies to any mode of transportation other than ocean transportation and is essentially the same as the CFR rule. CPT is used when the mode of transportation is not by water or, if water is used, the cargo is not handled over the rails of the ship. This may occur, for example, in the case of roll-on–roll-off (RORO) cargo or containerized multimodal shipments which also include ocean transportation. As with CFR, the exporter is responsible for packing for export and all transportation costs to the destination city. The importer is responsible for unloading the cargo from the carrier's truck, clearing customs and inland transportation beyond the destination city.

Carriage and Insurance Paid to (CIP): This INCOTERM also applies to any mode of transportation other than ocean transportation and is conceptually the same as the CIF rule. CIP may be used for ocean transportation only if the cargo is not handled over the rails of the ship as with RORO or multimodal containerized cargo which also includes ocean transportation. The exporter is responsible for packing the merchandise for export and all costs associated with transportation to the destination city, including the cost of insurance. The importer is responsible for unloading the cargo from the carrier's truck and any additional inland transportation costs to the importer's facilities.

Delivered at Terminal (DAT): This rule applies to any mode of transportation, as well as to situations where more than one mode of transportation is used. Here, the exporter is responsible for packing the merchandise for export and all other costs related to transporting the product to the terminal. Under this rule, a 'terminal' may be a wharf, warehouse, container yard, airport terminal, rail terminal or road terminal. The importer is responsible for unloading the cargo at the destination, import clearance and all associated duties and taxes.

Delivered at Place (DAP): This INCOTERM rule is similar to DAT above, but delivery is deemed to have occurred once the exporter makes the merchandise available at the designated place and it is ready to be unloaded by the buyer. In a DAP transaction, the seller is responsible for the final leg of transit and the buyer is responsible for unloading the cargo once it arrives at the importer's premises. The importer is also responsible for import clearance and all associated duties and taxes.

It should be noted that DAT and DAP are relatively new (2010) INCOTERMS rules and replace the 2000 rules, Delivered Ex-Ship (DES), Delivered at Frontier (DAF), Delivered Ex-Quay (DEQ) and Delivered Duty Unpaid (DDU), which are no longer used.

Delivered Duty Paid (DDP): DDP may be used for any mode of transportation and places maximum responsibility on the exporter. Under this rule, the seller packs the goods for export and transports them to the buyer's premises and covers all the costs associated with these tasks. In addition, the exporter is responsible for clearing the shipment and paying the import duties. The importer's only duty is to unload the merchandise once delivered to its premises.

TERMS OF PAYMENT

The global marketing manager has a number of options available for payment when conducting international transactions. The options vary tremendously in the risks they present to the buyer and the seller in the transaction (see Figure 11.5). For an exporter, the most favorable option is, of course, **cash in advance** in which the buyer pays the seller even before the product is shipped. With this method, the exporter does not bear any non-payment risk and has immediate access to the funds for capital investment or business operations. The importer, however, is placed at a significant disadvantage in terms of the risk of non-delivery of the merchandise after payment has been made. At the other extreme, **consignment sales** are the most advantageous for the importer. In such transactions, the exporter ships the product to the importer but only receives payment after the importer has been able to sell the product. In essence, payment to the exporter is deferred until the product is sold to the final consumer, and in some instances the exporter may have to pay for the return of the product if a sale is not consummated in a timely manner. A third option open to the global marketer is **open account**. With this method, the product is shipped and the buyer has a specified period of time, say 30 days, to remit payment to the seller. Open account is far more common in the case of domestic, as opposed to international, transactions.

The method of payment most commonly used in international transactions is the **letter of credit** (LC). An LC is an instrument issued by the importer's bank at the request of the importer and guarantees payment to the exporter provided the merchandise is shipped in accordance with precise instructions. The process begins with negotiation between the exporter and the importer on price and other aspects of the transaction. Once there is agreement, the exporter provides the importer with a pro forma invoice and detailed instructions on the terms of the sale which are presented to the importer's bank with a request that an LC be opened in favor of the exporter.

Once the request is made, the importer's bank (or **issuing bank**) will contact the exporter's bank (**advising bank**) and inform that institution that an LC has been opened in favor of the exporter. The advising bank will verify that the issuing bank is a bona fide financial institution and confirm that the information provided on the LC is consistent with that on the pro forma invoice. The advising bank will then notify the exporter that an LC has been opened in its favor and that the documents are in order. The advising bank will forward a copy of the LC to the exporter. Based on this notification, the exporter will proceed to ship the merchandise to the importer.

FIGURE 11.5   Risks for buyers and sellers

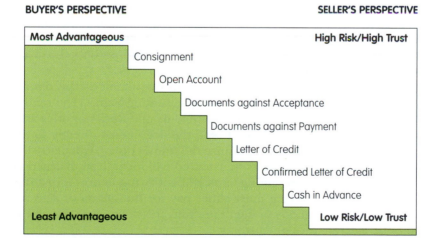

Source: Adapted from Chase Manhattan Bank (1984) *Dynamics of Trade Finance.* New York: Chase Manhattan Bank, p. 5

The LC guarantees that the importer's bank will pay the exporter the amount due for the product on the presentation of certain specified documents such as a bill of lading, a consular invoice and a description of the products. These documents are generated during the export process. The LC in essence substitutes the credit worthiness of the exporter for the credit worthiness of the issuing bank. Note that because it is providing a guarantee, the issuing bank may place a hold on funds in the importer's account of up to 100 percent of the value of the LC. The exporter, therefore, does not have to be concerned about non-payment by the importer as payment is guaranteed as long as the products are shipped in accordance with the LC's requirements. It should be noted that the product must be shipped exactly as specified in the LC if the exporter is to receive payment. For example, if the LC stipulates that the merchandise should be shipped in one crate containing a total of 12 units and the exporter instead ships two crates each containing 6 units, the issuing bank will not honor the terms of the LC and payment will not be made.

Once shipment has been made, the exporter will provide the relevant documents to the advising bank which in turn transfers them to the issuing bank. The issuing bank checks the documents against the LC and, if consistent, will remit payment to the advising bank. The advising bank in turn credits the exporter's account. The issuing bank will also release the documents to the importer, including the bill of lading which can be used to clear the merchandise through customs.

There are several types of LCs:

Revocable vs. irrevocable: An irrevocable LC cannot be modified or cancelled without the written consent of the exporter, i.e. the beneficiary. Revocable LCs, on the other hand, may be modified or cancelled by the importer and, therefore, do not provide the exporter with the same level of protection.

Confirmed vs. unconfirmed: With a confirmed LC, the bank guarantees payment even if the importer were to default. The bank assumes all the risk of the transaction, including the exchange rate risk, and therefore provides the exporter with an exceptionally strong guarantee. With an unconfirmed LC, the bank does not provide the exporter with such a strong guarantee. Clearly, an irrevocable and confirmed LC offers extremely strong protection for the exporter.

Revolving vs. non-revolving: LCs usually relate to one specific international transaction and are described as non-revolving. LCs that cover multiple shipments are said to be revolving.

Other payment options open to the firm are documentary collections, i.e. **documents against payment** and **documents against acceptance**. With documentary collections, the exporter retains the services of a bank in the importer's country to act on its behalf. The bank is instructed not to release documents pertaining to the export transaction until the importer has paid the exporter or signed a **draft** or **bill of exchange** promising to pay. In particular, the bank will not release the bill of lading to the importer as this is the certificate of title and allows the importer to clear the goods through customs and take possession. With documentary collections, if the importer does not take delivery of the goods, the exporter is able to ship them back to its home country or perhaps find another buyer in the importer's country. Should the goods need to be shipped back, the exporter will lose only the cost of transportation as opposed to the entire value of the shipment.

With documentary collections, the exporter uses its own bank as the remitting bank to transmit the documents to the importer's bank (or presenting bank). The remitting bank in these transactions is merely a conduit for the documents and does not offer any guarantees to the parties. While the exporter could well send the documents directly to the importer's bank, use of a remitting bank serves to legitimize the transaction, particularly if the exporter is not a well-known company. Documents transmitted will include an instruction letter from the exporter. Once received, the presenting bank will notify the importer that the documents have been received and that the firm must either pay for the goods or sign a draft. If the importer does not pay for the goods or sign the draft, the documents are not released and the goods cannot be cleared through customs.

Drafts or bills of exchange are legal documents in the importing country and are an official recognition of a commercial debt to the exporter. Because it is a legal document in the importer's country, it is easier to pursue the matter in court, should the importer default on the obligation. There are several types of drafts. **Sight drafts** require that the importer pay the exporter's invoice before the documents are released. These types of transactions are termed documents against payment. Payment is due immediately, i.e. on sight, and the exporter retains title until payment has been received. The exporter may also make use of a **time draft** in which the importer must sign a document promising to pay the exporter in a certain number of days, usually 30, 60, 90 or 180. Once the draft is accepted and signed by the importer, the presenting bank will release the documents. Transactions using time drafts are referred to as documents against acceptance.

MANAGEMENT OF FOREIGN EXCHANGE RISKS

Pricing decisions in international markets require that the global marketing manager consider the issue of foreign exchange risk. Unless the buyer and seller share the same currency, such as the euro, movements in foreign exchange rates will have a negative impact on one or other of the parties to the transaction. The global marketing manager has the option of quoting product prices in the currency of the home country, in the currency of the foreign buyer or in the currency of some third country. For example, an American exporter selling into a eurozone country will most likely choose to quote prices either in US dollars or in euros. If prices are quoted in US dollars, the exporter bears no currency risk. When the European importer remits payment, the exporter will receive exactly the price that was quoted. On the other hand, once there is a commitment to purchase, the European importer bears the foreign exchange risk as the euro may depreciate in value before payment is made. Of course, if prices are quoted in euros, then it is the US exporter who bears the foreign exchange risk. Also, the longer payment remains outstanding, the greater is the risk for the affected party.

To mitigate the impact of foreign exchange risk, the global marketing manager has several options:

Forward contracts: A company that is required to make a payment in a foreign currency on a specified date can enter into a **forward contract** and lock in the exchange rate. For example, if an Argentinean company has, say, 30 days to make a US$5 million payment to an American firm for merchandise it has imported, it has the option of waiting until the payment is due and simply purchasing the foreign exchange on the spot market. If the Argentinean peso depreciates over the 30 days however, the firm will have to surrender more local currency to secure the US$5 million payment. Alternatively, the Argentinean importer could use the **forward market** to purchase the US dollars at a **forward rate** well in advance of the due date for payment. A forward rate is an exchange rate at which two parties agree to exchange currencies on some specified future date. Based on macroeconomic, political and other considerations, bankers and currency traders form expectations about future spot currency exchange rates. To hedge its risks, the Argentinean importer could enter into a contract on the forward market to purchase US$5 million at the forward rate. This contract would require that the importer purchase the US dollars at the specified forward rate on the agreed-on date. Should the Argentinean peso depreciate within the 30-day period and be well below the spot rate at the time payment is to be made, the importer is still able to purchase the dollars required at the agreed-on forward rate. However, should the peso strengthen over the 30-day period, the importer will not be able to take advantage of the appreciation to reduce the amount of pesos required to secure the US$5 million payment. In using this strategy, the Argentinean importer needs to be aware that at any point in time the forward rate may be higher (a premium) or lower (a discount) than the spot rate so some analysis is required before entering into a contract.

Currency options: Companies may also use **currency options** to manage foreign exchange risks. A currency option gives the firm the right (but not the obligation) to purchase or sell an amount of foreign currency at a specified rate on a specified date. A currency option is, therefore, quite different from the forward contract discussed above which requires that the company complete the transaction on the terms agreed to. Currency options provide the company with greater flexibility. Consider again the case of the Argentinean importer in the example above. If in 30 days when payment is due the spot rate for the peso is ARS5.10/US\$ but the importer had purchased a currency option at a rate of ARS7.25/US\$, the firm would be better off not exercising the option. In this instance, the firm should simply purchase the US dollars on the spot market which would save the firm ARS2.15 for every US dollar purchased. If, however, the option price was lower than the spot price, the firm would save by exercising the option.

Futures contracts: The Argentinean importer seeking to purchase US\$5 million has a choice of using either a forward contract or currency options contract to lock in the exchange rate. For smaller amounts, however, the forward market is not a viable alternative. Forward contracts are only available for transactions in excess of \$1 million. For smaller amounts, the importer could purchase a **currency futures contract**. Currency futures contracts are conceptually similar to forward contracts in that they allow the firm to lock in the exchange rate that would apply to a transaction at some future point in time. Futures contracts are typically in amounts less than \$100,000, providing an opportunity for smaller players to manage foreign exchange risks.

EXPORT FINANCING

In order to secure major international contracts, exporters often need to put in place financing facilities which allow them to be competitive. As part of negotiations, an important foreign buyer may, for example, request credit terms that exceed what an exporter is comfortable agreeing to. If the exporter is unable to comply, this could easily jeopardize the potential sale. Buyers often look beyond product quality and price to consider factors such as credit availability in deciding between prospective suppliers. Access to financing can make the difference between success and failure in export markets.

The global marketing manager has a number of export financing options available. A facility with a **commercial bank** in the exporter's home country is one option open to the global marketer. This may take the form of a line of credit, an overdraft or a business loan which the exporter may use to finance the entire range of export activities from production to shipping. Most commercial banks, however, are not specialists in trade finance and tend to take a somewhat cautious approach to financing international transactions. Collateral requirements may be extremely strict and commercial banks may deal only with established business customers with pristine credit histories. Small and medium-sized firms may, therefore, experience some difficulty in accessing export financing through their local commercial banks.

Export transactions often create cash flow problems for the exporter because of the length of time it takes to collect foreign receivables. Apart from a line of credit or other facility from a commercial bank, the exporter could also use **forfeiting** and **factoring** as a financing option. With forfeit transactions, the exporter ships the merchandise to the importer and receives payment in the form of a promissory note which is guaranteed by a commercial bank in the importer's country. Once in receipt of the promissory note, the exporter sells it to a third party at a discount to its face value and immediately receives the cash. The exporter, therefore, does not have to wait for payment from the importer and has immediate access to the cash to fund ongoing operations. Forfeit transactions are without recourse to the exporter. In other words, the forfeit company cannot hold the exporter responsible if the importer does not pay. The size of the discount to face value demanded by the forfeit company will depend on several factors, such as the importer's credit history and the financial strength of the guaranteeing bank in the importer's country. It should be noted that forfeit transactions may be used to finance credit terms of several years with the exporter presenting the forfeit company a series of notes with different due dates.

The exporter may also make use of factoring as a means of financing its operations without exposure to the problems involved in selling on open account. With factoring, the exporter sells its accounts receivables to a third party (a factor) at a discount. Unlike forfeit transactions, factoring transactions are with recourse so the exporter remains liable should the importer not pay. It should also be noted that while forfeiters work with longer-term receivables (over 180 days to as long as seven years), factors will only handle short-term receivables (up to 180 days). Another key difference is that while forfeiting is essentially a one-time transaction, factoring transactions may be ongoing with the factor providing a range of services such as conducting credit checks on buyers, accounts receivable bookkeeping and collection services.[12] Also, factoring does not involve a bank guarantee, as does forfeiting, and, as a result, factors may not conduct business in some high-risk developing countries. A further distinction is that forfeiters tend to work with capital goods transactions, while factors specialize in transactions involving consumer goods.[13]

case study 11.2: Export Development Canada

Founded in 1944, Export Development Canada (EDC) is a Canadian Crown Corporation that provides financing and risk management services to Canadian exporters. In 2012, the EDC helped more than 7,400 Canadian companies do business in 87 countries. Some 30 percent of these transactions were in fast-growing emerging markets. Since inception, the EDC has been involved in financing transactions in as many as 200 countries around the world. The EDC is self-financing and operates on commercial principles. The Corporation provides a range of financing services for Canadian exporters, including pre-shipment financing, facilitating financing arrangements with commercial banks, equity financing to facilitate growth of an export business, financing solutions for foreign buyers of Canadian products, and foreign direct investment to allow Canadian firms to expand globally. For foreign firms, the EDC offers lines of credit for repeated purchases of Canadian goods, structures and arranges loan syndications for Canadian and foreign firms, and provides a bank guarantee program to cover Canadian and foreign banks involved in financing the export of Canadian products to customers in developing countries. The EDC has a niche position in the Canadian financial services industry, handling risky export financing deals that commercial banks avoid. Despite this niche position and the success achieved, the EDC has begun to revamp its business model. The corporation has begun to move into sectors left vacant by US and European banks reeling from the effects of the financial crisis that began in 2007. The organization's new strategy will see it financing major transactions around the world even when there is no private-sector Canadian company involved. The EDC plans to focus primarily on emerging market deals once dominated by European banks. With this new business model, the EDC would act as lead financier on, say, a major transportation or infrastructure project in South America, even if there are no other Canadian investors. The Crown Corporation does hope, however, that its involvement in such deals will open the door for Canadian professional services companies, such as engineering and construction firms, to participate. Having the EDC involved is expected to give these firms the confidence they need to compete for service contracts.

Critics of the new strategy argue that the EDC's access to cheap government-guaranteed financing gives it an unfair advantage in the marketplace and distorts the true level of risk involved in these types of transactions. Others argue that the EDC is a Crown Corporation and is effectively competing with the private sector. Proponents point out that the EDC has been consistently profitable and, as long as that is the case, the risks to Canadian tax payers are negligible. Proponents also suggest that while the Corporation has broadened its mandate it has remained true to its objectives and will not be taking business away from other Canadian banks.

(Continued)

---

[12]   Czinkota et al. (2009) op cit.

[13]   Czinkota et al. (2009) op cit.

(Continued)

Sources

EDC website: www.edc.ca/en/Pages/default.aspx, accessed March 16, 2013.

Greenwood, J. (2013) How Export Development Canada is the Next Big Bank in Waiting. Available at: http://business. financialpost.com/2013/02/22/how-export-development-canada-is-the-next-big-bank-in-waiting/, accessed March 26, 2013.

Discussion Questions

1. Do you believe this is a good strategic move for the EDC? Why/why not?
2. What will be the likely reaction of the major US and European banks to the EDC's entry into this market?

DUMPING

Dumping refers to the practice of selling a product in an export market at a price that is lower than the price charged in the exporter's home country and/or below the product's cost of production. Cheap imported products may, of course, have a deleterious impact on domestic firms and raise concerns about unfair foreign competition. Firms may engage in what is described as **predatory dumping** where the intention is to compete heavily on price in an effort to drive competitors out of the market. The exporting firm may sell its products at a significant discount in order to capture market share and force competitors to also reduce their prices in a bid to regain their share of the market. Over time, losses mount for all firms, eventually forcing some or all of the local competitors to exit the market. The foreign firm with greater access to financial resources is better able to withstand the losses. Predatory dumping is a deliberate tactic. In some situations, however, dumping may be unintentional. **Unintentional dumping** may occur, for example, if sharp fluctuations in the exchange rate between the exporting and importing countries result in a significant drop in the price of the product on the export market. In such circumstances, price may temporarily drop below cost of production but due to a factor that is clearly beyond the control of the exporter.

Governments may at times subsidize their exporters, giving them an unfair price advantage in international markets. Under WTO rules, however, **countervailing duties** may be imposed on products deemed to have been dumped and which threaten to cause, or have caused, material injury to domestic firms in the industry. The amount of countervailing duties imposed is equal to the dumping margin or the extent of the subsidy.

NON-PRICE PAYMENT OPTIONS

In some situations, the global marketing manager may need to consider the use of non-price payment options in order to complete a sale. Referred to as **countertrade**, these transactions require that the global marketer accept payment in kind rather than cash for all or a substantial part of the value of the goods exchanged. While most companies would prefer to receive payment in cash, countertrade may be the only way to complete a sale in some circumstances. If, for example, the target country has foreign exchange controls in effect, this would limit the amount of hard currency available to importers to conduct business with exporters. Rather than abandon the sale altogether, the global marketer in this case may consider payment in kind for some part or all of the value of the goods to be shipped. In other situations, debt problems or an inability to obtain trade financing may limit the importer's access to cash to conduct international transactions. It is still possible to conduct business with the importer, however, if the exporter is willing to consider non-price options.

FORMS OF COUNTERTRADE

For companies willing to accept payment in kind, there are several forms of countertrade that may be considered. The first is **barter** or the direct exchange of products of equal value. With a straight barter transaction, there is only an exchange of goods and money is not involved. There are two major problems with a straight barter transaction. First, there has to be a double coincidence of wants, i.e. Party A to the transaction must want the goods offered by Party B, and vice versa. If this is not the case, the transaction is unlikely to be completed. The second problem with a straight barter transaction is that the goods must be of roughly equal value. Again, if this is not the case, the transaction is unlikely to proceed. The second form of countertrade is referred to as a **compensation deal**. Compensation deals attempt to resolve the valuation problem inherent in straight barter by allowing for the exchange of some amount of cash in addition to the exchange of physical products. In this case, the cash payment is designed to equalize the value of the goods being exchanged.

A third form of countertrade is a **buyback** in which one party provides equipment or technology which is used by the other party to produce goods. The goods produced are subsequently used as payment for the technology or equipment supplied. With a buyback transaction, the supplier of the technology must sell the goods received in order to receive a cash payment. In some cases, it is stipulated that the goods received be sold in some third country in order not to disrupt the local market and depress prices. A fourth form of counter-trade is referred to as a **counterpurchase** or **offset** transaction. With an offset, two contracts are signed between the buyer and the seller. Under the first contract, the product is sold and the seller receives payment in cash. Under the terms of the second contract, however, the original seller agrees to purchase products from the original buyer up to some stated value and within a defined period of time. In essence, the original seller becomes the buyer on the second part of the transaction. The value of the products to be purchased under the terms of the second contract may be equivalent to the value of the first contract or some defined percentage. Offset transactions are typically used in the procurement of military equipment.

SUMMARY

This chapter has covered a number of topics relevant to global pricing strategies. The factors that influence the setting of global prices were discussed. These included demand conditions, competitive pressures, cost and the impact of government regulations. Various pricing strategies were also presented, including the key issue of subsidiary involvement in the pricing decision. The special topic of intra-corporate pricing was also discussed in this chapter, and in particular how these internal prices may be set and how they are used by multinational firms to minimize their tax burden, improve price competitiveness and incent employees.

The chapter next examined terms of sale and the responsibility of exporters and importers. Various INCOTERMS were defined and their role in clarifying international price quotations was examined. Terms of payment were also discussed in the chapter and the relative risks to the importer and exporter associated with various forms of payment were identified. It was also pointed out that unless the buyer and seller share the same currency, foreign exchange movements will put one or the other at risk. To address this issue, a number of approaches to the management of foreign exchange risk were presented. The argument was also made that in some situations credit terms may have an important bearing on whether a particular international transaction is eventually consummated. The sources of export financing and their importance were, therefore, discussed. The chapter concluded with a brief discussion of dumping and non-price payment options.

? discussion questions

1. What is price escalation? What strategies could a manufacturer use to mitigate its impact?

2. Based on the information provided in this chapter, can you identify and discuss four factors that should be considered when setting prices in international markets?

3. What is a polycentric pricing strategy and how does it differ from geocentric and ethnocentric approaches?

4. Distinguish between cost-plus and demand-oriented pricing. Which would you use if entering a competitive export market?

5. What is a transfer price? Discuss three methods that may be used by the multinational firm to determine a transfer price.

6. How could transfer prices be used to minimize the company's global tax burden?

7. What are INCOTERMS and why are they important in export transactions?

8. What is a letter of credit and how is it used in export transactions?

🌐 Real World Challenges

Caterpillar in Peru

The executives of Caterpillar Inc. were facing a tough business environment. The Illinois-based manufacturer of heavy earth-moving equipment had just posted a first quarter net loss of US$112 million compared to a profit of US$922 million a year ago. The firm in its press release cited a deteriorating global business environment, cut its 2009 profit forecast in half and announced the layoff of 25,000 employees. In speaking to reporters, the CEO of the firm, Jim Owens, noted that the increase in infrastructure spending announced in the USA would not be sufficient to offset the declines seen in private-sector projects. Jim indicated that Caterpillar, a US company, was more optimistic about its prospects in overseas markets.

PHOTO 11.1

On May 1, 2009, Juan Hernandez, VP of Global Business Development for Caterpillar, was tasked with turning around the company's desperate financial situation. Two weeks later, Jim asked Juan to make a presentation to the company's board of directors to report on his progress. Juan knew that Jim and other members of the board were on side with respect to targeting overseas markets – particularly in the developing world. This was clearly where the company's prospects for growth were greatest. In fact, the previous week Juan had received a proposal from an established mining company in Peru to purchase earth-moving equipment valued at US$25 million. The company had indicated, however, that foreign exchange was being rationed in Peru and paying in hard currency would be difficult. The firm was suggesting a countertrade transaction in which Caterpillar would receive payment in the form of iron ore from its mines. The Peruvian firm's geologists had identified a large iron ore deposit and environmental approvals were already in place. As Juan stared at the proposal, he knew that this was the problem he would face in implementing a turn-around strategy. Still, a US$25 million order would go a long way to reversing the company's profit shortfall and there may well be similar deals available in other Latin American and African countries.

As Juan walked into the meeting, he was still unsure about whether he should recommend that Caterpillar pursue the deal with the Peruvian mining company. A number of questions swirled in his mind. Caterpillar is not in the mining business – should the company deviate from its established business practices and accept payment in iron ore? With current short supplies and high prices, getting the ore sold would not be a problem, but timing of payment would be. It was clear from the Peruvian firm's proposal that the equipment was needed before the ore could be extracted and this would certainly delay payment. Extraction of the ore could take several months. What if iron ore prices declined in the interim? Also, mining is a risky business – what if the tonnage of ore extracted was less than the value of the equipment shipped? After all, geologists have been known to make mistakes, and even to distort the truth.

Source

Tita, B. (n.d.) Caterpillar Slashes Its Forecast. Available at: http://online.wsj.com/article/SB124030427865538569.html, accessed July 4, 2013.

Questions

1. State the problem that Caterpillar faces in Peru.
2. Identify the options available to Juan. Be sure to identify more than one.
3. Based on the options identified above, recommend a course of action for the company. Be sure to provide a rationale and make a decision.

FURTHER READING

Ernst & Young (2005) 2005–2006 Global Transfer Pricing Surveys: Global Transfer Pricing Trends, Practices and Analysis. *International Tax Services*, November.

Roslin, R.M. (2012) 'Setting prices for global markets: Global insights and perspectives', in T.C. Melewar and S. Gupta (eds) *Strategic International Marketing: An Advanced Perspective*. London: Palgrave Macmillan.

GLOBAL COMMUNICATION AND SALES STRATEGIES

12

LEARNING OBJECTIVES

After reading this chapter you should be able to:

- Discuss the elements of the communication model

- Discuss the role that culture plays in the process of communication

- Discuss the process of formulating a global communication strategy

- Discuss the role and appropriateness of advertising as a communication tool

- Discuss the role and appropriateness of public relations as a communication tool

- Discuss the role and appropriateness of sales promotion as a communication tool

- Discuss the role and appropriateness of corporate sponsorship as a communication tool

- Explain the process of personal selling

- Discuss the key issues involved in the management of an international sales force.

INTRODUCTION

This chapter focuses on global communication and the management of the firm's international sales efforts. In order to be successful in international markets, the global marketing firm must have in place an effective strategy for communicating with its customers and other stakeholders. This is generally a challenging proposition made even more so in an international context in which there may be significant cultural distance between the firm and its target audience. Communication messages that may be well received in one cultural context may not resonate with target audiences in another, or may even be offensive. Further, media that may be highly effective in one country may be less so in another or may not even be available to the global marketer. There is also the issue of differences in government regulations and the impact these may have on the firm's communication campaign.

Even large multinationals have a finite budget to allocate to communication. The global marketer must pay considerable attention to the financial resources available to implement the firm's communication strategy in a competitive global market. New products may fail to gain traction in international markets and established products may lose market share if not well supported with resources for advertising and promotion. Of course, the commitment of resources also necessitates that the firm has in place tools and approaches for measuring the effectiveness with which its communication objectives are being achieved. It should be recognized that the effectiveness of an international communication campaign will be driven to some extent by the selection of communication tools which are appropriate to the cultural context. These tools are also discussed in this chapter but we begin with a review of the basic model of communication.

ELEMENTS OF THE COMMUNICATION MODEL

The basic communication model is depicted in Figure 12.1. The **sender** (or source) in this model would be the global marketing firm which has a **message** that it wishes to communicate. This message may be, for example, the launch of a new product, a price reduction or other sales promotion, or in some special cases a product recall. This message is targeted at a **receiver**, the firm, organization or individual that receives the message. The receiver may be a final consumer, a channel member, government officials or even members of the investment community. In some situations, the receiver may be the company's own personnel. As illustrated in Figure 12.1, the message is conveyed from sender to receiver via a **channel** of communication. This channel may be electronic, such as television or radio, or may be much less sophisticated, such as outdoor billboard signs. The company's salespeople may also serve as the channel of communication between sender and receiver.

In order for the message to be understood, two processes are involved. First, the sender must **encode** the message or convert the abstract idea into a set of symbols that the receiver is able to understand. Second, the receiver must **decode** the message or convert the symbols back into the abstract idea originally conceived by the sender. The processes of encoding and decoding a message are, however, heavily influenced by the cultural framework of the sender and receiver respectively. As a result, messages may not be perceived quite in the way the sender intended. Communication may, of course, fail for other reasons. For example, the message may be transmitted though the wrong channel so that it never reaches the target audience. The global marketer's use of Internet-based advertising in a country with very low Internet penetration is a case in point. In other instances, the firm may not have identified the correct target audience and the communication, therefore, fails to reach those individuals the firm seeks to influence.

As illustrated in Figure 12.1, the communication process is also affected by **noise**. Noise in this context refers to anything that interferes with the accurate transmission of the message between sender and receiver. Language differences between the parties, or even differences in dialects of the same language, may create interference in the communication channel and negatively impact receipt of the message. As noted in an earlier chapter, translation errors are the source of numerous blunders in the international marketing literature. While amusing for the reader, they are much less so for the executives of the companies affected by the fallout.

FIGURE 12.1   The Basic Communication Model

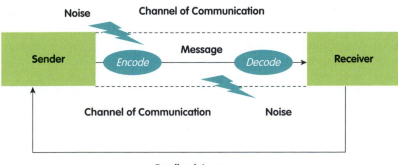

Even non-verbal language may create problems if the sender does not understand the culture of the receiver. A salesperson standing extremely close to a prospect may be quite acceptable in some cultures but may unnerve individuals from another.

Once decoded, the receiver will provide the sender with some form of feedback which will indicate the extent to which the message was properly received and decoded. This is shown as a feedback loop in Figure 12.1. Feedback may be provided to the source in the form of, for example, increased sales, brand awareness or traffic flow at retail outlets where the firm's products are sold. Based on the feedback received, the sender may need to modify the message, the way it is encoded or the channel of communication employed in order to increase the effectiveness of the communication process.

CULTURE AND COMMUNICATION

Culture plays an extremely important role in the process of communication.[1] As mentioned above, the cultural framework of the sender will influence the encoding of the message in international communication. Message content, choice of words and images will all be affected by the sender's cultural framework. The decoding of the message by the receiver will also be affected by culture. Selective perception is operative in international communication and consumers will, therefore, tend to filter out elements of the message that do not fit well with their own cultural frame of reference. In designing an international communication campaign, these and other differences need to be kept in mind.

PURPOSE OF COMMUNICATION

It should be noted that the **purpose** of communication varies depending on the cultural context. While several aspects of culture explain differences in communication, the individualism–collectivism dimension is thought to have the greatest impact. In individualistic cultures, communication is designed to influence, persuade, change attitudes or condition the behavior of the target audience. This is manifested, for example, in the nature of, say, American advertisements which emphasize persuasion, repetition and a hard-sell approach. In essence, the firm and the consumer are viewed as being on opposite sides of the sales counter, with the seller attempting to persuade the consumer to modify her purchasing behavior or attitude towards the firm and its products. The emphasis is on control. In contrast, communication in collectivist societies is designed to build trust and develop long-term relationships between the buyer and seller. This is seen, for example, in Japanese advertisements which tend to focus more on engendering positive feelings towards the firm and its brands, rather than providing a great deal of factual information to influence the purchase decision.

The above differences in purpose are reflected in a number of observable differences between advertisements from individualistic and collectivist countries. For example, if we consider television commercials we see a difference in the frequency and timing of verbal and visual mentions of the company's brand name. In a typical Japanese commercial, the name of the company, the brand name and the name of the product are mentioned much later in the ad when compared to the typical American commercial. In the Japanese commercial, more time is devoted to developing trust and understanding. The same is also observed in Chinese commercials where the brand name is mentioned much later than in US advertisements. Also, in advertisements from collectivist societies, the brand name is shown for a longer period of time, while in US advertisements the brand name is mentioned verbally more frequently, which is consistent with a hard-sell approach.

---

[1] This section draws heavily from de Mooij, M. (2010) *Global Marketing and Advertising: Understanding Cultural Paradoxes*, 3rd edn. London: SAGE.

FIGURE 12.2   The Hierarchy of Effects Model

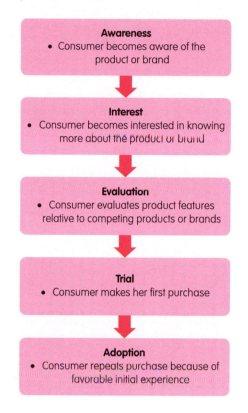

It should be noted that the US approach to persuasion is very much based on the way Americans process information. The USA is a low-context society and American consumers have been conditioned to the use of explanations, logical arguments and persuasive copy. In contrast, consumers from high-context cultures rely on signs, symbols and indirect communication in order to process information. In general, the approach to persuasion used in individualistic societies would not resonate well with consumers from collectivist cultures who, because of the difference in how information is processed, would find the hard-sell method very much a turn-off.

THE MECHANICS OF ADVERTISING

Most models of how advertising works are based on the assumption that advertising transports the individual from one stage to another. The process is deemed to be sequential and logical, i.e. there is a **hierarchy of effects** as the consumer is moved from awareness to trial and adoption (see Figure 12.2). The hierarchy of effects model has had a strong impact on the design of advertising campaigns in western countries with variants based on multiple hierarchies examining issues such as the degree of product involvement.

Advertising is generally viewed to work differently depending on the nature of the product. With high-involvement products such as cars, for example, the process follows a *learn-feel-do* schema in which the consumer first learns something about the product and then develops a feeling or passion for it before taking action, i.e. going to the retail outlet to purchase it. In the case of low-involvement products such as laundry detergent, advertising is believed to follow a *learn-do-feel* schema in which a positive (or negative) attitude towards the product is only developed after trial. With both high- and low-involvement products, knowledge precedes feeling and action. Advertising scholars argue that advertising works differently in collectivist societies. In countries such as

FIGURE 12.3   How Advertising Works in Western and Collectivist Societies

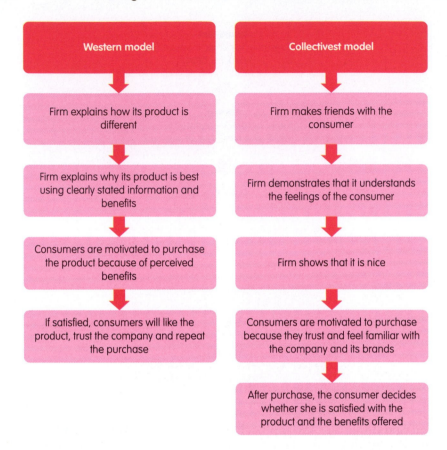

Japan, for example, the schema is likely to be *feel-do-learn*. Japanese advertising seeks to first build trust and create a bond with the consumer. The goal is to build *amae* (or dependency) which is done using an indirect approach. Feeling precedes the visit to the retail outlet to make the purchase and only after purchase do consumers truly learn about the product. The mechanics of advertising in western and collectivist societies are shown in Figure 12.3.

VISUAL CUES

There are also cultural differences in the **use of visual cues** that need to be considered in designing an international communication campaign. Visuals may be a strong tool of persuasion but standardized images are not universally understood in the same way across different cultures. The global marketer must, therefore, be aware of their interpretation in the specific cultural context of the target country. This was seen, for example, in the case of Volkswagen's advertisement for the Golf which aired in Italy and depicted a black sheep in a flock to represent the Golf owner as an independent and confident individual. In other countries, however, the image did not have the same interpretation. In some cultures, a black sheep symbolizes an outcast. It should also be recognized that in high-context societies consumers may read more into an image than was intended by the advertiser. Even simple images with explicit content may invite consumers from these societies to search for hidden meaning. In low-context societies with consumers who are conditioned to more explicit communication, this is unlikely to be a problem.

ADVERTISING STYLE

The following elements determine advertising style:

- appeal, i.e. values and motives that define the central message
- approach to communication, i.e. whether communication is explicit, implicit, direct or indirect
- form and execution, e.g. testimonial, drama or entertainment.

All elements of advertising style are impacted by culture. In the case of appeal, the advertiser is seeking to connect with some emotion that will make the product particularly desirable for the consumer. A status appeal, for example, may seek to convey quality and exclusivity, while an economy appeal may seek to communicate the product's low price and value for money. In low power distance societies, the use of status symbols is likely to be less effective compared to cultures with high power distance. This is seen, for example, in the case of US ads for Rolex watches which feature status sports such as golf, show jumping and sailboat racing. On the other hand, in cultures with low power distance, it is not atypical for a commercial to feature the young advising the old, as is seen in Procter & Gamble's commercial for Yes in Sweden. Such an egalitarian approach would probably not resonate well in high power distance societies.

The masculinity–femininity dimension is also important. Feminine societies are nurturing and caring, as is reflected in Volvo's advertisements which tend to focus on safety and protecting the family. Volvo, a Swedish brand,[2] has positioned itself as a car company passionate about safety. Masculine societies, on the other hand, are focused on success, being first and being the best. Playing to the combination of individualism and masculinity is a common strategy of American brands such as Nike.

In terms of approach, communication in individualistic societies is likely to be more direct than in collectivist cultures. Advertisements with a direct style of communication use words such as 'You' and 'We' and tend to be more verbal than visual. US ads generally fall into this category. On the other hand, indirect style communication tends not to address the target audience directly and in fact uses less words and more visual cues. For example, in advertising its Café Pilão, Sara Lee shows a cup of coffee that, despite a continuous stream of milk, does not seem to get any lighter. The message being conveyed in this Brazilian ad is that Pilão is a strong coffee. Similarly, Asian ads make use of less copy and more visuals in getting their message across.

The effectiveness of advertising forms varies depending on the culture. A form such as entertainment has been found to be effective in Japan but much less so in the USA. Entertainment is an indirect form of communication, the main purpose of which is to please the audience as opposed to sell the product. Given that ads in collectivist cultures aim to establish relationships and build trust, the entertainment form of advertising is likely to resonate with target audiences in countries such as Japan. Entertainment as an advertising form includes the use of humor or skits that involve the product. An example of humor is the use of Yoda, the Star Wars character, in a soup commercial. Yoda is shown levitating a kettle and Cup Noodles in a Japanese ad. In the ad, the 900-year-old Jedi master exhorts the audience to: 'Believe in your own power, you must.' He ends with: 'May the force be with, Japan.' As another example, at its product museum in Osaka Nissin, the manufacturer of the Cup Noodles brand uses humor in its display which shows the product surviving an explosion that destroys other items such as cell phones and hamburgers.

Announcements are another advertising form. Here only the facts are presented to the target audience with no use of people. The objective is simply to communicate the facts about the company and its brands. In some cases, the ad is simply a display of the products, while in others an attempt is made to convey product attributes. Advertisements that convey the product message tend to be aired in low-context, individualistic societies, given the need of

---

[2] Volvo was acquired by the Chinese firm Geely Motors on August 1, 2010. The new owners are not involved in Volvo's day-to-day operations and the brand is still viewed as being Scandinavian. See Mateja, J. (2012) Volvo Not Hindered by Chinese Ownership, North American Exec Says. Available at: http://wardsauto.com/management-amp-strategy/volvo-not-hindered-chinese-ownership-north-american-exec-says-0, accessed April 6, 2013.

consumers from such cultures for rational explanation if they are to be convinced to purchase. An example is a UK ad for the Kodak Hero 7.1 all-in-one Wi-Fi printer, which shows not only the machine but also what it is capable of delivering.

Pure display ads feature only the product as it would appear in a retail outlet. No attempt is made to explain or illustrate what the product is capable of or why it may be superior to other brands on the market. This is illustrated by ads for the Japanese product Atorrege which is used to treat a range of skin diseases and merely shows packages of the product as they would appear in the window of a retail outlet. This type of announcement ad is relatively culture-neutral and may be used effectively across a range of countries.

A third advertising form is the lesson. In this form, the aim is to lecture the target audience by presenting the facts and arguments that support purchase of the product. The presenter attempts to explain why he supports use of the product and you should too. This is usually accomplished with the use of visuals to demonstrate the advantages of the product. This form of advertising is particularly relevant to low-context societies such as the USA with consumers who seek facts and figures before making a purchase. In this advertising form, the presenter is often a dominant personality if the commercial is to be aired in a masculine society. In feminine cultures, the presenter is likely to be less pushy and more softly spoken. In those societies high on uncertainty avoidance, the presenter should exude expertise and confidence, while in low uncertainty avoidance cultures product expertise is best understated. Testimonials and endorsements are sub-forms in which the presenter suggests that he is a user of the product or has an opinion about the product and is, therefore, willing to endorse it. In western cultures, product endorsers are generally well-known personalities with sufficient expertise to be credible. Former NBA basketball player Michael Jordan, for example, has appeared in numerous sneaker commercials in support of Nike's Air Jordan sub-brand. However, credibility is much less important in the case of celebrity endorsements in Asia, with basketball players such as Yao Ming endorsing a range of products in China such as watches, consumer electronics, food and clothing.

PHOTO 12.1

FORMULATION OF A GLOBAL COMMUNICATION STRATEGY

With an understanding of how culture impacts the process, the global marketing manager is in a position to consider the development of a comprehensive communication strategy. Communication strategy development must consider a number of factors from identification of the target audience to budgeting and the measurement of effectiveness.[3] These issues are illustrated in Figure 12.4 and discussed in more detail below.

IDENTIFY THE TARGET AUDIENCE

The global marketer's first task is to identify the target audience. It needs to be clear who the communication will be designed to influence. In many cases, the target audience will be the final consumer or end user of the firm's products, but in other instances the target may

---

[3]   Czinkota, M., Ronkainen, I., Farrell, C. and McTavish, R. (2009) *Global Marketing: Foreign Entry, Market Development and Strategy Implementation*. Toronto: Nelson Education.

FIGURE 12.4   Development of a Global Communication Campaign

Target Audience

Communication Objectives

Budget Considerations

Media Strategy

Crafting the Message

Management of the Communication Process

Measuring Communication Effectiveness

be members of the wider community, government officials or prospective investors. In some instances, the communication may be targeted internally at the firm's own employees and managers. The target audience will have a direct bearing on all other aspects of campaign design, including the choice of media and promotional tools.

DETERMINE THE COMMUNICATION OBJECTIVES

The second step in the development of a global communication campaign is the determination of the objectives. Objectives will vary depending on the target audience. In the case of final consumers, the objective may be to create awareness which eventually leads to trial and adoption of the firm's products. In other instances, the firm may wish to remind its loyal customers of the benefits that they have received from the product over the years, and convince them that switching to a competing brand is not in their best interest. The objective of the firm's communication may also be to improve its image in the community. This is seen, for example, in the case of the BP oil spill in April 2010. Eleven workers were killed and some 200 million gallons of oil flowed into the Gulf of Mexico following an accident on a BP-leased Deepwater Horizon drilling rig. Ten months after the accident, BP launched an advertising campaign worth some $93 million to repair its corporate image.[4] In one of the television advertisements, BP spokesperson Iris Cross notes: 'I'm glad to report that all beaches and waters are open for everyone to enjoy!' She goes on to say: 'And the economy is showing progress, with many areas on the Gulf Coast having their best tourism season in years.'[5] While some have criticized BP for the amount of money spent on the ad campaign, clearly the company believed that salvaging its reputation in the USA and around the world was a worthwhile objective.

Whatever the global marketer's objectives in launching a communication program, it is important that they be well defined and measurable. If this is not the case, it will be virtually impossible for the firm to assess overall effectiveness.

---

[4] *Los Angeles Times* (2010) Gulf Oil Spill: BP's Ad Spending Climbs. Available at: http://latimesblogs.latimes.com/greenspace/2010/09/gulf-oil-spill-bps-ad-spending-climbs-.html

[5] Burdeau, C. (2012) BP Ad Campaign Following Gulf Oil Spill Deemed 'Propaganda' By Some. Available at: www.huffingtonpost.com/2012/01/08/bp-ad-campaign-gulf-oil-n_1192600.html

DEVELOP THE BUDGET

Once the target audience has been identified and the objectives have been developed, the firm next needs to assess the budgetary implications of the communication campaign. Companies utilize a variety of approaches in the development of a communications budget. One of the simplest is to base the budget for each country on historical (previous year) sales in that particular country market. With this approach, the company uses a **percentage of sales** to set the budget for the communication campaign. This method in essence ties communication expenditure to the historical performance of the country market and, therefore, fewer resources will be allocated to those markets where sales are weakest. This, of course, may not necessarily be in the best interest of the company. Some flexibility may be required, for example, if the product is a relatively new entrant to the market and while it has potential has not yet had sufficient time to become established. To overcome this weakness, companies may also generate a forecast of future sales in the market and then establish the communication budget as a percentage of that forecast. However, both the percentage of sales and the **percentage of future sales** methods ignore the impact of competition and company objectives.

An alternative approach is **competitive parity**. With this option, the company bases planned communication expenditure in the particular country on what its major competitors have spent in the past. While this approach ensures that the company will not be outspent in the specific country, accurate data on expenditures made by competitors in foreign markets may be somewhat difficult to collect. The approach also does not take into account the performance of the firm's own products in the target market or its own objectives in launching a communications campaign. This option may also prove to be problematic if the firm is up against companies that are substantially larger and better capitalized.

A third alternative open to the global marketer is the **objective and task method**. This approach involves basing the communication budget on the specific objectives the firm seeks to achieve in the country market and the identification of the individual tasks that must be completed in order to achieve those objectives. The costs associated with the completion of each of the identified tasks are then determined and aggregated to arrive at the total budget. The objective and task method is generally regarded to be a more logical approach to establishing a budget compared to the percentage of sales and competitive parity options. Expenditures are tied to specific objectives. If the goal of the company is merely to create awareness in the foreign market, then less funds will be allocated compared to a situation where the objective is to move the target audience through to the trial and adoption stages.

CHOOSE A MEDIA STRATEGY

With a clear understanding of the communication objectives and the resources to be allocated to the campaign, the global marketer should next consider the media strategy to be employed. It needs to be recognized at the outset that there may be binding constraints on the **availability** of media in the foreign market. Electronic media such as television and the Internet may not be viable options in countries with a sporadic electricity supply or low levels of Internet penetration. While a challenge for the global marketer, media will have to be selected that effectively reach the target audience and do so within the firm's budget. The **nature of the product** may also have an impact on the design of the firm's media strategy. In countries such as the USA and Canada, advertisements for cigarettes have been banned since the 1970s, and while advertisements for alcohol are permitted it is against the law to show the product actually being consumed on television. In Sweden, television advertising aimed at children under the age of 10 has been banned since 1991, making it illegal to advertise toys in that country. In Greece, advertisements for toy guns, tanks and other military equipment are completely banned, while ads for other types of toys cannot be aired between 7.00am and 10.00pm. Other countries in Europe, including Norway, Finland and Denmark, also have restrictive advertising policies.

In designing a media strategy, the global marketer must also consider the **media habits** of the target audience. It is important to identify the television programs viewed and the magazines and newspapers that are read by the firm's target audience. An understanding of media habits will also necessitate that data be collected on, for example, websites visited, time spent online and the audience's favorite radio programs. The more detailed and accurate the information available on the media habits of the target group, the greater the likelihood that the media strategy will be successful.

CRAFT THE MESSAGE

The global marketer must develop an understanding of what drives the behavior of the target audience and craft an appropriate message. **Motivations** may not always be obvious and more than likely will vary from country to country, even for the same product. In North America, for example, canned soups are purchased by women for their convenience. However, in other countries such as Italy and Brazil, women react negatively to purchasing canned soups. Italian and Brazilian women prefer to make their soups from scratch, believing it to be more nutritious and better for their families. Soup companies such as Campbell's may use the message of convenience when marketing in North America but such a message is unlikely to go over well with consumers in Brazil and Italy. In Brazil and Italy, the message has to be modified if it is to be effective. Indeed, in those countries canned soups are advertised as starters to which consumers could add their own special ingredients.

MANAGE THE COMMUNICATION PROCESS

The global manager must make a number of decisions with respect to the management of the communication process. A critical decision will revolve around the use of external experts and consultants. In many instances, the firm may not have in-house experts on all aspects of the communication process and may need to secure the services of consultants who specialize in media buying, ad design, etc. A list of the top global marketing communications firms is provided in Table 12.1. The firm also needs to make decisions with respect to the role of its subsidiaries in the communication campaign. The locus of control may well be at head office with country managers having little or no direct involvement. Alternatively, control may be localized in the foreign target market with little or no involvement from head-office personnel. Centralization will offer the firm greater control over its advertising message and all details associated with execution. Decentralization will, however, allow subsidiaries greater freedom which could result in a campaign that is better suited to local conditions.

MEASURE EFFECTIVENESS

It is essential that the global marketing manager measure the effectiveness of the company's communication campaign. A number of metrics may be used such as increased sales, market share and profitability. The firm may also assess effectiveness by measuring changes in consumer brand awareness, ad recall or coupon returns. Post-test of communications campaigns may be accomplished in a number of ways. The firm or its advertising agency may use **aided recall** in which the advertisement is shown to a group of respondents who are asked a number

TABLE 12.1   The Top Global Marketing Communications Groups by Revenue, 2011

Company	Notes
WPP Group (UK)	WPP owns four of the world's largest advertising agencies in JWT, Ogilvy & Mather, Young & Rubicam and Grey. These are partnered by the four global media networks Mindshare, MEC, Mediacom and Maxus, under the overall banner of Group M. WPP also controls a substantial portfolio of market research, PR, direct marketing, design and consultancy subsidiaries. WPP remains the world's biggest marketing services group with revenues of almost $16.5bn in 2012. The company has 160,000 employees operating out of 3,000 offices in 110 countries.
Omnicom Group	Omnicom is now the world's second largest marketing services group, controlling an extensive collection of different businesses led by the global advertising networks of BBDO, DDB and TBWA – three agencies with a reputation unequalled within the industry for consistently excellent creative work. The company also owns a global network of more than 175 marketing services companies; and a media group that offers media buying and planning services. Omnicom has over 5,000 clients in as many as 100 different countries.
Publicis Groupe (France)	Publicis Groupe is the third largest marketing communications group in the world. The company was formed in 1926 and has grown consistently over the years through a series of acquisitions. Publicis has shown itself to be a worthy rival to established giants WPP and Omnicom.
The Interpublic Group of Companies (USA)	Interpublic (IPG) is one of the big four international marketing communications organizations, alongside WPP, Omnicom and Publicis, but it has struggled off and on since the early 2000s with a series of challenges in different parts of its portfolio. These were largely attributed to integration issues with several of its acquisitions. The company has almost 44,000 employees in 100 offices around the world.
Dentsu (Japan)	No advertising agency dominates its home market as comprehensively as Dentsu, which controls around 30% of all mass media advertising in Japan and has a staggering portfolio of more than 6,000 clients. Despite the best efforts of its competitors to erode its dominance, it remains almost twice as big as its closest domestic rival.
Havas (France)	Havas was for years France's biggest advertising organization, until toppled by the phenomenal growth of arch-rival Publicis. It is now one of the last remnants of what was once a sizeable second tier of smaller international marketing organizations.

Source: Adapted from adbrands.net (n.d.) The Top 50 Marketing Groups Worldwide by Revenues. Available at: www.adbrands.net/agencies_index.htm, and company websites.

of questions such as: Have you seen this ad before? In what medium do you remember seeing it? Do you recall the name of the magazine or television program? The firm or its advertising agency may also use **unaided recall** to assess communication effectiveness. With this approach, respondents are asked more general questions such as: What advertisements do you remember seeing last evening? The idea here is to determine whether the firm's advertisement made a sufficient impression on respondents that they remember it without being prompted. In some instances, the firm may be interested in knowing whether its communication campaign has been successful at changing consumers' attitudes towards its products. **Attitude tests** may be used to measure any changes in respondents' attitude towards the company's product after being exposed to the advertisement. The technical aspects of administering the above tests do not differ significantly when used in an international as opposed to a domestic context. The global marketer may, however, find conducting advertising research in a global context to be more expensive and time-consuming. Further, agencies such as A.C. Neilsen which specialize in measuring the effectiveness of television advertisements may not be available in the country market of interest to the global marketer.

THE TOOLS OF COMMUNICATION

The global marketer has a number of communication tools available to reach the firm's target audience. These range from advertising to personal selling and each has its own set of advantages and disadvantages when used in a global context. These tools are not mutually exclusive and may be used concurrently in the firm's attempts to achieve its communication objectives.

ADVERTISING

Advertising is generally defined as any paid form of non-personal presentation of ideas, goods or services by an identified sponsor.[6] Based on this definition, to be considered advertising, the sponsor must be identified and the communication must be non-personal. A 30-second spot on television for Coca-Cola aired in Canada would be considered an advertisement as would an outdoor sign in a developing country. In both cases, there is no direct personal contact between a representative of the company and the audience, and in both cases it is clear who has sponsored the communication. Advertising is a one-way form of mass communication. It has the ability to reach large segments of the population at the same time but does not provide for interaction between the firm and its target audience.

In purchasing advertising, the global marketing manager must consider a number of factors. First is the issue of **reach,** or the number of different individuals or households that will be exposed to the firm's advertisement. Magazine and newspaper publishers may attempt to convince firms to advertise by referring to their circulation numbers or the number of copies of their publication sold over a specified period of time. Radio and television stations, on the other hand, may refer to the number of viewers/listeners who tune into specific programs. Also important to the global marketer in purchasing advertising time is **frequency** or the number of times individuals will actually be exposed to the firm's advertisement. Reach and frequency are often combined into one media-buying metric referred to as **gross rating points** (GRPs). The GRP is computed simply by multiplying the medium's reach (as a percentage of the market) and its frequency. In general, an advertising medium with a high GRP is superior to one with a lower GRP. However, purchasing advertising is not as simple as comparing GRPs. Cost is also a consideration. In the world of media buying, cost is usually expressed as **cost per thousand** (CPM) and represents the cost involved in reaching 1,000 individuals or households in the firm's target audience.

ADVERTISING ALTERNATIVES

In purchasing advertising media, the global marketer has a number of alternatives:

Television – this is a highly effective medium for reaching large segments of the population. It combines the visual and auditory and has the ability to engage and hold the attention of an audience. Further, by making appropriate choices with respect to programs and time of day, the medium can be targeted at specific segments of the market. Television is fairly widely available, even in developing country markets, making it a viable alternative for the global marketing firm. A major drawback of television is, however, its cost. While effective, it is an extremely expensive alternative.

---

[6]   Kotler, P. and Cunningham, P. (2004) *Marketing Management*, Canadian 11th edition. Harlow: Pearson Prentice Hall.

Radio – this is a lower cost alternative open to the global marketer. Radio stations tend to be local which allows the global marketer to more precisely target sub-regions within the target country that may offer greater market potential. Of course, a major drawback of radio is its lack of visual cues, making it less effective for demonstrating how products should be used or conveying the benefits that are derived from consumption.

Newspapers – in most countries, the global marketer will have access to at least one newspaper with a national circulation. In many countries, there may be several national newspapers, as well as numerous other papers with more local coverage. Newspaper ads are relatively inexpensive and because distribution is daily or sometimes weekly the global marketer will be able to make changes and keep the content up to date. Newspapers, as with other print media, are well suited for conveying complex ideas, although the lack of color may be a disadvantage in this respect.

Magazines – these provide the global marketer with an excellent way of targeting particular demographic and psychographic segments of the population. Many magazines are produced in full color, making them suitable for the presentation of more complex product information. Unlike newspapers, magazines tend to be kept by their purchasers for an extended period of time, giving the ads some longevity. However, publication is less frequent than newspapers and so the lead time for the ad to be in print is much longer.

PHOTO 12.2

Outdoor advertisements – billboards and posters are a relatively inexpensive means of advertising and may be very effective at reaching a local audience. Strategically placed outdoor advertisements may offer the firm good visibility over a relatively long period of time. It should be noted that billboards and posters do not provide the global marketer with an opportunity to present detailed product information and content may well be limited to a logo and picture of the product. For established brands, outdoor ads are an excellent complement to other advertising alternatives such as television. To be effective, billboards need to be placed in well-trafficked locations with good sight lines. In practice, however, billboard sites are often congested with several products competing for the attention of viewers.

Internet advertising – the Internet has become one of the most important media for advertisers. The medium's reach is, of course, global and it can incorporate not only text but also audio and video in communicating the firm's message. The medium is also interactive, allowing viewers to be more engaged in the presentation. The advertiser has the option to use search bars, games and various navigation tools to provide the user with the amount of information that she desires. This is particularly useful in the communication of more complex product information such as for products that require detailed usage instructions. Internet advertising is relatively inexpensive but its usefulness is, of course, dependent on its penetration in the specific target countries under consideration.

Social media – closely related to Internet advertising is the use of social media websites such as Facebook, Twitter, Orkut and LinkedIn. These Internet-based applications go beyond the ability to merely search for information, allowing people with similar interests to interact and share ideas and experiences. Being web-based, these sites are inherently global and scalable, i.e. they allow an infinite number of users around the world to connect with each other regardless of their physical location. While Facebook is the undisputed leader in this space, the number of social media websites has grown significantly in the last few years (see Figure 12.5), creating major advertising opportunities for the global marketing manager. While many companies rely on free social media tools, advertising expenditure on social media websites was projected to have increased from $7.7 billion in 2012 to $18.9 billion in 2014.[7] In 2014, North America accounted for the largest share of global advertising spend at around 49 percent, followed by Western Europe (Table 12.2).

---

[7] See www.go-gulf.com/blog/social-media-advertising/

PHOTO 12.3

TABLE 12.2   Global Social Media Ad Spending Share by Region

Region	2012	2013	2014
North America	49.7	48.8	48.9
Western Europe	24.6	23.2	20.9
Asia Pacific	20.6	22.9	23.7
Eastern Europe	2.5	2.8	2.8
Latin America	2.3	2.7	3.1
Middle East & Africa	0.3	0.4	0.6

Source: www.go-gulf.com/blog/social-media-advertising/

ADVERTISING APPROACH

In launching an advertising campaign, the firm has the option of implementing a **global** approach in which message content and execution are fairly uniform across all country markets. Another option is a **multi-domestic** strategy in which the firm adapts the advertising message and creative execution to the target country. A global approach offers the firm a number of advantages such as cost savings in the creation of content which, once developed, can be used in campaigns around the world. There will also likely be savings in media buying if the firm is able to centralize the process and, therefore, negotiate better rates. A global approach is also useful if the market for the firm's products is itself global and consumers are motivated to purchase by essentially the same factors. A global approach also allows the firm to exercise greater control over content and choice of media platform. A multi-domestic strategy, on the other hand, will likely produce content that resonates more completely with local consumers.

case study 12.1: Kraft's global approach

Kraft's Philadelphia cream cheese is a leader in its category and is sold in over 90 countries around the world. The product is supported by a global advertising campaign that was first introduced in Canada in 1994. The successful campaign speaks to Kraft's best of global, best of local strategy in marketing its top brands around the world and was developed by the ad agency J. Walter Thompson (JWT). The advertisements feature angels promoting the product from their heavenly vantage point with the memorable tagline: 'When it's Philadelphia, it's Heaven.' Of course, the heaven metaphor complete with angels, for the consumer, translates into pure wholesome goodness. The character of the angels was also adapted to the specific country market. In Japan, for example, the angels are portrayed as being truly angelic and perfect, while in other markets such as Canada they are portrayed as being more folksy and down to earth. In the UK and Germany, the angels are portrayed as hip and contemporary in order to appeal to younger consumers. The 'Heaven'

PHOTO 12.4

campaign has been rolled out in a number of markets across Asia, Europe, Latin America and the USA. The ads, supported by a product sampling program and point of sale displays, were used in Brazil when Philadelphia cream cheese was first introduced to that country. Locally produced 30-second television spots were used with a local television personality joining the cast of angels. Within six months of launch, the brand led its category in that country.

Source

www.kraft.com/foodfun_071304.html, accessed November 19, 2006.

Discussion Questions

1. Do you believe that a standard global approach would have been effective for Kraft in this product category?
2. Why do you believe this ad campaign has been so successful for Kraft?

Spotlight on Research 12.1   Implementing Advertising Strategy

Fastoso and Whitelock (2012) focus on the issue of how firms implement advertising strategy across national borders. They argue that the literature has emphasized the strategic issues around localization versus standardization, ignoring important implementation considerations. In their paper, the authors seek to develop a conceptual model that multinational firms may use to implement international advertising strategies. They also appeal to contingency theory to derive and test a set of hypotheses with respect to the factors that should guide a firm's choice of implementation approach. Based on their review of the literature, the authors contend that choice of implementation approach will be contingent on both environmental (cultural homogeneity and economic integration) and company-specific (subsidiary size and country of origin of the parent company) factors. Following researchers such as Ghemawat (2003) and Peebles et al. (1977), the authors propose four strategic approaches to implementing advertising strategy:

National campaign transference in which an advertising campaign is transferred from a national market for which it was initially developed to some other market for which it was not.

Option clustering through international campaign development in which the advertising campaign, from inception, is designed to be international.

Pattern implementation in which core features of the advertising campaign are pre-set to be used in more than one country.

Localization in which the firm develops an advertising campaign that is specific to each country.

Hypotheses

The authors test the following hypotheses:

H1. In a culturally homogeneous region, clustering and pattern implementation will be employed to implement international advertising strategies more frequently than national campaign transference and localization.

H2. Clustering and pattern implementation will be employed to implement international advertising strategies in an economically integrated region more frequently than in a region with no such integration.

H3. Large subsidiaries will use the pattern implementation option to implement international advertising more frequently than small/medium subsidiaries.

H4. Small/medium subsidiaries will use the clustering option to implement international advertising more frequently than large subsidiaries.

H5. Clustering and pattern implementation will be employed to implement international advertising strategies more frequently by companies of US origin than by those of other origins.

Method

The context for this study is Latin America with an emphasis on the Mercosur countries of Argentina, Brazil, Uruguay and Paraguay. The authors utilized a web-based survey of subsidiary managers in their data collection efforts, arguing that online surveys offer the advantages of fast turn-around times, flexibility and the minimization of coding errors. Seven universities in the Mercosur countries assisted in data collection by emailing the researchers' questionnaire to alumni of their executive MBA programs. The online questionnaire used was developed in both South American Spanish and Portuguese (for Brazilian respondents). Of the roughly 4,874 former students contacted, 264 responses were received from respondents holding positions with specific responsibility for the implementation of advertising decisions in their national markets. The authors found that the response rate for Brazil was substantially lower than that for the other countries and opted to exclude Brazilian responses from the analysis. Responses from an additional 31 managers were excluded because they were currently working in the multinational's home market. As a result, the analysis was conducted on 182 responses.

Respondents were asked to consider only the most recent advertising campaign for their company's main brand, measured in terms of advertising expenditure. They were also asked if the campaign was developed for local use only with no external guidance (a localization strategy) or for local use only but based on centrally defined advertising parameters (i.e. a pattern implementation strategy). Other options provided to respondents were whether they had adopted or adapted a campaign from another country (i.e. a national campaign transference strategy) or had used or created a campaign intended from the outset for a group of countries (a clustering approach). In the case of the latter three strategies, information on the specific countries with which the campaign shared common elements was used to code responses into three categories – 'Mercosur wide standardization', 'Latin America wide standardization' and 'Standardization at the broader geographic level'.

Results

The authors find support for H1. Clustering and pattern implementation were found to be used more frequently within culturally homogeneous regions than at broader international levels. Clustering was used by

(Continued)

(Continued)

67 out of 87 respondents (77 percent) and pattern implementation by 26 of 29 respondents (90 percent). Statistical analysis did not find support for H2. Clustering and pattern implementation should be used more frequently in economically integrated regions if this hypothesis is to be supported. The results indicate, however, that within the Mercosur context, only 13.8 percent of respondents used a clustering strategy (compared to 63 percent in the broader Latin American context). While 55 percent of respondents used pattern implementation within a Mercosur context compared to only 35 percent for Latin America, the result was not found to be statistically significant (Chi-squared = 1.385, $\rho = 0.239$).

In terms of the contingency factors, the researchers do find support for H3. Large subsidiaries do use pattern implementation more frequently than small/medium subsidiaries. Roughly 38 percent of large subsidiaries (≥ 500 employees) use pattern implementation versus only 20 percent of small and medium-sized subsidiaries – a result that is statistically significant (Chi-squared = 6.000, $\rho = 0.014$). The authors also find support for H4, as small and medium-sized subsidiaries were found to use a clustering strategy more frequently than large subsidiaries. Roughly 55 percent of small and medium-sized subsidiaries used this approach compared to 40 percent of large units, and again the result is statistically significant (Chi-squared = 3.904, $\rho = 0.048$).

With respect to the multinational's country of origin, the researchers find only partial support for H5. Firms of US origin were found to use a clustering strategy more often than those of other origin (53.3 percent vs. 41.7 percent; Chi-squared = 17.778, $\rho = 0.001$) but they use pattern standardization less frequently (21.3 percent vs. 36.7 percent). Relative to firms of other origin, US multinationals are more likely to use a localization strategy.

Implications

Based on the above, the authors conclude that:

1. Given the choice between a group of countries characterized by economic integration and cultural similarity (the Mercosur) versus one group showing cultural similarity only (Latin America), multinationals would prefer to implement their standardization strategy in the less homogeneous group of countries.
2. The study provides confirmation for the theoretical expectation that cultural similarity fosters standardization.
3. The study also provides support for the regionalization/semi-globalization paradigm and the theory of regional multinationals (Ghemawat, 2003; Rugman and Verbeke, 2004; Douglas and Craig, 2011) in the context of international advertising decisions.

Sources

Douglas, S.P. and Craig, C.S. (2011) 'Convergence and divergence: Developing a semiglobal marketing strategy', *Journal of International Marketing*, 19, 1: 82–101.

Fastoso, F. and Whitelock, J. (2012) 'The implementation of international advertising strategies: An exploratory study in Latin America', *International Marketing Review*, 29, 3: 313–35.

Ghemawat, P. (2003) 'Semiglobalization and international business strategy', *Journal of International Business Studies*, 34, 2: 138–52.

Peebles, D.M., Ryans, J.K. and Vernon, I.R. (1977) 'A new perspective on advertising standardization', *European Journal of Marketing*, 11, 8: 569–78.

Rugman, A.M. and Verbeke, A. (2004) 'A perspective on regional and global strategies of multinational enterprises', *Journal of International Business Studies*, 35, 1: 3–18.

PUBLICITY AND PUBLIC RELATIONS

Publicity may be defined as any editorial comment or published news item about a company, its business strategies or positions on important policy issues that is not paid for by the firm. **Public relations** (PR), on the other hand, may be defined as the marketing communications function that seeks to earn public understanding and acceptance of the firm's strategies in the marketplace and its position on critical policy issues. A magazine article written by an independent author would be considered to be publicity, while a company press release announcing, say, the opening of the firm's new office in Pakistan would be considered public relations. Public relations is a communication function performed by the company's PR staff and paid for by the firm. As a result, the company has complete control over what is communicated and how it is communicated. This is not the case for publicity. While the firm does not pay for publicity, it also has little or no control over what is to be reported or how the information is communicated.

SALES PROMOTION

Sales promotion refers to any inducement or incentive offered by the firm to generate an increase in sales. The impact of a company's sales promotion efforts is usually temporary with sales returning to more normal levels once the incentive is withdrawn. Incentives that are typically used in a sales promotion campaign include:

Price discounts – cashback or rebates on the purchase price of the product are usually effective in reducing inventories of slower-moving items and getting consumers to try a new product.

Coupons – coupons are also effective at stimulating trial of a new product and moving inventory through the marketing channel. Coupons typically provide consumers with a percentage discount off the regular price and are usually valid for a specified period of time.

Product samples – providing prospective consumers with free samples of the product is also a form of sales promotion. Allowing consumers to experience the product free of charge is often an excellent strategy, particularly when there are several entrenched brands on the market.

SPONSORSHIP

The company may also communicate with its target audience and influence their choices by associating with an event or cause that is generally viewed as worthwhile and socially responsible. Major sporting events such as the Olympics provide firms with a tremendous opportunity to achieve global visibility. Similarly, important causes such as the fight against cancer or AIDS and efforts to combat drunk driving provide companies with an opportunity to associate with issues that resonate with the target audience. In societies where consumers place a great deal of emphasis on trust, sponsorship is likely to be an effective promotional tool.

case study 12.2: Ryanair's charity calendars

Ryanair is an Irish discount airline that began operations in 1985. In 2011, the company posted a profit of €503m on traffic of almost 76 million passengers. In 2002, the airline became No. 1 in Europe for customer service, scoring the highest among European airlines for punctuality, fewest cancellations and fewest lost bags. In 2008, the company launched its first cabin crew charity calendar. The calendar featured scantily-clad Ryanair flight attendants and would become an annual publication raising money for various causes. The 2011 calendar, for example, raised over €100,000 for the German charity Tafel, while the 2012 edition raised a similar amount for the Irish charity DEBRA Ireland. Overall, the Ryanair calendar has raised over €500,000 for various European charities.

PHOTO 12.5

In December 2012, however, the Swedish Advertising Ombudsman (Reklamombudsmannen) reported that it had received complaints from angry Swedes denouncing the sexual content of the calendar. Many believed that the images of the women in lingerie – accompanied by the text 'Our prices are red hot … and our staff' – were offensive to women. Based on the complaints received, the Swedish Advertising Ombudsman launched an investigation and determined that the Ryanair advertisements were sexist. The Ombudsman noted that the women who modeled for the calendar had 'no relation' to the company's product and that 'through their clothing and poses the women are being portrayed as pure sex objects'. The ads were deemed a breach of Article 4 of the International Chamber of Commerce (ICC) Consolidated Code of Advertising and Marketing Communication. Despite the complaints, however, Stephen McNamara, a Ryanair spokesman, stated that 'we will continue to support the right of our crew to take their clothes off to raise money for those who need it most'. The Reklamombudsmannen ruling was sparked by complaints from 56 individuals and two pro-gender equality organizations.

Sources

Gee, O. (2012) Ryanair Slammed for Sexist Bikini Calendar. Available at: www.thelocal.se/39174/20120217/#. UVomRKI3uSp, accessed April 1, 2013.

Ryanair website: www.ryanair.com/en/about

Discussion Questions

1. Do you agree with Ryanair's decision to continue publishing the cabin crew charity calendar despite the Ombudsman's ruling?
2. Do you believe that the controversy surrounding the calendar will have a negative impact on Ryanair's core business?

PERSONAL SELLING

Unlike promotional tools such as advertising, personal selling involves direct face-to-face, two-way communication between the firm and its target audience. The approach is highly effective because it allows for immediate feedback from the prospect and the opportunity for the sales person to overcome objections. However, personal selling is time-consuming and expensive and is, therefore, better suited to business-to-business markets and to more expensive and technologically advanced consumer products such as cars and high-end electronics.

FIGURE 12.6   The Personal Selling Process

The sales process is generally regarded to consist of a series of steps, as outlined in Figure 12.6. The **prospecting** stage involves developing a list of leads through a process of cold calls or through the firm's own analysis of the market, such as discussions with trade association representatives in the case of industrial products. The next stage in the process is the **pre-approach** in which the leads generated are qualified. The prospecting stage may generate hundreds or even thousands of leads. Given that the firm has limited resources, it will not be possible for the company to follow up on all of them simultaneously. The firm is, therefore, well advised to establish a set of criteria against which to assess potential prospects.

The third stage in the process is the **approach**, i.e. face-to-face meetings and interactions with the sales prospect. An understanding of the culture of the host country is critical at this stage. Nuances of language and the use of non-verbal cues must be understood to increase the probability of closing the sale. The next stage is the **presentation**. The style of presentation utilized will also be influenced by cultural factors. Germans, for example, are more likely to be influenced by a logical, information-rich presentation with a focus on facts and figures. In other cultures, effective presentations will be less formal and more engaging with a reliance on visual cues. The fifth stage in the personal selling process is **overcoming objections**. Regardless of how well thought out the firm's presentation, it is likely that prospects will voice objections to some or all of what is presented. In some cultures, objections may not be voiced directly in order not to offend the presenter. It is also possible that objections will be raised only towards the end of the negotiations when seemingly all major points have already been agreed to. This is often the case with Chinese buyers. Western firms may also encounter situations in which it is necessary to overcome objections, not from one individual, but from an entire team involved in the process. A great deal of patience will, therefore, be required as the presenter works to overcome these multiple objections.

The sixth stage in the process is **closing the sale**. Again, in some cultures the close may be a long, drawn-out process as the buyer haggles over seemingly minor aspects of the deal. In some countries such as the UK, Australia and the USA, there is an expectation that the salesperson will explicitly ask for the sale, both early in the process and often.[8] The salesperson should also be aware that in some cultures techniques such as stalling for time or providing misleading information may all be part of the sales process and these can significantly complicate efforts to close the deal. The final stage in the process of personal selling is **following up**. Keeping in touch with the new customer is critically important as it demonstrates the firm's long-term commitment to the foreign market. Demonstrating this commitment is particularly important in geographic markets such as Asia, the Middle East, Latin America and parts of Europe.[9] In some cases, the firm may have to rely on its distributors or agents to maintain contact with the new customer. While this may be satisfactory, the firm should still seek out opportunities to maintain more direct face-to-face communication, such as at trade shows and conventions.

[8]   Czinkota, M., Ronkainen, I., Farrell, C. and McTavish, R. (2009) *Global Marketing: Foreign Entry, Market Development and Strategy Implementation*. Toronto: Nelson Education.

[9]   Czinkota et al. (2009) op cit., p. 495.

ORGANIZATION AND MANAGEMENT OF AN INTERNATIONAL SALES FORCE

The global marketing manager must give some consideration to how the international sales force will be organized and managed across the various country markets. As noted above, the personal selling process is very much influenced by the culture of the target country. Given that personal selling is culture bound, it is unlikely that the firm will be able to utilize a uniform approach across all the country markets in which it operates. The approach used will more likely have to be crafted for each individual target market. The sales management process involves three major functions, as illustrated in Figure 12.7.[10]

FIGURE 12.7 The Sales Management Process

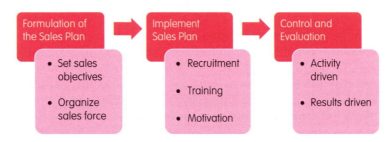

Formulation of a **sales plan** involves the setting of objectives and organization of the sales force. Sales management objectives need to be established within the context of the firm's overall strategic plan (discussed in the following chapter). In other words, the firm's global strategy will drive the approach that it takes to management of its personal selling resources in the various countries in which it operates. If the firm's objective is to introduce new products to the foreign market, the objectives of the sales team may well focus on **missionary selling** which involves getting the company's promotional message out to the target audience. For companies with an established presence in the foreign country, the objective of the sales force will involve more **relationship selling** in which the firm attempts to strengthen its ties with its customers. The objectives established will, of course, drive other aspects of sales management, including the selection of appropriate salespeople and how they are trained and motivated. Recruitment and training issues are discussed more fully in Chapter 15.

The global marketing company has a number of options in terms of organization of its global sales force, as illustrated in Figure 12.8. For example, the global marketer may consider an organizational structure based on the nationality of the sales staff employed. The firm may opt to utilize expatriate sales professionals, host-country nationals or sales professionals from a third country. Expatriates will already be familiar with the company's internal policies and its products but would lack knowledge of the foreign market. In some cultures, expatriate salespeople may also experience some difficulty in being accepted by local buyers which may hinder their effectiveness, particularly in the short term. Host-country nationals, on the other hand, will be intimately familiar with the target country but will lack an understanding of the corporate culture and technical aspects of the company's products. Sales professionals from third countries were neither born in the firm's home country nor in the target country. Such professionals would, therefore, lack an understanding of the way the company does business at home as well as of the culture of the foreign buyer. Third-country sales professionals will also likely require extensive training on the technical aspects of the firm's products.

---

10   Czinkota et al. (2009) op cit., p. 496.

FIGURE 12.8   Organization of the Sales Force by Nationality

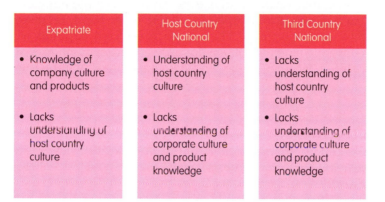

The global marketer could also consider other forms of international sales force organization such as the use of geographic region, product type or customer characteristics. One could also consider sales potential or even language in selecting the most appropriate organizational structure. For most companies, however, the organization of the international sales force tends to follow the structure used in the domestic market. In other words, if the domestic sales team is organized by type of product, this tends to be the structure used in foreign markets.[11]

Having formulated the sales plan, the global marketing manager must next consider its **implementation**. The recruitment, training and motivation of the global sales team are the major considerations. Much depends, however, on whether the firm has opted to employ expatriates, third-country nationals or nationals of the target country. Expatriates and third-country nationals will be asked to work in a culturally different environment over a long period of time. Such assignments are not right for everyone, making the screening and recruitment function critical for success. Individuals selected for such positions need to be open to learning about other cultures and may perhaps have to learn and work in another language. Depending on the organizational structure, the individuals selected may have to work and make decisions without a great deal of head-office support.

Prior to deployment to the target country, it is essential that sales staff be properly trained. This process will involve training on the products to be marketed in the target country. A great deal depends on the technical sophistication of the product and the availability of head-office technical specialists to whom prospects could be referred. It is reasonable for prospects to expect that sales professionals will be able to answer at least basic technical questions about the products they sell. Training should also include an orientation to the company's policies, including how prospects should be approached and the all-important issue of ethical behavior in the foreign country. Expatriate deployment is taken up again in more detail in Chapter 15.

Motivation of sales professionals is closely tied to compensation in many countries, such as the USA and Canada. In other cultures, however, factors other than financial reward may be major drivers. In some countries, titles, opportunities for foreign travel and advanced training may be highly valued by prospective employees. In many instances, it is a combination of monetary and non-monetary rewards that will need to be negotiated. It is, therefore, important for the global manager to consider the culture of the target country in crafting an appropriate strategy to motivate the sales team.

The global marketing manager must also consider how the company's overseas sales team will be controlled and evaluated. Depending on the size of the overseas sales operation, it may be important for the firm to recruit a sales manager for the target country. This individual would generally report to a senior marketing or sales executive at head office. In terms

[11]   Hill, J.S. and Still, R.R. (1990) 'Organizing the overseas sales force: How multinationals do it', *Journal of Personal Selling and Sales Management*, 10, 2: 57–66.

of evaluation, there are two options – to evaluate **activity** or to evaluate **results**. Activity objectives may, for example, relate to some expectation about the number of sales calls that should be made each month. Results metrics, on the other hand, relate to the profitability of the salesperson's client portfolio. The approach selected depends to some extent on the culture of the target country. In Asian countries, there may be less of an emphasis on bottom-line profitability, whereas in the West that, most likely, will be the focus.

SUMMARY

This chapter has examined the topic of global communication. The basic communication model was first described and the point was made that the process is heavily influenced by the cultural framework of the firm and its target audience. Several points of difference were discussed in terms of high-context versus low-context societies and how these differences impact the communication process. Other salient differences between masculine versus feminine and collectivist versus individualistic cultures were also presented. The basic point made was that the global manager must understand the cultural context if communication with the target audience is to be effective.

This chapter also argued in favor of a logical and systematic approach to the development of a communication campaign. The various elements of such an approach were discussed, beginning with an understanding of the target audience and proceeding to measuring the effectiveness of the communication campaign. Various approaches to developing a communication budget were also discussed as part of this process and the need to manage and control the execution of the strategy was emphasized. An important part of this discussion was the various communication tools open to the global marketer such as advertising, public relations and personal selling. The merits and demerits of each in an international context were presented.

 Real World Challenges

Ford's Advertising Nightmare in India

Kendrick James knew that he would have to act quickly. His assistant had just emailed him images that could only mean trouble for him and his team. As Managing Director for Ford, India, Kendrick could already visualize the potential fallout from the images he was viewing. Without much thought, he immediately placed a call to Janet Hobson, Creative Director and Managing Partner of JWT India. JWT India is a unit of WPP – the world's largest advertising agency. 'How could you allow this to happen?', shouted Kendrick on hearing Janet's voice on the line. Knowing exactly what Kendrick was referring to, Janet tried to assure him that she and her team were looking into the matter. Kendrick had always assumed that by hiring one of the world's largest and most respected advertising agencies, there would be no need for him to micromanage Ford India's advertising strategy. He had argued in favor of having creative content for the Indian market developed locally as opposed to having to deal with the slow-moving bureaucracy at Ford's head office. At the time, it made sense and he was able to convince senior management at Ford USA that his was the correct approach. By retaining the Indian subsidiary of a global advertising agency, Kendrick believed he would have the best of both worlds – culturally sensitive creative content executed with the highest standards of professionalism.

Still furious, Kendrick ended the call with Janet and began to check his social media accounts. As expected, the images had gone viral. Everywhere he looked he saw the images that had been uploaded to an industry website by someone at JWT India. One image showed the ex-Italian Prime Minister Silvio Berlusconi in the front seat of a Ford Figo, winking and flashing a peace sign, with three scantily clad women tied up in the trunk. Another image shows Paris Hilton also sitting in the front seat of the Figo winking, and with socialites Kim, Kourtney and Khloe Kardashian similarly bound in the trunk. The images prominently featured the Ford logo and carried the tagline: 'Leave your worries behind with Figo's extra-large boot' – a reference to the car's generous trunk. So much for culturally sensitive creative content, thought Kendrick. The ads appeared on the Internet just a few days after the government of India had approved new laws to punish sex crimes following the sexual assault of a student on a bus that sparked protests in India and condemnation around the world. The treatment of women in India was a hot button issue and these images had clearly placed Ford on the wrong side of the debate.

In the days that would follow, Janet Hobson and several members of her team would be fired by JWT India and the company would issue an apology stating: 'We deeply regret the publishing of posters that were distasteful and contrary to the standards of professionalism and decency at JWT … These posters were created by individuals within the agency and did not go through the normal review and oversight process.' WPP would similarly condemn the ads with: 'We deeply regret the publishing of posters that were distasteful and contrary to the standards of professionalism and decency within WPP Group.' While these apologies would go a long way in terms of putting the immediate crisis behind them, Kendrick knew that he needed to rethink his approach to management of the firm's communication process. He did not have much time as he had just been summoned to the US head office for a meeting with the Senior VP of Global Marketing and other senior executives to discuss the situation.

Sources

Bhushan, N. (2013) Ford's Ad Firm Fires Executives Over Spot Featuring Bound Women in Berlusconi's Trunk. Available at: www.hollywoodreporter.com/news/fords-ad-firm-fires-executives-431511, accessed April 6, 2013.

Reuters (2013) Ad Agency Sacks Employees Following Sexist Ford Ads Controversy. Available at: http://ibnlive.in.com/news/ad-agency-sacks-employees-following-sexist-ford-ads-controversy/381674-25-162.html, accessed April 5, 2013.

The Associated Press (2013) Ford Motor in Hot Water for Sexist Berlusconi Ad. Available at: www.cbc.ca/news/business/story/2013/03/25/business-ford-berlusconi.html, accessed April 6, 2013.

Discussion questions

1. State the problem that Ford faces in the Indian market.
2. Identify the options available to Kendrick. Be sure to identify more than one.
3. Based on the options identified above, recommend a course of action for the company. Be sure to provide a rationale and make a decision.

? discussion questions

1. What is meant by 'noise' in the basic communication model? In an international context, what are some factors that would generate noise in the communication process?

2. How do advertisements from western and collectivist societies differ in terms of the purpose of communication? How is this difference manifested in the execution of advertising campaigns by firms from these societies?

(Continued)

(Continued)

3. How do the mechanics of advertising differ in collectivist and western societies?

4. How does the masculinity–femininity dimension of culture impact the design of a firm's global communication campaign?

5. Describe the steps involved in the process of personal selling. How does culture impact the use of this communication tool in a country such as India?

FURTHER READING

de Mooij, M. (2010) *Global Marketing and Advertising: Understanding Cultural Paradoxes,* 3rd edn. London: SAGE.

Hill, J.S. and Still, R.R. (1990) 'Organizing the overseas sales force: How multinationals do it', *Journal of Personal Selling and Sales Management,* 10, 2: 57–66.

GLOBAL MARKETING STRATEGY AND IMPLEMENTATION

LEARNING OBJECTIVES

After reading this chapter you should be able to:

- discuss the steps in global strategy planning

- discuss the benefits and challenges involved in the design and implementation of a global account management system

- discuss strategies that may be used by local firms in defending their domestic market against foreign entrants.

INTRODUCTION

To achieve success in global markets, the firm must have a coherent strategy. Strategic objectives for foreign markets must be defined and the various elements of the marketing mix must be implemented in a way that ensures that the firm's objectives are achieved in an efficient and cost-effective manner. Without a global marketing strategy, the result for the company will most likely be financial losses, a tarnished corporate reputation and discouraged managers and employees. This chapter examines the process of developing a global marketing strategy. The issues discussed are important in terms of the firm's decisions in areas such as identifying its sources of competitive advantage in international markets and selecting an appropriate organizational structure. Decisions will also have to be made in terms of which elements of the marketing mix are adapted and which are standardized to facilitate foreign market entry. Country selection and the location of value-added facilities such as manufacturing and R&D are also key decisions that the firm needs to make.

The firm's strategic decisions are not made in a vacuum. Competitors will most certainly react to the firm's attempts to build market share and profitability and a well thought-out strategy must, therefore, anticipate a response from competitors. Local companies also need to consider situations in which they have to react to competitive threats presented by multinational firms from other countries. In such situations, the firm's strategic response may well have implications for profitability in its core home market or even for its very survival as a going concern. Strategic alternatives for addressing competitive threats at home are also discussed in this chapter.

THE PROCESS OF GLOBAL STRATEGY PLANNING

In a rapidly changing and competitive environment, planning becomes essential if the firm is to survive and grow. Planning allows the firm to anticipate and react to shifts in environmental factors that could impact market share growth and overall profitability. The unanticipated entrance of a new competitor to the market, shifts in consumer preferences, regulatory changes in important international markets and the emergence of new technologies are just some of the factors that could negatively impact the firm's performance abroad. A global strategic plan requires that the company set objectives, assign responsibilities for specific activities and commit resources to the international markets of interest. The process of global strategic planning also necessitates that the firm carefully examine its own capabilities and match them with the opportunities that are presented by foreign markets. It also becomes necessary for the firm to consider its product portfolio and determine whether there is a good fit with the needs of the foreign markets of interest.

The process of developing a strategic plan may be visualized as a sequence of four steps, as illustrated in Figure 13.1. These are discussed in more detail below.

DEFINE THE BUSINESS

While it may seem obvious, the first step in the development of a global strategy is to define the business for which the strategy is being developed. Strategic planning is usually undertaken at the level of the **strategic business unit** (SBU). SBUs represent groupings within the organization based on, for example, the type of customers to be served (e.g. government or industrial) or the products or services demanded by those customers. Fundamental questions need to be asked such as: 'What business are we really in?', 'Who are our competitors?' and 'Who are our customers?' While these questions may seem obvious for an established business, taking the time to answer them will force executives to avoid erroneous assumptions.

FIGURE 13.1   The Global Strategy Planning Process

FORMULATE THE GLOBAL BUSINESS STRATEGY

The second step in the process of strategic planning is the formulation of a global strategy. To accomplish this task, the firm must select a strategic orientation and adopt a country focus.

Porter's generic strategies

Michael Porter, a noted business strategy scholar, has proposed a framework of generic business strategies based on the source of the firm's competitive advantage.[1] When Porter suggests that a particular firm has a competitive advantage, he is referring to a situation in which the firm has some distinctive competence which closely matches the needs of consumers. As a result of this distinctive competence, the firm is able to out-compete other firms in its industry, delivering superior value for customers. Porter argues that a firm's competitive advantage may come from low cost or from differentiation. He argues, further, that these sources of competitive advantage may be levered in markets that are either narrow or broad. The result is a set of four generic strategies illustrated in Figure 13.2.

FIGURE 13.2   Porter's Generic Strategies

Competence	Market Scope	
	Narrow	*Broad*
Low Cost	**Cost Focus**	**Cost Leadership**
Differentiation	**Focused Differentiation**	**Differentiation**

If the firm's competence lies in being a low-cost manufacturer, it may opt to pursue a **cost leadership** strategy. The firm positions itself as the firm with the lowest costs in the industry across a broad range of market segments. This position may be based on the firm having more advanced technologies or more efficient manufacturing facilities than the competition. This competence allows the firm to have the lowest cost per unit in the industry and to pass these savings on to its customers. For this strategy to be sustainable over the long term, there must be barriers to other firms in the industry acquiring the same (or superior) technology or manufacturing facilities. If the source of competitive advantage is easily replicable, the firm will not enjoy a leadership position for very long.

Some firms, rather than competing on cost, may have a broad range of products with unique features that are highly valued by consumers. Product uniqueness across a broad range of market segments is a major source of competitive advantage for the firm and it is said to be pursuing a **differentiation** strategy. Consumers are generally willing to pay a higher price for unique products and this strategy, therefore, may be quite lucrative for the firm. As with low cost, however, this source of competitive advantage will not be sustainable if the firm's unique product features are easily replicated by other firms.

If the firm has a distinct low-cost advantage but only in a narrow segment of the market, it is said to be following a **cost focus** strategy. Again, the firm is able to lever its cost advantage to provide lower prices to a fairly limited segment of the market. To be effective, the firm's low-cost advantage must not be easily replicated by other firms, but also the market segment being addressed must provide for an adequate financial return. It should be recognized that the small size of the market does put the company following this strategy at greater financial risk.

If, on the other hand, the firm's competitive advantage stems from the uniqueness of its products, but these appeal only to a narrow segment of the market, it is said to be pursuing a **focused differentiation** strategy. Companies may, for example, produce high-end products that appeal to only a small segment of the market but for which consumers are prepared to pay a premium price. Such markets, although relatively small, may be particularly lucrative for companies able to deliver a superior and unique product.

---

[1] Porter, M.E. (1985) *The Competitive Advantage: Creating and Sustaining Superior Performance*. New York: Free Press. (Republished with a new introduction, 1998.)

The 7S framework

Porter's model of competitive advantage has been criticized by some strategy scholars for being too static and for not adequately capturing the realities of today's **hypercompetitive** global markets (D'Aveni et al., 1995).[2] Markets today are characterized by shortened product life cycles, compressed product design cycles, new technologies, the entry of new players into the market, the constant repositioning of incumbents and the redefinition of market boundaries. In hypercompetitive markets, it is not possible for firms to build and sustain a competitive advantage for any length of time. Industries are in a constant state of disequilibrium with a steady increase in the level of uncertainty, dynamism, heterogeneity of players and hostility.

Noted management scholar Richard D'Aveni and his colleagues have proposed a model to assist companies in the development of strategies to compete in hypercompetitive global markets. The key idea behind their 7S framework is that firms need to disrupt the strategies of their competitors and create for themselves a series of temporary advantages. This disruption is achieved through vision, capabilities and tactics, as illustrated in Figure 13.3. In terms of vision, successful companies focus on creating disruptions that satisfy their stakeholders, recognizing of course that not all disruptions are positive for the firm. In this regard, the most important stakeholders are the firm's customers. The authors of the framework argue that to satisfy customers, firms need to:

- identify needs that the customer has not yet been able to articulate
- find new, previously un-served, customers
- create customer needs that previously did not exist
- predict changes in customer needs before they take place.

Incremental increases in customer satisfaction are not enough to create disruptions in hypercompetitive markets. Strategic soothsaying is also part of the vision for disruption and involves developing an understanding of the evolution of the market and associated technologies that can create opportunities for temporary advantage.

To be successful in hypercompetitive markets, according to the 7S framework, the firm needs to develop two capabilities – speed and surprise. The firm must create a series of advantages and must do so quickly to blunt any response from competitors. Once an opportunity for an advantage is recognized, the firm needs to move quickly to capitalize on it given that the same opportunity may be simultaneously recognized by other firms in the industry. If the firm is the only player in the industry to recognize the opportunity, then the element of surprise becomes important in extending the time during which the advantage may be maintained. Of course, once the firm's advantage is more widely recognized, competitors will move quickly to neutralize it.

With the firm's vision for disruption and its capabilities of speed and surprise, the company uses a series of dynamic tactics to disrupt the market and create a competitive advantage. Tactics such as shifting the rules of the game by the introduction of revolutionary new technologies or product designs can throw competitors off track and create a clear advantage for the firm. The firm may also use signaling to disrupt the market. For example, a major deep-pocketed player in an industry publicly stating that it plans to fight to defend its position may cause other firms to reconsider their own competitive actions. The firm may also upset the equilibrium of the industry by the use of simultaneous or sequential strategic thrusts to confuse opponents and keep them guessing.

The 7S framework is a useful platform that may be adopted to devise a number of strategies to continuously disrupt the market and create a series of temporary advantages for the firm in global markets.

---

[2] This section draws heavily from D'Aveni, R.A., Canger, J.M. and Doyle, J.J. (1995) 'Coping with hypercompetition: Utilizing the new 7S's framework', *The Academy of Management Executive*, 9, 3: 45–60.

FIGURE 13.3   The 7S Framework

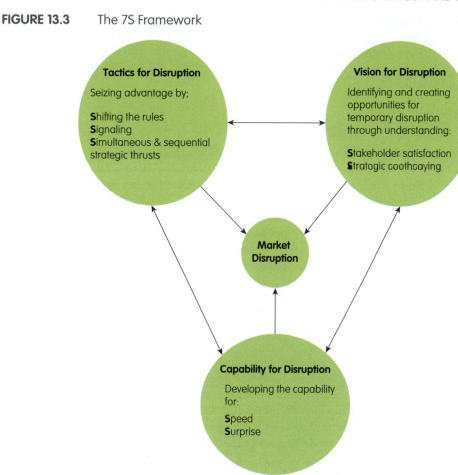

Adapted from: D'Aveni, R.A., Canger, J.M; Doyle, J.J (1995) Coping with hypercompetition: Utilizing the new 7S's framework, *The Academy of Management Executive*, Aug, 9, 3; 45-60.

Country market focus

Apart from deciding on a strategic orientation, the firm also needs to consider its **country market focus** as it develops its global strategy. There are, of course, hundreds of potential target countries around the world but with limited resources the firm will have to make choices. A framework was presented in Chapter 7 that screens prospective countries based on a set of macro- and micro-level criteria. It was argued that the firm should begin with a large number of countries and apply a set of screening criteria in order to arrive at a more limited number of country possibilities. The approach essentially groups countries with similar characteristics. Also, part of this framework was an internal assessment of the company's capabilities to ensure that these match the requirements of the country markets identified.

The clustering approach advocated above will lead to the identification of countries with similar characteristics. However, such a **country focus** approach carries certain risks for the firm. Because the countries are similar, weakness in one market may be associated with weakness in all of the other foreign markets in which the firm operates. To mitigate this risk, some firms choose a deliberate strategy of **country diversification** seeking to build a diverse portfolio of country markets, thereby reducing their reliance on any one. Of course, the firm's marketing program becomes more complicated the greater the number of countries in which it is engaged. Advertising copy would most likely have to be tailored to each market and product lines may have to be adapted to each country. Further, excessive country diversification may prove to be quite taxing for the management of the firm. Empirical research has demonstrated that a diversification strategy tends to lead to higher sales in foreign markets whereas a focused approach results in higher profitability. Some researchers have also argued that high-growth markets require more attention from management and tend to benefit from a focused approach, while markets characterized by instability and competitive rivalry tend to benefit from diversification.[3]

DEVELOP THE GLOBAL MARKETING STRATEGY

The third step in the strategic planning process is the development of the firm's global marketing strategy. There is currently very little agreement on what constitutes a global marketing strategy. The literature has, however, been dominated by three major perspectives (Zou and Cavusgil, 2002).[4] The first is the **standardization** view which focuses on the key standardization vs. adaptation/localization decision (see Figure 13.4). Firms are assumed to benefit from standardization of the key components of their marketing programs: pricing, promotion, distribution and product strategies, across all country markets in which they operate. Proponents of the standardization perspective argue in favor of homogeneous global demand, which makes the optimal global marketing strategy one in which the firm sells a standardized product using standardized marketing programs. The approach allows the firm to exploit economies of scale in production and marketing, provide consistency in dealing with customers around the world and capitalize on good ideas by implementing them across all country markets.

Early work by Keegan (1969)[5] sought to provide a simple conceptualization of the standardization vs. localization decision. According to this author, the firm could consider a **product–communication extension** approach in which the firm uses its home-country pricing policies, advertising appeals and products in all foreign markets entered. In other words, all elements of the marketing mix are standardized as the firm enters new foreign markets. This approach works well if competitive conditions and consumer preferences are more or less the same across all countries. For example, although Coca-Cola does make minor adaptations to its product in different countries, its approach to marketing strategy does tend to be fairly standardized. According to Keegan, firms may also pursue a **product extension–communication adaptation** approach. Here, the same product is marketed around the world but the communication strategy is adapted to the various markets targeted. In other words, the same product is positioned differently depending on the country. We see this, for example, with the Minolta Maxim single reflex camera which is identical in features and design but is advertised in Europe and Japan as a camera for the serious amateur, while in the USA it is positioned to appeal more to families and older adults.[6] Keegan also envisioned that the firm could use a strategy of **product adaptation–communication extension** in which the product's use conditions change depending on the country but its positioning does not vary. For example, Exxon's 'Put a Tiger in Your Tank' advertisements have been used in countries around the world but changes are made to the gasoline by the use of various additives to reflect differences in climate and performance requirements in the different country markets.[7] Keegan's fourth approach is dubbed **dual adaptation** and involves the simultaneous adaptation of both the firm's product and communication strategies. Benetton, the Italian apparel manufacturer, has adopted a dual adaptation strategy in Southeast Asia. Consumers' body

[3]   Johansson, J.K. (2003) 'Global marketing: Research on foreign entry, local marketing, and global management', in B. Weitz and R. Wensley (eds) *Handbook of Marketing*. London: SAGE.

[4]   Zou, S. and Cavusgil, S.T. (2002) 'The GMS: A broad conceptualization of global marketing strategy and its effect on firm performance', *Journal of Marketing*, 66, 4: 40–56.

[5]   Keegan, W.J. (1969) 'Multinational product planning: Strategic alternatives', *Journal of Marketing*, Jan.: 58–62.

[6]   Johansson (2003) op cit.

[7]   Johansson (2003) op cit.

proportions and color preferences have necessitated that the firm make adjustments to its product line. At the same time, however, the firm's well-known politically charged ads also needed to be modified as they did not resonate with retailers or their customers.[8] Finally, Keegan suggested a fifth approach, **product invention**, which he argued is suitable for truly global firms. The approach involves developing entirely new products for foreign markets.

The second major global marketing strategy perspective focuses on the **configuration and coordination** of the firm's value chain activities. From this perspective, the firm's global marketing strategy is in essence a way of exploiting the comparative advantages of particular host countries and capitalizing on the synergies that may exist between country markets. Proper configuration of value-added activities necessitates that the firm give consideration to the concentration of these activities. For example, will after-sales service be concentrated in one country or in multiple countries? In which countries will manufacturing take place? Where will the firm's product design and development activities be located? In the case of product development and engineering, the firm may decide to locate these activities in countries with a depth of world-class technical talent, while it may opt to manufacture in countries with a large pool of low-cost workers. From this perspective, the firm seeks to exploit location-specific advantages that exist in countries around the world. According to this perspective, consideration must also be given to cross-national coordination. The firm needs to make decisions with respect to the degree of head-office control, how knowledge will be shared across the global enterprise and how the firm will capitalize on potential economies of scale and scope.

FIGURE 13.4   Elements of a Global Marketing Strategy

Source: Adapted from Zou, S. and Cavusgil, S.T. (2002) The GMS: A broad conceptualization of global marketing strategy and its effect on firm performance, *Journal of Marketing*, Oct, 66, 4: 40–56.

The **integration** view is the third major perspective of global marketing strategy. This perspective seeks to address how the firm competes in global markets. The central idea is that

---

8   Johansson (2003) op cit.

the company needs to determine if it will compete in all major markets in the world or take a more limited view. Participation in all major markets allows the firm to coordinate its competitive responses across its various target countries. The company will, for example, be able to respond to an attack by competitors in one market by launching its own counterattack in several other countries. This, however, may require that the firm cross-subsidize or divert resources from one market to shore up its position in another. The company's operations, according to the integration view, are interdependent.

★ Box 13.1

Not all executives will be equally interested in or committed to pursuing international opportunities. The drive to pursue foreign opportunities and solve complex international market problems requires that managers have a **global mindset**. Levy, Beechler, Taylor and Boyacigiller (2007) define a global mindset as 'a highly complex cognitive structure characterized by an openness to and articulation of multiple cultural and strategic realities on both global and local levels, and the cognitive ability to mediate and integrate across this multiplicity'. According to these authors, global mindset is a multidimensional continuum with executives falling somewhere along the range between high and low levels. As a cognitive process, global mindset impacts managers' ability to process information and make decisions. A global mindset allows executives to focus on information emanating from their local and global environments and to interpret, integrate and use this information to make strategic decisions. Individuals with a global mindset are open and nonjudgmental when presented with new information and will attempt to garner new insights from multiple sources regardless of their culture or national origin. This characteristic may lead them to question existing mental models. Executives with a global mindset are likely to arrive at complex, innovative and nonconventional solutions that do not attempt to merely simplify global realities. This ability is important in today's complex and rapidly changing global marketing environment. Having a global mindset may not necessarily lead to better managerial decisions though. As Levy et al. (2007) point out, the heavy demands on the processing of information may eventually overwhelm these decision makers and have a deleterious impact on the quality of their strategic decisions.

Source

Levy, O., Beechler, S., Taylor, S. and Boyacigiller, N. (2007) 'What we talk about when we talk about "global mindset": Managerial cognition in multinational corporations', *Journal of International Business Studies*, 38: 231–58.

IMPLEMENT THE GLOBAL MARKETING STRATEGY

The fourth step in the process of strategic planning is implementation and control of the global marketing strategy. Effective implementation requires international commitment on the part of the firm, the design of an appropriate organizational structure and effective staffing. As with any strategy, the firm must also put in place control mechanisms to ensure that objectives are being realized.

Commitment to global markets

Having defined its objectives and designed a global marketing strategy, the firm's executives must determine whether they are in fact committed to its execution. Senior management must be fully aware of the financial resources that would need to be invested in pursuing global markets, as well as of the human resource commitment the firm will be required to make.

The firm's executives must also recognize that pursuing international markets is not an easy undertaking. The process is time-consuming and there will be setbacks. If there is no commitment from senior management, the result will be a rapid withdrawal from international markets as problems begin to surface.

Organizing for global expansion

The manner in which the firm is organized for global market expansion will have a significant impact on the potential for success. The organizational structure adopted has a bearing on the firm's ability to react quickly to international marketing opportunities, service its overseas customers, support its foreign subsidiaries and control the execution of its marketing strategy. There is no one perfect structure that will provide the firm with optimal results. Instead, the firm has the option of choosing from a number of alternative organizational structures, each with its own inherent advantages and disadvantages. These structures are described below.

FUNCTIONAL STRUCTURE

In a functional structure, each division specializes in a particular activity such as marketing, finance, production or research and development (see Figure 13.5). This is an extremely simple structure in which the heads of the various functional divisions report to the chief executive officer (CEO). Efficiency in the execution of the various functions is the goal of this organizational structure and it is achieved by the grouping of the various functional teams into a coherent unit. As will be noticed from Figure 13.5, a small export marketing department may be established to handle overseas orders early in the firm's process of internationalization. It may be expected, however, that as international markets become a more important component of the firm's corporate strategy, some attempts will be made to create a specialized international division that would function as a separate strategic business unit. Such a division would be a standalone unit within the firm and would compete with other divisions for resources and would have a stronger voice in areas such as product development that would have a bearing on international customers and markets.

FIGURE 13.5   Functional Organizational Structure

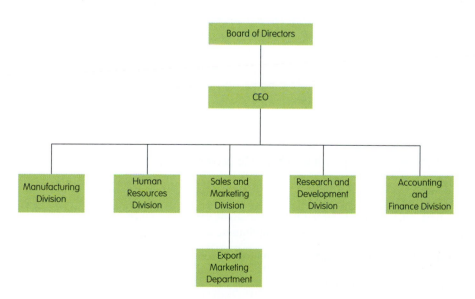

Spotlight on Research 13.1   International Commitment

In their article, da Rocha et al. (2012) seek to answer the following research question: How do small established entrepreneurial firms from an emerging economy develop and show international commitment in their foreign operations? The authors make the point that the notion of commitment is central to a number of theoretical frameworks, including the Uppsala internationalization process model, the network theory of internationalization and the literature dealing with international entrepreneurship, born globals and export marketing. They point out, however, that there is no agreement on when and how commitment comes into play in the internationalization process and researchers are also divided on how the commitment construct is manifested. There is also little agreement in the literature with respect to the factors that influence commitment and its outcomes. For these and other reasons, the authors suggest that there is a significant gap in the international commitment literature. They argue that their research contributes to our understanding of the construct by: (a) focusing on commitment in small, entrepreneurial firms; (b) focusing on commitment to foreign direct investment by small firms; (c) combining contributions from various streams of research including the resource-based view of the firm; and (d) focusing on firms from an emerging market – Brazil.

Method

The authors select Brazil as the focal point of this study because of that country's growing global economic importance and cultural dissimilarity from other emerging markets such as China and India. The authors are attempting to build theory (as opposed to test existing theory) and, therefore, opt to use a case study approach. Three small entrepreneurial firms were selected for the analysis. The firms, Brazilian steakhouses, were well established in their domestic market and had begun to expand abroad in the 1990s. Because the firms were similar, the researchers were able to control for the impact of industry, size, timing of internationalization, and foreign market effects. Issues related to international commitment could, therefore, be more effectively examined. Data on these three firms were collected over the course of several years beginning in the 2000s. Two rounds of in-depth interviews were conducted with the management of the firms, along with information retrieved from company websites and articles published in business magazines and newspapers. Data were collected on company history and the background of the entrepreneur, as well as on the company's international activities through 2009. Data were also collected on variables specific to pre-internationalization, including entry mode selection, foreign market selection, marketing strategies adopted and outcomes. Data on the factors influencing international commitment, the manifestations of international commitment and outcomes of international commitment were also collected.

In total, the researchers collected some 153 pieces of documentation which were used to reconstruct past events. Combined with the results of the interviews, the authors were able to use triangulation in their data collection process. Data analysis for this study took place over several years and involved going back and forth between the case studies and existing theoretical frameworks. In essence, the researchers followed an abductive approach to theory development. Comprehensive reports were subsequently developed for each case and comparative tables constructed. Pattern-matching logic was employed and the authors continued to make comparisons with the existing literature.

Propositions

Based on the results of the case analysis, the authors offer a number of propositions.

Internationalization triggers:

P1a. When established entrepreneurial firms from an emerging economy are pulled to internationalization by attractive business proposals (reactive motives), commitment tends to be lower from the start.

P1b. When the trigger to internationalization is opportunity discovery, commitment tends to be higher from the start.

P1c. Opportunity discovery by the entrepreneur in established firms from an emerging economy combined with a latent desire to internationalize tends to be a key factor in engendering international commitment.

Resource availability and goal congruence:

P2a. Resource availability is not a sufficient condition to international commitment if a firm's strategic goals do not contemplate growth through internationalization.

P2b. Congruence with a firm's strategic goals tends to be a mediator between entrepreneurs' desire to internationalize and commitment.

Resource allocation:

P3a. When established entrepreneurial firms from an emerging economy start their internationalization process, the allocation of financial resources may be a lesser manifestation of international commitment than the allocation of managerial resources to a new foreign venture.

P3b. In established entrepreneurial firms from an emerging economy, a critical manifestation of international commitment is the designation of a family member to manage firm operations abroad.

P3c. As the international commitment of established entrepreneurial firms from an emerging economy increases, financial resources become more critical than managerial resources.

Planning for internationalization:

P4a. In established entrepreneurial firms from an emerging economy, preparatory activities to internationalization are a manifestation of commitment.

P4b. Preparatory activities tend to delay the beginning of international activities of established entrepreneurial firms from an emerging economy.

P4c. The extent of preparatory activities by established entrepreneurial firms from an emerging economy tends to limit the geographic scope of their initial foreign markets.

Outcomes of commitment:

P5. International commitment tends to have a positive impact on the international performance of established entrepreneurial firms from an emerging economy, which in turn reinforces commitment.

P6. Knowledge acquisition and transfer, as well as opportunity development, tend to increase pari passu with international commitment among established entrepreneurial firms from an emerging economy.

Implications

The following are the major implications of the study:

1. According to the authors, their research suggests that international commitment is the result of a complex interaction of several factors. Resource availability, predetermined strategic goals, the personal interests of the entrepreneur and family attitudes towards international expansion combine and lead to some measure of international commitment in the case of small entrepreneurial Brazilian firms. The authors argue in favor of more research into this interaction effect.
2. da Rocha et al. (2012) do not find support for the antecedents of international commitment typically discussed in the literature. Factors such as international orientation, global vision and global mindset were not found to be important in the context of their study. The authors suggest that this may be the result of Brazil's history of economic insularity and the size of its domestic market that made venturing abroad much less of a priority. Also interesting is the conclusion drawn by the authors that in the case of emerging market economies, the most critical resource to facilitate internationalization is managerial talent devoted to the process. While resource allocation is important to firms from both developed and

(Continued)

(Continued)

emerging markets, the availability of dedicated managerial talent may be more of a constraint in the case of the latter.

3. The authors of this study also note that commitment to a network or relationships with other firms did not seem to be central to the internationalization of the Brazilian firms in their analysis. The authors suggest that this may be the result of the nature of the industry in which these firms operate. The ability to replicate the unique characteristics of a Brazilian steakhouse in a foreign country may be what gives these firms a competitive advantage, making it less important to lever the knowledge base of other firms in a network.

4. The researchers also argue that the speed and scope of internationalization need to be interpreted differently in the case of established entrepreneurial firms, and in particular firms from emerging economies which have fewer examples to inspire them. In this case, rapid internationalization may not reflect greater international commitment. Delayed entry that results from more detailed preparation may in fact be a better indicator of commitment to foreign markets.

5. With respect to performance, the da Rocha et al. (2012) study indicates that the relationship between commitment and performance may well be a continuous process, with greater commitment leading to better performance which in turn serves to deepen the firm's commitment to foreign market expansion. This is similar to the interaction between knowledge acquisition and commitment suggested by the Uppsala model.

6. Opportunity discovery in the da Rocha et al. (2012) study seems to occur at various points in the process of internationalization and was not linked to international performance. Opportunity development seemed instead to be linked to knowledge acquisition and international commitment, a relationship that the authors suggest is deserving of more in-depth investigation.

Source

da Rocha, A., Cotta de Mello, R., Pacheco, H. and de Abreu, I. (2012) 'The international commitment of late-internationalizing Brazilian entrepreneurial firms', *International Marketing Review*, 29, 3: 228–52.

Discussion Questions

Read the complete article and answer the following questions:

1. Do you believe that the case study method is the best approach to use in the development of a theory to explain international commitment? Justify your answer.

2. The authors of this research suggest that in the case of small entrepreneurial Brazilian firms, international commitment is the result of a complex interaction of several factors, including resource availability, predetermined strategic goals, personal interests of the entrepreneur and family attitudes towards international expansion. What factors would you hypothesize drive international commitment in multinational companies from the developed world? How would you test your hypothesis empirically?

PRODUCT STRUCTURE

The firm may also opt for a product divisional structure in which the focus is on specific products or product categories. Functional activities associated with each product are in essence rolled under the same division (see Figure 13.6). Each division will also have responsibility for both domestic and foreign markets in which its products are sold. In this organizational structure, the marketing function is distributed across the various product categories and no attempt is made to develop an independent international marketing unit. There is significant duplication of effort inherent in the product division structure which could lead to inefficiencies and problems of coordination.

FIGURE 13.6   Product Organizational Structure

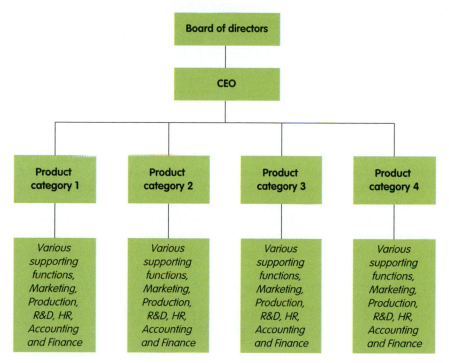

GEOGRAPHIC STRUCTURE

A third organizational form open to the firm is a geographic structure. With this approach, subsidiaries are established for each of the firm's major geographic markets (Figure 13.7). All of the various functional activities are again rolled up under the regional subsidiaries

FIGURE 13.7   Geographic Organizational Structure

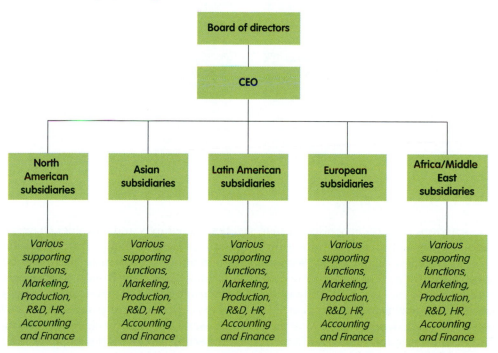

and duplicated across the organization. This organizational structure allows the firm to focus more directly on its key geographic markets and develop marketing programs that are more precisely crafted for each. Again, this structure does lead to significant duplication of effort across the organization and lost opportunity to exploit synergies across the various country markets. The structure may, however, be optimal if there are significant differences between the markets in terms of product needs or regulatory requirements.

CUSTOMER STRUCTURE

If there are significant differences in customer characteristics or buyer behavior, the firm may wish to consider a customer divisional structure (see Figure 13.8). Divisions within the organization serve specific customer types, regardless of their location or the products ordered. As with the product and geographic forms, all associated functional activities are rolled up under each division and duplicated across the organization. For this organizational structure to be useful, the customers served should be different, such as individual consumers, industrial buyers (i.e. businesses) and government departments. Each of these segments will have different needs and a different approach to the process of buying which could justify a dedicated divisional structure.

FIGURE 13.8   Customer Organizational Structure

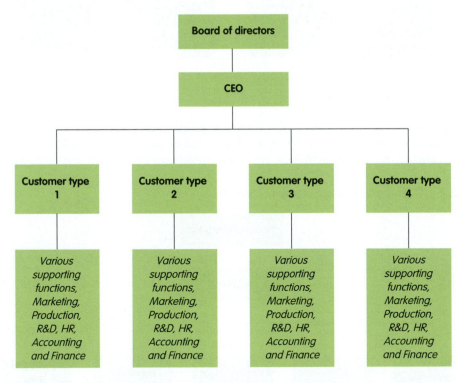

MATRIX ORGANIZATION

In some instances, the firm may discover that, say, both geography and customer characteristics are important. In such a situation, the firm may wish to combine both of these structures in a matrix organization (Figure 13.9). With a matrix organizational structure, there will be dual reporting relationships. The customer division, for example, will have responsibilities across all geographies, while each geographic division will have responsibilities across all customer types. Matrix organizational structures in essence consist of two intersecting structures. Any two structures could be used, depending on what the firm sees as the most critical elements of its market. The firm may, for example, also create a matrix of intersecting product and geography structures.

FIGURE 13.9   Matrix Organizational Structure

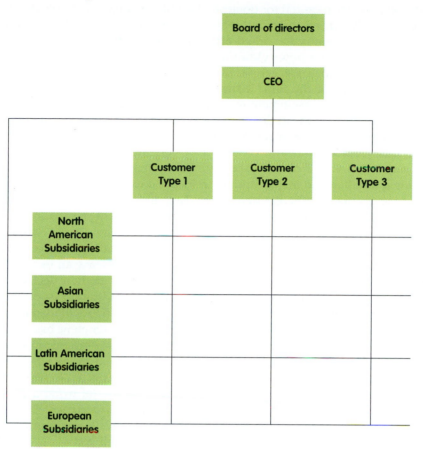

TRANSNATIONAL AND NETWORK ORGANIZATIONS

Globalization has produced a further evolution in organizational structure. Transnational organizations, for example, distribute their value-added functions across several geographies. Companies such as Ericsson from Sweden may locate their telecommunications R&D in one country, their manufacturing in another with global sales and marketing in a third. Some companies have also adopted a horizontal network structure in which the traditional hierarchical arrangement of a single decision maker at the top of the international division has been replaced by a much flatter arrangement. In horizontal network organizations, local managers are involved not only in the implementation of global strategy but also in its development. Managers at head office and those in the various countries are virtually indistinguishable in their job functions. Flows are from the country subsidiary to the head office and between the various subsidiaries.[9]

Staffing

According to Gröschl et al. (2009), an organizational structure is only as effective as the people who are hired to staff the various positions.[10] Staffing for international positions is more

---

[9]   Johansson, J.K. (2003) *Global Marketing: Foreign Entry, Local Marketing, and Global Management*. New York: McGraw-Hill/Irwin.

[10]   This section draws heavily on Gröschl, S., Dowling, P.J., Festing, M. and Engle, A.D. (2009) *International Human Resource Management: A Canadian Perspective*. Toronto: Nelson Education.

complex than filling domestic vacancies. Candidates for international assignments need to possess skills that are not required for domestic jobs. For example, individuals deployed from the home-country office need to have the ability to transfer their technical and managerial skills to a new foreign country (so-called **effectiveness skills**), as well as have the **coping skills** needed to survive in a new cultural environment. **Expatriate failure**, defined as the premature return of an expatriate, represents the result of a poor staff selection process and carries a significant cost for the firm. It should be noted that return of the expatriate prior to the normal period of the assignment may be a poor measure of failure. An expatriate, for example, may lack effectiveness in the overseas position but is never recalled by head office. This individual may generate poor results and cause long-term harm to the prospects of the overseas subsidiary but the posting would not be classified as a failure if the individual is not recalled prematurely. The cost of expatriate failure may be direct or indirect. The direct costs are easily quantified and include airfare, relocation expenses, salary and training costs. The indirect costs are more difficult to measure. They may include soured relationships with key government officials in the host country or a failure to build positive relationships with important local clients and channel members. The poor performance of the expatriate may also surface in the form of morale and retention problems among staff of the overseas subsidiary.

Several factors affect the decisions of expatriates to stay in or leave an international assignment. These factors moderate expatriate performance and impact their decision to stay in or leave the overseas posting. An inability to adjust to the foreign culture is, of course, a major factor. This inability to adjust may relate not only to the expatriate but also to the accompanying spouse and children. The length of the international assignment has also been found to have an impact on expatriates' ability to adjust and their performance overseas. Longer assignments provide expatriates with more time to adjust. The average length of an assignment for Japanese firms is 4–5 years and expatriates are not expected to be operating at full capacity until the end of their third year. There are also a number of workplace-related issues that may impact the process of adjustment and expatriate performance. These include job autonomy, level of organizational support from head office as well as within the host-country subsidiary, and the extent to which skills are actually being utilized.

Selection is the process of evaluating potential candidates for a position and deciding to whom it should be given. Several criteria are used in the selection of personnel for international assignments (see Figure 13.10).

FIGURE 13.10   Expatriate Selection Criteria

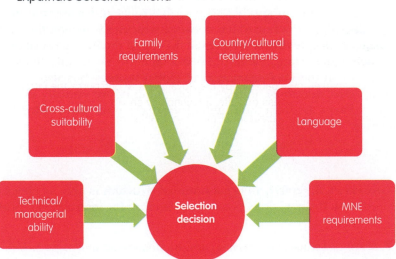

Source: Adapted from Gröschl, S., Dowling, P.J., Festing, M. and Engle, A.D. (2009) *International Human Resource Management: A Canadian Perspective.* Toronto: Nelson Education.

Technical/managerial ability: The individual's ability to perform the job is, of course, an important selection criterion. An individual's technical and managerial skills can easily be assessed based on past performance. In most instances, candidates being considered for overseas assignments would be employees of the parent company, making it relatively easy to check past performance evaluations and consult with candidates' superiors and direct reports.

Cross-cultural suitability: Given the importance of the cultural environment in determining expatriate success, the selection process should factor in the candidate's cross-cultural suitability. Ability to empathize with the culture of the host country, positive attitude, adaptability, emotional stability, maturity and diplomacy are all important considerations in the selection process.

Family requirements: Spouses and other family members play an important role in the expatriate's adjustment to the foreign country and his performance. Many of the duties and responsibilities involved in setting up a new house in the foreign country may well fall to the accompanying spouse, who may also have primary responsibility for ensuring the physical, emotional and educational well-being of the children. In many instances, the expatriate's spouse or partner will not be able to work in the country and this individual may have given up a successful career along with friends and other social supports at home. Despite the importance of the family, very few firms actually include this as a consideration in the selection process, preferring to focus only on the expatriate.

Country/cultural requirements: Expatriate candidates from the firm's home country will generally require a work permit in order to take up the foreign posting. In some cases, this may require the firm to prove that a host-country national, with similar qualifications, is not available. Some governments have refused work permits and entry visas on this basis. Further, if a work permit is issued, it is likely that an accompanying spouse will not be able to work in the host country which, as pointed out above, may lead to expatriate failure. The firm should also recognize that some countries in the Middle East may be reluctant to issue a work permit to a female candidate, regardless of her qualifications and experience.

case study 13.1: The Royal Bank of Canada

'The rules are very clear', he said. 'You cannot displace Canadians to hire people from abroad.' This was the reaction of the Canadian immigration minister in response to news that the Royal Bank of Canada had laid off a number of Canadian employees and replaced them with workers from India. The Royal Bank of Canada is Canada's largest bank as measured by assets and market capitalization. The firm employs some 80,000 employees and has more than 15 million personal, institutional, business and public sector clients. The company operates out of offices across Canada, the USA and 49 other countries around the world.

The controversy was sparked by a decision by the Royal Bank to outsource the information technology operations of its Dexia investor services business to iGate, a technology services firm that operates mainly out of India. In discharging its obligations under its contract with Royal Bank, iGate brought in a number of workers from India who were to be trained on the Dexia system by existing bank employees. Once trained, the Indian workers were to have taken over the positions held by the Canadian IT employees. Roughly 45 bank employees were to have been affected by the arrangement. Under Canadian law, companies are able to hire foreign workers. The Temporary Foreign Worker Program allows companies to fill vacancies with foreign workers but only if no suitable Canadian can be recruited. To use the program, companies must first request a labor market opinion from Human Resources and Skills Development Canada (HRSDC) to demonstrate a shortage of the specific skills required for the job. Companies must also demonstrate best efforts to find qualified Canadians. If the company is able to prove its case, an application must then be submitted for a special work visa.

(Continued)

(Continued)

Word of the Royal Bank's plans to outsource the IT positions created a public relations nightmare for the company, with angry Canadians making use of social media to voice their dissatisfaction with the bank's decision. HRSDC also took the matter seriously and initiated an investigation of iGate's application, also reviewing public statements made by the Royal Bank on the matter. In the wake of the controversy, the bank issued a public apology and has vowed to provide alternative and comparable jobs for the IT professionals displaced by the outsourcing initiative.

Sources

Coyne, A. (2013) 'RBC outsourcing controversy an economic fraud', *The National Post*, April 10, 2013. Available at: http://fullcomment.nationalpost.com/2013/04/10/andrew-coyne-rbc-outsourcing-controversy-an-economic-fraud/, accessed April 17, 2013.

Curry, B., Robertson, G. and Cousineau, S. (2013) 'Why Ottawa is pushing for answers over RBC move to outsource jobs', *The Globe and Mail*, April 8, 2013. Available at: www.theglobeandmail.com/report-on-business/economy/jobs/why-ottawa-is-pushing-for-answers-over-rbc-move-to-outsource-jobs/article10870961/, accessed April 17, 2013.

Mcintosh, J. (2013) 'Royal Bank apologizes to outsourced workers', *The Canadian Press*, April 11, 2013. Available at: www.thestar.com/business/2013/04/11/rbc_chief_issues_open_letter_apology_to_canadians_over_outsourcing.html, accessed April 17, 2013.

Discussion Questions

1. In this era of globalization, should countries impose restrictions on the employment of foreign workers by multinational companies? Why/why not?
2. Should the Royal Bank have apologized to Canadians for its outsourcing decision? Why/why not?

Language: The ability to communicate in the host-country language is clearly an important selection criterion for home-country (and third-country) expatriates. Often associated with cross-cultural suitability, companies vary in the amount of emphasis they place on host-country language capability in the selection process. Although it is a barrier to cross-cultural communication, US multinationals, for example, tend to rank language ability quite low on their list of desirable expatriate qualities.

MNE requirements: In addition to the above, several other firm-specific factors may come into play in the selection of an expatriate. The ratio of home-country nationals to host-country and third-country nationals may be a consideration in some situations. Employment tends to be a sensitive issue. For political reasons, companies may wish to be seen as providing relatively more opportunities to host-country nationals. Further, if the firm has a local joint venture partner, the selection process may become more complex. Each firm may have its 'favorite' candidate, making final selection very much a negotiated outcome. In addition, if knowledge transfer is a key component of the joint venture arrangement, the ability of the candidate to train her counterparts and subordinates also becomes a key requirement for selection.

Control

Implementation of the firm's global marketing strategy necessitates that control mechanisms be put in place to ensure that objectives are being met and the overall plan is on track. Negative variances between planned and actual results need to be identified early and corrective action taken as required. The type of action taken will, of course, be determined by the underlying cause of the sub-optimal results. In addition to correcting errors, the control process also provides management with an excellent vehicle for learning what works and what doesn't and for incorporating best practices into future iterations of its global marketing strategy.

In general, there are several types of controls used by organizations (see Figure 13.11). **Feed-forward** controls are preventative in nature and seek to identify and correct problems before they actually occur. This is largely done by ensuring that objectives are clear, responsibilities are well defined and the required inputs are in place before implementation actually begins. **Concurrent** controls, on the other hand, focus on interventions during the implementation process. In essence, these types of controls seek to correct problems while implementation is still ongoing, recognizing, of course, that there may be limits to what can be changed once the process is already underway. **Feedback** controls focus on the results achieved after process execution, comparing these to what was originally intended.

FIGURE 13.11   Types of Controls

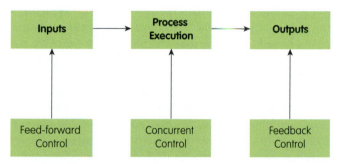

The controls put in place to monitor the effectiveness with which the global marketing strategy is implemented may be either **output** or **behavioral** in nature. Behavioral controls focus on influencing the behavior of the individual so that she does what is required to ensure realization of the objectives. The onus is placed on the properly trained and oriented individual to make the adjustments required to ensure that the strategy's objectives are realized. Output controls, on the other hand, rely on administrative systems and procedures to ensure that problems are identified and corrective action is taken. Training and socialization in the corporate culture are important aspects of behavioral controls, as is open communication within the organization. In contrast, output controls rely more on budgets and the careful monitoring of program expenditures.

GLOBAL ACCOUNT MANAGEMENT

The increasing globalization of customers presents a challenge for the various organizational structures discussed above. The global marketer must attempt to provide its most important global customers with a single point of contact and seamless service regardless of geographic location. To accomplish this, firms need to extend the national account management function across their countries of operation. **Global account management** (GAM) may be defined as 'an organizational form and process in multinational companies by which the worldwide activities serving a given multinational customer are coordinated centrally by one person or team within the supplying company' (Montgomery and Yip, 1999).[11]

From the perspective of the global marketing firm (i.e. the supplying company), the major benefits of a global account management system may be summarized as follows:

- consistency in the application of the company's policies in all countries in which it operates
- the potential to increase sales volumes by coordination of the marketing and selling functions across country markets

---

[11] Montgomery, D. and Yip, G. (1999) 'Statistical evidence on global account management programs', *Thexis*, 16, 4: 10–13.

- the potential to more effectively use marketing strategies and programs across geographic locations
- greater efficiency as a result of providing key accounts with a single point of contact
- establishment of a control mechanism relative to key accounts, to reduce the probability of account turnover
- improved two-way communication with key accounts which should lead to improvements in the firm's understanding of their requirements and better quality goods and services provided to these important global clients
- provision of a means to preempt both local and global competitors from securing business from the firm's important customers (Harvey et al., 2002). [12]

Global account management significantly simplifies the customer's interactions with the global marketing firm and provides important benefits but it does present the supplying firm with a number of challenges. A global account management system is typically implemented alongside the firm's existing organizational structure, such as one that is geographically focused. As a result, sales executives based in the various countries may perceive that their autonomy is being undermined by the head-office-based global account management team and may react negatively to its involvement (Birkinshaw et al., 2001).[13] 'Ownership' of important accounts has implications for compensation and is, therefore, important to executives and sales professionals in the various country subsidiaries. In some cases, staff in the country offices may actually be called upon to implement policies crafted by the GAM team, further adding to the tension between the two groups. It is also possible that, because of the overlapping authority structure, the GAM arrangement may serve to undermine the relationship between the country-based sales team and local representatives of the global customer. These relationships may have been cultivated over many years.

Companies also need to carefully examine their motivations for launching a GAM strategy. If the motivation is to keep a global customer but the GAM strategy is implemented without strong commitment and support from senior executives and the heads of functional departments, it is unlikely to be successful. To be workable, there must be an internal champion and the GAM team should be well resourced and supported. If the infrastructure is not in place to support the GAM team, it is unlikely to achieve its objectives, which may lead to customer disappointment. If, on the other hand, the motivation is to salvage a worsening relationship with a key global customer, implementation of a GAM strategy may also not work, unless the underlying reasons for the poor supplier–customer relationship are also addressed. These reasons may include poor product quality, uncompetitive prices or a history of poor customer service. In this case, a GAM strategy will only serve to mask the problem.[14]

The global marketing manager also needs to be fully aware that implementation of a GAM strategy will involve increased costs. Not only will new resources be needed to support the unit, as mentioned above, but there is also more than likely going to be duplication given that the new GAM team will be essentially carrying out a function already performed at the country level. Quite apart from these explicit costs however, a GAM strategy will also be costly to the firm in other ways, such as the increased length of time required to make decisions, time spent resolving conflicts between the GAM team and their country-based

---

[12]   Harvey, M., Myers, M.B. and Novicevic, M. (2002) 'The managerial issues associated with global account management', *Thunderbird International Business Review*, 44, 5: 625–47.

[13]   Birkinshaw, J., Toulan, O. and Arnold, D. (2001) 'Global account management in multinational corporations: Theory and evidence', *Journal of International Business Studies*, 32, 2: 231–48.

[14]   Harvey et al. (2002) op cit.

counterparts, as well as time invested in setting up a new organizational unit and selection of a management team.[15]

Figure 13.12 illustrates a step-by-step GAM implementation plan that may be followed should senior management make the decision to proceed. It is recommended that the GAM team be assembled first and that team members be part of the process of developing the goals and objectives of the unit. This is particularly important when team members have worked with major global clients and have knowledge of their corporate aspirations and expectations. Goals established for the GAM unit must be well defined and measurable, and an assessment must be done of the strategic fit between these goals and those of the firm's major global clients. As noted above, the GAM unit must be well resourced if it is to accomplish its objectives. The next step in the development of a GAM implementation plan is, therefore, to consider the infrastructure needs of the new unit. These include IT, accounting and financial management functions.

FIGURE 13.12   GAM Implementation Plan

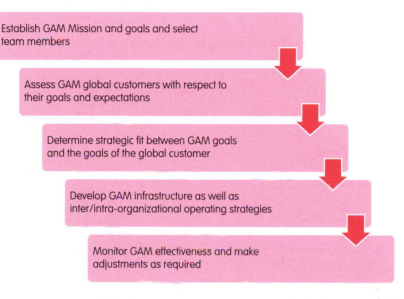

Source: Adapted from Harvey, M., Myers, M. and Novicevic, M. (2002) The managerial issues associated with global account management, *Thunderbird International Business Review*, Sep/Oct, 44, 5; 625–47.

It is also necessary to develop policies, systems and procedures to facilitate coordination between the GAM unit and the global customer base, as well as between the GAM team and other parts of the supplier organization. In terms of the latter, procedures will need to be put in place for resolving the inevitable conflicts that will arise between the GAM team and managers in the country subsidiaries. It would also be helpful to anticipate and discuss some of these potential problems in advance and arrive at negotiated, mutually agreeable solutions.

The final step in the process of developing a GAM implementation plan is to design an appropriate monitoring and control mechanism to measure effectiveness and provide a basis for adjustments as required. The monitoring and control mechanism should at a minimum provide answers to the following questions:

- Is the supplier receiving the expected benefits?
- Is the customer satisfied with the supplier's global coordination of the account?

---

[15]   Harvey et al. (2002) op cit., p. 640.

- Does the GAM unit provide a superior alternative to the old approach to account management and other alternatives that may be available?

COMPETITIVE STRATEGIES FOR LOCAL FIRMS

To this point, we have considered the strategies of multinational firms expanding into foreign markets. In this section, we turn our attention to the case of a local firm under attack by foreign multinationals in its home market. In many instances, the foreign multinational entering the local market will be considerably better capitalized than the local firm and have a depth of global marketing experience that puts it in a strong position. The correct strategic response for the local firm in such a situation depends on two factors:

- the extent of globalization in the firm's industry
- the extent to which the firm's assets are transferable (or only locally relevant).[16]

The strategic options open to the local firm are illustrated in Figure 13.13.

FIGURE 13.13   Competitive Strategies for Local Companies

	Firm's Competitive Assets are Customized to the Home Market	Firm's Competitive Assets are Transferable Abroad
High Pressure to Globalize	**Dodger** *Sells out to a global player or becomes part of a global alliance*	**Contender** *Upgrades capabilities to compete with global firms in niche markets*
Low Pressure to Globalize	**Defender** *Leverages local assets to compete with global firms in areas where they are weak.*	**Extender** *Expands into overseas markets that are similar to its home market*

Source: Adapted from Dawar, N. and Frost, T. (1999) 'Competing with the giants: Survival strategies for local companies in emerging markets', *Harvard Business Review*, 77 (March–April): 119–29.

If the local firm's strategic assets are customized to the home market and are not easily transferred to foreign markets but the firm is in an industry that faces strong pressures to globalize, then the appropriate response is to sell out to the global competition. This is referred to as a **dodger** strategy and is seen, for example, in the case of Škoda, the Czech automaker. With the collapse of communism and the implementation of market reforms in Eastern Europe, this company recognized that it was not in a strong position to compete with western automakers. Rather than let Škoda go out of business, the government of Czechoslovakia opted to bring in a strong foreign partner. Škoda became a wholly-owned subsidiary of Volkswagen in 1991. As a result of this transaction, Škoda gained access to new automotive technologies, management practices and distribution options, becoming a major emerging brand with an improved reputation across Europe. In 2012, the company delivered roughly 939,000 vehicles to customers in China (25 percent), Germany (15 percent)

---

[16]   Czinkota, M., Ronkainen, I., Farrell, C. and McTavish, R. (2009) *Global Marketing: Foreign Entry, Market Development and Strategy Implementation*. Toronto: Nelson Education.

and Russia (11 percent), as well as to customers in other countries across Europe and Asia.[17]

If, on the other hand, the local firm's assets are customized to the home market but it is in an industry that faces only weak pressures to globalize, then a **defender** strategy is the best option. With such a strategy, the local firm leverages its assets to compete with the foreign competition in areas where local knowledge is required and the foreign multinational is likely to be weak. This approach was used by chocolate manufacturers in Latin America.

PHOTO 13.1

With the entry of Mars and Hershey into their market, local manufacturers such as Arcor and Nacional de Chocolates maintained their business by selling bite-sized chocolates that were affordable to low-income consumers instead of the larger (and more expensive) bars sold by their foreign rivals. The local firms also ensured that their products were crafted to suit the tastes and preferences of the local market and would be available in retail outlets in remote areas.

If the local firm's assets are easily transferred to new foreign markets and it operates in an industry that faces strong pressures to globalize, then a **contender** strategy may produce the best results. With this approach, the local firm upgrades its capabilities and begins to aggressively tackle new foreign markets competing with other multinational companies, including those targeting its home market. For example, while the major players in the aircraft manufacturing business such as Airbus and Boeing have been competing in the market for larger planes, the niche market for aircraft carrying 70–110 passengers has been overlooked. The segment is fast growing with demand up significantly in Europe and North America. The Canadian firm Bombardier has moved to capitalize on growth in this niche segment of the market and competes head to head with Brazil's Embraer for regional jet customers around the world. In essence, both Bombardier and Embraer now compete with the major players in the industry by focusing on an underserved segment of the global market.

Finally, if the firm's strategic assets are transferable aboard but there is only weak pressure to globalize, then an **extender** strategy should be considered. With an extender strategy, the local firm expands into foreign markets but the focus is on those markets that are similar to its home market. Jollibee Foods Corporation, for example, defended its position in the Philippines market against McDonald's by customizing its products and services to the tastes of its local customers. The firm would eventually extend its reach to tackle foreign markets with a sizeable Filipino population such as Hong Kong and California, USA. The firm now has a network of 450 restaurants in seven countries.

SUMMARY

This chapter has focused on the development of a global marketing strategy. The strategic choices made by the firm have a major bearing on its success in international markets.

---

[17] *2012 ŠKODA Annual Report* (2012) Available at: http://new.skoda-auto.com/SiteCollectionDocuments/company/investors/annual-reports/en/skoda-auto-annual-report-2012.pdf, accessed April 16, 2013.

The process of strategy formulation was discussed as a series of four interrelated steps: defining the business; developing the firm's overall business strategy; developing the international marketing strategy; and implementing the international marketing strategy. As part of this process, a number of generic business strategies were discussed based on the type of competitive advantage the firm possesses, i.e. cost or product differentiation and market scope. The point was also made that these generic strategic approaches are static and do not reflect the dynamism of today's hypercompetitive markets. To address this problem, the 7S framework was presented, which argues that sustainable competitive advantage does not exist and that the firm needs to focus on market-disrupting tactics that will provide it with a series of temporary advantages.

The discussion next considered the key elements of an effective international marketing strategy. The issue of standardization versus localization was flagged as a critical decision for the firm, as was the configuration of its value-added activities. The firm, in other words, needs to think about the extent to which it will adjust elements of its marketing mix, such as production and communication strategies, in order to cater to the requirements of the host country. Decisions also have to be made regarding where value-added activities such as production, product design and customer support will take place, such as in low-wage jurisdictions or countries with a significant pool of technical talent. In the development of an international marketing strategy, the firm also needs to decide on the geographical scope of its activities, i.e. whether participation in international markets will be fairly circumscribed in terms of the number of countries targeted or be more broad based. Given that global markets are highly competitive, the firm, as part of its international strategy, should think about the approach that would be used to defend itself against competitors.

A number of implementation issues were also addressed in this chapter, including the design of the firm's organizational structure and the recruitment of staff for overseas assignments. The notion of commitment to global markets was also touched on briefly and the point made that without commitment implementation is unlikely to be successful. Firms will quickly withdraw from international markets as the inevitable challenges begin to surface. The chapter concluded with a discussion of strategies that may be used by local firms to defend themselves against attacks from foreign multinationals.

? discussion questions

1. What factors would you consider in selecting employees for an overseas assignment in Saudi Arabia?

2. What is a hypercompetitive market? Describe a strategic framework that a firm may use to compete in such markets.

3. Describe the three major perspectives of international marketing strategy that currently dominate the literature.

4. What is global account management (GAM)? From the perspective of the supplying company, what are the benefits of implementing a GAM system?

5. What are two challenges that firms are likely to face in the implementation of a GAM system?

6. What strategic options are open to a local firm that is under attack in its home market by a major foreign multinational?

Real World Challenges

FEMSA and the Mexican Beer Market

It was certain to happen at some point, Ricardo said to himself, as he steered his BMW 5-series through the crowded streets of Mexico City. As VP, Marketing for FEMSA, he knew that his company would soon face significant challenges. The beer market in Mexico is concentrated in the hands of a few local breweries and FEMSA is a major player. Founded as a brewery in Monterrey, Mexico, in 1890, FEMSA had grown to become an integrated beverage company with revenues in 2008 of over US$12 billion. The firm maintains operations in nine countries in Latin America – Mexico, Guatemala, Nicaragua, Costa Rica, Panama, Colombia, Venezuela, Brazil and Argentina. FEMSA operates six breweries in Mexico, eight in Brazil and employs roughly 122,000 people. FEMSA Cerveza is the business unit responsible for the firm's 35 high-quality premium beer brands which include Carta Blanca, Tecate, Tecate Light, Superior, Sol, Dos Equis Lager, Dos Equis Ambar, Indio, Bohemia and Noche Buena. While this business unit had clearly been a major success, Ricardo was bothered by recent news that Anheuser-Busch InBev, the Belgian powerhouse, was poised to take on the Mexican market.

Anheuser-Busch InBev is one of the world's top five consumer product companies. The company owns four of the ten top-selling beer brands in the world and is No. 1 or No. 2 in over 20 key global markets. Overall, the company owns almost 300 brands including global brands such as Budweiser, Stella Artois and Beck's. The firm employs 120,000 people worldwide and had revenues in 2008 of over US$39 billion. InBev already has a strong presence in Brazil with roots going back to 1885. The Brazilian brewery AmBev was created in 1999 by the merger of two breweries – Brahma and Antarctica. In 2004, AmBev merged with the Belgian firm Interbrew to create InBev and in 2008 acquired Anheuser-Busch. The new firm was renamed Anheuser-Busch InBev and Anheuser-Busch retained two seats on the company's board. Given the firm's history in Latin America, Ricardo was not surprised that sooner or later InBev would turn its attention to the Mexican market. As he pulled into his driveway, Ricardo considered that the entire global beer industry was changing and that a few dominant players were beginning to emerge. FEMSA had to worry not only about InBev but also about other giants in the marketplace such as Molson Coors which was created in 2005.

Ricardo decided to call a meeting of his management team to consider his company's options. He knew that the management of FEMSA was committed to remaining an independent company. How then could FEMSA defend itself against companies such as InBev? What would be the best strategy for FEMSA in a rapidly globalizing beer market? Maybe the company should forget the beer market and concentrate on its FEMSA Comercio business unit which operates convenience stores, or its Coca-Cola FEMSA unit which bottles Coca-Cola products. Ricardo fired off an email to the management team requesting an urgent meeting and settled in with a bottle of Bohemia to watch soccer on TV.

Sources

www.ab-inbev.com/index.cfm

www.euromonitor.com/The_global_beer_market_a_world_of_two_halves

www.femsa.com/en/business/cerveza/

Questions

1. State the problem that FEMSA faces in Mexico.
2. Identify the options available to Ricardo. Be sure to identify more than one.
3. Based on the options identified above, recommend a course of action for the company. Be sure to provide a rationale and make a decision.

FURTHER READING

Birkinshaw, J., Toulan, O. and Arnold, D. (2001) 'Global account management in multinational corporations: Theory and evidence', *Journal of International Business Studies*, 32, 2: 231–48.

D'Aveni, R.A., Canger, J.M. and Doyle, J.J. (1995) 'Coping with hypercompetition: Utilizing the new 7S's framework', *The Academy of Management Executive*, 9, 3: 45–60.

Harvey, M., Myers, M. and Novicevic, M. (2002) 'The managerial issues associated with global account management', *Thunderbird International Business Review*, 44, 5: 625–47.

Keegan, W.J. (1969) 'Multinational product planning: Strategic alternatives', *Journal of Marketing*, Jan.: 58–62.

Zou, S. and Cavusgil, S.T. (2002) 'The GMS: A broad conceptualization of global marketing strategy and its effect on firm performance', *Journal of Marketing*, 66, 4: 40–56.

THE MARKETING STRATEGIES OF EMERGING MARKET MNES

LEARNING OBJECTIVES

After reading this chapter you should be able to:

- Define and explain the terms 'emerging market' and 'emerging market multinationals'

- Discuss the challenges to the growth and development of emerging market multinationals

- Discuss the rise of emerging market multinationals and their growing importance in the global economy

- Describe how emerging market multinationals may be classified

- Discuss the sources of competitive advantage for emerging market multinationals

- Discuss the process by which emerging market multinationals internationalize

- Discuss the marketing strategies employed by emerging market multinationals.

INTRODUCTION

This chapter examines the international marketing strategies of emerging market multinational enterprises (EMMNEs). Much of the literature on international marketing has been derived from research on multinational companies from developed countries. Researchers believe, however, that multinationals from emerging markets possess characteristics not shared by their developed country counterparts and that these features result in differences in their approach to the process of internationalization and the implementation of international marketing strategy.

In the last few years, there has been a growing interest in the strategies of EMMNEs. High-profile acquisitions by companies from China, India and other developing countries have sparked controversy in the developed world and made for attention-grabbing headlines in the business press. Tata Motors, for example, purchased the Jaguar and Land Rover brands from Ford Motor Company for $2.3 billion, signaling the entrance of this Indian firm as a major player in the automotive industry. That Ford would relinquish Jaguar, its iconic luxury British brand, to an Indian firm took many by surprise. Similarly, Lenovo Group's acquisition of IBM's personal computer business for close to $2 billion generated considerable interest among industry professionals. This acquisition of a leading American firm by a Chinese multinational also prompted US government officials to express their reservations.

High-profile acquisitions, such as the ones noted above, and other evidence of performance in global markets, are quite interesting given that EMMNEs have historically been viewed as technologically backward and lacking in international marketing skills. Further, these firms are based in countries with weak institutional structures, high levels of corruption and political instability, making their rapid progress all the more surprising. Both academics and business professionals are now seeking to understand how firms from such environments have become such a dominant force in international business. Whatever the reasons, it is clear that these firms now have global aspirations and present a major competitive threat to multinationals from developed countries. In the words of GE's chief executive officer, Jeff Immelt: 'GE has tremendous respect for traditional rivals like Siemens, Philips, and Rolls-Royce. But it knows how to compete with them; they will never destroy GE. By introducing products that create a new price-performance paradigm, however, the emerging giants very well could.'[1] This chapter is devoted to understanding the international strategies of this new class of multinational enterprises.

WHAT ARE EMERGING MARKET MULTINATIONAL ENTERPRISES?

EMMNEs may be defined as companies originating from emerging markets and which are engaged in outward foreign direct investments where they exercise control over assets and engage in value-added activities in foreign countries (Luo and Tung, 2007).[2] It should be noted that some researchers explicitly exclude state-owned companies from their definition of EMMNEs, as such firms tend to be more focused on promoting their home-country government's foreign policy agendas than on the maximization of shareholder value.[3] Other analysts, however, adopt a much less restrictive definition and make no distinction between state- and privately owned enterprises. Companies that primarily invest in tax havens in countries such as the Cayman Islands and the Virgin Islands as a means of avoiding taxes in their home countries are normally excluded from the definition of an EMMNE. Also excluded are companies that engage in so-called **round-tripping investments**, i.e. using funds on the books in their own foreign subsidiary to make investments back in their home country for the purpose of receiving preferential treatment from their governments.

As noted above, EMMNEs originate from emerging markets. The term emerging markets was coined in 1981 by then World Bank economist Antoine van Agtmael who was attempting to find a positive name for an equity mutual fund that would invest in the shares of developing country companies.[4] The term was considered to be less pejorative than other terms such as Less Developed Countries (LDCs) or Third World Countries that were in common use in prior decades. In essence, emerging market economies refer to a group of countries such as China, India, Brazil, Russia and South Africa that have recently undergone significant economic reforms and structural changes. As a result of these changes, emerging market economies have experienced rapid rates of growth and the prospect for continued growth remains strong despite their relatively weak institutional frameworks. These countries are also characterized by a growing middle class, as well as by political and social transformations. Emerging market economies are generally considered to be countries that are part way between developing and developed country status. There is no one list of emerging market countries. Various institutions, such as the International Monetary Fund, Standard and Poor's and Dow Jones, maintain their own list of emerging market economies. While there is overlap, these lists are by no means identical (see Table 14.1 for illustrative examples). The so-called BRIC countries (Brazil, Russia, India and China) are arguably the most important of the emerging market economies.

---

[1] Immelt, J.R., Govindarajan, V. and Trimble, C. (2009) 'How GE is disrupting itself', *Harvard Business Review*, 87, 10: 56–65.

[2] Luo, Y. and Tung, R. (2007) 'International expansion of emerging market enterprises: A springboard perspective', *Journal of International Business Studies*, 38, 4: 481–98.

[3] Luo and Tung (2007).

[4] *The Economist* (2008) Ins and Outs. Available at: www.economist.com/node/12080703, accessed April 22, 2013.

TABLE 14.1   Illustrative Lists of Emerging Market Countries

The Emerging Market Global Players (EMGP) project	FTSE	S&P
Argentina	**FTSE advanced emerging countries:**	**European:**
Brazil	Brazil	Czech Republic
Chile	Czech Republic	Hungary
China	Hungary	Poland
Hungary	Malaysia	Russia
India	Mexico	Turkey
Israel	Poland	**Asia Pacific:**
Korea	South Africa	China
Mexico	Taiwan	India
Poland	Turkey	Indonesia
Russia	**FTSE secondary emerging countries:**	Malaysia
Slovenia	Chile	Philippines
Taiwan	China	Taiwan
Turkey	Colombia	Thailand
	Egypt	**Latin America:**
	India	Brazil
	Indonesia	Chile
	Morocco	Mexico
	Pakistan	Peru
	Peru	**Middle East & Africa:**
	Philippines	Egypt
	Russia	Morocco
	Thailand	South Africa
	UAE	

Sources: www.vcc.columbia.edu/content/emerging-market-global-players-project; www.ftse.com/Indices/FTSE_Emerging_Markets/index.jsp; www.sp-indexdata.com/idpfiles/citigroup/prc/active/factsheets/Factsheet_SP_Global_BMI.pdf

CHALLENGES TO EMMNE DEVELOPMENT AND GROWTH

EMMNEs face a number of obstacles to their development and growth. The home-country environments from which many of these firms have emerged have been less than supportive of their domestic development and global ambitions. Political and institutional frameworks in many of these countries tend to be weak, resulting in suboptimal government policies and a regulatory environment that fails to provide firms with clear and consistent operational guidelines. The lack of transparency in government policies and regulations along with a weak judicial system paves the way for corruption in many of these societies and increases the burden on domestic firms attempting to conduct business in these countries. In many instances, the above problems are compounded by deeply rooted social tensions and a history of violence. Many emerging market economies have also historically been beset by serious macro-economic challenges, including excessive debt, rampant inflation, high levels of unemployment and underemployment, and exchange rate instability. These countries are also marred by serious infrastructure deficits that create challenges for the physical movement of goods and for normal business operations. Further, several of the countries classified as emerging have historically relied on natural resources, with little emphasis on advanced manufacturing and technology.

It is also the case that EMMNEs operate in a home environment in which distribution channels are relatively underdeveloped, and, while there are a large number of consumers, they are generally considered to be unsophisticated. EMMNEs for the most part do not possess strong global brands, revolutionary technologies or particularly strong global management expertise. The above country- and firm-level characteristics have contributed to an image of EMMNEs as being unsophisticated and backward. The stereotypical view of these firms is that they are only proficient at manufacturing cheap products and that this competence stems exclusively from the availability of cheap labor in their home countries. EMMNEs have historically not been considered a competitive threat to multinationals from the advanced countries. In fact, when countries such as Brazil and India began to embrace economic reforms and modernization, the fear was that multinationals from the developed world would quickly put local firms out of business with their advanced technologies, quality products and globally recognized brands.[5]

case study 14.1: Haier Group Appliances

The Haier Group is a major player in the home appliances market. The company was founded in Qingdao, China, in 1984 and currently has 80,000 employees around the world and customers in 100 countries. The firm has five R&D centers, 61 trade companies, 21 industrial parks in various countries and is ranked first by Euromonitor among global home-appliance brands. The Boston Consulting Group ranks the Haier Group 8th on its 2012 list of most innovative companies. In 2012, the company reported an annual turnover of 163.1 billion yuan. The company was originally founded as the Qingdao Refrigerator Plant in 1984 and was renamed the Haier Group in 1992. In the early to mid-1980s, Haier was a small money-losing enterprise producing low-quality products for the local market. In fact, in 1984 the company posted a loss of some US$500,000, and, unable to secure credit from the regional banks, was forced to borrow from farmers in the villages around the plant.

Zhang Ruimin was appointed the company's plant director in 1984 and set about the process of transforming the organization. In order to improve plant efficiency, discipline and product quality, the new plant director instituted policies that prohibited employees from arriving late for work or leaving early for home. Plant hygiene was also improved and a rule was adopted that if defective products were produced, 20 percent would be deducted from the salaries of all employees involved. In one oft-quoted example in 1985, Ruimin is reported to have received a number of customer complaints about the quality of the firm's refrigerators. In response, he instructed employees to line up 76 of the defective appliances while others looked on. A number of employees were subsequently issued with sledgehammers and ordered to destroy the defective products. This would be a turning point in the company's quest to become a quality manufacturer.

With a culture of quality beginning to form and with the entry of a number of global appliance manufacturers into the Chinese market, Haier would soon find it necessary to focus on international expansion. Supported

---

5   Ramamurti, R. (2012) 'Competing with emerging market multinationals', *Business Horizons*, 55: 241–9.

by the Chinese government, the firm would take its first steps towards internationalization in 1996 by expanding into Indonesia and several other South East Asian countries before tackling the US market. According to Zhang Ruimin, now CEO of the company, 'In the globalization era, there are two categories of companies: one is the international company, and the other is one taken over by the former group. There isn't a third category'.

PHOTO 14.1

Sources

Liu, H. and Li, K. (2002) 'Strategic implications of emerging Chinese multinationals: The Haier case study', *European Management Journal*, 20, 6: 699–706.

Haier website: www.haier.net/en/about_haier/

Smith, F.O. (2008) 'A "BRIC" house: Emerging multinationals pose threat to established global players', *Manufacturing Business Technology*, 26, 9: 12.

Discussion Questions

1. Why would Haier begin its process of internationalization by expanding into markets in South East Asia?
2. Was it important for Haier to secure a strong position in the Chinese market before expanding overseas?
3. Do you agree with the then plant director's approach to improving product quality? Would such an approach work in western countries?

THE RISE OF THE EMMNE

EMMNEs represent the fourth wave of multinational expansion that the world has witnessed. Prior to World War I, the major multinationals were European, particularly the British, French, Dutch and Germans. Multinationals from these countries levered the colonial dominance of their home countries to control a significant share of world investment. Following World War II, a second wave of multinational expansion became evident. This time it was firms from the USA that would rise to prominence and capture a controlling share of global investment as European dominance began to wane. In the late 1980s and 1990s, we witnessed the rise of Japanese firms with their aggressive expansion into the USA, Europe and across Asia. Some analysts now believe that multinationals from countries such as China, India, Russia, Brazil and even some parts of Africa will soon dominate international business in much the same way that multinationals from the developed world have dominated in previous decades.[6]

EMMNEs are now seen as a competitive threat to developed country multinationals around the world and in almost every industrial sector. The stereotypical view of emerging markets has now been replaced by a new perspective that sees these markets as fast growing, dynamic and representative of tremendous business opportunities. It is clear that EMMNEs have secured home-field advantage in these markets with a rapidly expanding

---

[6] Ramamurti (2012) op cit.

middle class and are now challenging developed country multinationals in markets around the world. Some scholars have argued that the competitive threat facing western multinationals from EMMNEs is much deeper and broader than that posed by the rise of Asian countries such as Japan, Taiwan and Korea several decades ago.[7] The current threat comes simultaneously from a number of countries and from regions as diverse as Latin America, Asia, Eastern Europe and even Africa. Interestingly, it is not only in their home countries that EMMNEs pose a threat to developed country multinationals. Having survived economic reforms in their home countries and established a firm foothold in those markets, many EMMNEs have expanded into neighboring countries. As noted earlier, the Haier Group expanded into Indonesia, Malaysia and the rest of South East Asia, challenging established companies such as Whirlpool not only in China but also in these regional markets as well. Similarly, Brazilian multinationals expanded into other Latin American countries, while firms from South Africa have worked to cement their positions in the rest of Africa. This is obviously not positive news for developed country multinationals, many of which are now looking to emerging markets as a source of growth. These multinationals from the Triad (the USA, Japan and Western Europe) are contending with slow economic growth and unfavorable demographics at home and are highly motivated to seek opportunities outside these markets.

THE IMPORTANCE OF EMMNEs

The significance of EMMNEs has been steadily increasing over the last few years. As Chattopadhyay, Batra and Ozsomer (2012)[8] report, the number of EMMNEs on the Fortune list of the top global 500 companies has increased from 44 in 2005 to 113 in 2010. Further evidence of the growing significance of EMMNEs comes from UNCTAD data which show that the top 100 firms from emerging markets increased their foreign sales by 48% and their foreign employment by 73% in 2005, compared to just a 10% increase in foreign sales and employment for companies based in the developed world.

EMMNEs are expanding internationally at a rapid pace that has taken many by surprise. For example, EMMNEs undertook 1,100 mergers and acquisitions in 2006 valued at close to US$128 billion. These deals cut across industry sectors and included Mittal Steel's US$32 billion acquisition of European steel-maker Arcelor and the US$17.2 billion acquisition of Canada's Inco by Brazilian mining company, Vale. Several other deals in excess of $1 billion have also been

FIGURE 14.1   EMMNE Competitive Advantage

7   Ramamurti (2012) op cit.

8   Chattopadhyay, A., Batra, R. and Ozsomer, A. (2012) *The New Emerging Market Multinationals: Four Strategies for Disrupting Markets and Building Brands*. New York: McGraw-Hill.

TABLE 14.2   Examples of World-class EMMNEs

Name of company	Country of origin	Industry
Grupo Arcor	Argentina	Arcor is one of the world's largest candy manufacturers. The company was founded in 1951.
Grupo Bimbo, S.A.B. de C.V.	Mexico	Bimbo is a leader in the bakery category. The company was established in 1945.
JBS S.A	Brazil	JBS is one of the world's most dominant companies in the meat and meat products industry. The company was founded in 1953.
Tenaris	Argentina	Tenaris is a leading supplier of tubes and related products to the energy industry. The company was founded in 1948.
Braskem	Brazil	Braskem produces a number of chemical and petrochemical products. Founded in 2002.
Haier	China	Leading manufacturer of home appliances and consumer electronics. Founded as Qingdao Refrigerator Company in 1984.
Bharat Forge	India	Global leader in metal forming. Founded in 1961.

recorded, including Tata Group's 2007 acquisition of UK–Dutch Corus Group for US$12.2 billion and China National Petroleum Corporation's 2005 acquisition of PetroKazakhstan for US$4.1 billion. It should also be noted that the activities of EMMNEs are not confined to one or two sectors but span a wide range of industries from telecommunications to IT services and power generation. As illustrated in Table 14.2, many of these companies have become world leaders in their respective categories. Haier, for example, has become the fourth largest player in the global white goods industry and many other EMMNEs aim to become global leaders. Infosys and Tata Consulting, both Indian firms, aim to become the next Accenture, while Chery Automobile and Geely of China aspire to become the next Honda or Toyota, and Brazil's Petrobras has its sights set on becoming the next Shell.[9]

A TYPOLOGY

As noted above, EMMNEs originate from a number of different countries and are active in a diverse range of sectors. Despite this heterogeneity, some scholars argue that EMMNEs actually fit into four major categories, depending on the extent of their international diversification and whether they are state- or non-state owned[10] (see Figure 14.1). **Niche entrepreneurs** are non-state-owned firms that are highly specialized in a sector or particular product category. One example is ZTE, a Chinese manufacturer of handsets and one of the world's leaders in the production of mobile phones. Originally a state enterprise, ZTE is now publicly traded on the Hong Kong Stock Exchange and has subsidiaries in

PHOTO 14.2

---

[9]   Ramamurti (2012) op cit.

[10]   Luo and Tung (2007) op cit.

FIGURE 14.2   An EMMNE Typology

	State owned	Non-state owned
Narrow international diversification	Commissioned specialist	Niche entrepreneur
Broad international diversification	Transnational agent	World stage aspirant

Source: Luo and Tung (2007)

a number of countries such as Australia, Germany and the USA. Another example is Arçelik A.S., a manufacturer of home appliances based in Turkey with production facilities in a number of countries including Russia, China and South Africa. The company is the leader in the freezer, refrigerator and washing machine segment in the UK and the second-ranked brand in dishwashers in France. Arçelik is also publicly traded. Niche entrepreneurs do not receive funding from their home-country governments and do not have any real depth of industrial experience.

World stage aspirants are also non-state-owned and do not receive funding from their home governments. Unlike niche entrepreneurs, however, firms in this category operate across a wide range of industries and geographies. One example is the Thai conglomerate Charoen Pokphand which operates businesses in the areas of agro-industry and food processing, retail and telecommunications. The firm is also active in plastics, automotive products, pharmaceuticals, information technology, real estate development and financial services. There are over 100 companies in this group and its operations are scattered across Asia, including China, the Middle East, North America and Europe.

Transnational agents are state-owned companies that have made significant international investments but which are subject to instructions from their home-country governments. Companies in this category generally operate in sectors that are of strategic interest to their home-country governments and which support economic development at home. For many, this would include sectors such as oil, natural gas and other natural resources. Transnational agents expand abroad to take advantage of a superior investment climate in foreign countries and so are clearly focused on growing the business while supporting the objectives of the state, which is usually their largest shareholder. Hindustan Petroleum is an example of a firm in this category. The company is classified as a government of India enterprise and is also a Fortune 500 company. Hindustan Petroleum is an integrated oil refining and marketing company which supplies 10 percent of India's refining capacity and is active in retailing, aviation, bulk fuels, lubes and alternative energy.

The fourth category of EMMNE is the **commissioned specialist**. Firms in this category are also state owned but they focus on a narrow range of business activities and geographies while discharging their obligations to their home-country governments. The commissioned specialist has a dual role of pursuing international expansion, as would be the case with any other multinational, and being an instrument of government policy. One example is the Sinopec Group, a Chinese state-owned enterprise in the petroleum and petrochemical business. Sinopec Group essentially operates and manages state assets in the petroleum sector and owns a controlling interest in China Petroleum & Chemical Company (Sinopec Corporation) which is listed on the New York, Hong Kong, London and Shanghai stock exchanges.

The above typology is useful in better understanding the motivations, behaviors and performance outcomes of EMMNEs. For example, commission specialists and transnational agents receive substantial funding from their home-country governments and are mandated to further the state's agenda, whether or not this conflicts with the firm's profit-maximization objective. In contrast, niche entrepreneurs and world-stage aspirants do not enjoy the same level of institutional support from their governments but are also not subject to the same level of political interference in their operations. The typology presented above suggests that there are likely to be significant differences in the international expansion decisions made by commission specialists and transnational agents, on the one hand, and niche entrepreneurs and world-stage aspirants, on the other. Political interference is likely to lead to differences in the quality of decisions made in areas such as the management of overseas subsidiaries, choice of host-country location and choice of foreign joint-venture partners. Further, given the government support available to transnational agents and commission specialists, one may also expect that there will be differences in risk-taking behavior when compared to firms in EMMNE categories that do not receive such support. Similarly, EMMNE categories which pursue broad international diversification may have access to greater opportunities but also face greater risks than those EMMNEs that are more narrowly focused. As a result, we may observe that world-stage aspirants and transnational agents engage in a higher degree of global integration and conduct broader value-chain activities overseas, such as the establishment of foreign R&D facilities.[11] It should be noted that the impact of ownership on the internationalization motives, entry-mode strategies and performance outcomes of EMMNEs has not received much attention in the academic literature (Lin and Farrell, 2013).[12]

EMMNEs' COMPETITIVE ADVANTAGES

EMMNEs possess a number of competitive advantages that account for their continued success in international markets. First, EMMNEs have developed **unique insights** into the needs of their customers in the developing world and have demonstrated a willingness to adapt their products to the needs of the market. Generally, EMMNEs tend to supply products which are sturdy, easy to operate and maintain and, most importantly, cheap. Such products appeal to developing country consumers who are often extremely price sensitive and focused on value for money. In some cases, EMMNEs have also shown a willingness to add special features to their products, features that may be of little importance to consumers in the developed world. We see this, for example, in the case of Haier, the Chinese white goods manufacturer. When engineers from this company went into the rural areas of China to repair washing machines, they often discovered that the machines were being used to wash not just clothes but also vegetables. Western multinationals that sell washing machines in China were also aware of the 'problem' but dismissed it as being attributable to unsophisticated and uneducated consumers who obviously did not know better. The Haier engineers, on the other hand, saw the situation differently and made modifications to their washing machines so they would actually do a better job of washing vegetables. The result was a significant increase in sales of their machines in China.

As noted above, EMMNEs are low-cost producers. While it is true that they operate in countries with lower wage costs than their developed country counterparts, other factors do contribute to their **low-cost structure**. EMMNEs are more likely to operate in second-tier cities where real estate costs are lower; they are also more likely to base their manufacturing operations on the use of second-hand equipment or they may fashion cheaper versions of more expensive western machines at home rather than import them from the West. EMMNEs are also more likely to use a higher proportion of labor to capital in their production operations as would be expected given the abundance of labor in their home countries. EMMNEs also tend to adopt flatter organizational structures with fewer layers of management, and the managers and workers who are employed receive lower salaries and benefits than their counterparts employed by multinationals in the developed world.

The low-cost structure of EMMNEs relates not only to familiar consumer nondurable products but also to their approach to product innovation. These firms are becoming more adept at new product development that is accomplished faster and cheaper than firms in more developed countries. Tata Motors, for example, is now well known for the Nano – a city car

---

[11]   Luo and Tung (2007) op cit.

[12]   Lin, X. and Farrell, C. (2013) 'The internationalization strategies of Chinese state and private sector enterprises in Africa', *Journal of African Business*, 14, 2: 85–95.

that originally retailed for less than $2,000. Regarded as the cheapest car in the world, the Nano was targeted at Indian consumers who typically ride motorcycles and is the product of what has been termed '**frugal engineering**' or '**frugal innovation**'. To bring the Nano to market at the $2,000 price point, Tata Motors levered technologies from the developed world and combined them with its own set of innovations. Tata is reported to have contributed 28 of the 59 patents filed on the Nano[13] but the firm did partner with, for example, Germany's Bosch for the car's engine management system and Johnson Controls of the USA for the seating system. Japan's Toyo contributed the technology used in the engine cooling system.[14]

EMMNEs operate in **institutionally immature business environments** and have learned how to cope and even thrive. These firms must deal with government policies and regulations that change frequently and with little warning, as well as with inept and sometimes corrupt government officials. They learn to move quickly in such environments and to adapt to constant change. EMMNEs have also learned to survive and thrive in an environment of deficient physical infrastructure. Roads and other aspects of their home-country's infrastructure such as electricity supply are often not well developed, requiring that the EMMNE find ways around these constraints. Solutions may be as simple as the use of backup generators or may require that the firm completely rethink its business model. Companies that were formed and became dominant players in such a home environment tend to be highly competitive in more operationally predictable developed countries.

In some instances, EMMNEs have access to considerable **state resources** that provide a major competitive advantage in overseas markets. This is clearly seen in the case of Chinese multinationals such as China National Offshore Oil Company (CNOOC) which has been involved in several high-profile acquisitions in the West, including the 2013 purchase of Canadian Nexen Inc. for $15 billion. CNOOC is a Chinese state-owned company and as such has access to a significant pool of capital. It should also be noted that, in many cases, governments in emerging markets may use their natural resources, large populations or rapid growth to attract foreign investment. In order to invest, however, foreign multinationals must often agree to partner with a local firm and transfer their knowledge and technology. EMMNEs benefit tremendously from such government interventions, acquiring knowledge and skills that improve their competitiveness both at home and abroad.

THE INTERNATIONALIZATION STRATEGIES OF EMMNES

The process of internationalization was discussed in Chapter 7. In that chapter, a number of models were advanced to explain the process and pattern of internationalization and the point was made that most of these are specific to multinationals from developed countries. One framework was discussed, however, that is designed to explain the internationalization behavior of EMMNEs. The springboard model or latecomer perspective was developed by Luo and Tung (2007) and argues that EMMNEs use outward investment as a springboard to overcome disadvantages in their home countries. In essence, these firms make a series of aggressive, high-risk acquisitions in the developed world to give them access to strategic assets. Once acquired, these assets provide EMMNEs with a competitive advantage that may be exploited both at home and abroad. According to this model, EMMNEs' internationalization is spurred by a number of factors that may include a weak institutional framework at home that imposes limits on growth, the arrival of global rivals in their home market or a change in technology that impacts their core business. The drivers of EMMNE internationalization are discussed in more detail below.

It is important to understand that, for EMMNEs, international expansion is a recursive activity that is part of the firm's long-term strategy to become a major global player. Each successive foreign acquisition is designed to correct or compensate for a weakness in the

---

[13]   Anonymous (2010) 'Tata Technologies Limited; Tata Technologies explains Nano frugal engineering', *Asia Business Newsweekly*, August 17, p. 31.

[14]   Prahalad, C.K. and Mashelkar, R.A. (2010) 'Innovation's holy grail', *Harvard Business Review*, 88, 7–8: 134.

firm's competence, such as its ability to develop and manage global brands, to create innovative products or to access foreign customers. When EMMNEs are pursuing acquisitions in developed countries, therefore, their targets are likely to possess advanced manufacturing technologies or strong global brands. In many instances, these developed country targets are in financial trouble and, as a result, are willing to entertain takeover bids from EMMNEs. It also needs to be recognized that compared to multinationals from the developed world EMMNEs are new to the process of internationalization. As latecomers, these firms are under considerable pressure to move quickly and aggressively to overcome their deficiencies and catch up to their developed country rivals.

Box 14.1

Noted strategy scholar Ravi Ramamurti offers a few tips to developed country multinationals on dealing with the EMMNE challenge:

- Take the EMMNE threat seriously. Awareness of the potential challenge must exist at the highest levels within the organization.

- Exercise patience when formulating and implementing strategies in emerging markets. A short-term orientation is unlikely to produce satisfactory results. It may take up to a decade to find the right business model, develop a workable portfolio of products for those markets and price them appropriately.

- Strive to become deeply engaged in emerging markets. Western firms should seek to become an Indian firm when operating in India and a Chinese firm when tackling the Chinese market. Developed country multinationals should seek to address all key segments of these markets and not just the premium segment or the urban segment.

- Demonstrate a willingness to learn from their competitors and their customers in emerging markets. Developed country multinationals must learn how to make products more cheaply and how to appeal to low-income consumers in emerging country markets.

- Conduct R&D in emerging markets and innovate specifically for those markets. Western firms must be prepared to develop products and services specifically for consumers in emerging markets – innovations that could potentially be transferred to other emerging markets and perhaps even back to developed country markets around the world.

- Develop a strategy that sees emerging markets as places with talent that may be used to produce goods and services that may be sold around the world; as markets with a large and growing middle class; and as centers of innovation. Developed country multinationals that are able to develop a comprehensive strategy that levers all three will reap unique synergies.

Source

Ramamurti, R. (2012) 'Competing with emerging market multinationals', *Business Horizons*, 55: 241–9.

Expand Your Knowledge

Criavegna, L., Fitzgerald, R. and Kundu, S. (2013) 'Operating in emerging markets,' Financial Times (FT) Press, New York: Pearson.

This book provides practical approaches for companies interested in pursuing opportunties in emerging markets.

In some cases, EMMNEs may use international expansion as a springboard to counter the attacks of developed country multinationals that have entered their home market. As noted earlier, EMMNEs generally possess a strong home-country position and may derive most of their revenues from their domestic market. Incursions by advanced country multinationals may, therefore, force EMMNEs to react by pursuing opportunities in developed countries. **Institutional voids** are also a major catalyst for the international expansion of EMMNEs. These refer to weaknesses in the home-country environment that place limits on the growth and development of EMMNEs and include poor enforcement of commercial laws, a judicial system that is not transparent, a lack of intellectual property protection and underdeveloped markets. Political instability, corruption, government bureaucracy and government interference are also factors that lead EMMNEs to pursue international opportunities.

It is also the case that EMMNEs, while they may lack technology and the capacity to innovate, have the ability to go into the market and purchase much of the advanced technology and expertise they need. EMMNEs have expertise in the mass production of standardized products that has been developed over many years, serving as OEM partners to multinationals from developed countries. Access to advanced technologies and expertise in mass production are competitive advantages that can be exploited in other emerging and developing markets and, therefore, serve as a springboard for international expansion. The demand for technologically standardized products is very high in emerging and developing country markets, making expansion into these markets an attractive proposition for EMMNEs. With their emphasis on low-cost manufacturing, EMMNEs are able to offer customers in emerging and developing country markets a better value proposition than more established developed country multinationals that may have been in those markets for many years. This is discussed in more detail in the following section.

THE MARKETING STRATEGIES OF EMMNEs

The study of EMMNEs is still very much in its infancy and little is currently known about the marketing strategies of EMMNEs.[15] Indeed, much of the marketing theory developed over the past few decades has been based on the study of US multinationals and there is concern that these theories do not fully explain the behavior of EMMNEs. How did these firms transform themselves from low-cost manufacturers of their own weak consumer brands or from contract manufacturers of branded products of the dominant developed country multinationals into major competitors in their own right? How did a company such as Haier capture a 5 percent share of the white goods market and become the fourth largest player in that space? How did Huawei, also a Chinese firm, become the number one challenger of Cisco Systems in the telecommunications industry? How could Wipro and Infosys, two Indian firms, post higher levels of profitability than their major developed country rivals, EDS and Accenture? What about companies such as Samsung and Hyundai from Korea, and their ability to compete head to head with major rivals in the smartphone and auto sectors, respectively?

The above questions have been taken up in a recent book by Chattopadhyay, Batra and Ozsomer (2012).[16] The authors utilize a case-study approach, interviewing executives from some 39 EMMNEs, including HTC (Taiwan), LG Electronics (South Korea), Haier (China), Pollo Campero (Guatemala) and Natura (Brazil). State-owned multinationals were excluded from the study. The authors make the point that after many years serving as contract manufacturers, OEM and private label suppliers, EMMNEs now have the vision, confidence and expertise to become global players in their own right. These firms no longer want to stand in the shadow

---

[15] Fan, Y. (2008) 'The rise of emerging market multinationals and the impact on marketing', *Marketing Intelligence and Planning*, 26, 4: 353–8.

[16] Chattopadhyay, A., Batra, R. and Ozsomer, A. (2012) *The New Emerging Market Multinationals: Four Strategies for Disrupting Markets and Building Brands*. New York: McGraw-Hill.

of developed country multinationals but instead want to build global businesses and their own global brands. A company such as Taiwan's Hon Hai/Foxconn Technology Group, for example, has for many years served as a contract manufacturer of Apple's iPods and iPhones, earning the 3–8 percent gross margin typical of firms in that industry. This company now has its sights set on developing its own base of brand-loyal global customers and on earning the 40 percent gross margin that Apple enjoys.

From the case studies of the EMMNEs included in their research, the authors have identified four strategies that are used by these firms in building their global businesses (see Figure 14.3). The authors note that while the four strategies are conceptually distinct, in the real world there may be some overlap. The strategic alternatives proposed are based first on the customer segment the EMMNE chooses to focus on, i.e. emerging markets that are similar to its own home country or dissimilar developed country markets. Penetration of similar emerging market countries is likely to be faster and easier for the EMMNE than penetration of developed country markets. The latter are likely to require more time and a much higher level of resource commitment than the former.

Strategic alternatives are also dependent on the competence that the EMMNE levers in addressing the above market segments. In this regard, the EMMNE may opt to rely on its existing competence such as low-cost leadership to extend the firm's activities into new customer segments. The authors refer to this as **mechanistic extension**. This option requires that the firm have mastery of a narrow but extendable technology, that it be committed to its focus on cost cutting to maintain its advantage, and is able to find customers in international markets that are similar to those in its home country. Alternatively, the EMMNE may opt to rely on **dynamic evolution** in which the firm develops new capabilities such as product design for global markets, R&D, global brand management expertise or advanced manufacturing technologies. This option will require that the firm develop the ability to generate insights into the needs of foreign customers and have the competence to lever these insights. Rather than emphasize extendable technologies and cost cutting, the focus with this option will be on flexible manufacturing capabilities, innovation and R&D.

FIGURE 14.3   EMMNE Marketing Strategies

	Customer Segment	
	Focus on Similar Emerging Markets	*Focus on Dissimilar Developed Country Markets*
Mechanistic Extension	**Knowledge Leverager**	**Cost Leader**
Dynamic Evolution	**Niche Customizer**	**Global Brand Builder**

Source: Adapted from Chattopadhyay, A. Batra, R. and Ozsomer, A. (2012) *The New Emerging Market Multinationals: Four Strategies for Disrupting Markets and Building Brands.* New York: McGraw-Hill.

Based on the customer segment to be addressed and the competence to be levered or developed, four strategic options are possible:

> *Cost leaders* – these EMMNEs lever their existing low-cost structure and large-scale volume to extend their operations to developed country markets. EMMNEs in this category have taken advantage of their country's low manufacturing costs and large domestic markets to create large-scale operations. These firms are relentless in driving down manufacturing costs and have mastered the art of frugal engineering. They essentially market low-priced products to price-sensitive consumers in both developed and developing countries. Cost leaders typically service their own large domestic market and maintain contract manufacturing arrangements with firms in the developed world, allowing them to reap the economies of large-scale production. In essence, firms in this category

exploit the competitive advantage normally associated with firms in emerging markets, i.e. cheap labor, abundant natural resources and a large domestic market. Arçelik, a Turkish manufacturer of home appliances, and Mahindra Tractors of India, have become world leaders based on this strategy. Mahindra Tractors, for example, is now the largest tractor manufacturer in the world based on number of units sold. Other companies in this category include the Indian pharmaceutical company Ranbaxy and Turkey's Temsa.

Knowledge leveragers – EMMNEs in the knowledge leverager category capitalize on their experience in building products that are able to stand up to the harsh physical conditions found in emerging markets. These firms manufacture tough, rugged products that can be sold to the less affluent customers found in emerging markets similar to their home countries. In essence, these firms, based on many years of operating in a harsh environment, have acquired knowledge and skills that may be extended to other emerging market environments where conditions are similar. The products and brands marketed by the knowledge leverager are low-priced, functional and durable and, therefore, appeal to cost-conscious consumers in emerging markets outside the firm's home country. In addition, the knowledge leverager is already adept at managing in an institutionally immature environment and is able to adjust to volatile economic conditions, corruption, bureaucracy, capricious government policies and political interference. Mahindra and Mahindra is an example of a knowledge leverager. This Indian firm is a major player in the utility vehicle market, manufacturing rugged cars, trucks and commercial vehicles that are well suited to the poor road conditions found in most emerging markets.

Niche customizers – the previous two strategies are not new. One would expect EMMNEs to follow a strategy based on low wages in their home countries or one that focuses on similar consumers in other emerging markets. We do, however, observe EMMNEs that develop and lever entirely new capabilities to exploit opportunities in developed and emerging markets. Niche customizers use dynamic evolution to target consumers in emerging markets that are similar to their home countries. These EMMNEs focus on small, neglected and underserved segments of the market primarily (but not exclusively) in developing markets. Marico, an Indian company in the health and wellness industry, is an example of a niche customizer. The firm is a leader in the haircare industry and targets markets in South Asia, the Middle East and Africa.

Niche customizers lever their capabilities in frugal innovation to adapt and customize their product offerings for a well-defined geographic market. As with the knowledge leveragers, niche customizers also make use of their experience in manufacturing low-cost products for the poorer segments of the market in developing countries, and, because they typically own their production facilities, they can be flexible in responding to changes in customer needs. Further, because they are adept at managing in institutionally immature markets, this category of EMMNE has little difficulty adapting to the business environment in other developing countries. It is important to note that niche customizers have a distinct advantage over multinationals from the developed world that may also be interested in pursuing emerging markets. In entering emerging markets, developed country multinationals typically use a standardized product approach which leaves them vulnerable to niche customizers that are willing to adapt their products to the needs of consumers in these markets. Also, niche customizers focus on smaller underserved market segments that are unlikely to attract the attention of large multinationals from developed countries, or they may focus on segments which developed country firms simply don't understand. Savola Foods of Saudi Arabia, for example, has built a successful business in the edible oils, pasta and sugar market but does not compete directly with major companies such as Unilever.

Global brand builders – firms in this category utilize a marketing strategy that stresses the development of innovative technologies and products and the targeting of consumers in the more advanced countries. Global brand builders utilize a strategy of focused innovation in addressing markets in developed countries. They take advantage of the low manufacturing cost structure of their home markets, as well as of low-cost home-country R&D in the implementation of their marketing strategies. Global brand builders are also prepared to supplement these competences with overseas licensing agreements and foreign acquisitions in order to fill holes in their design and engineering skills. While global brand builders may tackle markets in the more advanced countries, they typically focus on a very narrow segment of the market. For example, the Taiwanese company, HTC, is focused on the smartphone market and has become a leader in the manufacture of Android and Windows mobile devices. Founded in 1997, the firm has become the third largest handset maker after Apple and Samsung and has become known for innovation in the smartphone market.

Natura is another company categorized as a global brand builder. This Brazilian firm has discovered approaches to sustainably harvesting indigenous plants from the Amazon forests. The firm has also developed competences in the identification and extraction of active ingredients used in the manufacture of a range of cosmetics. Natura has successfully sold its line of skincare products in France, the USA and the UK. As with HTC, Natura levers its competences in low-cost R&D and low-cost manufacturing to build market share in developed country markets. It should be noted that despite the fact that their research is reasonably sophisticated, companies such as Natura and HTC do not conduct R&D on the same scale as developed country multinationals such as L'Oreal or IBM. These companies have, however, learned how to focus their R&D efforts in precisely those areas where they have the greatest impact and create the most value for their customers. Chattopadhyay, Batra and Ozsomer (2012) point out that in 2009 Natura invested only 3 percent of its net income in R&D, which was much less than its developed country rivals. Despite this relatively low investment, the company was able to produce a new product every three working days, which is on a par with developed country multinationals such as 3M. In fact, in 2010 almost 66 percent of Natura's billings came from products that were launched in the previous two years. This figure has been relatively consistent for the company over the years.

SUMMARY

This chapter has focused on a new class of multinational enterprises that some scholars and industry practitioners argue are poised to become the dominant force in international business. These emerging market multinationals originate from countries such as India, China, Russia and Brazil which are in the process of reform and are currently grappling with a range of political, institutional and macroeconomic challenges. EMMNEs have been able to adapt to these home-country problems and have embarked on a process of rapid internationalization. Further, these firms have been able to penetrate both developed and other emerging market countries in the absence of the traditional firm-specific advantages possessed by Triad multinationals. EMMNEs typically do not possess, for example, advanced technologies, global brands or superior international marketing expertise. Despite these country- and firm-level constraints, EMMNEs have gone on to challenge developed country markets in their home countries and around the world.

This chapter has presented a typology of EMMNEs and discussed the springboard model which attempts to explain their internationalization. It was argued that these firms internationalize to overcome the limitations imposed by their home-country environments and do so through a series of aggressive moves. These strategic moves include the acquisition of targets in developed countries which allow EMMNEs to fill in the gaps in their capabilities. It was pointed out that EMMNEs already possess a number of competitive advantages that may be levered to address markets in both developed and developing countries. An ability to operate in institutionally immature environments, frugal innovation, low-cost manufacturing capabilities, insights into the behavior of emerging market customers, and access to state resources in some cases are among the advantages that provide EMMNEs with a competitive edge.

In the above discussion of EMMNE strategy, the point was made that little is really known about their approach to international marketing and global brand development. This knowledge deficit has been partially addressed by a new conceptual model that relates EMMNE competence to the customer segments to be targeted. Based on a case study of EMMNEs from a number of countries, the authors of this study argue that these firms may employ mechanistic extension or dynamic evolution when targeting developed country markets with dissimilar customers or emerging market countries with customers similar to those in their home markets. The authors of the study argue further that strategies predicated on mechanistic extension are consistent with expectations of how these firms should behave but strategies based on dynamic evolution are new.

? discussion questions

1. What are emerging market multinationals (EMMNEs) and why are they important in the study of global marketing?

2. What can developed country multinationals do strategically to defend against the challenge presented by emerging market multinationals?

3. Describe a model that may be used to explain the internationalization of emerging market multinationals.

4. Emerging market multinationals generally do not possess firm-specific assets such as strong global brands and advanced technologies. What then are their sources of competitive advantage?

5. How did the Haier Group become the fourth largest player in the global white goods industry?

6. Explain the global brand-builder strategy used by firms such as Natura from Brazil.

7. What are the key differences between emerging market multinationals that follow a cost leader strategy and those that utilize a global brand-builder strategy?

Real World Challenges

The Deal for Smithfield Foods

Charles Patrick was a bit apprehensive as he put together notes for a meeting with the US Committee on Foreign Investment. This would probably be the most important meeting of his long executive career at Smithfield Foods and he was decidedly nervous. As president and CEO of the company, Charles had been asked to appear before the Committee to provide information on a potential acquisition of his company by Shuanghui Group of China. Charles knew that much depended on the outcome of this meeting, including the fate of the company where he had worked for 20 years and thousands of its employees and customers around the world. He needed to consider every angle and formulate a consistent position before his 8.00am meeting tomorrow. If the Committee on Foreign Investment voted 'no', the deal would be dead and that would have potentially serious implications for Smithfield. Charles was well aware that Charoen Pokphand Foods of Thailand and Brazil's JBS SA had both walked away from the purchase of Smithfield Foods, leaving Shuanghui as the only suitor. He stared again at the press release announcing the acquisition which was subject to regulatory approval. The Chinese company had offered to acquire Smithfield for $4.7 billion ($7.1 billion including debt). If the deal is approved, Smithfield would cease to trade on the US stock market as an independent company and would become a wholly-owned subsidiary of Shuanghui.

Founded in 1936, Virginia-based Smithfield Foods is one of the world's largest hog producers. The firm brings some 8 million animals to market each year, owns 460 farms and has contracts with an additional 2,100 farms across 12 US states. Along with four other firms, Smithfield Foods controls 73 percent of the US pork-processing industry. The company's major brands include household names such as Armour, Farmland and Healthy Ones. Most of Smithfield's sales are generated in the USA. The company experienced losses in 2008 and 2009 as hog farmers were hit with rapidly escalating grain prices brought on by increased demand for corn for ethanol production which pushed up prices. An industry-wide glut of hogs also squeezed Smithfield's margins and made the company a target for acquisition. Shuanghui, on the other hand, is China's largest hog producer and is privately held. Unlike some other emerging market multinationals, it is not controlled by the state, although the company's chairman is well connected in Communist Party circles. The company was founded in Henan Province, China, in 1969 and now produces over 2.7 million tons of meat per year and operates facilities in 13 Chinese provinces. The company has annual revenues of $6.2 billion and assets of $3.5 billion.

As Charles considered his position, he began to reflect on the possible reasons Shuanghui would acquire Smithfield at a 31 percent premium to the company's closing share price on the day the announcement was made. Charles was aware that Shuanghui had been implicated in a case in which Chinese food inspectors discovered clenbuterol in some of its pork products. Clenbuterol is an additive which speeds up muscle growth in pigs but is banned in both China and the USA as it causes nausea, vomiting, headache and an irregular heartbeat in humans. Death may sometimes occur. In announcing the acquisition, Shuanghui had indicated that it intended to export Smithfield pork products to China and not import Chinese pork into the USA. On announcing the deal, Shuanghui's chairman declared: 'Together we will be able to meet the growing demand in China for pork by importing high-quality meat products from the USA, while continuing to serve markets in the United States and around the world.' Clearly, this approach would make sense given that demand for pork was increasing in China as its middle class expanded but demand was falling in the USA. In fact, if this was indeed the intention, then marketing a well-respected American brand in China would go a long way to restoring consumer confidence in Shuanghui's products. Prior to the acquisition, Smithfield already exported 25 percent of its output to China. Charles wondered, however, whether this was in fact going to be the strategy going forward. Once they acquired Smithfield's managerial and technical expertise and knowledge of the US market, what would prevent Shuanghui from exporting Chinese pork to the USA? Economic growth was slowing in China after all, so who could predict whether demand from the middle class would continue to be robust? Charles also wondered whether his management team would face any pressure from the company's new bosses to lower quality standards in the US operation. This was a major consideration given that Smithfield had built a solid reputation for quality over its many years of operation.

Shuanghui had also pledged that it would be business as usual at Smithfield after the acquisition and that it would keep the existing management team in place. The union representing Smithfield workers was also

(Continued)

(Continued)

supportive of the deal as Shuanghui had insisted that all existing collective agreements would remain in place after the acquisition. Again, Charles wondered whether the company's workers and their union could rely on this once Shuanghui better understood the economics of production in the USA. Would there be pressure to renegotiate these agreements and attempt to reduce wages and benefits?

As Charles continued work on his presentation, he was well aware that the Shuanghui offer was not the only option available. While two potential suitors had already walked away, institutional investors, Starboard Value LP and Continental Grain, had been pushing to break up Smithfield into separate businesses to unlock shareholder value rather than simply accept Shuanghui's single all-cash transaction. Continental, for example, had proposed that the company be split into three businesses. The first would sell pork and packaged meats, the second would operate hog farms and a third division would be based outside the USA. The Continental proposal was tabled after Smithfield reported disappointing results that trailed its major rivals, Tyson Foods and Hormel Foods. Would such reorganization solve the company's performance problems or was it too late for that to be a consideration? As Charles glanced at the clock in his office, he smiled. Given the number of Smithfield shares he owned, if the Committee voted in favor of the all-cash acquisition he stood to benefit personally to the tune of some $4 million. He, however, quickly brushed aside those thoughts, recognizing that the position he articulated in the morning should reflect what was best for the company, its shareholders and all the company's stakeholders. It was on that basis that he needed to decide whether he supported the deal.

Sources

Bloomberg (2013) Shuanghui Agrees to Acquire Smithfield Foods for $4.72b. Available at: www.bloomberg.com/news/2013-05-29/shuanghui-group-said-to-near-agreement-to-buy-smithfield-foods.html, accessed July 14, 2013.

Bloomberg (2013) Smithfield Investor Urges Hog Farmer to Consider Breakup. Available at: www.bloomberg.com/news/2013-06-17/smithfield-investor-urges-u-s-hog-producer-to-consider-breakup.html, accessed July 14, 2013.

English.caixin.com (2013) Dissecting Shuanghui's Big Deal with Smithfield Foods. Available at: http://english.caixin.com/2013-06-04/100537120.html, accessed July 14, 2013.

Kavilanz, P. (2013) Smithfield Foods Bought by Chinese Meat Producer. Available at: http://money.cnn.com/2013/05/29/news/companies/smithfield-foods/index.html, accessed July 14, 2013.

Kesmodel, D. (n.d.) Chinese Firm Agrees to Buy Smithfield. Available at: http://online.wsj.com/article/SB10001424127887324412604578512722044165756.html, accessed July 14, 2013.

WSJ.com (2013) The Smithfield Deal: China Bringing Home the American Bacon. Available at: http://blogs.wsj.com/corporate-intelligence/2013/05/29/the-smithfield-deal-china-bringing-home-the-american-bacon/, accessed July 14, 2013.

Discussion questions

1. State the problem that Charles faces.
2. Identify the options available to Charles. Be sure to identify more than one.
3. Based on the options identified above, recommend a course of action for the company. Be sure to provide a rationale and make a decision.

FURTHER READING

Accenture (2008) Multi-Polar World 2: The Rise of the Emerging-Market Multinational. Available at: www.accenture.com/sitecollectiondocuments/pdf/mpw2.pdf

Chattopadhyay, A., Batra, R. and Ozsomer, A. (2012) *The New Emerging Market Multinationals: Four Strategies for Disrupting Markets and Building Brands*. London: McGraw-Hill.

Fan, Y. (2008) 'The rise of emerging market multinationals and the impact on marketing', *Marketing Intelligence & Planning*, 26, 4: 353–8.

Ramamurti, R. (2012) 'Competing with emerging market multinationals', *Business Horizons*, 55: 241–9.

THE FUTURE OF GLOBAL MARKETING

INTRODUCTION

This final chapter of the text examines the future of global marketing. The forces shaping the development of the discipline will be discussed, as will careers in global marketing and the skills and attitudes required to be successful. It is clear that the environment within which global marketing managers must operate is constantly changing. The sub-prime financial crisis that rocked the USA and the global economy in the latter part of the 2000s is a case in point, as is the sovereign debt crisis that engulfed the European Union beginning with peripheral countries such as Greece and Ireland. These macro-economic shocks have continued to take their toll on business and consumer confidence with a resultant decline in the level of global economic activity. Austerity measures imposed to rein in public sector debt have created significant hardship for consumers and sparked social unrest in numerous countries across Europe. Coordinated efforts by central banks around the world to utilize conventional and unconventional monetary tools to stimulate the global economy have raised concerns about asset prices, inflation and the prospects for more robust economic growth.

It is not just Europe and the USA that currently face severe macro-economic headwinds. Japan has been mired in recession for over two decades as it continues to grapple with the fallout of the collapse of its real estate and stock market bubbles in the 1980s, and even the fast-growing emerging market economies discussed in the previous chapter have seen their economic growth rates moderate. China, for example, having posted double-digit growth rates for many years, has seen its growth decline to the high single digits in part due to weakened global demand. These and other challenges complicate the implementation of global marketing strategy but also create opportunities for the astute global marketer. In this chapter, we will attempt to delineate the skills and attitudes that are required to be successful in the global marketing environment of the future.

FORCES SHAPING THE DISCIPLINE OF GLOBAL MARKETING

It is difficult to predict the challenges that will be faced by global marketing managers in the years and decades ahead, or what new opportunities may suddenly emerge. What is certain is that global marketing as a discipline will continue to be shaped by the forces of globalization and that international markets will continue to be fast paced and dynamic. To be successful in the future, global marketers will need not only the technical skills and knowledge to respond positively to an increasingly complex international business environment, but also a range of non-technical skills.

It may be useful to look back at how the field of global marketing has evolved before attempting to predict its future trajectory. Noted international marketing scholars Michael Czinkota and Coskun Samli have suggested that the field of international marketing has evolved through four phases since the mid-1940s[1] (see Figure 15.1). According to these scholars, the period 1945–1964 was characterized by acute product shortages and strong demand as countries struggled to rebuild in the aftermath of World War II. With product shortages, little effort was required for companies to sell their products in foreign markets and indeed marketers made a relatively minor contribution to their firms' overall sales and profitability. Proactive international marketing approaches were not used at this time. Trade liberalization efforts under GATT were slowly opening up foreign markets and the concept of international marketing was only beginning to take shape. In general, companies did not have global ambitions at this stage and many were in fact quite inward-looking.

FIGURE 15.1   The Development of International Marketing

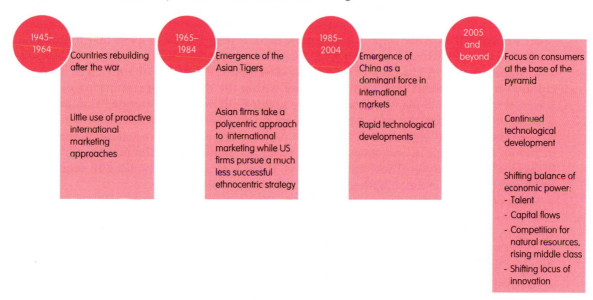

The years 1965–1984 saw the emergence of international organizations. During this period, the so-called Asian Tigers (Hong Kong, Singapore, Taiwan and South Korea) began to exert their influence on foreign markets using Japanese-style marketing techniques. Companies from Japan and the four Tigers transitioned from producers of cheap imitation products to innovators with their own global brands. These included companies such as Hyundai and

[1] See Czinkota, M.R. and Samli, C.A. (2012) 'An analysis of the people dimension in international marketing', in T.C. Melewar and S. Gupta (eds) *Strategic International Marketing: An Advanced Perspective*. London: Palgrave Macmillian. See also Czinkota, M.R. and Samli, C.A. (2007) 'The remarkable performance of international marketing in the second half of the twentieth century', *European Business Review*, 19, 4: 316–31.

Samsung. As noted by Czinkota and Samli (2012), it is at this time that differences in marketing approach began to appear between US companies on the one hand and companies from Japan and the four Tigers on the other. While US firms remained mired in an ethnocentric approach, Asian companies were committed to a polycentric orientation, catering to the unique needs of customers in the various country markets in which they operated. US firms attempted to merely extend their domestic strategies to foreign markets which proved to be a much less successful strategy. It is during this period that we see the emergence of international marketing strategies and their implementation.

The years 1985–2004 saw Asian firms and particularly those from China take on a more important role in international markets by emphasizing low prices, improved product quality and delivery efficiency. Trade liberalization was proceeding apace as was European unification and the privatization of state enterprises in many parts of the world. During this time, products were becoming increasingly sophisticated and technology was advancing at a rapid pace. The Internet, for example, brought consumers in countries around the world closer to the companies and brands that interested them and allowed firms in third-world countries to participate more fully in the global economy. During this period, international marketers were forced to deal with increasingly technical problems as their companies' products entered new foreign markets.

The final period in the evolution covers the years post-2005. As noted above, it is difficult to predict what new challenges will confront the discipline of global marketing in the years ahead or what new opportunities may surface. The following trends may, however, offer some guidance.

Rise of the developing country consumer: In the coming years, we may expect to see firms focus more on reaching the poorer segments of the world's population, i.e. the large mass of consumers at the base of the pyramid. As growth in the developed world slows, companies will have to seek out opportunities in developing country markets. These markets are characterized by large and growing populations but low per capita incomes. These characteristics necessitate that companies make adjustments to their marketing strategies in order to capitalize on the opportunities presented. It may also be argued that international marketing theories which have been formulated for developed country markets may not apply and entirely new frameworks will need to be developed. These new theories will have to be culture or group specific and developed from within the developing country markets themselves, if international marketers are to truly understand how they operate.[2] Companies will need to recognize that the nation can no longer be taken as the basis of segmentation as the base of the pyramid segment in fact crosses national boundaries. For example, the Chinese in Indonesia, Singapore and Malaysia have more in common than the Malays, Chinese and Indians within Malaysia. Tackling consumers at the base of the pyramid will require some rethinking of international marketing theory and application.

Technology: One may expect that in the coming decades technological progress will proceed at an ever-increasing pace, leading to the development of entirely new products that appeal to consumers around the world. Technology may be expected to impact all facets of business from communication to improved manufacturing processes, business models and data analytic techniques. New technologies may be expected to drive down the cost of products, speed up the product development process and empower consumers around the world to make more informed purchase decisions. It is likely that the global marketer will, in the future, face even more compressed product life cycles, increased competitive pressures and a more demanding consumer.

Shifting balance of economic power: The balance of economic power is shifting away from the Triad to a diverse group of developing countries around the world. Consulting firm Accenture makes reference to a new multi-polar world in which developing countries such

---

2   Fletcher, R. and Chikweche, T. (2012) 'Future directions in international marketing: The decade ahead', in T.C. Melewar and S. Gupta (eds) *Strategic International Marketing: An Advanced Perspective*. London: Palgrave Macmillan.

as India and China will make up an increasingly significant share of global trade, investment and output.[3] In the coming decades, we will see multiple centers of economic power driven by a confluence of mutually reinforcing trends such as rapid advances in communication technologies, government policies to increase economic openness and the increasing size and reach of multinational enterprises as they seek out new markets around the world. Accenture views this multi-polarity as a deeper form of globalization but one in which the emerging market economies play an active role in shaping the direction. According to the authors of the Accenture study, the new multi-polar world is characterized by five key dimensions:

- **Talent** is becoming a global commodity for which firms will have to compete. As western societies grapple with the impact of an aging population, developing countries boast rapidly growing populations with a significant percentage of young people. According to the Accenture report, about 97 percent of the 438 million people to be added to the global workforce by 2050 will come from developing countries. Western multinationals are increasingly looking to developing countries to recruit skilled workers but so too are emerging marketing multinationals as they become more competitive in markets around the world.

- **Capital flows** will also reflect the shifting balance of power around the world. Developed countries have historically been the major source of foreign direct investment. This is changing as emerging marketing multinationals expand and seek new foreign markets. The percentage of global investment accounted for by emerging market countries may be expected to increase significantly in the coming decades. Portfolio investment flows into emerging market economies are also expected to increase as global investors seek out higher returns in markets with superior growth prospects.

- **Competition for natural resources** is also likely to intensify in the coming decades as emerging market economies such as China attempt to sustain their high rates of economic growth. Energy, minerals and water are all likely to be the focus of increased competition for many years into the future. Accenture notes that since 2000 emerging market countries have been responsible for 85 percent of the increase in world energy demand and that these countries will continue to account for the bulk of energy demand up to 2030. At the same time that global demand for resources is increasing, supply has become more constrained. Regions of the globe such as Sub-Saharan Africa will continue to attract interest not only from traditional western multinationals but also increasingly from state-owned enterprises in China (Lin and Farrell, 2013).[4]

- **A rising middle class in emerging countries** is another characteristic of the new multi-polar world. Rising incomes and employment in these countries are creating a burgeoning middle class. Emerging market countries are expected to account for 50 percent of world consumption by 2025, when adjusted for purchasing power. China, for example, has become one of the top three markets for cars in the world and figures significantly in other product categories such as mobile phones. Mexico has become the second largest soft drinks market in the world, illustrating the point that an increasing number of consumers in the emerging markets are experiencing growing incomes and economic prosperity.

- **The locus of innovation** is also shifting. Innovation has historically been centered in the Triad with its advanced technology, sophisticated consumers and highly skilled workers. This is changing and will likely continue to change over the coming decades. The Accenture report notes that many emerging market countries are moving up the value chain at an unprecedented pace as they increase their investment in R&D and education and make strategic investments in exciting new industries. Indeed, clusters of innovation are springing up in geographic locations such as Beijing, Bangalore, Greater Seoul and Krakow.

The above trends will have an important bearing on the environment that the global marketing manager will have to face. To compete effectively, the global marketer will need a range of skills, as discussed below.

---

[3]   Accenture (2008) Multi-Polar World 2: The Rise of the Emerging-Market Multinational. Available at: www.accenture.com/sitecollectiondocuments/pdf/mpw2.pdf

[4]   Lin, X. and Farrell, C. (2013) 'The internationalization strategies of Chinese state and private sector enterprises in Africa', *Journal of African Business*, 14, 2: 85–95.

Real World Challenges

Product innovation at Heinz

In late 2009, Mike Pretty was appointed to the position of Vice President, Global Ketchup, Health & Wellness, and Marketing Development for the HJ Heinz Company. According to a press release, in this new role Pretty 'will lead the Global Tomato Ketchup Taskforce, reporting directly to Heinz Chairman, President and Chief Executive Officer Bill Johnson. He will work with the country marketing teams around the world to drive volume and share growth, especially in key developed markets, where it is imperative that Heinz continue to increase the level of innovation on flagship products. He will also facilitate best practice sharing across Heinz business units with the goal of driving the development and implementation of exciting new product and packaging ideas'. In his new role, Mr Pretty will also be involved in the Heinz Marketing Academy, a training program designed to enhance the marketing skills of the company's employees. He will, however, continue to be based in the Heinz Wattie office in Auckland.

PHOTO 15.1

Mike Pretty started his career at Heinz Wattie in New Zealand in 1989 as a project manager for the company's pet food division. He excelled and was assigned increasingly important roles across the organization, becoming Director of Marketing in 2002. Prior to joining Heinz Wattie, however, Mr Pretty worked in the UK as a graduate trainee at one of Europe's largest dairy companies. After two years in this position, he got the urge to travel and planned to visit New Zealand, Australia and the USA before returning to the UK. This itinerary would not materialize and Mr Pretty would end up staying in New Zealand and joining the Heinz organization.

Sources

Boardroom Insiders website: www.boardroominsiders.com/executive-profiles/8132/H.J.-Heinz-Company/Mike-Pretty, accessed May 12, 2013.

Heinz Corporate website: www.heinz.com/our-company/corporate-governance/executive-management.aspx, accessed May 12, 2013.

Heinz Watties website: www.heinzwatties.co.nz/What-s-New/Heinz-Wattie-s-marketer-appointed-to-key-role-in-Heinz, accessed May 12, 2013.

THE KNOWLEDGE AND SKILLS OF THE GLOBAL MARKETING MANAGER

The activities in which the global marketing manager is engaged have been discussed throughout this book. In essence, the global marketer is responsible for the design and execution of the firm's marketing strategy in all the various foreign markets in which it operates. The global marketing manager is also responsible for the coordination of marketing activities across these markets as the firm attempts to take advantage of the synergies that may exist from operating in multiple countries. To perform these activities successfully requires that the global marketer adjust to changes taking place in the external environment as these have a bearing on the outcomes realized.

KNOWLEDGE REQUIREMENTS

The knowledge required of the global marketing manager may be categorized as follows:[5]

- country market knowledge
- cross-border transactions knowledge
- cross-cultural knowledge (see Figure 15.2).

FIGURE 15.2   Hard Skills Required of the Global Marketing Manager

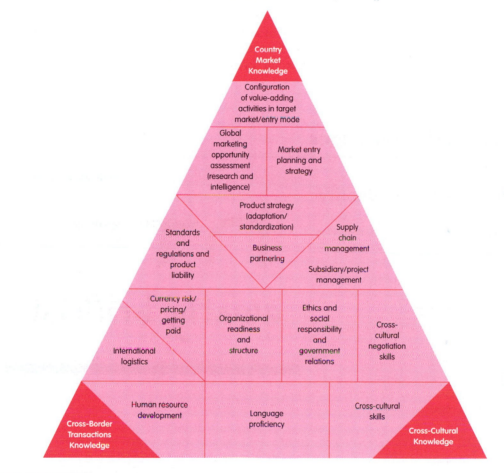

Source: Cavusgil (1998).

These three knowledge bases are interrelated and give rise to a menu of more specific bodies of knowledge/skills that are central to success as a global marketing manager. These have all been discussed in previous chapters of this text. For example, consideration of how the firm's value-chain activities should be configured and what market entry strategy should be employed has been addressed, as has the identification and analysis of global

---

[5]   Cavusgil, S.T. (1998) 'Perspectives: Knowledge development in international marketing', *Journal of International Marketing*, 6, 2: 103–12.

market opportunities and the selection of foreign business partners. The global marketer's ability to understand the rules and regulations that govern the marketing of the firm's products in the foreign country was also flagged as important when considering entry into new foreign markets.

Also important are strategies and tools for the management of exchange rate risk, such as the use of forward contracts and currency options; and the setting of foreign prices and techniques such as letters of credit and documentary collections to ensure that the firm is paid for products shipped. Understanding the logistical issues involved in getting products to final consumers in disparate foreign countries is also an important body of knowledge. Figure 15.2 also suggests that the global marketing manager should develop an understanding of cross-cultural issues and have some facility with the languages of the firm's host countries. As discussed in a previous chapter, the design of the global firm's organizational structure and the management of expatriate and host-country personnel have a bearing on the overall success of the international venture. The global marketing manager should have some appreciation of the organizational issues related to the firm's efforts to operate in foreign markets.

Real World Challenges

HTC updates its brand identity

In January 2013, Benjamin Ho became HTC's third chief marketing officer in two years. HTC, the Taiwanese manufacturer of smartphones, has been struggling in recent years with sales down some 41 percent in the fourth quarter of 2012 compared to the previous year. HTC has been losing market share to major rivals such as Apple and Samsung. In an interview with the *Wall Street Journal*, Mr Ho promised to adopt a bolder approach to the company's marketing efforts. He noted that the company would be retiring its tagline 'Quietly Brilliant' from its product ads, stating 'We have a lot of innovations but we haven't been loud enough'.

PHOTO 15.2

Benjamin Ho joined HTC following stints as vice president of business strategy and marketing for Taiwanese telecom operator FarEasTone Telecommunications Co. and as VP and chief marketing officer for Motorola Asia Pacific Ltd. He has also served as director at BBDO Greater China, Dentsu and Young and Rubicam International. In his new role of chief marketing officer at HTC, Ho will report directly to the company's CEO and has been tasked with leading HTC's next wave of brand building and with creating awareness of the company and its products. Benjamin earned a Business Studies and Marketing Diploma at Stamford College in Singapore.

Sources

Dou, E. (2013) 'HTC's marketing chief takes bolder approach', *Wall Street Journal*. Available at: http://blogs.wsj.com/digits/2013/03/25/htcs-marketing-chief-taking-bolder-approach/, accessed May 13, 2013.

HTC website: www.htc.com/www/about/newsroom/2012/2012-11-28-HTC-appoints-Benjamin-Ho-Chief-Marketing-Officer

Whittaker, Z. (2013) HTC Hires New Marketing Chief in Bounce Back Hopes. Available at: www.zdnet.com/htc-hires-new-marketing-chief-in-bounce-back-hopes-7000008020/, accessed May 13, 2013.

As has been stressed in this text, operating outside of the firm's home market will bring the firm's managers head to head with thorny ethical issues. It is imperative that the global marketing manager has some training on and appreciation for what is, and is not, considered ethical behavior in the foreign countries in which the firm does business as well as in the home country. The global marketer also needs to develop skill in dealing with foreign government officials and other stakeholders in the host countries to ensure that the firm is positioned in the best possible light.

SKILL REQUIREMENTS

To be successful, the global marketing manager requires a range of skills. These skills may be categorized as being either 'hard' or 'soft'. As Griffith and Hoppner (2013) point out, hard skills relate to technical or administrative processes such as forecasting demand for the firm's products in foreign markets, the application of analytical models to assess alternative country markets and the ability to understand local languages. The global marketer's ability to analyze and understand the economic, cultural, political and social conditions in the firm's home and host countries is also categorized as a hard skill. In essence, hard skills embody both technical knowledge and the ability to make managerial decisions. Hard skills can be codified and can, therefore, be easily transferred or taught. Soft skills, on the other hand, are non-technical and not easily codified. These skills relate more to the individual's ability to interact with others and include intuition, flexibility and the ability to learn. Soft skills are central to the global marketing manager's ability to adjust strategy to changes taking place in the international business environment, and, as argued by Griffith and Hoppner (2013), are more important than hard skills in the manager's role as decision maker.[6]

SOFT SKILLS

The literature suggests that there are several soft skills that are required to be effective in the role of global marketing manager (see Figure 15.3):[7]

FIGURE 15.3   Soft Skills Required of the Global Marketer

---

[6] Griffith, D.A. and Hoppner, J.J. (2013) 'Global marketing managers: Improving global marketing strategy through soft skill development', *International Marketing Review*, 30, 1: 21–41.

[7] This section draws heavily from Griffith and Hoppner (2013).

Tacit knowledge: The global marketing manager develops tacit knowledge from making decisions regarding the day-to-day activities of the firm's international operations. In essence, tacit knowledge is a subconscious cognitive process that results from the manager's exposure to various stimuli in the global marketplace. Tacit knowledge allows the global marketer to determine what information is relevant to a specific managerial decision or whether a proposed solution is appropriate. As Griffith and Hoppner (2013) point out, tacit knowledge is particularly useful when the global marketing manager must bypass detailed in-depth analysis of a problem in order to quickly arrive at a plausible solution. Tacit knowledge is critical in situations in which the global marketer must make adjustments to strategy based on unanticipated changes in the external environment.

Experience: Managers develop experience by being exposed to a range of business problems and their solutions. The global marketer must acquire experience in international marketing more generally but must also acquire more specific country-level experience by being exposed to operations in a number of host countries. Exposure to specific international marketing problems and how they were solved is also part of the experience that global marketers should thrive to acquire. The more experience a global marketer possesses, the more likely it is that she will be able to respond effectively to changes in the international environment. An experienced global marketer confronted with a change in the environment is more likely to have seen similar problems before and be in a better position to decide on an appropriate course of action. Experienced global marketing managers are likely to be in a better position to decide what specific marketing actions are workable in particular country markets and how best to lever firm resources to better serve customers in these markets.

Learning: Learning refers to the process by which an individual develops the mental models that guide his actions. These models are refined over time as actions are taken and new information from the individual's environment is fed back and incorporated. To be effective, the global marketing manager must have the capacity to incorporate new information into his strategic decision making. This new information may be related to the culture of the host countries in which the firm does business or their political, trade or economic situations. An individual's ability to learn has a direct impact on his ability to make adjustments to the firm's strategy based on shifts in the international business environment.

Unlearning: Unlearning is the process of dismantling existing mental models and the acquisition of a new logic to guide the actions of the individual. Existing mental models may have to be discarded if they are rooted in information now known to be inaccurate or obsolete. The literature suggests that unlearning is just as important as learning in managerial decision making. Learning enhances the logic used by managers in decision making but simultaneously creates mental barriers to solving problems that arise in a constantly changing business environment. Unlearning is essential if a marketer must transition from the firm's domestic operations to its global operations. Taking on international marketing responsibilities requires that the manager unlearn the decision-making routines that may have worked well in the firm's domestic operations in favor of new routines geared to global markets. For global marketers to be effective in a future characterized by constant change, the ability to unlearn is considered an essential skill.

Intuition: Some scholars have suggested that intuition is a desirable soft skill for managers making strategic decisions on behalf of their companies. Intuition may be defined as a sense of certainty about a particular decision or course of action without a clear understanding of how that conclusion was arrived at. In essence, the manager knows but is unable to articulate how he knows. Analysts have argued that managers who use their intuition in making strategic decisions tend to make decisions that are more profitable for their firms than managers who do not use this soft skill.

Self-efficacy: Bandura (1995)[8] defines self-efficacy as the belief in one's ability to organize and execute actions which are required to manage particular situations. In the literature,

---

[8] Bandura, A. (1995) 'Exercise of personal and collective efficacy in changing societies', in A. Bandura (ed.) *Self-efficacy in Changing Societies*. Cambridge: Cambridge University Press.

self-efficacy has been associated with a number of desirable traits such as the setting of high individual goals, the motivation to achieve the goals established and the ability to remain on task even when faced with obstacles and setbacks. In seeking candidates for positions as global marketing managers, self-efficacy has been identified as an important factor in the selection process. Self-confident global marketers are more likely to expend the energy required to overcome the challenges posed by a constantly changing international business environment. They are much less likely to be fazed by obstacles to internationalization such as disputes with potential joint venture partners, hostility towards foreign firms, indifferent host-country government officials or the myriad other problems associated with establishing a new enterprise in a foreign country.

Flexibility: Flexibility may be defined as an awareness that in any given situation individuals have numerous options and alternatives available to them. Such individuals are able to consider a number of alternative approaches to solving a particular problem and do not remain wedded to only one course of action. Managers who are inflexible tend to restrict their options to those that may have been employed in the past and fail to see new alternatives that may in fact represent a superior solution to the problem under consideration. In making strategic decisions, global marketing managers who are flexible are likely to consider a range of possible alternatives, including options that may have worked in the firm's home country as well as in foreign markets around the world.

Problem prioritization: The ability to prioritize problems is considered a core soft skill of successful global marketing managers. This skill relates to the individual's ability to identify and rank issues that have a bearing on the ability of the firm to achieve its strategic objectives. It allows the global marketing manager to order the problems being addressed in terms of their potential impact on firm objectives, i.e. deciding which problems require urgent attention and which may be solved at some later date. In a complex and constantly changing international environment, new problems may be expected to surface with some regularity and may stem from competitive threats posed by new entrants to the market, regulatory changes in the target host countries or production or distribution issues that impact the firm's ability to service its foreign customers. As Griffith and Hoppner (2013) note, global marketers with this soft skill are likely to be better prepared to act when problems of differing importance emerge.

Ability to work under pressure: It is not enough for the global marketing manager to be able to prioritize problems. Dealing with the most urgent ones may require that the manager also have the facility to work well under pressure. Pressure is a result of the changes and challenges the manager encounters, as well as demands that are placed on the individual. Tight deadlines, the magnitude of the potential loss if the wrong decision is made and the impact on the manager's own career all contribute to the pressure the individual faces. Indeed, globalization is itself a major contributor to the pressure managers face when asked to make strategic decisions. Global marketing managers who have found ways to cope with these pressures are likely to be better decision makers than managers who are unable to meet this challenge.

Tolerance for ambiguity: In making strategic decisions, the global marketing manager is unlikely to possess complete information about the external environment. Decisions still have to be made, however, despite the fact that all relevant information may not be available. Some managers have a greater capacity than others to cope with situations in which complete information is lacking. Global marketers with a higher tolerance for ambiguity are likely to be more effective in making decisions in a complex international environment.

CAREERS IN GLOBAL MARKETING

Individuals interested in a career in global marketing have a range of options. Opportunities often exist with multinational companies with operations in a range of foreign countries. Typically, new recruits would be required to spend some time on domestic projects before being assigned international duties. This is particularly the case with individuals with limited or no prior international experience. It may take several years for new recruits to learn the culture of the parent company, its products and business systems, but this learning curve must be navigated if the individual is to be successful on foreign assignments. It is important to note that international experience is often essential if individuals are to be eventually promoted to senior executive positions within a multinational company.

In considering a career in global marketing, individuals should not restrict their choices to large multinational organizations. Small and medium-sized companies are also increasingly involved in international operations and provide excellent career choices for some people. Small and medium-sized companies may provide the individual with greater flexibility to make decisions, learn and grow than will large multinationals with their more bureaucratic organizational structure. On the other hand, the scope of foreign market assignments may be more limited in the case of small and medium-sized companies.

A third career option is, of course, self-employment. With the requisite knowledge and skills, some people opt to establish their own import–export operations or trading companies. Again, this may be a viable option for those with access to capital and industry contacts in foreign markets. Many home-country governments provide financial and technical assistance to individuals interested in establishing export operations.

Real World Challenges

LComm in the Chinese market

PHOTO 15.3

Albert Yong graduated with a degree in business management from the University of Ottawa, Canada, and has since held positions in both large multinational companies and small startups and has also been an entrepreneur. Born in China, Albert moved to Hong Kong at the age of 6 and lived there for ten years before moving to Canada. Following graduation from university, Mr Yong held a number of positions in various telecommunications companies and would eventually open his own retail operation marketing telecommunications products. In 2004, Albert joined LComm Wireless as the firm's Director of Asian Markets. At the time, LComm was a small Canadian company with some 30 employees that provided in-building wireless infrastructure systems for sensitive areas. The company's clients included nuclear plant operators, universities, hospitals and government departments. The company's technology is unique. For example, LComm installed the first full wireless voice and data communication in the elevators of Scotia Plaza in downtown Toronto, Canada. In emergencies, the system provides a live video link to the security desk and allows staff to see inside the cab and speak to the occupants. Passengers are also able to see the security guard on duty on a 15-inch screen inside the elevator cab. This was the first system of its kind anywhere in the world.

As Director of Asian Markets, Yong's mandate was to introduce and establish a beachhead for the firm's products in the mainland Chinese market with subsequent expansion to other markets in Asia. At the time, China was in the midst of a construction boom but the concept of a system that could provide both wireless voice and data services over one integrated network was new to Chinese property owners and developers. Despite a significant commitment of time devoted to networking with prospective clients, securing adoption proved to be a challenge for Albert. His break came, however, when a major hotel agreed to purchase LComm's wireless solution. With one fully installed system, Albert was finally able to showcase the product's features in a live environment to other prospective clients and further adoptions followed. LComm was eventually acquired and Albert left the organization to join the Remington Group, a Toronto-based real estate developer. As Vice President, Retail Leasing and Broker Relations, Mr Yong is hoping to help this company deepen its commitment to the global market. Remington is already active in the condominium market in China as part of a joint venture partnership.

Albert credits his university training in international marketing for the success he has achieved in his career to date. In his words: 'My international marketing courses helped me to identify and categorize what I was observing and to lay out the elements of a comprehensive strategy … The international marketing courses I took help me to think in a more logical and systematic way and appreciate the need for solid data.' His advice to recent graduates is to have an open mind, to be creative and prepared to move quickly to seize opportunities as they present themselves.

Source

Yong, A. (2013) My career in global marketing. Interviewed by C. Farrell [by telephone], Toronto, Ontario, Canada, May 14, 2013.

SUMMARY

This chapter has examined the future of global marketing. The forces that have shaped the development of the field in the post-war era were discussed and an attempt was made to identify the forces that are most likely to impact its future development. The point was made that while predictions are difficult to make, it is likely that the discipline will need to adjust to an increasingly dynamic and complex international business environment. This environment will necessitate that global marketing managers possess the knowledge and skills required to adapt to this constantly evolving and competitive global environment. These knowledge bases and skills were identified and discussed. The chapter concluded with a brief look at a few career options open to individuals interested in the discipline.

? discussion questions

1. What are 'soft' skills and why are they important to success as a global marketing manager?

2. The balance of economic power is shifting away from the Triad. What factors are driving this transition to a multi-polar world?

INDEX

Page numbers in *italics* indicate figures. Page numbers in **bold** indicate tables.